Constitutional &
Administrative Law
2013–2014

Routledge Q&A series

Each Routledge Q&A contains approximately 50 questions on topics commonly found on exam papers, with comprehensive suggested answers. The titles are written by lecturers who are also examiners, so the student gains an important insight into exactly what examiners are looking for in an answer. This makes them excellent revision and practice guides. With over 500,000 copies of the Routledge Q&As sold to date, accept no other substitute.

New editions publishing in 2013:

Civil Liberties & Human Rights
Company Law
Commercial Law
Constitutional & Administrative Law
Contract Law
Criminal Law
Employment Law
English Legal System
Equity & Trusts
European Union Law

Evidence
Family Law
Jurisprudence
Land Law
Medical Law
Torts

Published in 2012:

Business Law 2012–2013
Intellectual Property Law 2012–2013

For a full listing, visit http://cw.routledge.com/textbooks/revision

Routledge Questions & Answers Series

Constitutional & Administrative Law

2013–2014

Helen Fenwick, BA, LLB

Professor of Law at the University of Durham

AND

Gavin Phillipson, BA, LLM (*Cantab*), *Solicitor*

Professor of Law at the University of Durham

Routledge
Taylor & Francis Group

LONDON AND NEW YORK

Eighth edition published 2013
by Routledge
2 Park Square, Milton Park, Abingdon, Oxon OX14 4RN

Simultaneously published in the USA and Canada
by Routledge
711 Third Avenue, New York, NY 10017

Routledge is an imprint of the Taylor & Francis Group, an informa business

© 2013 Helen Fenwick and Gavin Phillipson

The right of Helen Fenwick and Gavin Phillipson to be identified as authors of this work has been asserted by them in accordance with sections 77 and 78 of the Copyright, Designs and Patents Act 1988.

First edition published by Cavendish Publishing 1993
Seventh edition published by Routledge 2011

British Library Cataloguing in Publication Data
A catalogue record for this book is available from the British Library

Library of Congress Cataloging in Publication Data
Fenwick, Helen.
  Constitutional & administrative law / Helen Fenwick, Gavin Phillipson.—8th ed.
    p. cm.—(Routledge questions & answers series)
  ISBN 978–0–415–62892–1 (pbk)—ISBN 978–0–203–08393–2 (ebk)
  1. Constitutional law—Great Britain—Examinations, questions, etc.   2. Administrative law—Great Britain—Examinations, questions, etc.   I. Phillipson, Gavin.   II. Title.   III. Title: Constitutional and administrative law.
  KD3989.6.F46 2013
  342.41—dc23

                                                                    2012024620

ISBN: 978–0–415–62892–1 (pbk)
ISBN: 978–0–203–08393–2 (ebk)

Typeset in TheSans
by RefineCatch Limited, Bungay, Suffolk

Printed and bound in Great Britain by the MPG Books Group

Contents

Table of Cases

Table of Legislation

INTERNATIONAL LEGISLATION

STATUTORY INSTRUMENTS

EUROPEAN LEGISLATION

Guide to the Companion Website

http://cw.routledge.com/textbooks/revision

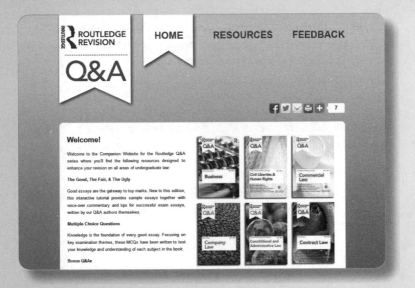

Visit the Routledge Q&A website to discover even more study tips and advice on getting those top marks.

On the Routledge revision website you will find the following resources designed to enhance your revision on all areas of undergraduate law.

The Good, The Fair, & The Ugly

Good essays are the gateway to top marks. This interactive tutorial provides sample essays together with voice-over commentary and tips for successful exam essays, written by our Q&A authors themselves.

Multiple Choice Questions

Knowledge is the foundation of every good essay. Focusing on key examination themes, these MCQs have been written to test your knowledge and understanding of each subject in the book.

Bonus Q&As

Having studied our exam advice, put your revision into practice and test your essay writing skills with our additional online questions and answers.

Don't forget to check out even more revision guides and exam tools from Routledge!

Lawcards

Lawcards are your complete, pocket-sized guides to key examinable areas of the undergraduate law.

Routledge Student Statutes

Comprehensive selections; clear, easy-to-use layout; alphabetical, chronological, and thematic indexes; and a competitive price make *Routledge Student Statutes* the statute book of choice for the serious law student.

Introduction

This book is intended to be of help to students studying constitutional and administrative law who feel that they have acquired a body of knowledge, but do not feel confident about using it effectively in exams. This book sets out to demonstrate how to apply the knowledge to the question and how to structure the answer. Students, especially first-year students, often find the technique of answering problem questions particularly hard to grasp, so this book contains a large number of answers to such questions. This technique is rarely taught in law schools and the student who comes from studying science or maths A levels may find it particularly tricky. Equally, a student who has studied English literature may find it difficult to adapt to the impersonal, logical, concise style that problem answers demand. It is hoped that this book will be particularly useful at exam time, but may also prove useful throughout the year. The book provides examples of the kind of questions that are usually asked in end-of-year examinations, along with suggested solutions. Each chapter deals with one of the main topics covered in constitutional and administrative law or public law courses and contains typical questions on that area. The aim is not to include questions covering every aspect of a course, but to pick out the areas that tend to be examined because they are particularly contentious or topical. Many courses contain a certain amount of material that is not examined, although it is important as it provides background knowledge.

PROBLEM AND ESSAY QUESTIONS

Some areas tend to be examined only by essays, some mainly – although not invariably – by problems, and some by either. The questions chosen reflect this mix, and the introductions at the beginning of each chapter discuss the type of question usually asked. It is important not to choose a topic and then assume that it will appear on the exam paper in a particular form unless it is in an area where, for example, a problem question is never set. If it might appear as an essay or a problem, revision should be geared to either possibility: a very thorough knowledge of the area should be acquired, but also an awareness of critical opinion in relation to it.

LENGTH OF ANSWERS

The answers in this book provide useful guidance for students writing assessed essays, which typically are around 2,000 words. In relation to exam questions, there are a number of reasons for including answers of the length found in this book. Some students can write long answers – about 1,800 words – under exam conditions; some students can nevertheless write two very good and lengthy essays and one reasonable but shorter one. Such students tend to do very well, although it must be emphasised that it is always better to aim to spread the time evenly between all three essays. Therefore, some answers indicate what might be done if very thorough coverage of a topic were to be undertaken.

EXTRA MARKS/COMMON PITFALLS
Certain essays also provide points that could be made to obtain extra marks as well as pointing out common mistakes students sometimes make.

EXPRESSING A POINT OF VIEW
Students sometimes ask, especially in an area such as constitutional law, which can be quite topical and politically controversial, whether they should argue for any particular point of view in an essay. It will be noticed that the essays in this book tend to do this. In general, the good student does argue for one side but he or she always uses sound arguments to support his or her view. Further, a good student does not ignore the opposing arguments; they are considered and, if possible, their weaknesses are exposed. Of course, it would not be appropriate to do this in a problem question or in some essay questions but, where an invitation to do so is held out, it is a good idea to accept it rather than sit on the fence.

EXAM PAPERS
Constitutional and administrative law exam papers normally include one question on each of the main areas. For example, a typical paper might include problem questions on public order, police powers, judicial review (probably natural justice), and essay questions on parliamentary sovereignty, conventions, the parliamentary process, the Executive, freedom of expression and judicial review. Therefore, the questions have to be fairly wide-ranging in order to cover a reasonable amount of ground on each topic. Some answers in this book therefore have to cover some of the same material, especially where it is particularly central to the topic in question.

SUGGESTIONS FOR EXAM TECHNIQUE
Below are some suggestions that might improve exam technique; some failings are pointed out that are very commonly found on exam scripts.

(1) When tackling a problem question, do not write out the facts in the answer. Quite a number of students write out chunks of the facts as they answer the question – perhaps to help themselves to pick out the important issues. It is better to avoid this and merely to refer to the significant facts.

(2) Use an impersonal style in both problem and essay answers. In an essay, you should rarely need to use the word 'I' and, in our view, it should not be used at all in a problem answer. (Of course, examiners may differ in their views on this point.)

Instead, you could say 'it is therefore submitted that' or 'it is arguable that'; avoid saying 'I believe that' or 'I feel that'.

(3) In answers to problem questions, try to explain at the beginning of each section of your answer what point you are trying to establish. You might say, for example: 'In order to show that liability under **s1** will arise, three tests must be satisfied.' You should then consider all three, citing the relevant case law, come to a conclusion on each, and then come to a final conclusion as to whether or not liability will arise. If you are really unsure whether or not it will arise (which will often be the case – there is not much point in asking a question to which there is one very clear and obvious answer), then consider what you have written in relation to the three tests. Perhaps one of them is clearly satisfied, one is probably satisfied and the other (arising under, for example, **s1(8)**) probably is not. You might then say: 'As the facts give little support to an argument that **s1(8)** is satisfied, it is concluded that liability is unlikely to be established.'

(4) If you make a point, *always* if at all possible substantiate it by citing a case or a statutory provision. If it cannot be supported in that way, as it is speculative, seek to support it by citing academic writing.

(5) It cannot be emphasised enough that the main points raised by a question have to be covered before interesting, but less obvious, issues can be explored.

Common Pitfalls

The most common mistake made when using Questions & Answers books for revision is to memorise the model answers provided and try to reproduce them in exams. This approach is a sure-fire pitfall, likely to result in a poor overall mark because your answer will not be specific enough to the particular question on your exam paper, and there is also a danger that reproducing an answer in this way would be treated as plagiarism. You must instead be sure to read the question carefully, to identify the issues and problems it is asking you to address and to answer it directly in your exam. If you take our examiners' advice and use your Q&A to focus on your question-answering skills and understanding of the law applied, you will be ready for whatever your exam paper has to offer!

The Characteristics of the British Constitution

INTRODUCTION

This chapter concentrates on six particular issues that arise from the distinctive characteristics of the British constitution: the nature of constitutions in general and the sense in which the UK can be said to have/not to have a constitution; the significance of parliamentary sovereignty; the nature of constitutional conventions; the principles of the rule of law and the separation of powers; the significance of the devolution settlement; and the desirability of a new codified constitution. These areas are sometimes treated in textbooks as discrete areas, but they are clearly interlinked and will therefore be considered here together. The significance of the previous Labour Government's reform package, and continued under the Coalition, including the Constitutional Reform Act 2005, Constitutional Reform and Governance Act 2010 and most recently the Fixed Term Parliaments Act 2012, is considered here in general terms, although the significance of the Human Rights Act 1998 is discussed much more fully in Chapters 2 and 9. The sovereignty of Parliament and the impact of European Union (EU) law on the UK constitution are fully considered in Chapter 2.

Checklist ✔

Students should be familiar with the following areas:

- the debate about the nature and functions of a constitution, and the argument that the UK does not indeed possess one under certain definitions;

- the nature and role of constitutional conventions;

- certain of the most significant conventions – those relating to the exercise of the royal prerogative, to the working of the Cabinet system, to the relationship between the Lords and the Commons, and to those regulating proceedings in Parliament;

- the doctrine of parliamentary sovereignty and the modification to the traditional view represented by the impact of EU law;

- the concept of the rule of law and the impact upon it of the **European Convention on Human Rights (ECHR)** and the **Human Rights Act 1988 (HRA)**;

- the doctrine of the separation of powers, and the effect upon this of the **ECHR** and **HRA** and of the **Constitutional Reform Act 2005**;

- the benefits and defects of the un-codified UK constitution;

- devolution to Scotland, Wales and Northern Ireland, including the **Scotland Act 2012** and the introduction of primary legislative powers for the Welsh Assembly; the 'West Lothian' or 'English' question and possible solutions;

- the constitutional significance of the **HRA**;

- the significance of ongoing reform of the House of Lords including the draft **House of Lords Reform Bill 2012** and of the **Freedom of Information Act 2000** for the overall balance of powers within the constitution;

- the significance of further constitutional reform, as enacted in the **2010 and 2012 Acts**;

- a brief outline of the Coalition Government's plans for further constitutional reform.

QUESTION 1

Would you agree that there is no justification for distinguishing between strict law and convention in the UK constitution and that, therefore, conventions should be codified in legal form?

How to Answer this Question

This question is often asked in one form or another and is reasonably straightforward. It requires the student to consider why features of the constitution that are not strict laws should be maintained. It should not degenerate into a list of the main conventions; rather, conventions should be used as examples. Clearly, it is crucial at the outset to try to distinguish between law and convention.

Answer Structure

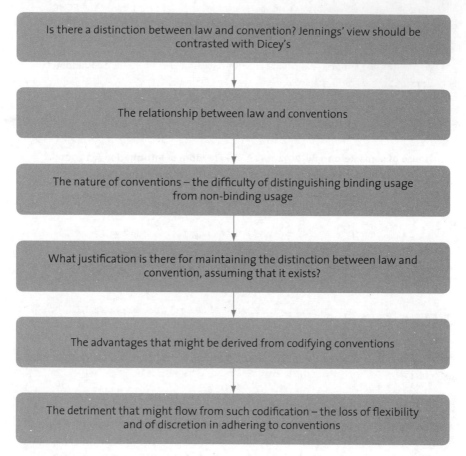

Is there a distinction between law and convention? Jennings' view should be contrasted with Dicey's

The relationship between law and conventions

The nature of conventions – the difficulty of distinguishing binding usage from non-binding usage

What justification is there for maintaining the distinction between law and convention, assuming that it exists?

The advantages that might be derived from codifying conventions

The detriment that might flow from such codification – the loss of flexibility and of discretion in adhering to conventions

Essentially, the matters above should be discussed.

ANSWER

Dicey wrote that conventions could be clearly distinguished from laws, in the sense that no court would apply a sanction for their breach (*The Law of the Constitution*, 1971). However, this distinction was attacked as artificial by Sir Ivor Jennings in *The Law and the Constitution* (1959), on the basis that law and conventions both ultimately rest on 'general acquiescence'. The distinction put forward by Dicey, however, finds some support in case law. In *Madzimbamuto v Lardner-Burke* (1969), the Privy Council held that the convention under which the UK Parliament needed to obtain the consent of the Southern Rhodesia Government before legislating for that colony had no effect in limiting the powers of the UK Parliament. Similarly, the Canadian Supreme Court in *Re Amendment to the Constitution of Canada* (1982) held that conventions are not enforced by the courts:

the only sanctions for breach of a convention are political ones. Most constitutional writers have accepted this distinction between law and convention, and the general view may be summed up by Marshall and Moodie: conventions may be described as 'rules of constitutional behaviour which are considered to be binding by and upon those who operate the Constitution but which are not enforced by the law courts . . . nor by the presiding officers in the Houses of Parliament' (*Some Problems of the Constitution*, 5th edn, 1971, pp 22–23). Most conventions are based on usage that continues because statesmen would find it politically inconvenient to depart from it. It may then be argued that conventions depend on acquiescence for their very existence, whereas laws do not cease to exist because they are widely disobeyed. The road traffic laws are frequently violated, but no one doubts that they remain valid laws.

It follows that if, for example, the government were to be defeated on a vote of confidence in the House of Commons but refuse to obey the convention that it should therefore resign, the courts would not recognise this breach of convention by declaring that government ministers were not legally entitled to exercise the powers of their office.[1]

However, having postulated a distinction between law and convention, it must be accepted that there are exceptions to it. In particular, it would be going too far to say, as Dicey did, that conventions are never *recognised* by the courts. For example, in *Liversidge v Anderson* (1942) and *Carltona Ltd v Commissioner of Works* (1943), the courts supported the refusal to review the grounds on which executive discretionary powers had been exercised on the basis that a minister is responsible to Parliament for the exercise of his power. In *Attorney General v Jonathan Cape Ltd* (1976), Lord Widgery CJ considered the doctrine of collective Cabinet responsibility at some length, coming to the conclusion that the maintenance of the doctrine was in the public interest and, therefore, could justify restraint on the disclosure of Cabinet discussions (although no restraint was granted in the instant case due to the lapse of time since the discussions took place). Equally, it must be remembered that not all legal rules are justiciable.

Assuming that, to an extent, the distinction between strict law and convention holds good, why, as De Smith asks (in *Constitutional and Administrative Law*, 8th edn, 1998), maintain a distinction at all? Why not codify conventions of the constitution in legal form – either in a statute or as part of a written constitution? Several Commonwealth constitutions have already undertaken this codification would have the advantage of clarifying certain of the most significant constitutional rules. The informality associated with conventions may be disadvantageous in that it may sometimes be very difficult, if not impossible, to ascertain whether a certain usage has crystallised into a conventional rule. Of course, some conventions are formulated in writing, such as the agreement in

---

1   Answers gain much greater credibility by being able to use a concrete example in this way.

1930 that the Governor General of a dominion should be appointed by the Crown exclusively on the advice of the dominion government concerned, but those that have gradually evolved will often be uncertain in scope and, unlike laws, their meaning will not be resolved by their interpretation in the courts. For example, the conventions governing the Queen's prerogative power to appoint a prime minister,[2] while relatively clear in the event that a general election produces an overall majority in the House of Commons for one party, are notoriously unclear where no one party has such a majority. While the process proceeded fairly smoothly after the hung parliament produced by the 2010 general election, this was mainly because the Conservatives were both the largest single party, *and* the only ones who could put together a viable Coalition agreement. Matters would have been much more uncertain had the numbers and the politics allowed for a viable Lib–Lab Coalition, but the Conservatives had been the largest party. As Turpin and Tomkins point out (*British Government and the Constitution*, 6th edn 2007, p 359) it is by no means clear whether in such circumstances the Queen should appoint a minority Conservative prime minister or a PM representing a Lib–Lab Coalition. This difficulty could be avoided if the constitutional functions of the monarch in this situation were set out in legal form.

Uncertainty arises not only as to the scope of some conventions, but as to whether or not they have come into being at any particular time, or whether it may be said of a custom that it is merely a non-binding usage. Moreover, it is arguable that conventions should be enshrined in law because otherwise they may be more readily violated. Conventions are binding if those to whom the usage applies consider that they are under an obligation to comply with them. But although, in practice, many conventions do seem to be regarded as binding, lack of certainty as to the scope or existence of some, as already considered, may lead to behaviour that would be regarded in some quarters as unconstitutional. The absence of an enacted constitutional code means that 'unconstitutional' has no definition. Such a code would mean that unconstitutional behaviour could be more readily identified and would be clearly illegal. If the resulting code were made non-justiciable, its value would largely lie in its clarification of conventions, thereby precluding some disputes. This was essentially the course taken recently when the conventions governing relations between the House of Lords and House of Commons were partially codified in a Report of the Joint Committee on Conventions (2005–06, HL Paper 265-I/HC 1212-I) which was recognised by resolutions passed in both Houses. The result is not binding in any way on either House and in some cases, the only formulation for a given convention was found to be a very general one, but there was thought to be some value in enhancing clarity in this area nevertheless.

. . . .

2   It is important that candidates differentiate clearly between the legal *power* – to appoint the prime minister – and the convention governing its proper *exercise* – that the leader of the party best able to command a majority in the House of Commons should be appointed. Students frequently confuse the two.

However, codification might achieve a desirable clarity in some areas, but at the expense of the present flexibility. Conventions allow the constitution to evolve and keep up to date with changing circumstances without the need for formal repeal or amendment of law. Further, conventions may not always be followed and, although this can be seen as a weakness, as argued above, it can also be seen as a strength that, in certain circumstances, rigid adherence to conventions is not required as it would be if they were enshrined in a legal code. Conventions have been able to lose their binding force or undergo a change in content without the need for any formal mechanism being followed. They may disappear gradually if they are no longer observed. If a convention has been established by express agreement, as recently with the Sewell Convention, it may be superseded or modified by agreement. For example, decisions taken by the prime minister or the Cabinet about the way the Cabinet is to operate may be superseded by new decisions. Such flexibility has been politically convenient in the past and will, presumably, continue to be so.

The doctrine of collective Cabinet responsibility provides an example of the advantage to be derived from the indeterminate nature of conventions. Under the doctrine, ministers are collectively responsible to Parliament for their actions in governing the country and, therefore, should be in accord on any major question. A minister should resign if he or she is in disagreement with the policy of the Cabinet on any such question. Examples of such resignations include Sir Thomas Dugdale's in 1954, due to his disagreement with the government as to the disposal of an area of land known as 'Crichel Down' (this resignation is not always cited as an example of policy disagreement, but such appears to have been its basis), and Sir Anthony Eden's in 1938, over Chamberlain's policy towards Mussolini. However, there appears to have been some blurring and weakening of the doctrine dating from the mid-1970s. In 1975, the Labour Cabinet was divided on the question of whether the UK should remain in the Common Market. It was agreed that, in the period before the referendum on the question, Cabinet ministers should be able to express a view at variance with the official view of the government that the UK should remain a member of the Common Market. Moreover, the present, Coalition Government appears to operate with a greater degree of internal dissent and argument than would be thought appropriate in a single-party government. In particular, and as in 1975, the Coalition Agreement (2010) explicitly permitted members of the Government to campaign on different sides during the 2011 referendum on the voting system for general elections, and this agreement was used to the full during a bitterly partisan campaign.[3]

3   When discussing matters where there are recent examples from current affairs, students will gain credit for citing them; not only does this show that students can do more than regurgitate a textbook, it also demonstrates real understanding.

If the convention of collective responsibility were enshrined in a statute, departure from it, as in 1975 and 2011, might be less readily undertaken even if the provisions of the statute were made non-justiciable. In any event, it would be difficult and probably undesirable to define the convention, as discretion in complying with it may be said to be endemic in it. Political inconvenience would clearly arise and it might be argued that the democratic process would be endangered if ministers could not, at times, express their views on exceptionally important issues with some freedom. Therefore, it may be argued that no advantage would be gained by enacting such a statute: such crystallisation of the convention would clearly reduce its value.

Of course, in particular instances, the enactment of conventions has been called for after they have been violated; the need for flexibility has been outweighed by the need for clarification and certainty. For example, in 1909, the House of Lords ignored the convention that it must defer to the will of the House of Commons. This led to the enactment of the Parliament Act 1911, which defined the relationship between the two Houses and ensured that the House of Lords would defer to the Commons.

In some instances where a convention seems to embody a clear rule, the need for flexibility is certainly less pressing and the argument for codification more compelling. Arguably, certain constitutional functions of the monarch (such as rules governing government formation, Parliament and assent to Bills) should be enacted in order to avoid uncertainty as to when the Queen may be acting unconstitutionally.

Thus, it may be concluded that if codification were undertaken, it should be confined to conventions of a sufficiently definite nature, which should be codified in order to reduce the potential for disagreement as to their scope.

QUESTION 2

'While the UK has a set of relatively stable rules, procedures and practices under which its governance is carried out, it has no Constitution, in the sense in which that term is understood by most other countries in the world.'

▶ Discuss.

How to Answer this Question

It is important that students do *not* adopt the simplistic line of assuming that this question refers simply to the written/unwritten distinction, but instead tease out carefully the requirements of a constitution in the sense argued for in the question, and then apply these systematically to the UK system.

Answer Structure

The requirements of constitutionalism – power allocation and power separated by law; power only to be exercised by law; laws to be made in accordance with specified procedures; limitations on the content of laws; entrenched rights

↓

The overriding requirement that the constitution be above the power of government and, therefore, not susceptible to ordinary change

↓

The application of the above to the UK constitution; partial compliance but no form of higher law save sovereignty itself; constitutional statutes under the *Thoburn* doctrine

↓

Conclusion: thesis broadly correct, but overstated somewhat by Ridley

ANSWER

The claim that the UK has no constitution in the second sense advanced in the question has been put forward most forcefully by Ridley ((1988) 41 *Parlt Aff* 340). In essence, it distinguishes a merely descriptive definition of a constitution as that body of rules and arrangements which regulates the government of a country and its relations with its citizens from what is argued to be the more important one – the constitution as a form of higher law that limits and controls the powers of government. Ridley and others argue that to qualify as what Anthony King calls a 'capital C' Constitution (in *The British Constitution*, 2007, Chapter 1) a constitution must have particular characteristics. These may be used as a measure against which to judge the existence or non-existence of the UK constitution.

There are perhaps two essential characteristics or purposes of constitutions. The first is that constitutions are necessary in order to control the power of the State; the second is that constitutions ensure that the power of the State derives from a legitimate source. As to the first notion, constitutions may be seen to exercise such control by the fact they distribute power amongst the different organs of government, according to law. This represents a limitation on State power by separating out different types of power and assigning them to different and separate organs of government. This is the doctrine of the separation of powers, which, broadly speaking, demands: first, that each part of government should be separate and to an extent independent of the others; second, that each organ should be vested with only one main function of government; and, third, that each organ should be able to check the actions of the others.

A further very simple aspect of a constitution is that power must be exercised only through the making of laws, as opposed to the exercise of arbitrary power. This represents a basic limitation on government because, since the rules must be announced in advance, the government cannot simply act as it pleases; instead, it must be able to point to some law justifying its actions. Liberal constitutions also usually limit governments not only as to the *form* by which they must exercise power, but also as to the *substance* of what powers may be exercised. Thus, under many constitutions, there are some laws that the government *cannot make at all*: broadly, those that would infringe what are seen as fundamental human rights. The First Amendment of the US Constitution states simply (inter alia): 'Congress shall make no law abridging the freedom of speech or of the press.' This is the notion of entrenched rights – a ring fence around certain basic liberties that the government is not allowed to cross. Most Western countries have constitutions that declare the existence of such liberties and forbid governmental interference with them, except perhaps in cases of grave national emergency.

Implicit in all of the above ideas is the notion that constitutions are in some way superior to and beyond government; they state what form the government shall take, and what it may and may not do. They are 'above' governments in specifying matters that are prior to the formation or election of any government, and they also bind all governments. From this requirement flows another: namely, that the constitution should be *entrenched*, so that it is not readily alterable by the government of the day. If the constitution were not in some way entrenched, then any government could simply remove the limitations on its power that the constitution imposed and the basic idea of controlling the power of government would be lost.

We may now turn to the application of these ideas of constitutionalism to the UK. The UK constitution does allocate power amongst the different organs of government. The doctrine of parliamentary sovereignty states that Parliament, and only Parliament, may make new laws. Similarly, the judges must give effect to all valid Acts of Parliament and may not question the desirability of their content. However, looking a little closer at the idea of allocation of powers in Britain, a fundamental problem appears: some of the most important powers in the British State are allocated not by *law*, but by *convention* – that is, a traditional understanding about how things should be done, which is accepted by those it applies to, but which cannot be enforced legally.[4] Thus, in theory, the Queen holds all of the prerogative powers of government – to declare war, to make peace, to dismiss ministers, etc. In practice, of course, these powers are exercised by ministers, either

---

4   Students very often miss this simple but crucial point about the UK constitution.

collectively or individually. However, there is no law of the constitution stating that this is the case. The *law* in fact states that all of these powers belong to the Queen. The idea that these powers are exercised by her only in a formal way is a constitutional convention. Furthermore, some of the most important 'checks and balances' in the constitution, required by the notion of separation of powers, exist only by virtue of convention.[5] For example, the whole notion of responsible government – that the government is accountable to Parliament is only a convention.

What about controls on how laws may be made and what they may say? Laws may only be made through Acts of Parliament that comply with all specified formalities: resolutions of the Commons alone, for example, are not laws binding on the courts (*Stockdale v Hansard* (1839)). Furthermore, the courts enforce a basic notion of legality: government action impinging on citizens must be justified by reference to some law that empowers the specific act done, as in *Entick v Carrington* (1765). However, the ability of Parliament to enact what laws it pleases means that it can pass – and does increasingly pass – laws that give government very wide discretionary powers, so that it will be difficult for the courts to find that any particular actions are not justified in law (see e.g. the Legislative and Regulatory Reform Act 2006 granting sweeping powers to ministers to repeal by order primary legislation imposing a 'burden'). As to the notion of more substantive limitations on government rule in the form of entrenched rights, we may note immediately that there is no comprehensive system of entrenched rights in the UK, and orthodox constitutional doctrine tells us that Parliament is competent to legislate on any matter whatever. This remains the case under the Human Rights Act, which specifically preserves the power of Parliament to legislate incompatibly with the ECHR rights it protects (ss 3(2) and 4(6)). Of course, legislation removing these rights would be in violation of the UK's obligations under the ECHR but the UK, at least in theory, can withdraw from this treaty and certainly Parliament may simply repeal the HRA. At the time of writing it seems likely that the Conservatives will bring forward lelegislation to do at least the latter, should they win the next general election.

It has recently become apparent that the courts will not apply Acts of Parliament that conflict with rights deriving from European Union law (*Factortame Ltd and Ors v Secretary of State for Transport (No 2)* (1991)), so that insofar as rights are protected by EU law, they do have a special status. However, EU law does not at present provide a set of basic civil and political rights (the EU Charter of Rights being the subject of a UK opt-out). It should be noted that a few judges have recently, and mainly speaking extra-judicially, suggested that there may be basic rights and freedoms embedded in the common law, particularly

5   Again, many students argue that the UK constitution has 'checks and balances', but fail to note that many of them are not legally enforceable.

the ability of the courts to engage in judicial review of executive action – a basic requirement of the rule of law – which the judges would not allow Parliament to remove; the most recent example was the now well-known comments to this effect by Lord Steyn in *A-G v Jackson* (2006), at [102].[6] Comments to like effect were made by Lord Hope in *AXA General Insurance v Lord Advocate* [2011] UKSC 46 at [51], in dicta that appear to apply to the UK as well as the Scottish Parliament.

Finally, what of the notion that the constitution must in some way be above or beyond the powers of government? One matter – parliamentary sovereignty itself – appears to be a matter of 'higher law', in that it is generally accepted that Parliament is unable to restrict its continuing sovereignty. This point has been thrown into some doubt as the courts have, in effect, allowed Parliament to restrict its own powers to legislate contrary to EU law. Nevertheless, there is little doubt that this restriction is ultimately one that Parliament could remove through withdrawal from the EU and probably also through the simple expedient of stating an express intention that a given Act should prevail over EU law. But, on the orthodox view, no other rule in the constitution is immune from change by an ordinary Act of Parliament. Thus, so-called constitutional principles are in theory as readily changeable as rules relating to the licensing of public houses. The only, minor caveat to be entered to this is that, according to the line of reasoning taken in *Thoburn* (2002) the *courts* could and should recognise certain Acts, including the 1972 Act, as 'constitutional statutes', which cannot be impliedly repealed, but must be expressly repealed by Parliament. Essentially these are those that affect fundamental rights or 'the relationship between citizen and State in some general, overarching manner'.

Even under this view, Parliament can remove constitutional statutes such as the **Scotland Act 1998**, granting devolution to Scotland, by ordinary repeal – although this may be politically impossible. More fundamental attacks on democracy, e.g. restricting the franchise, through express repeal of the **Representation of the People Act** and its replacement with a more restrictive statute, could also be undertaken by Parliament. Hence, the basic notion, noted above, that the constitution should establish the source of governmental power and, in a democracy, establish that source as the people, is only partly fulfilled in the UK. The source of ultimate *legal* power in the UK is Parliament, *not* the people. Thus, the 'no constitution' thesis appears to be fairly readily made out, at least if it is taken to mean that 'the constitution' must consist of a form of 'higher order' law. Alternatively, it has been suggested that the UK has a constitution, but consisting of only one rule: 'What the Queen enacts in Parliament is law.'

In conclusion, there appears to be a strong argument that the basic thesis in the question is correct. Ridley, however, arguably goes too far in further claiming that the term 'constitution' does not even have a normative or conventional meaning in the UK. He

---

6   Essays gain much greater credibility by giving specific examples of this sort.

claims that there are no parts of the system to which any special sanctity attaches, so that no one may confidently claim that a given change to the system of government or to the rights of the citizen is 'unconstitutional'. However, if the government were, for example, to procure the passage of legislation allowing for the dismissal by prime ministerial fiat of any judge, commentators would have no hesitation in using the term 'unconstitutional' to describe such actions, even if they would not contravene domestic law.

Common Pitfalls

There are two very common faults in answering questions like the above. The most obvious is simply that, rather than seeking to answer the question, the student simply writes about the different sources of the constitution (i.e. just describes it) without *analysing* it, and so fails to address the question at all (such an answer will either fail or at best get a third-class mark). The other problem is that, when the question *is* addressed, the question of what amounts to a constitution is discussed at a very simplistic level of written/ unwritten, or (more accurately) codified/uncodified; in other words, no assessment is made of the key *purposes* or *functions* of a constitution and whether the UK constitution may be said to satisfy those purposes.

QUESTION 3

Do statutes of great constitutional significance, such as the Scotland Act 1998 and the Human Rights Act 1998, amount to a form of 'higher law' constitution for the UK?

How to Answer this Question

Students must briefly explain what is meant by a 'higher law' constitution and then consider whether either of these two important statutes amounts to one. It is important to look at specific aspects of both statutes, but also their broader normative significance.

Answer Structure

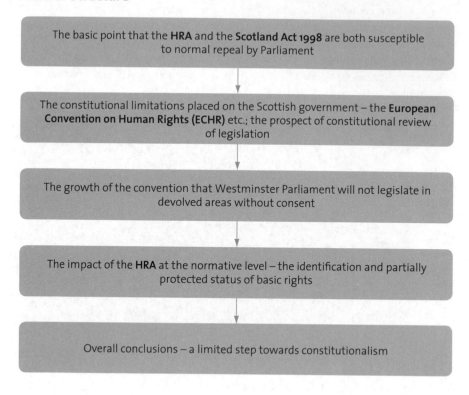

The basic point that the **HRA** and the **Scotland Act 1998** are both susceptible to normal repeal by Parliament

The constitutional limitations placed on the Scottish government – the **European Convention on Human Rights (ECHR)** etc.; the prospect of constitutional review of legislation

The growth of the convention that Westminster Parliament will not legislate in devolved areas without consent

The impact of the **HRA** at the normative level – the identification and partially protected status of basic rights

Overall conclusions – a limited step towards constitutionalism

ANSWER

The notion of a 'higher law' constitution may be distinguished from a merely descriptive definition of a constitution as that body of rules and arrangements which regulates the government of a country and its relations with its citizens: the constitution as a form of higher law that limits and controls the powers of government. Constitutions in this sense amount to 'higher law' because they are in some way superior to and beyond both governments and ordinary law; they state what form the government shall take, and what it may and may not do. From this requirement flows another: namely, that the constitution should be *entrenched* so that it is not readily alterable by the government of the day. If the constitution were not in some way entrenched, then any government could simply remove the limitations on its power that the constitution imposed and the basic idea of controlling the power of government would be lost.[7]

---

7   It is crucial that students define what the notion of 'higher law' means in this context: without a clear definition the entire essay will lack focus.

The traditional doctrine of parliamentary sovereignty, which allows Parliament to repeal and replace any law, of whatever constitutional importance, and the absence of a codified constitution of special status, as found, for example in the USA and Germany, has generally led observers to pronounce that the UK has no form of 'higher law' other than parliamentary sovereignty itself. More recently, EU law may have attained this status, following the decision in *Factortame Ltd and Ors v Secretary of State for Transport (No 2)* (1991) that the European Communities Act 1972 prevailed over a subsequent, incompatible statute. How far has this changed in the UK following devolution and the advent of the HRA? The first point to make is that neither change has, in terms, created any 'higher' system of law. Both the Scotland Act 1998 and the HRA specifically affirm that they do not affect Parliament's continued ability to reverse the changes that they make, either wholly or in part. Thus, the HRA makes no attempt to entrench itself, and further provides quite specifically that if the courts find a piece of legislation passed either before or after the HRA to be incompatible with one or more of the Convention rights, this will not affect the validity or continuing effect of that legislation (ss 3(2) and 4(6)). Similarly, the White Paper on Scottish devolution (Cm 3658) proclaims that 'The United Kingdom is and will remain sovereign in all matters', and this basic statement of principle is clearly enacted in the legislation. Section 28(7) of the Scotland Act states that the grant of legislative powers to the Scottish Parliament 'does not affect the power of the United Kingdom Parliament to make law for Scotland'. Moreover, Westminster may repeal or modify the Scotland Act itself by ordinary legislation.[8]

These two pieces of legislation introduce substantive, rights-based limitations on governmental power (the HRA) and devolution of that power to a specified region (the Scotland Act). These are matters that, in most countries, would be part of 'higher' constitutional law, subject to change only through extraordinary procedures themselves specified in the constitution. Instead, the opposite is provided for: following devolution and since the introduction of the HRA, Parliament is still, as a matter of law, able to invade basic rights or the legislative autonomy of Scotland as easily and readily as it may change the rate of income tax.

Thus, on one level, the charge that the UK lacks any framework of 'higher law' retains its basic force. But, on another level, its applicability to the UK has become more problematic. To take Scotland first, its Parliament and thus its government for most matters are now limited by what is in effect a codified constitution, made up of the Scotland Act itself, the ECHR and EU law. This is because the Scotland Act provides that Acts of the Scottish Parliament or Executive that are outside the powers devolved to it by the Act or which infringe Convention rights or EU law will be ultra vires (s 29), and further that the courts have what can only be described as a power of constitutional review,

---

8   Students should spell out precisely, and with relevant statutory references, the provisions in the two statutes that explicitly preserve the Westminster Parliament's continuing sovereignty.

being empowered to strike down legislation of the Scottish Parliament or actions of its Executive on those grounds. Of course, in the areas that are not devolved, the Scots continue to be governed by the unrestrained and unconstitutionalised Westminster government and Parliament. However, the day-to-day experience of the Scottish people is now to live under a government that, in most areas, is constrained by a written constitution that protects basic rights, specifies the electoral system and sets the basic shape of government. Those entrenched matters are above and beyond the reach of the Scottish Government and Parliament (since neither may alter the Scotland Act itself). Of course, the Westminster Parliament still has the theoretical right to legislate in the devolved areas against the will of the Scottish Parliament and even to abolish the devolved institutions entirely, but no one seriously expects either to occur: the system would be unworkable if Westminster were to interfere in the devolved matters in this way, while the outright abolition of devolution has become virtually a political impossibility. Thus, the day-to-day experience of the Scottish people is now to live under a codified constitution for the first time.

There is moreover some doubt as to whether Scottish judges would uphold Westminster's claimed legislative omnicompetence (see *MacCormack v Lord Advocate* (1953)). Furthermore, the Scottish Claim of Right 1989, the foundation of the Scottish constitutional convention that laid the basic principles for devolution, affirmed the 'sovereign right of the Scottish people to determine [their] form of government' – a clear rejection of the notion that sovereignty over Scotland lies with Westminster. It is possible, therefore, that Scottish judges in the future will make findings at least to the effect that devolution, bolstered as it was with emphatic democratic endorsement by the Referendum of 1997, is an entrenched principle that may not be unilaterally removed or modified by the Westminster Parliament.

Moreover, it is clear that the term 'unconstitutional' has started to have a very clear and definite meaning, certainly in relation to the government of Scotland, but also in relation to Westminster. In relation to the former, it now means 'legislation or administrative decisions which violate the legal constraints on the government of Scotland' – there is no doubt as to that. Legislation on rights-related matters now falls to be discussed, and eventually adjudicated upon, in constitutional terms. As to Westminster, as devolution and the new Scottish Government have become firmly entrenched, a convention has become established to the effect that the Westminster Parliament will not legislate in the devolved areas without the consent of the Scottish Parliament, just as such a convention developed during the period of the Stormont Government of Northern Ireland between 1920 and 1972. Indeed, such an understanding is set out in a memorandum of understanding drawn up between the UK Government and the devolved administrations (the so-called Sewell Convention) and Westminster has not, to date, legislated in the devolved areas without the consent of the Scottish Parliament (known as 'legislative consent motions'). It is notable in particular that, when Westminster was considering the Scotland Bill passed in May 2012, the Government made clear that it would not be passed without the consent of the Scottish Parliament, which was eventually granted by motion in April 2012. Devolution has thus become constitutionalised: in a very concrete way as far as Scotland and its Government are concerned; in a conventional but nevertheless real way for the Westminster Parliament. Moreover, the passage of the Scotland Act 2012, containing what observers described as the largest transfer of financial powers to Scotland since the Treaties of Union in 1707, underlines the direction of travel in favour of greater autonomy for Scotland.[9]

Much the same may be said of the HRA. We have noted that it is not in any formal way entrenched; nevertheless, for the first time, the rights of the UK citizenry have been authoritatively identified and stated to be fundamental. Executive actions are unlawful if they infringe such rights, unless primary legislation inescapably mandates or authorises the infringement (s 6). *Daly* (2001) confirms that this requires courts to assess for themselves whether Executive decisions have infringed Convention rights, affording a far higher level of protection for those rights than was available under judicial review, although there has been some vacillation about this point in some of the decided cases (see, for example, I. Leigh [2002] PL 265). For the first time, statutory construction fully and unequivocally recognises the importance of basic rights – courts have to read both past and future legislation into conformity with the Convention rights if possible (s 3(1)). Cases such as *A* (2001), *Ghaidan v Mendoza* (2004) and *AF (No 3)* (2009) indicate the radical force of this provision, and how far it subordinates normal canons of statutory interpretation to the overriding imperative to uphold Convention rights if possible, although other cases, such as *Re W and B* (2002), indicate a less activist approach. Ministers now have to make a statement when introducing legislation into Parliament that it does not infringe Convention rights, or that they believe it does, but they wish to proceed in any event (s 19). Statements of the latter kind would amount to a declaration that the UK intended quite deliberately to violate its Treaty obligations and breach international law; this requirement will inevitably act as a powerful deterrent against the introduction of such legislation (only one negative statement has been made, in relation to the ban on political broadcasts in the Communications Act 2003). Clear and serious legislative infringements of the Convention are still extremely unlikely, and inadvertent infringements will be avoided by the need to scrutinise the Bill prior to making the statement to Parliament mentioned above.[10]

Meanwhile, ambiguously worded legislation that may infringe rights can be dealt with via the interpretative obligation of the courts noted above. Together, and depending upon how rigorously the courts enforce the interpretative injunction in s 3(1) of the HRA (as indicated above, the cases to date indicate that it is being taken very seriously,

---

9 Students should show some awareness of the significance of the recently passed **Scotland Act 2012**.

10 The **section 19** requirement is important, and should not be omitted in discussions of the constitutional significance of the **HRA**.

although the outcomes vary), this adds up to quite a strong guarantee that legislation will no longer, in practice, infringe basic rights. All of this, however, can be removed, simply by repeal of the HRA. While this was official Conservative policy the Conservatives had promised instead a British Bill of Rights, which would also ensure that basic rights would remain to an extent constitutionalised. Neither seems likely during the current Parliament under the Coalition Government, although, should the Conservatives win the next general election, it would seem highly likely that they would seek to repeal the HRA.

In conclusion, therefore, while no higher basic norms have, as a matter of law, been created, the effect of the canvassed reforms may in practice be indistinguishable. The basic ability of Parliament to remove so-called constitutional guarantees, perhaps only by express repeal, will still remain, at least as a matter of strict law. However, any suggestion that the concept of 'constitutionalism' at the normative, conventional level cannot be deployed in the UK will lose much of its force, as certain notions of devolved power at least attain an authoritatively declared basis and – as is likely – become fenced round by strong inhibitory conventions. In that sense, these reforms inject a modest dose of normative constitutionalism into the UK polity while leaving us formally still in search of a constitution.

QUESTION 4

How far does the Rule of Law find recognition in the UK, and how far has this been strengthened by the Human Rights Act 1998?

How to Answer this Question

This question is a common one. It is important to give specific examples of how the rule of law has been affected by the HRA.

Answer Structure

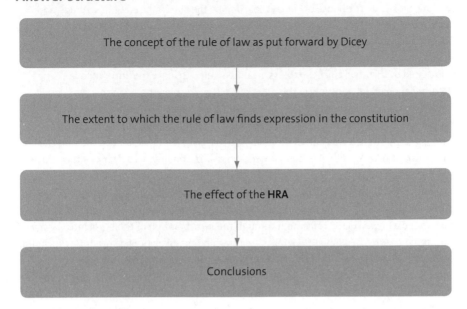

The concept of the rule of law as put forward by Dicey

The extent to which the rule of law finds expression in the constitution

The effect of the **HRA**

Conclusions

ANSWER

The Constitutional Reform Act 2005 states in s 1 that 'it does not affect the existing constitutional principle of the rule of law'. The rule of law is seen as being one of the most fundamental aspects of the UK constitution, although there is strong academic disagreement as to everything but the core meaning of the concept. This essay will consider Dicey's exposition of the rule of law, as still one of the more influential analyses. It will be argued that the HRA has strengthened aspects of the rule of law, albeit within limits determined by the doctrine of parliamentary sovereignty.

The concept of the rule of law as influenced by Dicey (*The Law of the Constitution*, 1971) appears to encompass the following notions: first, that powers exercised by government must be founded on lawful authority as opposed to being arbitrary; second, that citizens should be equal before the law; and, third, that the law should be clear. Can it be said that these notions find expression in the UK constitution?[11]

Historically, constitutional lawyers in this country have prided themselves on their adherence to the rule of law, as upheld by judges in a number of famous cases. One of these is *Entick v*

11   Clearly, answers must define what they mean by 'the Rule of Law'; Dicey's definition, though not uncontentious, is a good starting point.

Carrington (1765), in which agents of the king, acting under a warrant issued by the Secretary of State, broke into the house of Entick, alleged to be the author of seditious writings, and removed certain of his papers. It was found that because the action was justified by no specific legal authority, it was a common trespass, for which the Secretary of State was liable in damages. If government is under the law, in the sense that any actions it takes must be authorised by law, then since the courts are empowered to make the authoritative determination of what the law is, this must mean that the government is in a sense under (and therefore obliged to obey) orders of the courts, expressed in the form of injunctions. The normal sanction for failure to obey an order of the court is a finding of contempt of court. Perhaps surprisingly, it was only in the case of *Re M* (1993) that it was settled that ministers of the Crown were obliged to obey court orders and risked a finding of contempt if they did not.

The notion, expressed in both of the above cases, that exercises of governmental power, particularly those that impact upon the liberty of the citizen, must have a basis in law, has now found a powerful reinforcement through the incorporation of the ECHR into UK law through the HRA. The Convention rights are now binding on all public authorities, including courts, which act unlawfully if they act incompatibly with them (s 6(1)). Under s 3(1) of the HRA, 'So far as it is possible to do so, all legislation must be construed compatibly with the Convention rights', although if any primary legislation cannot be so construed, it remains valid and of full effect – the courts are given no strike-down power. Certain Convention rights permit interferences with them in limited circumstances: Art 2 (right to life); Art 5 (personal liberty); Art 8 (privacy); Art 9 (freedom of religion); Art 10 (freedom of expression); and Art 11 (freedom of assembly and association). In order for such interferences to be lawful under the ECHR, the government must first show that the interference was 'prescribed by' or 'in accordance with the law' – that is, that it had a basis in existing domestic law. In other words, an identifiable legal basis authorising the interference must be shown: mere Executive discretion cannot suffice. It was on this basis that the UK was held to be in violation of Art 8 of the ECHR in the case of *Malone v UK* (1985). The UK was found to have fallen short of this standard much more recently in the case of *Gillan v UK* (2010). This Strasbourg case followed the very disappointing decision of the House of Lords in *Gillan* (2006); this judgment, made when reviewing the exercise of a very broad discretionary power – the notorious power to stop and search without reasonable suspicion in the former section 44 of the Terrorism Act 2000 – showed how easily the supposed rule-of-law prohibition on such broad coercive powers may be abridged by Parliament and winked at by the courts. The unanimous finding by Strasbourg in *Gillan v UK* that the powers granted were so broad and open to abuse that they failed the 'in accordance with law' requirement in Article 8 ECHR was an eloquent condemnation of both the power itself and the failure of the House of Lords to uphold rule of law principle. The Protection of Freedoms Act 2012 repeals section 44 and enacts a more restrictive power in its place.[12]

---

12 *Gillan* was an important case because it is the first time that a modern British statute has been found not to meet the Strasbourg standard of the qualities law must have.

It could be said that arbitrary power, although apparently contrary to the rule of law as expounded by Dicey, is exercised by ministers in the sense that legislation is often enacted conferring on them or other government officials a broad discretion to act as appears appropriate in any particular circumstance. Section 336(5) of the Communications Act 2003 (replacing the similar power under s 10 of the Broadcasting Act 1990) provides an example of a very widely drafted discretion: the Home Secretary can order Ofcom, the independent broadcasting regulator, by notice to direct broadcasters to 'refrain from including in their licensed services any matter or descriptions of matter, specified in the notice'. Once a discretion of this width is granted to a minister, might it be said that he or she can act in a manner that is unregulated by the law? Clearly, in a narrow sense, the minister is acting within the law because the discretionary power is lawfully granted. However, such an answer largely begs the question at issue. To some extent, it may be said that the minister is indeed able to exercise arbitrary power in the sense that any specific action has no specific legal authority; the only check on such actions is represented by the availability of judicial review. Where the exercise of the power in question would impact on a right protected by the ECHR, as in the example given above (Art 10) then, under s 3(1) of the HRA, the courts will be obliged to construe the power granted narrowly, so that it no longer authorises interference with Convention rights, if that is possible, and to quash actions that do infringe Convention rights (s 6(1)) unless the statute in question clearly mandates or authorises such infringement (s 6(2)). This considerably reduces the broad discretion that is prima facie granted by such statutes, and which the House of Lords in *Brind* (1991) refused to read as impliedly restricted by reference to the Convention rights. The HRA therefore overrules *Brind*.

However, where no Convention right is arguably engaged by the exercise of statutory authority, such powers, however broad, will not be affected by the HRA. However, the courts are prepared to invalidate a minister's actions, according to the House of Lords in *Padfield v Minister of Agriculture* (1968), where he or she purports to act within a broadly drafted power, on the ground that the actions do not promote the policy and objects of the statute conferring the power.

What of the notion that the law applies equally to all citizens, which implies that no one is above the law? The notion could be attacked by citing numerous exceptions to it. Members of Parliament enjoy complete civil and criminal immunity in respect of words spoken during 'proceedings in Parliament' by virtue of the Bill of Rights 1688, while judges also enjoy various legal privileges. Diplomatic and consular immunities arise under the Diplomatic Privileges Act 1964 and the Consular Relations Act 1968, and these have been left undisturbed by s 16 of the State Immunity Act 1978. However, it might be suggested that these examples of exemptions granted and recognised by law support the argument that the rule of law exists in the UK constitution, as they imply that there is a need to create exceptions to a general principle that would otherwise apply to all of the groups mentioned. It is notable that in *A v Secretary of State* (2004), one of the key grounds for finding the legislative scheme allowing for detention without trial in

Belmarsh Prison of terrorist suspects incompatible with the Convention, was that it unlawfully discriminated between nationals and non-nationals.[13]

Furthermore, Parliament is free to enact legislation nullifying a decision taken in the House of Lords, as it did in the War Damage Act 1965, which followed the decision in *Burmah Oil Co v Lord Advocate* (1965). Article 7 of the ECHR, now binding on all public authorities save Parliament under s 6(1) of the HRA, states: 'No one shall be held guilty of any criminal offence on account of any act or omission which did not constitute a criminal offence under national or international law at the time when it was committed.' This Article reinforces the protection against non-retroactivity in criminal law, a crucial aspect of the rule of law but, since it is incorporated through the HRA, could simply be overridden by Parliament and therefore remains subject to parliamentary sovereignty.

Aim Higher ★

Students who want to make a more nuanced impact of the effect of the HRA on the rule of law could note that the HRA may paradoxically be said to undermine the rule of law by adding further uncertainty to the law. The Act requires all legislation to be read and given effect in such a way as to be compatible with the Convention rights 'So far as it is possible to do so'. Potentially, therefore, all legislation that touches on ECHR issues is now open to reinterpretation; a considerable period of uncertainty will thus ensue. The case of *A* (2001) is a good example: the statutory provision in question, s 41 of the Youth Justice and Criminal Evidence Act 1999, was given a radically different meaning from that which appears on its face; it is difficult to know in advance which other statutory provisions might be thus judicially re-shaped, thus rendering their meaning uncertain until so determined.

QUESTION 5

Would you agree that the notion of the separation of powers is somewhat overshadowed in the UK constitution by the doctrine of parliamentary sovereignty? Take account of the impact of the Constitutional Reform Act 2005 and Constitutional Reform and Governance Act 2010 in your answer.

How to Answer this Question

Clearly, the assumption that parliamentary sovereignty is the dominant feature of the constitution should be tested. The question of how far the doctrine has been affected by

---

13   ***Belmarsh*** is such an important case that examiners may well expect to see a mention of it outside the particular area of law it dealt with.

the UK's membership of the EU should be touched on, but cannot be considered in detail if the separation of powers is to receive adequate coverage. Obviously, it amounts to a very important issue in itself (which is considered in Chapter 2), but it would not be appropriate to examine it in detail here. In considering the doctrine of the separation of powers, comparisons can usefully be made with other jurisdictions, such as the USA. Mention of specific aspects of the Human Rights Act 1998 (HRA), specific European Convention on Human Rights (ECHR) Articles and relevant case law is essential in dealing with the final part of the question.

Answer Structure

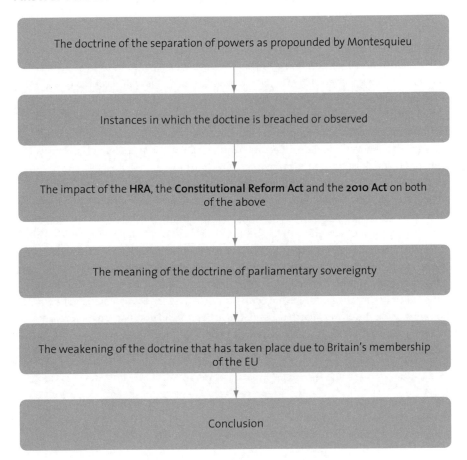

The doctrine of the separation of powers as propounded by Montesquieu

Instances in which the doctine is breached or observed

The impact of the **HRA**, the **Constitutional Reform Act** and the **2010 Act** on both of the above

The meaning of the doctrine of parliamentary sovereignty

The weakening of the doctrine that has taken place due to Britain's membership of the EU

Conclusion

ANSWER

The doctrine of the separation of powers, originally developed by Montesquieu and his followers, encompasses the notion that the three main organs of government are the legislature, the Executive and the judiciary, and that only one class of function should be in the hands of each body. For example, the judiciary should apply, not create, law. Thus, a system of checks and balances between each branch of government will be provided. It is not hard to find examples of the violation of this doctrine. Judges can create law, in the sense that they can declare and develop the common law. Declaring the common law sometimes means creating it, as the common law often has to meet fresh situations that have never previously been addressed. In *Shaw v DPP* (1962), for example, the House of Lords declared that the common law included a doctrine known as 'conspiracy to corrupt public morals', although no precedents were cited demonstrating that it had ever existed except as a variant of the power exercised by Star Chamber judges to punish offences against conventional morality.

In the UK as in all constitutions that follow a parliamentary, rather than presidential system, ministers, who are members of the Executive, sit as members of the House of Commons, which is the legislative body. More importantly, it is well accepted by constitutional observers that the Executive can effectively determine the legislative output of Parliament, theoretically a separate body.[14] However, if the doctrine of separation of powers is not interpreted in an over-rigid manner, it may be argued that some aspects of government do reflect recognition of its existence. Under the House of Commons Disqualification Act 1975, civil servants must resign their posts if they wish to stand for election to the House of Commons, as must professional full-time judges. Further, the number of government ministers permitted to sit in the House of Commons is limited to 95. Moreover, the growing significance of judicial review does not suggest that the separation of powers is irrelevant. Judicial review is generally recognised as an important and necessary check on the exercise of official power. Here again, the HRA has clearly had an impact: s 6(1), which makes it unlawful for a public authority to act in violation of a Convention right, represents a significant shift in power from the Executive to the judiciary – for the first time, the courts are able to strike down actions not because they are outside the powers used to justify the actions or did not follow a fair procedure, but on the substantive basis that they violated human rights: *ex p Limbuela* (2005) is a striking example. The freedom of action of the Executive – the area of discretion that it enjoys – is, as a corollary, substantially curtailed.[15]

The HRA has already had a more specific impact in terms of the separation of functions between the Executive and the judiciary. An example of what Stevens refers to as 'the casual British attitude to the separation of powers' ((1999) OJLS 366) was the power of

14 Students often make the point that in the UK ministers sit in the House of Commons: but if this alone means that the UK has no proper separation of powers then the same applies to the many parliamentary systems around the world, including e.g. in Canada, Australia, India, Italy and Germany.

15 It is important that students can clearly and succinctly capture the difference between judicial review under the **HRA** and the 'ordinary' heads of judicial review.

the Home Secretary to set sentences to be served by juvenile killers. A challenge to the Secretary's power to set such tariffs was launched before the European Court of Human Rights, in reliance upon Art 6(1) of the ECHR, which provides: 'In the determination of his civil rights and obligations, or of any criminal charge against him, everyone is entitled to a fair and public hearing within a reasonable time by an independent and impartial tribunal established by law.' In *T v UK; V v UK* (2000), the Court found that the Secretary, as a party politician, could not be considered an 'independent' tribunal. The UK was obliged to implement that judgment as a matter of international law. This was followed by similar decisions by the House of Lords under the HRA in *Anderson* (2003) and the Scottish decision in *Starrs v Ruxton* (2000), which also indicate the bolstering effect which Article 6 is now having on the independence of the judiciary, a vital aspect of the separation of powers.[16]

A more systematic reorganisation of the UK constitution, in line with separation of powers principles, has been brought about by the Constitutional Reform Act 2005 (CRA). The Act brought in a number of reforms designed to rationalise the UK's hitherto rather ad hoc arrangements for its highest court, the position of the head of the judiciary (the Lord Chancellor) and his involvement with other organs of government and judicial appointments. In brief, the CRA provided that the Lord Chancellor ceases to be the head of the judiciary; that function is now held by the most senior judge – the Lord Chief Justice (s 7(1)). It provided for a new Supreme Court, to end the anomaly whereby the UK's highest court – the House of Lords – was merely a committee of its upper legislative chamber; this ended the violation of the separation of powers represented by the presence of the Law Lords in the second chamber of Parliament. The CRA also formally brought about the end of the Lord Chancellor's role in the judicial and legislative arms of government; he is no longer a judge and does not now take the judicial oath (s 17); it also provided that he is no longer the Speaker of the House of Lords (s 18), which now chooses it own Speaker. Perhaps most importantly, the Act put in place a new system for judicial appointments, designed to bolster judicial independence. Previously, the most senior judiciary (the Law Lords, the Court of Appeal judges, the President of the Family Division and the Master of the Rolls) were appointed by the Queen on the advice of the prime minister. High Court, circuit and district judges were appointed by the Queen on the advice of the Lord Chancellor, as were recorders. In relation to the most senior positions (Law Lords and Court of Appeal judges), there was a system of 'secret soundings', whereby the Lord Chancellor would consult confidentially with existing judges at this level as to the merits of possible candidates for promotion. This system had been subject to widespread criticism for its lack of transparency and for its tendency to limit membership of the senior judiciary to a small elite of senior barristers, overwhelmingly white, male and upper class (see, for example, K. Malleson (2004) PL 102). The CRA created

---

16 Answers on recent changes to the separation of powers very often deal with nothing but the **CRA 2005** it is important to deal with other important changes, such as the cases described in this paragraph.

a full Appointments Commission, with a carefully balanced membership. Lord Mance, an existing Law Lord, has described its composition as 'more nuanced and subtle than any found in any other European jurisdiction' ((2006) 25 CJQ 155). The Commission does not actually appoint, but makes recommendations to the Lord Chancellor, who, in the case of the most senior appointments, then puts these to the Queen. Thus, formally speaking, senior politicians are still involved in the process; however, the Lord Chancellor's power to reject names suggested is highly restricted and figures from the Ministry of Justice show that it has been used extremely sparingly.

The somewhat complex provisions of the Act indeed only allow the Lord Chancellor to ultimately reject one candidate recommended by the Commission in relation to each position it is filling. The Act therefore considerably strengthens the independence of the judiciary, both symbolically and practically, even if it has not as yet led to greater diversity in appointments. Moreover the Act specifically provides that the Lord Chancellor and other ministers have a duty 'to uphold the continued independence of the judiciary' (s 3(1)) and, specifically, 'must not seek to influence particular judicial decisions through any access to the judiciary' (s 3(5)). It is valuable to have so important a principle both of the separation of powers and of the rule of law (which is heavily dependent upon the independence of the judiciary) enshrined in statute.

Finally, the Constitutional Reform and Governance Act 2010 introduced a very modest strengthening of the separation of powers, in terms of introducing further checks on the Executive. It gave Parliament a heavily qualified legal right to give its consent before treaties signed by the UK Government come into force; however, as reports by the Public Administration Select Committee in particular pointed out, the provisions are so full of exceptions that it remains perfectly possible to bypass the parliamentary approval procedural.

Overall, it must be acknowledged that the separation of powers in Britain is less clearly apparent than under some systems. This is partly because of the doctrine of parliamentary sovereignty, which is the most prominent feature of the UK constitution in a way that marks it out from other constitutions. Parliament can legislate on any subject and therefore could pass laws severely curtailing civil liberties without facing the possibility that such legislation might be declared unconstitutional. The HRA specifically declares that the incompatibility of any legislation with the incorporated Convention rights will not render that legislation void or deprive it of effect (ss 3(2) and 4(6)). Parliament's full powers to invade Convention rights are thus maintained, at least as a matter of law.

The potential for parliamentary sovereignty simply to overwhelm other principles of the constitution may be seen in the saga of the Regulatory Reform Bill 2006. As originally introduced, the provisions were startling: they 'empower[ed] any Minister by order to make provision amending, repealing or replacing *any* legislation, primary or secondary, for *any* purpose, and to reform the common law to implement Law Commission recommendations'. The Bill thus would have given ministers 'a . . . general power to legislate', as one critical Select Committee report put it. In this instance, Parliament's unlimited power would have enabled it effectively to hand over the power to legislate to the Executive. The episode thus reveals the potential for the separation of powers to be *legally* undermined – but at the same time shows its potency as a *political* principle. Although passed by the Commons, the Bill raised widespread protests, in and out of Parliament: the powers were amended in the Lords so that such Orders could be made only for the purpose of 'removing or reducing any burden, or the overall burdens, resulting directly or indirectly for any person from any legislation'. This, while still a very wide power, at least avoided the wholesale transfer of law-making power to the government that the original proposals had allowed for.[17]

Although it may be argued that parliamentary sovereignty has been weakened by Britain's membership of the EU (*Factortame v Secretary of State for Transport (No 2)* (1991)), it may be concluded that, despite this, parliamentary sovereignty is still the dominant feature of the constitution, and therefore to an extent undermines the separation of powers, although it is submitted that it is far from rendering it unimportant. The HRA and the CRA have strengthened the separation of powers to a significant degree, but of course both remain subject to the doctrine of parliamentary sovereignty.

QUESTION 6

How far has Scottish devolution affected the unitary nature of the UK and its 'unwritten' constitution?

How to Answer this Question

Questions on devolution often focus upon the whole scheme, requiring comparison of the settlements for Scotland, Wales and Northern Ireland, and often requiring the candidate to comment on the asymmetric nature of the scheme. Another popular topic is the issue of the unresolved 'West Lothian' or 'English' question, whereby Scottish MPs continue to vote on matters solely affecting England, whereas English MPs now no longer vote on the broad swathe of areas devolved to Scotland, and a specific question on this topic is included below. Where a more specific question is asked, it will often focus upon the constitutional implications of devolution to Scotland, the most significant of the schemes.

---

17 Answers on the separation of power rarely mention this statute and the original proposals; however, it concerned far more important matters than some of the largely symbolic changes made by the **CRA 2005**.

Answer Structure

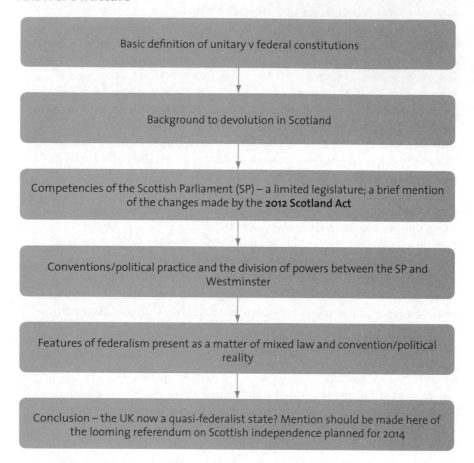

Basic definition of unitary v federal constitutions

Background to devolution in Scotland

Competencies of the Scottish Parliament (SP) – a limited legislature; a brief mention of the changes made by the **2012 Scotland Act**

Conventions/political practice and the division of powers between the SP and Westminster

Features of federalism present as a matter of mixed law and convention/political reality

Conclusion – the UK now a quasi-federalist state? Mention should be made here of the looming referendum on Scottish independence planned for 2014

ANSWER

A unitary constitution is one in which there is a central legislature, with competence to legislate for the whole of the State in all areas, without restrictions upon it deriving from the sharing of legislative power with provincial legislatures. The doctrine of parliamentary sovereignty, still probably the central feature of the UK constitution, logically implies a unitary State;[18] moreover, up until recently, the UK, unlike many other states, had no provincial legislative bodies, with power to make laws for particular regions of the State, such as those that exist in Canada, the USA and Germany. The

---

18 It is essential to have a clear explanation of what a 'unitary' State means and to make the link with parliamentary sovereignty.

'unwritten' – more properly, 'uncodified' – nature of the UK constitution means, at its most basic, that whilst reforms such as Scottish devolution are readily introduced through the ordinary legislative process, such constitutional provisions have no special status, and can be repealed, with none of the special procedures required for changes in the constitutions of other countries, such as referenda or two-thirds majorities in the legislature.

A unitary constitution can be contrasted with federalism as seen, for example, in the constitutions of the USA, Canada and Germany. Federalism may be defined as having three key characteristics. First, there exist both federal and state or provincial legislatures, and, crucially, each have *exclusive* areas of competence: *both* are limited legislatures with a defined area of competence. Thus, typically, federal legislatures are competent to legislate on matters such as defence, macroeconomic policy and national transport policy and regulation; provincial legislatures deal with matters such as education, health policy and housing. Because both legislatures have independent areas of power, neither are competent to dissolve the other. Second, there must be a written constitution, which defines and limits the jurisdiction of both federal and provincial legislatures. Third, there must be a Supreme, or Constitutional Court, which has the power to review the vires of Acts of both legislatures and annul them as unconstitutional if they have strayed into areas reserved for the other legislature.[19]

Whilst the UK has always been a unitary State, it has also always recognised the special status of Scotland within the union, preserving in the Treaties of Union Scotland's separate legal system, its separate established church – the Presbyterian Church of Scotland – and its separate education systems. While the Westminster Parliament was sovereign and thus legislated for Scotland, many Bills were known as 'Scottish' Bills, that is, concerned with Scottish affairs only. Scotland thus had quite a high degree of what can be referred to as executive devolution and had always preserved its separate legal system, church, and education system.

Following a rising tide of opinion in favour of change, the Scottish Constitutional Convention proposed a Parliament for Scotland that would exercise substantial legislative powers and this proposal was accepted by the incoming Labour Government. The legislation putting in place the Scottish Parliament (SP) was not passed until the proposal that there should be a Scottish Parliament had been put to the Scottish people in a referendum. The question of whether there should be such a parliament and that it should have tax-raising powers was approved in a referendum by over 70 per cent of those who took part, on a reasonable turnout of 60 per cent. As discussed further below, this is of great political-conventional significance, although not relevant in strict law.

....

19 A *clear* definition of federalism must also be offered, in order to make clear the central contrasts with devolution.

What then are the competencies of the Scottish Parliament? The first point to note is that the legislation is designed quite explicitly so as *not* to produce a federal system. The White Paper *Scotland's Parliament* (Cm 3658, 1997, para 4.2) stated: 'The United Kingdom Parliament is and will remain sovereign in all matters.' This intention is made plain in the Scotland Act (SA); s 28(7) states, 'This section does not affect the power of the Parliament of the United Kingdom to make laws for Scotland.' This provision can only have been included for the sake of absolute certainty: as a matter of orthodox constitutional law, Parliament could not have restricted its own powers by giving them away to the new Scottish Parliament. Moreover, the SA makes it clear that the Scottish Parliament is, unlike Westminster, a limited legislature. Section 29(1) states: 'An Act of the [SP] is not law so far as any provision of the Act is outside the legislative competence of the [SP].'

Instead of setting out the specific powers that were to be shared with Scotland, a different route was taken: those powers that were not to be shared (known as 'reserved powers') are specified, so that anything not mentioned is deemed to be devolved. The competence of the SP is thus defined negatively – the Scottish Parliament may not legislate on 'reserved matters' (SA, Sched 5), which are retained at Westminster (contrast the Scotland Act 1978). The areas reserved to Westminster include: UK constitutional issues; foreign and defence policy; fiscal, economic and monetary system (that is, macroeconomic issues, including interest rates and the currency); common markets for UK goods and services; employment and social security; and transport safety and regulation. The powers thus devolved include: all areas of education; local government; land development and environmental regulation; many aspects of transport policy; the Scottish NHS, the legal system (civil and criminal law excepting areas covered by EU law and the ECHR); agriculture and fisheries; sports, arts and culture. Some minor new areas of competence were added by the Scotland Act 2012. More importantly, the 2012 Act gives the Scottish Parliament the power to vary the level of income tax in Scotland – a power estimated to correlate to £5.3 billion of tax (*Guardian*, 21 March 2012). Moreover stamp duty, aggregates levy and the landfill levy are also now wholly devolved. Per s 29 of the Act, the SP may not legislate contrary to EU law or the ECHR nor for the territory of another country and nor may it alter the terms of the SA itself (with a few minor exceptions). Clearly then the Scottish Parliament is not a legislature within a federal system: it has no legally exclusive competence, since the Westminster Parliament retains its ability to legislate for the whole of the UK, while the SP can be abolished by the Westminster Parliament.

In certain other respects, however, the SP *does* follow the model of a legislature in a federal system: the vires of its legislation can be raised either post or pre-enactment; the final determinant of 'devolution issues' is now the new Supreme Court, per the Constitutional Reform Act 2005. Up until recently, there had been no cases in which legislation of the Parliament had been annulled by the courts. However, there were two cases in 2012 in which Scottish Courts determined that an Act of the SP was 'not law': *Cameron v Cottam* 2012 SLT 173 and *Salvesen v Riddell* [2012] CSIH 26. Both concerned breaches of Convention rights; there has not yet been a successful challenge on the basis that legislation of the Scottish Parliament trespasses on the reserved areas: the most recent challenge on this ground – *Logan v Harrower* 2010 JC 1 – failed. Moreover in *AXA General Insurance Ltd, Petitioners* [2011] UKSC 46 (SC) the Supreme Court held that Acts of the SP may not – as the lower Scottish courts had ruled – be challenged on common law grounds of irrationality or abuse of discretion. Lord Hope allowed for challenge but only for fundamental breach of the rule of law, such as abolishing judicial review – a ground that increasing numbers of Supreme Court justices appear to believe also applies to the UK Parliament.

Having surveyed the legal position, which, as we have seen, firmly precludes the creation of any kind of federalism, it is necessary to examine the position as a matter of convention or political practice.[20] As noted above, the SA expressly reserves to the Westminster Parliament the right to legislate on all matters, including those devolved to the SP. However, as Tam Dalyell, MP, remarked at the time of the passing of the Act, '[this] may conceivably be true in an arcane legal sense, but in the political reality of 1998 it is palpably misleading and about as true as it would be to say that the Queen can veto any legislation' (HC Deb vol 305, col 366, 28 January 1998).

The problem would arise if the Westminster Parliament were to wish to legislate in one of the devolved areas in order to overturn the policy of the Scottish Executive or Parliament, or in opposition to their wishes. If the Executive were to threaten to resign if the Westminster Parliament passed the legislation in question, this would be likely to make the Government very reluctant to press forward with its legislation for fear of provoking a political crisis in Scotland. If a Scottish Executive were to resign in protest, precipitating an election, the fear of the UK Government would be that such an action would ignite a wave of nationalist sentiment, threatening the break-up of the United Kingdom, or at least aggressive demands for further devolution. It is at this point that the strict legal position becomes far less important than political realities. There has indeed been express recognition of the de facto surrender by Westminster over the devolved areas by the UK Government. A memorandum of understanding signed between the UK Government and the Scottish Executive states that '. . . the UK Parliament would not normally legislate with regard to devolved matters except with the agreement of the devolved legislature'. This convention, known as the Sewell Convention, has been faithfully followed by Westminster; whilst Westminster *has* passed legislation intruding into the devolved areas, this has only taken place with the consent of the SP. It is notable in particular that, when Westminster was considering the Scotland Bill passed in May 2012, the Government made clear that it would not be passed without the consent of the Scottish Parliament, which was eventually given by means of a legislative consent motion in April 2012.

....

20 A good 2:1 essay needs to include both these important perspectives: the legal position needs to be set out clearly before being contrasted with the politico-conventional position. This applies to many areas of the UK constitution.

In the result, one may put forward an argument that what we have in the UK is now a form of quasi-federalism.[21] At this point, we must recall the three components of federalism defined above: (a) legislatures with separate and distinct areas of competence; (b) that those limits are fixed by the constitution; and (c) that there is a Supreme Court with power to review the vires of legislation of each body. Given the existence and strength of the Sewell Convention, we may say that, at the conventional level, (a) is satisfied – the SP legislates for Scottish, devolved matters, the UK Parliament for the reserved areas only (and needs the permission of the SP to legislate for the devolved areas). As for point (b), the constitution for these purposes would be the **Scotland Act**. While it is clearly not 'higher law' in the sense that it remains subject to ordinary express repeal, if it becomes impossible to repeal or amend it as a matter of political reality without the consent of the SP, then it becomes a form of de facto higher law. In this respect, the fact that the SP was set up with the clear backing of the Scottish people as approved in a referendum is of great significance: it makes its abolition, or emasculation, without the consent of the Scottish people, virtually politically impossible. As for (c), the Supreme Court is at present the JCPC, soon to become the new UK Supreme Court. Of course, whilst this body has full powers to review and indeed strike down Acts of the SP that exceed its vires, it has no power to do so in relation to Acts of the Westminster Parliament. Nevertheless, it is plausible to assume that courts will develop an interpretative presumption to the effect that the latter does not intend to legislate in the devolved areas without the consent of the SP, as the Sewell Convention states. This could lead to a position in which courts are prepared to read Westminster legislation that *did* intrude into such matters without consent as narrowly as possible, so as to prevent such intrusion.

In conclusion, then: it is clear law that devolution to Scotland has not altered the legal basis of the UK constitution. It remains a unitary system: the UK Parliament retains full legislative competence in relation to Scotland, so that no power has, strictly speaking, been 'transferred' to the Scottish Parliament; moreover the **Scotland Act**, whilst doubtless a 'constitutional statute' under the *Thoburn* doctrine, remains subject to express repeal at least, by Parliament. However, the UK Parliament, as a matter of expressly declared, and so far faithfully followed, constitutional convention is now a limited Parliament – it will not legislate in the areas devolved to Scotland without the consent of the Scottish Parliament. Further the **Scotland Act** plainly has a special status as a matter of political fact – it will be impossible to repeal it or modify it in a way that reduces the scope of devolution without the consent of the Scottish Parliament. The fact that a referendum on Scottish independence is to be held in 2014, despite the fact that the Scottish Parliament probably lacks the power to authorise it, shows the strength of political imperatives in this area trumping strict legal considerations. Viewed through this second lens then, devolution to Scotland has introduced a convention of federalism and a marked degree of codification to the UK constitution.

....

21 Students sometimes endorse the notion of 'quasi-federalism' in essays, but such arguments often lack precision; to make out the case properly it is necessary to go back to the definition of federalism set out earlier in the essay.

QUESTION 7

'England is the gaping hole in the devolution settlement' (Hazel). Do you agree and how would you solve the 'English' or 'West Lothian' question?

How to Answer this Question

Questions like this are very likely indeed to be asked over the next few years. This question focuses specifically on the 'West Lothian' question; sometimes, however, this issue should be addressed as part of a more general question, which will ask you to examine the asymmetry or 'muddle' of Labour's devolution programme, in which case it should be treated as a very important part of the answer, but to be considered alongside other issues such as the differential grants of power to the Welsh and Scottish devolved institutions, the special features of Northern Irish devolution and so on.

Answer Structure

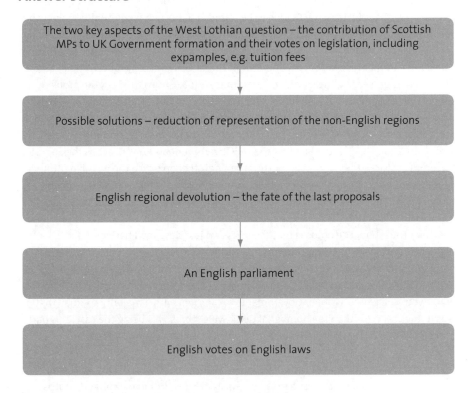

The two key aspects of the West Lothian question – the contribution of Scottish MPs to UK Government formation and their votes on legislation, including expamples, e.g. tuition fees

Possible solutions – reduction of representation of the non-English regions

English regional devolution – the fate of the last proposals

An English parliament

English votes on English laws

ANSWER

Brigid Hadfield has observed that 'England is the only UK nation all of whose laws are made and all of whose policies are formulated by a UK body and never by a solely English-elected body' ((2005) PL 286, 291). This situation of course arises because of the successful Labour programme of devolution to Scotland, Wales and Northern Ireland, which provides for democratic institutions in those nations, directly elected only by voters of that nation, which exercise, particularly in the case of Scotland, a very substantial area of power over domestic law and policies. At a simple level, therefore, the 'gaping hole' referred to by Hazel is simply the absence of any equivalent representative body in England, elected by the English. But this absence has further problematic consequences, collectively termed the 'West Lothian' or 'English' question. In what follows, the different aspects of this issue will be systematically set out and analysed; possible solutions will then be mooted and their desirability assessed, before a conclusion is reached on the best way forward.

The English question arises not only because of the above-noted facts, but because the UK Parliament, as a result, has to serve as the Parliament for England, but with the problematic feature of containing a significant proportion of MPs from the non-English nations. Out of a total of 646 MPs (due to be reduced to 600), 117 represent non-English constituents: Scotland has 59 (a number recently reduced from 72 in partial recognition of the English question), Wales has 40 and Northern Ireland has 18. There are two distinct consequences that follow from this: first, what might be termed the government-formation issue; second, the legislation-legitimacy issue.[22] As to the first, the problem is simply that it is possible that, in future, there will be a UK Government that only holds power due to the presence in Westminster, as part of the governing party's majority, of Scottish and Welsh MPs (hereafter the 'Celtic MPs'). There would be nothing wrong with such a situation, save for the fact that the UK Government also has to act as the English Government (since there is no other). Thus the English people face the possible future of being governed by an administration that is a minority one in terms of seats: in blunt terms, by a Labour Government when they voted Conservative.

The point that should be noted is that the situation just described has not in fact happened since devolution was introduced. Under a Conservative Government, the problem could not practically arise, because the Conservatives tend to do much better in England than Scotland and Wales. The only circumstances in which it would be likely to occur would be where a Labour Government was formed with a majority so small that it was numerically less than the number of Celtic MPs it had. This being the case, this part of the English question is strictly a potential, rather than an actual, problem.[23]

In contrast, the second part of the question has already materialised. This more well-known aspect points out that, as a result of legislative devolution in Scotland, Scottish MPs at Westminster can and do vote on legislation passed at Westminster that only applies to England (hereafter 'English laws' or 'English Bills'), while English MPs cannot

---

22 Students commonly miss the first of these, yet it is potentially far more important than the second.
23 In areas like this, it is essential that students display some awareness of the relevant party-political factors. Constitutional law cannot be studied in isolation from politics!

vote on equivalent laws applying to Scotland, because such laws are now passed by the Scottish Parliament. This, it is submitted, is a conspicuous constitutional unfairness in principle. The problem is at its most acute where legislation, which does not command a majority among English MPs, is yet passed because of the votes of Scottish MPs; in such a situation, it may be said that legislation has been imposed upon England that its representatives, as a whole, did not vote for. Instead, Scottish MPs, who are, as Hadfield puts it, 'Unelected by [English voters] and unaccountable to [them]' (ibid, 286) determine the policies that will apply to those voters. Notoriously, this is precisely what happened in relation to two highly controversial government Bills – those introducing foundation hospitals and student tuition (or 'top-up') fees in England: because of large rebellions from its backbenchers, the then Labour Government needed the votes of Scottish MPs to get both these policies through. Salt was rubbed into English wounds by the fact that neither policy would apply in Scotland

What then are the possible solutions and how satisfactory would they be? In short order, they may be summarised as: first, reduction of the representation at Westminster of the Scottish (and possibly Welsh) MPs; second, English regional devolution; third, an English Parliament; fourth, the policy popularly known as 'English votes for English laws'. The first provides no real answer to the problem, and, taken further than it already has been, would simply unfairly reduce the representation of Scottish MPs in the Westminster Parliament, which still decides many crucial issues relevant to the UK as a whole, including macroeconomic policy, virtually all taxation issues, immigration and citizenship and energy policy; moreover, of course, it forms the UK Government and holds the UK Government to account on issues such as the conduct of foreign policy and the deployment of UK forces abroad.

The second possible solution would be to introduce some form of devolution to the English regions; this would at least seek to address the democratic deficit whereby English voters have no representative body specifically to represent them. It should be noted, of course, that in one English region – London – this has already been implemented, with some success, in the form of the London Mayor and Assembly. There are, however, three problems here. The first is, bluntly, that it has been tried and resoundingly rejected by the voters in the North-East of England in 2004. The second problem is that it seems inconceivable that any such scheme would grant anything like the kinds of powers to regional assemblies that the Scottish Parliament has. Certainly the 2003–04 scheme did not offer the regions anything close to the powers of even the Welsh Assembly. The third problem, as a result of the second, is that the proposed solution simply does not deal with the problem: the UK Parliament would remain the legislature for England, with Scottish MPs voting in it. Neither the government formation, nor the legislative questions would thus be ameliorated by this 'solution', much less answered by it.

The third mooted solution is an English Parliament, which might, although it would not need to, lead to a federal UK. It was briefly put forward by former Conservative leader

William Hague and is clearly the most comprehensive solution. Practically speaking, the main drawback with this solution is simply that there seems to be little public support for it. The other objection to it is that the federation created by an English Parliament – whether a quasi-federation or a legal federation (which would require the UK Parliament to lose its sovereignty) – would be unbalanced and dominated by England and would 'rival' the Westminster Parliament (see Report of the Royal Commission on the Constitution in 1973 (Cmnd 5460)).

It is suggested, however, that these objections are unpersuasive. The Westminster Parliament, which in some senses acts as a federal Parliament for the UK (in that it decides policies normally decided by the federal legislature), is *already* dominated by English MPs and thus English voters. Thus if this is a problem in this respect, it already exists, and the introduction of an English Parliament would make no difference to it. As for the contention that the English Parliament would 'rival' the Westminster Parliament, the question is why this would matter? The English Parliament would undoubtedly be a major institution, and would have to be given a huge budget to dispense. But why this would be problematic does not seem to be stated. This solution, then, is less problematic than generally assumed and if English voters ever want it, they can vote for it.

However, the most likely solution and one requiring far less constitutional upheaval (and expense) would be some variant of the policy of 'English votes for English laws': all Bills introduced into Westminster would have to somehow be 'tagged' as either 'UK' in nature (e.g. if a Bill implemented a treaty) or as affecting only Wales, or only Scotland, or only England. In the last case, Scottish and Welsh MPs would be barred from voting on it. If this new system were enshrined in law, issues around court-enforceability would arise. However, it could, at least as a first step, be adopted merely by resolution of the House of Commons, as a constitutional convention to be followed by all MPs. The Coalition Government has recently set up the McKay Commission to examine such a possibility. The solution seems elegant because of its economy and simplicity: effectively a new, but intermittently existing, English Parliament would be created within the Westminster Parliament; the latter would morph into the former whenever an English Bill was being considered.

What then are the objections to this seemingly simple solution? First, it is said that defining an 'English Bill' would be, practically speaking, impossible: legislation considered by Westminster often involves Scotland, Wales and England, so that it would be impossible to disentangle it into its constituent parts. It is doubtful that this is a persuasive argument. Bills covering devolved areas would not extend to Scotland anyway. The greater use of framework Bills for Wales, whereby only the bare bones of principle are set out and the Welsh Assembly then passes detailed delegated legislation to flesh out the policies, would also force the use of separate Bills for Wales, thus going a long way towards obviating the problem, while enhancing the powers of the Welsh Assembly. Moreover, the 'yes' vote in the 2011 referendum on giving primary legislative powers to the Welsh Assembly will mean that more Bills passed by Westminster will deal with only England. Overall, it is concluded, the definitional problem is far from insuperable.[24]

The second, and most important, objection is known as the 'in–out' government scenario. In brief, were Scottish MPs to be prevented from voting on 'English laws', the possible scenario could arise of a government that was dependent upon Scottish MPs for its majority, losing that majority when Parliament was dealing with an English Bill. Since much of the important work of Westminster consists of dealing with Bills mainly or exclusively affecting England, this, it is said, would fatally undermine that government. Once again, however, it is argued that this objection is more apparent than real. First of all, the scenario would arise only in one limited circumstance: the election of a Labour Government with a very small majority. But, more importantly, it may be argued that this objection is simply spurious: a government, one of the main concerns of which is the formation of English policy, *ought* to be fatally undermined if it has no majority among English MPs. Moreover, as Hadfield observes (ibid, 301), if such a government cannot pass legislation concerning England, which does not command a majority among English MPs, this is not a problem, but a desirable outcome: 'Why should [such legislation] become law?' In reality, all that this objection amounts to is the observation that a Labour Government with no majority among English MPs (which has very rarely happened, historically) would no longer be able to impose legislation upon England without the support of a majority of English MPs. Thus put, the 'problem' sounds rather a desirable state of affairs.

In conclusion, then, 'the English question' is a real problem, although minor compared to the situation of Wales and Scotland, prior to devolution. While an English Parliament would be the most complete solution, it is at present unlikely to be implemented. As at least a temporary and much more easily implemented measure, 'English votes for English laws', in some variant or other, represents a practical and economical solution; its disadvantages have been greatly overplayed.

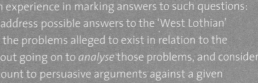

Common Pitfalls

There is a very common experience in marking answers to such questions: students, in seeking to address possible answers to the 'West Lothian' question, consider only the problems alleged to exist in relation to the possible solutions without going on to *analyse* those problems, and consider whether they really amount to persuasive arguments against a given solution. This is particularly noticeable in relation to the English Parliament solution (in which the objections of the Royal Commission are often treated as decisive) and the arguments against English votes for English laws.

---

24 This objection is commonly advanced in student essays, but seldom critically analysed. When doing so, it is vital to show awareness of how recent greater devolution to Wales removes some of the force of the original objection.

Parliamentary Sovereignty, the Human Rights Act and the European Union

2

INTRODUCTION

Textbooks on constitutional law often deal with parliamentary sovereignty and European Union (EU) law in separate chapters. However, exam questions on sovereignty will now often have explicit EU dimensions, and will, in any event, almost invariably require explanation of the impact of EU law on the traditional doctrine. Therefore, this chapter deals with the traditional view of parliamentary sovereignty and the impact of EU law together. The impact of the Human Rights Act 1998 (HRA) on sovereignty is also a very topical subject and we include a question specifically devoted to that complex issue, as well as including consideration of its significance in some of the other essays, where relevant. Thus, four main issues are covered in this chapter: the nature of parliamentary sovereignty and possible legal limitations on it; the impact of EU law on the traditional doctrine of parliamentary sovereignty; the means by which EU law can take effect in the UK (direct and indirect effect); and the impact of the HRA on sovereignty. Questions on sovereignty and on the applicability of EU law in the UK may be of the problem or essay type, although essays are probably more common. Both are included here.

Checklist ✔

Students should be familiar with the following areas:

- the traditional doctrine of parliamentary sovereignty – the doctrine of implied repeal; possible authority for departure from the doctrine – *AG for New South Wales v Trethowan* (1932);
- the main academic arguments surrounding the possible limitations on Parliament, including possible self-limitation;
- the effect of **ss 2(1), 2(4)** and **3(1)** of the **European Communities Act 1972**;
- the primacy of Community law – *Costa v ENEL* (1964);
- the direct and indirect effect of Community law; the *Francovich* principle;
- the purposive approach to domestic legislation supposed to implement an indirectly effective Community law;

- the partial entrenchment of **s 2(1)** of the **European Communities Act** – *Macarthy's v Smith* (1981); the *Factortame* litigation; *Secretary of State for Employment ex p EOC* (1994);

- the alternative and broader explanation given for the above in the case of *Thoburn* (2002);

- the implications of the **European Union Act 2011**

- the implications of the above for protection of a Bill of Rights;

- the extent of protection for the **HRA** – whether the normal doctrine of implied repeal will fully apply; recent case law under the Act;

- implications of the decision in *Jackson* for all of the above.

Note in relation to the *Factortame* litigation: *Factortame* (1990) refers to the first decision of the House of Lords (HL), cited in the Tables as [1990] 2 AC 85; *Factortame* (1990) (ECJ) refers to the decision of the European Court of Justice (ECJ) on interim relief, cited in the Tables as [1990] 3 CMLR 1, ECJ; *Factortame (No 2)* (1991) refers to the second decision of the HL, cited in the Tables as [1991] 1 AC 603; *Factortame (No 3)* (1992) refers to the decision of the ECJ on the substantive issue, cited in the Tables as [1992] QB 680.

QUESTION 8

'... Once an instrument is recognised as being an Act of Parliament, no English court can ... question its validity' (*per* Sir Robert Megarry VC in *Manuel v AG* (1983)). What role do the courts have in determining what is an Act of Parliament?

How to Answer this Question

This is a fairly demanding question and requires careful analysis of the recent *Jackson* case in the House of Lords.

Answer Structure

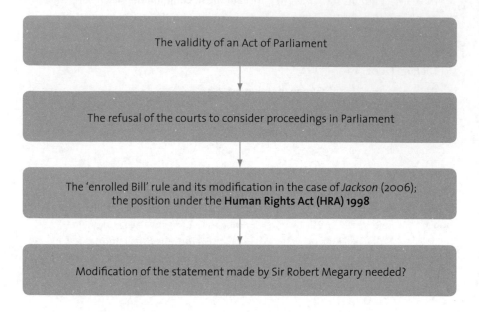

The validity of an Act of Parliament

The refusal of the courts to consider proceedings in Parliament

The 'enrolled Bill' rule and its modification in the case of *Jackson* (2006); the position under the **Human Rights Act (HRA) 1998**

Modification of the statement made by Sir Robert Megarry needed?

ANSWER

This question raises the issue of whether the judges will ask whether what appears to be an Act of Parliament is valid, in the sense that it has been passed in accordance with lawful procedure. It does not raise the broader question of parliamentary sovereignty, namely, when, if ever, courts will refuse to obey an admittedly valid Act of Parliament. Of course, it might be argued that the first aspect is embodied in the second; in other words, the lack of validity of a statute might merely be one ground among others that could be put forward as a reason for disapplying the provision in question. Nevertheless, the issues are distinguishable in that a negative answer to the first question will preclude the second, although a positive answer will still leave the second question open. In one instance, a court is confining itself to asking the narrow question: what is an Act of Parliament? In the other, a court may be accepting that there are circumstances in which an Act of Parliament accepted as valid will yet not be applied.[1] Only the first of these two questions will be considered in what follows, in which it will be argued that the courts will in general decline jurisdiction to examine the authenticity of purported Acts of Parliament, but that a minor adjustment to this rule has been established by the decision of the House of Lords in *Jackson v AG* (2006).

---

1   Note the way that the Introduction very carefully delineates the precise scope of the question to be addressed.

In determining whether the courts will question the validity of a statute, it is unhelpful to ask whether it has been recognised as such, because to say so begs the question as to what the recognition of an Act of Parliament involves. An Act of Parliament is an expression of the sovereign will of Parliament; if, however, Parliament is not constituted as Parliament, or does not function as Parliament within the meaning of the law, it would seem to follow that it cannot express its sovereign will in the form of an Act of Parliament. However, the courts have declined opportunities to declare an Act a nullity where it has been asserted that something that appears to be an Act of Parliament and which bears the customary words of enactment is not authentic. In *Edinburgh and Dalkeith Railway Co v Wauchope* (1842), the court was asked to find that the legislation in question, a Private Act, had been improperly passed and was therefore invalid, in that standing orders had not been complied with. Lord Campbell said, obiter, that if, according to the Parliament Roll, an Act has passed both Houses of Parliament and has received the royal assent, a court can neither inquire into the manner in which it was introduced into Parliament nor into what passed in Parliament during its progress through the various parliamentary stages. This rule, now known as 'the enrolled Bill rule', was relied upon in *Pickin v British Railways Board* (1974): Mr Pickin had sought to challenge a Private Act of 1836 on the basis that Parliament had been misled by fraud. The House of Lords held that he was not entitled to examine proceedings in Parliament to show that the Act had been passed due to fraud. That action therefore failed.

The rationale for this refusal is partly the fear that such an enquiry, which could for example involve determining whether the House of Commons' own Standing Orders had been complied with, could bring the courts into conflict with Parliament, which would undoubtedly have made its own enquiry on the matter, the finding of which could differ from that made by the courts. The other reason is Article 9 of the Bill of Rights 1688, which provides that 'Freedom of speech and debates or proceedings in Parliament ought not to be impeached or questioned in any court or place out of Parliament', the most important effect of which is to confer complete civil and criminal immunity upon those speaking during proceedings in Parliament. However, Article 9 has also been construed so as to forbid any 'questioning' in the courts of the procedures used in Parliament to pass legislation: hence the refusal to consider finding an Act of Parliament to be invalid on the grounds of defective procedure, deception of the House, and so on.[2]

Perhaps, after *Pickin's* case, the possibility still remains that a court might be prepared to take note of an assertion that a Bill had not obtained a majority at the final reading in the House of Commons, although this would risk collision with the privilege of the House not to have its internal proceedings investigated. Generally speaking, then, the

---

2   Students are often aware of the 'enrolled Bill rule' but rarely make the important link with **Article 9** of the **Bill of Rights**.

courts will decline jurisdiction to declare an apparently authentic Act of Parliament a nullity.

There are, however other circumstances in which a court might treat a purported statute as nugatory: a Bill to prolong the life of a Parliament beyond five years might be passed in the Commons but not in the Lords (such a Bill is explicitly excluded from the 1911 Parliament Act procedure) and receive the royal assent. It would state that it had been passed in accordance with the Parliament Acts; if so, a court might treat it as a nullity as 'bad on its face'; its defective nature would be apparent without needing to inquire into proceedings in Parliament. This has been taken further by the House of Lords in the recent decision in *Jackson* (2006). In this case, the Hunting Act 2004 was challenged on the basis that it had been passed without the consent of the House of Lords under the 1911 Parliament Act, as amended by the 1949 Act. It was argued that because the 1949 Act had used the very procedure for bypassing the Lords contained in the 1911 Act to modify the 1911 Act (by reducing the Lords' power of delay from two years to one year), it was not a valid Act of Parliament. Therefore the Hunting Act, passed under the 1949 Act, was not a valid Act either. This argument was rejected by the House of Lords, relying largely on the clear statement in the 1911 Act that measures passed under the Parliament Act procedure 'shall become an Act of Parliament', thus disposing of the notion that measures passed under that procedure amounted only to delegated legislation. However, a clear majority of the Lords accepted that a Bill that used the 1949 Act to modify the 1911 Act in order to allow its use to pass a Bill extending the life of a Parliament beyond five years would not be a valid Act of Parliament. Such a Bill is explicitly excluded from the Parliament Act procedure in the 1911 Act. Moreover, to use that procedure first to repeal the prohibiting clause in the 1911 Act and then to pass a Bill under the Parliament Act procedure to extend the life of a Parliament, thus indirectly circumventing the provision designed to ensure that this could not happen without the consent of the Lords, would, the majority held, also be contrary to the intention of the 1911 Act and would thus not be accepted by the courts as a valid Act of Parliament.[3] This indicates something of a departure from the literalism of the enrolled Bill rule and a determination to protect the public from the dangers of tyranny driven by a majority in the House of Commons. However, the House of Lords was clear in rejecting the broader notion put forward by the Court of Appeal in the same case that the Parliament Act procedure may not be used to effect 'major constitutional change.' In doing so, their Lordships again relied on the wording of the 1911 Act, which allows for 'any Bill' to be passed using the procedure save those specifically excepted. It was also pointed out that the purpose of the passage of the 1911 Act was precisely to allow for legislation making a fundamental constitutional change, namely Home Rule for Ireland. Despite this, however, their Lordships did not leave the matter completely clear: Lord Carswell said, at para 179:

---

3   We have read numerous essays by students over the last few years dealing with *Jackson*; remarkably few
     however, manage *accurately* to state the 'two step' procedure discussed in *Jackson*; the point often
     missed is that the **Parliament Act** procedure is used in *both* of the two steps.

Despite the general lack of enthusiasm for the proposition espoused by the Court [of] Appeal, however, I incline very tentatively to the view that its instinct may be righ[t] that there may be a limit somewhere to the powers contained in section 2(1) of the 1911 Act, though the boundaries appear extremely difficult to define.

One specific limit may be that an Act passed under the Parliament Act procedure could not validly abolish the House of Lords. For if that were done, then once the Lords was abolished, the life of Parliament could be extended without the consent of the Lords (since it would no longer exist). In this way, the Commons and Monarch would, by two steps, have achieved an extension of the life of Parliament without the consent of the Lords – precisely contrary to what Lord Nicholls terms 'the express legislative Intention' of the 1911 Act.

If a court were asked to disapply a statute not because something in its background was alleged to render it invalid but due to other factors, it would, according to the traditional doctrine of parliamentary sovereignty, decline to do so except where the other factor consisted of incompatibility between the statute before it and a subsequent statute. This doctrine includes the notion that Parliament cannot bind its successors because the latest expression of Parliament's will must prevail.

In *Ellen Street Estates Ltd v Minister of Health* (1934), it was argued that the Acquisition of Land (Assessment of Compensation) Act 1919 prescribed a certain manner for authorising the acquisition of land. It provided in s 7 that other statutes 'shall have effect subject to this Act'. If s 7 were to apply to subsequent enactments, provisions of the Housing Act 1925 that were inconsistent with the 1919 Act would have no effect. However, Maughan LJ held, obiter, that Parliament cannot bind itself as to the form of future enactments. Thus, the courts will not give effect to a statute that is in conflict with a later statute, on the basis that the earlier statute has been impliedly repealed to the extent of its inconsistency.

In conclusion, the traditional 'enrolled Bill rule' appears broadly still to stand, denying the courts the ability to find an apparent Act of Parliament invalid. But the decision of the House of Lords in *Jackson* certainly introduces at least a narrow qualification to that rule in relation to legislation extending the life of Parliament by the 'two step' procedure, and possibly legislation that outright abolished the House of Lords itself.

QUESTION 9

Would you agree that, under our current constitutional arrangements, a Bill of Rights could not be protected from repeal and that the Human Rights Act 1998 makes no attempt to so protect itself?

How to Answer this Question

In answering this question, it should be borne in mind that a number of different forms of protection could be suggested for the Bill of Rights short of entrenchment.

Answer Structure

> The doctrine of parliamentary sovereignty

> The danger of erosion of the **Human Rights Act 1998 (HRA)** and of any Bill of Rights due to implied repeal by subsequent enactments

> The attempt to prevent inadvertent implied repeal through ministerial statements of compatability

> The construction of subsequent enactments so as to avoid conflict with the **HRA** under **s 3**; a comparison with the approach of the courts to protecting EC legislation from repeal under **s 2(4)** of the **European Comunities Act 1972**; an assessment of case law so far on **s 3**

> The consequences of this approach – the partial protection of the **Convention** rights

> The preclusion by the **HRA** of the possibility of the judiciary using the more radical approach taken in *Secretary of State for Transport ex p Factortame Ltd and Others (No 2)* (1981) to protect the Convention

> The implications of *Thoburn* (2002); dicta suggesting the possibility of limits to sovereignty in *Jackson* (2006)

> Conclusion: the possibility of entrenchment by means of a new constitutional settlement

ANSWER

The adoption of a Bill of Rights intended to exist for all time is incompatible with the doctrine of parliamentary sovereignty: under that doctrine, a purported Bill of Rights would in fact have the same status as other enactments in that it would be vulnerable to express and (possibly) implied repeal. This, indeed, was the stance taken by the White Paper (Cm 3782) on incorporation of the European Convention on Human Rights (ECHR); the HRA makes no attempt to entrench the Convention into UK law, and indeed explicitly states that incompatibility between Convention rights and either future or past UK legislation will not affect the validity or continuing effect of that legislation. Under the doctrine of sovereignty, no Parliament may bind its successors or be bound by its predecessors, and the courts cannot question the validity of an Act of Parliament (see *Pickin v British Railways Board* (1974)). It follows that Parliament can repeal or amend any statute and that where a later statute is incompatible with a former, it repeals the former to the extent of its incompatibility. Thus, the adoption of a Bill of Rights appears to include the unconstitutional notion of limiting the legislative competence of successive Parliaments.

Express repeal of all or part of the Bill of Rights might be undertaken by a subsequent Parliament out of sympathy with its aims, while implied repeal – which might at times be unintentional – could gradually and insidiously erode it. For example, a Bill that, in future, sought to *entrench* the provisions of the ECHR would contain a clause protecting the right to privacy – Art 8. If a subsequent enactment dealt with an aspect of privacy (such as the use of newly developed surveillance devices) in terms that clearly allowed for violations of the rights guaranteed by Art 8, this Act would prevail. The Bill of Rights might eventually become almost worthless – in fact, worse than worthless, because it could be used by government to cloak erosions of freedom, while at the same time raising expectations that it could not fulfil. This danger cannot be ruled out in relation to the HRA.

However, arguably, certain forms of protection for enactments, even amounting to a weak form of entrenchment, already exist in our constitution and are utilised by the HRA. (The word 'protection' is used as being wider than 'entrenchment'.) Legislation that is of doubtful compatibility with the ECHR may be prevented from impliedly repealing the protected rights by virtue of s 3(1). This strongly worded section instructs the courts that in interpreting both previous and future legislation, so far as is possible, they must read and give effect to it in such a way as to make it consistent with the Convention rights. This amounts to a form of protection that may be as strong as judges care to make it although, of course, s 3 could in future be expressly repealed or modified. Just how much protection can be afforded by such an approach can be illustrated by reference to the stance judges have taken in relation to the protection of EU law from implied repeal. The equivalent provision to s 3 of the HRA is s 2(4) of the European Communities Act 1972, which reads as follows: '... any enactment passed or to be passed ... shall be construed and have effect subject to the foregoing provisions of this section.' The words 'subject to' appear to suggest that the courts must allow Community law to prevail over a subsequent Act of Parliament. The 'foregoing provisions' are those of s 2(1), importing Community law into national law.

The House of Lords in *Pickstone v Freemans* (1988) found that a purposive interpretation of the domestic legislation would be adopted; in other words, the plain meaning of the provision in question would be ignored and an interpretation would be foisted upon it that was not in conflict with EC law. The House of Lords followed a similar approach in *Litster v Forth Dry Dock Engineering* (1989). These decisions provide authority for the proposition that Parliament cannot by plain words impliedly depart from the provisions of European Communities law (except by repealing part or all of the European Communities Act 1972). Probably, it could do so only by stating expressly that it was so acting. In *Macarthy's Ltd v Smith* (1981), Lord Denning accepted that an express provision that the instrument in question should prevail over inconsistent Community law would be obeyed. Clearly, such a ruling involves a departure from the rule (deriving from the dictum of Maughan LJ in *Ellen Street Estates Ltd v Minister of Health* (1934)) that Parliament cannot bind itself as to the form of future enactments. Thus, partial entrenchment of the 1972 Act has occurred, as confirmed in *Factortame (No 2)*. Section 18 of the European Union Act 2011, providing that EU law 'falls to be recognised and available in law in the United Kingdom only by virtue of' the 1972 or other Act does not affect this conclusion, as it addresses only the *source* of authority in UK law of EU law, not its effect on other, later statutes. [4]

There appear to be at least some instances of this approach being followed in some of the cases under the HRA. The House of Lords' decision in *A* (2001) concerned the interpretation to be given to s 41 of the Youth Justice and Criminal Evidence Act 1999, which forbade any evidence to be given in a rape trial of the woman's sexual history, including any previous sexual history with the alleged rapist, except in very limited circumstances. This raised an issue of compatibility with Art 6 of the ECHR, which provides, inter alia, that: 'In the determination of . . . any criminal charge against him, everyone is entitled to a fair and public hearing within a reasonable time by an independent and impartial tribunal established by law.' Lords Steyn and Hutton were prepared to hold that given the very strong wording of s 3(1) and *Pepper v Hart* (1992) statements in Parliament to the effect that declarations of incompatibility (indicating that the attempt to ensure compatibility using s 3(1) had failed) were to be a remedy of last resort, the only way in which Parliament could legislate contrary to a Convention right would be by 'a clear limitation on Convention rights . . . stated in terms'. This approach led them simply to read into the relevant part of s 41 words that were not there,

----

4   As the only recent statute explicitly dealing with sovereignty, it is important that the EU Act 2011 is referenced wherever relevant. The paragraph in the text is an instance of a very concise but clear summary of section 18.

namely, that evidence was to be admitted where that was necessary to achieve a fair trial. It may be noted that Lord Hope considered that this approach went too far, crossing the line from interpretation to legislating. He considered, in what is certainly the more usual understanding of the word 'interpreting', that the judge's task was limited to identifying specific words that would otherwise lead to incompatibility and then reinterpreting those words, clearly not something that Lords Steyn and Hutton – and, for that matter, Lord Slynn – undertook.

Lord Hope's approach arguably found more support from the House of Lords in *Re W and B* (2002), in which their Lordships emphasised the importance of not stepping over the boundary from statutory interpretation to 'statutory amendment'. A more activist approach, arguably involving the rewriting, rather than the reinterpretation of legislation occurred in *Ghaidan v Mendoza* (2004). However, the decision in *Bellinger v Bellinger* (2003) clearly indicated that the courts will sometimes refuse to engage even in relatively straightforward reinterpretation of legislation, in terms of linguistics, where it is felt that the change is complex and significant enough to require consideration by Parliament. In contrast, in the recent decision in *Secretary of State for the Home Dept ex p MB* (2007), the House of Lords read into the **Prevention of Terrorism Act 2005** a broad saving to the effect that a clear rule preventing disclosure of sensitive evidence to the suspect in 'control order' cases was to be read as qualified by the requirement not to act incompatibly with **Art 6** of the **ECHR**. This exercise was repeated, more boldly, in *Secretary of State for the Home Department v AF (No 3)* [2009] 2 WLR 423, in order to read into the same statutory scheme a requirement that at least the gist of the evidential case against the suspect must be disclosed to him. Thus, the approach taken in *AF, MB, A* and *Mendoza* shows that at least in some areas of rights protection, Parliament has, through s 3(1), succeeded in imposing a requirement of express words upon such of its successors that wish to legislate incompatibly with the **Convention** rights.[5]

The line of reasoning taken in *Thoburn* (2002) represents a possible alternative route to the protection of the **HRA** from implied repeal. In that decision Laws LJ held that Parliament could not bind itself in any way and had not done so in the **1972 Act**. Rather the explanation for *Factortame* was that the *courts* had recognised the **1972 Act** as but one example of what he called 'a constitutional statute', essentially those that affected fundamental rights or 'the relationship between citizen and State in some general, overarching manner'. The legal consequence of recognising a statute as 'constitutional' was simple: 'Ordinary statutes may be impliedly repealed. Constitutional statutes may not.' Clearly, the **HRA** is a 'constitutional statute' under this analysis;[6] indeed, it was one

---

5   Most students can provide a reasonable summary of the **HRA** case law; however, few are able to make the connection made here, between this case law and the notion of a requirement of *form* – express words – for Parliament to override the **Convention** rights.

6   The *Thoburn* analysis is often cited by students: but what a good 2:1 answer needs is the approach taken here: *citation* and *application* of the definition of 'constitutional statute' that it advanced.

of the examples instanced by the judge. It is too early to say whether this revised view of sovereignty has won general acceptance amongst the senior judiciary, but if it does, the HRA will have gained through common law the protection from implied repeal that Parliament refused to give it.

Depending then upon the approach of the judiciary, the incorporated ECHR may turn out to be at least partly protected from implied repeal, while its express repeal remains unlikely. The HRA may therefore, contrary to the assertion in the question, be said to endow the Convention rights with at least the *potential* for some protection against future repeal, although the Act appears to rule out expressly the wholesale suspension of implied repeal engineered in the area of EU law.

Although this is not an issue in relation to the HRA, there is, finally, the possibility that a future Bill of Rights could be given substantial procedural protection from repeal. It is generally thought that if a Bill of Rights for the UK were enacted containing a provision that it could not be repealed except in accordance with a procedure such as a two-thirds majority, the courts would not give effect to it. However, De Smith suggests that Parliament could redefine itself so as to preclude itself as ordinarily constituted from legislating on a certain matter. The argument is based on the redefinition of Parliament under the Parliament Acts of 1911 and 1949: if Parliament could make it easier for itself to legislate on certain matters, equally, it could make it harder, thereby entrenching certain legislation, although this analogy has been attacked as unsound by Munro (*Studies in Constitutional Law*, 2nd edn, 1999) The only authorities that would support this proposition come from other constitutions: *AG for New South Wales v Trethowan* (1932) and *Harris v Minister of the Interior* (1951). There are contrasting dicta on this point in *Jackson*. Lord Steyn (at [81]) appeared to be open to the 're-definition' theory:

> . . . apart from the traditional method of law making, Parliament acting as ordinarily constituted may functionally redistribute legislative power in different ways. For example, Parliament could for specific purposes provide for a two-thirds majority in the House of Commons and the House of Lords.

In contrast, Lord Hope specifically rejected such a possibility (at [113]):

> . . . it is a fundamental aspect of the rule of sovereignty that no Parliament can bind its successors. There are no means whereby . . . it can entrench an Act of Parliament.

There are instances where Parliament has sought to impose requirements of this manner – purporting to prevent Parliament from doing certain things unless first approved in a referendum, as in the case of the Northern Ireland Act 1998 and the recent European Union Act 2011. However, even where such provisions are enacted, they could be regarded as simply subject to implied repeal, were Parliament to ignore the requirements. Alternatively, such 'referendum locks' could simply be expressly repealed by a later Parliament, acting under its ordinary procedure. Thus, the point of whether such locks bind a future Parliament cannot be regarded as settled.

Therefore, a proposal that the Bill of Rights be fully entrenched would be constitutionally controversial and probably impossible without a written constitution that could be regarded as establishing a new legal order within the UK.

Aim Higher ★

Students could make the more sophisticated point in an essay like that above that parallels between the **HRA** or other domestic protection of rights and EU law must be treated with caution. In 1972, the UK was signing up to a legal order in which the supremacy of EU law had already been firmly established by the European Court of Justice (ECJ) (for example, in *Costa v ENEL* (1964)) and was arguably necessary if the purposes of the Community were to be achieved. No such situation applies in relation to the **European Convention**, and indeed the White Paper expressly disclaims any such comparison (**para 2.12**). In practice, many judges may not be prepared to go as far to protect the **Convention** as they have to protect the law of the Community as the case law above indicates. Even if a *Litster*-style approach were to be generally adopted, the courts would at least occasionally be bound to come across provisions that are not capable of a compatible construction. In such a case, the incompatible statute would have to stand: the **HRA** expressly seeks to preclude judges from taking the further radical step of disapplying incompatible statutes, the step taken in the EC context in the case of *Secretary of State for Transport ex p Factortame (No 2)* (1991).

QUESTION 10

In March 2001, Parliament passes the Parental Leave Act (PLA), s1 of which provides that men or women are entitled to five months' parental leave on 80 per cent of full pay after the birth of their baby. Section 2 provides that any employer who fails to provide the said parental leave shall be liable in damages which shall be equivalent to the salary that would have been paid. Section 3 provides that no Bill to amend or repeal the Act shall be laid before Parliament, unless the Equal Opportunities Commission (EOC) has approved the changes.

In 2002, a European Community Regulation is passed allowing men and women equal access to parental leave and making provision that an employer who refuses to grant such leave will be liable in damages.

In 2003, a Bill amending s 1 of the Parental Leave Act 2001, with the effect that men are no longer entitled to parental leave, is laid before Parliament without the approval of the EOC, and without repealing section 3, is enacted as the Parental Leave Amendment Act 2003.

▶ Advise Mr B, who asks for parental leave in 2004 but is refused it by his employer.

How to Answer this Question

A problem question is commonly set in this area, which will usually involve conflict between two statutes, thereby requiring discussion of the doctrine of implied repeal. It will often also involve conflict between domestic law passed subsequently to directly enforceable European Community law. In many instances, the statute in relation to which implied repeal is raised as an issue could be considered as a 'constitutional statute' under the *Thoburn* analysis, although this is not a possibility here.

Applying the Law

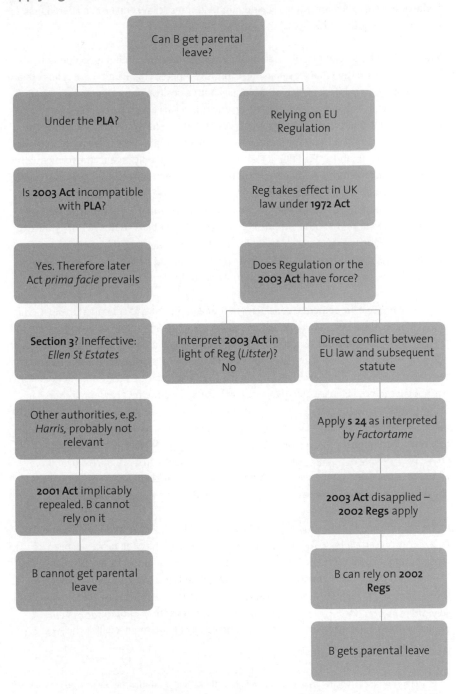

ANSWER

In addressing this question, Mr B's position under domestic law will be considered first before examining the relevance of the 2002 EC Regulation.

Under the traditional doctrine of parliamentary sovereignty, Parliament is competent to legislate on any matter whatsoever and no court is competent to question the validity of an Act of Parliament. This lack of legal restraint has both a positive and a negative aspect. It means that while Parliament can legislate on any subject, it cannot bind successive Parliaments. If it could, then clearly each successive Parliament would not be free to legislate on any matter. That aspect of sovereignty means that where there is inconsistency between a previous and a subsequent statute, the latter impliedly repeals the former to the extent of its inconsistency. Authority for this proposition derives from *Ellen Street Estates Ltd v Minister of Health* (1934), in which it was argued that the Acquisition of Land (Assessment of Compensation) Act 1919 prescribed a certain manner for authorising the acquisition of land. It provided in s 7 that other statutes 'shall have effect subject to this Act'. If s 7 were to apply to subsequent enactments, provisions of the Housing Act 1925 that were inconsistent with the 1919 Act would have no effect. However, Maughan LJ held that Parliament cannot bind itself as to the substance or form of future enactments.

If a court were to be prepared to consider whether Parliament had consulted the EOC, this would breach 'the enrolled Bill rule' expressed in *Edinburgh and Dalkeith Railway Co v Wauchope* (1842). The court was asked to find that the legislation in question, a Private Act, had been improperly passed and was therefore invalid because standing orders had not been complied with. Lord Campbell said, obiter, that if according to the Parliament Roll, an Act has passed both Houses of Parliament and has received the royal assent, a court can inquire neither into the manner in which it was introduced into Parliament nor into what passed in Parliament during its progress through the various parliamentary stages. This rule was relied upon in *Pickin v British Railways Board* (1974): Mr Pickin had sought to challenge a Private Act of 1836 on the basis that Parliament had been misled by fraud. The House of Lords held that he was not entitled to examine proceedings in Parliament to show that the Act had been passed due to fraud. That action therefore failed.

In the instant case, the 2003 Act expressly repeals s 1 of the 2001 Act and therefore, on the face of it, Mr B can claim no redress. Section 3 of the 2001 Act has not, however, been repealed and it could therefore be argued that the later Act is invalid as, in passing it, Parliament did not follow the correct consultative procedure as laid down in s 3. However, the doctrine of implied repeal set out above and, in particular, the dictum of Maughan LJ in *Ellen Street Estates v Minister of Health* (1934) would suggest that s 3 of the 2001 Act is impliedly repealed as inconsistent with the expression of Parliament's will in the 2003 Act.[7]

---

7   It is important that students set out the answer under the orthodox position, before going on to consider the position taking into account the ECA 1972.

Is there any authority on which Mr B could rely in order to escape the conclusion that the 2003 Act, although not enacted in accordance with s3 of the 2001 Act, will nevertheless be followed? If any can be found, he could rely on s1 of the 2001 Act in order to claim leave or damages from his employer. In this instance, it would not be possible to claim that the 2001 Act is a 'constitutional statute' and therefore, under the analysis of Laws LJ in *Thoburn*, immune from implied repeal. In *AG for New South Wales v Trethowan* (1932), the Privy Council upheld the statutory requirement of a referendum before two Bills could be presented for the royal assent. Although, as commentators have argued, this decision may be of limited application as involving a non-sovereign legislature (a view in accordance with that of Lord Evershed MR in *Harper v Home Secretary* (1955)), it does suggest that a class of legislation *may* exist for which it may be appropriate to delineate the manner or form of any subsequent amendment or repeal. For example, s1 of the Northern Ireland Act 1998 provides that Northern Ireland will not cease to be part of Her Majesty's dominions without conducting a poll in Northern Ireland, while the recent European Union Act 2011 sets out a set of 'referendum locks' preventing further extensions to the powers of the EU without a referendum. If a future Act of Parliament were to purport to act contrary to these guarantees without first conducting the relevant polls it is at least arguable that the courts would hold the later statute to be invalid, as occurred in the South African case of *Harris v Minister of the Interior* (1951). This view receives some support from Slade LJ in *Manuel v AG* (1983), although he did not finally resolve the issue. In a Canadian case, *Drybones* (1970), the Canadian Supreme Court took the view, obiter, that it had the power to render inoperative statutes passed after the Bill of Rights 1960 that were incompatible with it.

However, these decisions are of doubtful persuasive authority when the attempt is made to apply them in the British constitutional context. In *Harris*, for example, the wording of the Speaker's certificate on the face of the instrument in question indicated that the specially prescribed procedure had not been followed; moreover, the ruling did not encompass the legal effect of a self-imposed procedural requirement.[8] It may, therefore, be determined that the weight of authority is against upholding a requirement that Parliament cannot legislate without first complying with a procedural requirement such as that laid down by s3 of the 2001 Act. Therefore, under the doctrine of implied repeal, the 2003 Act will prevail; under domestic law, Mr B cannot seek redress from his employer. However, in 2002, the EC passed the Regulation allowing men or women parental leave. Can Mr B rely on that Regulation despite the 2003 Act?

Under s2(4) of the European Communities Act 1972, 'any enactment passed or to be passed ... shall be construed and have effect subject to the foregoing provisions of this section'. The words 'subject to' appear to suggest that the courts must allow Community law to prevail over a subsequent Act of Parliament. '[T]he foregoing' are those provisions referred to in s2(1) giving the force of law to 'the enforceable Community rights' there defined. Section 3(1) provides that questions as to the meaning or effect of Community law are to be

---

8   Note the careful distinguishing of the *Harris* authority that is undertaken here.

determined 'in accordance with the principles laid down by any relevant decision of the European Court'. Regulations have direct applicability and are binding on all member States without requiring implementation or adoption by national law. It is clear from judgments of the European Court of Justice (ECJ) (see *Costa v ENEL* (1964) and *Amministrazione delle Finanze dello State v Simmenthal SpA* (1978)) that Community law should prevail over national law in all circumstances. Thus, on the face of it, Mr B can rely on the 2002 Regulation. It does not matter that he is seeking to rely upon it in an action against a private body, his employer: regulations, unlike directives, have horizontal as well as vertical effect. However, there is clearly a direct conflict between it and the subsequent 2003 Act and, according to the doctrine of implied repeal, the 2003 Act should take precedence over the former instrument. When a conflict has arisen between Community law and a subsequent domestic enactment, the UK courts have where possible adopted what has been termed a 'purposive' approach. In *Pickstone v Freemans* (1988), the House of Lords determined that the plain meaning of the domestic provision in question would be ignored and an interpretation would be placed upon it that avoided a conflict with Art 141 (ex 119) of the EC Treaty. However, there seems to be no means of resolving the conflict between the 2003 Act and the 2002 Regulation in this manner due to their complete incompatibility.

In such a situation, it now seems to be clear, following the decision in *Secretary of State for Transport ex p Factortame Ltd (No 2)* (1991), that the incompatible UK legislation should be set aside, or 'disapplied'. The House of Lords initially determined that as a matter of UK law, no domestic court had power to make an order conferring rights upon the applicants that were directly contrary to UK legislation. However, following a reference to the ECJ, the House of Lords accepted that the Community now imposes the requirement, accepted by Parliament when it passed the 1972 Act, that EU law should override inconsistent domestic legislation, whenever passed. It therefore made an order 'disapplying' the incompatible legislation. In *Secretary of State for Employment ex p EOC* (1994), the House of Lords followed *Factortame* in finding that judicial review was available for the purpose of securing a declaration that UK primary legislation is incompatible with EU law. It was found that certain provisions of the Employment Protection (Consolidation) Act 1978 were indirectly discriminatory and were, therefore, in breach of Art 141 (ex 119) and the Equal Pay and Equal Treatment Directives.

It appears to follow from *Factortame* and the EOC case that Parliament has effectively succeeded in partially entrenching s 2(1) of the European Communities Act by means of s 2(4), due to the imposition of a requirement of form (express words) on future legislation designed to override Community law. Section 18 of the European Union Act 2011, providing that EU law 'falls to be recognised and available in law in the United Kingdom only by virtue of' the 1972 or other Act does not affect this conclusion, as it addresses only the *source* of authority in UK law of EU law, not its effect on other, later statutes.

Thus, as no express words are used in the 2003 Act (such as 'these provisions are intended to take effect notwithstanding any contrary provision of Community law') and assuming that on a straightforward interpretation of its provisions, the meaning of the 2002 Regulation is clear, it would seem that it will prevail over the 2003 Act. If so, it will be the duty of the domestic court to give it effect according to the above decisions.

It therefore appears that Mr B may rely upon the 2002 Regulation to claim redress from his employer either immediately before the domestic courts or after a reference to the ECJ.[9]

QUESTION 11

Article 141 of the Treaty Establishing the European Union provides: 'Each Member State shall, during the first stage, ensure and, subsequently, maintain the application of the principle that men and women should receive equal pay for equal work.'

In 2004, the UK government takes the view that the principle of equal pay for work of equal value is inappropriate in a free market economy and that, therefore, severe restrictions should be placed upon the ability to bring an equal value claim. The Equal Pay Amendment Bill 2004 is therefore laid before Parliament and duly passed as the (fictional) Equal Pay Amendment Act 2004. Section 1 of the 2004 Act provides that the guarantee of equal pay for equal work 'shall only apply where the claimant has been in the same employment for a minimum of five years'. Section 2 provides: 'It is hereby declared that in the event of a conflict between any provision of EU law and the provisions of this Act, the provisions of this Act shall prevail.'

If a UK judge was faced with a claimant employed for less than five years who wished to bring an equal value claim against her employer would the judge apply Article 141 or the 2004 Act?

(Note: you are not asked to decide the likely outcome of the case or to consider the other provisions of the Equal Pay Act 1970.)

How to Answer this Question

A problem question in this area usually concentrates on the issue of conflict between a post-accession domestic instrument and the previous directly effective Community law. The first part of this question consists of the type of question that is commonly set; it concerns the most direct conflict possible between Community law and domestic law, and is quite straightforward. It turns on the question of whether or not Community law is subject to the rule of express repeal. The second part concerning the issues raised by the concept of indirect effect is more demanding. However, it raises a very important constitutional issue, which is likely to appear more frequently on constitutional law papers in future: the extent to which UK judges can and will implement an indirectly effective instrument through the vehicle of domestic legislation, regardless of the wording of the domestic instrument in question.

9   Note how these last two paragraphs first of all conclude the immediate question, and then the overall one the question poses.

Applying the Law

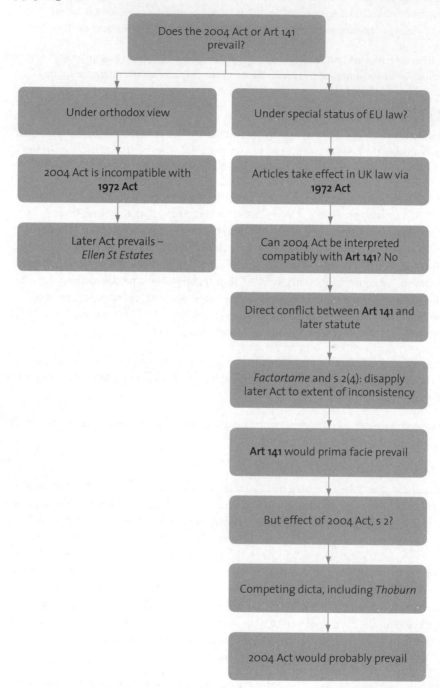

ANSWER

This question postulates a conflict between a domestic statute and EU law, given effect in UK law via s 2(1) of the **European Communities Act 1972**. In order to decide which would prevail, it is necessary to examine the special status of EU law in the UK legal order.

Under the traditional doctrine of parliamentary sovereignty, Parliament is competent to legislate on any matter whatsoever and no court is competent to question the validity of an Act of Parliament. This lack of legal restraint means that while Parliament can legislate on any subject and is free to amend or repeal any previous enactment, it cannot bind successive Parliaments. It follows that where there is inconsistency between a subsequent and a former statute, the later statute impliedly repeals the former to the extent of its inconsistency. Authority for this proposition derives from *Ellen Street Estates Ltd v Minister of Health* (1934) and *Vauxhall Estates Ltd v Liverpool Corp* (1932).

However, **Section 2(4)** of the **ECA** provides that: '. . . any enactment passed or to be passed '. . . shall be construed and have effect subject to the foregoing provisions of this section.' The words 'subject to' appear to suggest that the courts must allow Community law to prevail over a subsequent Act of Parliament. '[T]he foregoing' are those provisions referred to in s 2(1) giving the force of law to 'the enforceable Community rights' there defined. **Section 3(1)** provides that questions as to the meaning or effect of Community law are to be determined 'in accordance with the principles laid down by any relevant decision of the European Court'.

Section 2(4) of the **1972 Act** and the Community doctrine of the primacy of EU law flowing from the Treaty and from judgments of the European Court of Justice (ECJ) (see *Costa v ENEL* (1964)) require that Community law should prevail over national law. In *Amministrazione delle Finanze dello Stato v Simmenthal SpA* (1978), it was held that conflict between provisions of national law and directly applicable Community law must be resolved by rendering the national law inapplicable, and that any national provision or practice withholding from a national court the jurisdiction to apply Community law even temporarily was incompatible with the requirements of Community law. Furthermore, the ECJ made it clear in *Costa v ENEL* (1964) that Community law would prevail over both subsequent and previous domestic law. Thus, s 2(4) of the **1972 Act** appears to import a departure from the traditional doctrine of parliamentary sovereignty, in that a limitation as to the subject matter of future legislation (at least as long as the UK remains part of the EU) seems to have occurred. The alternative analysis, whereby EU law only has the effect that it has in UK law because of the **1972 Act** was affirmed by Parliament via **section 18** of the **European Union Act 2011**; under this analysis, were the **1972 Act** to be repealed or amended, parliamentary sovereignty would be reasserted in its traditional form. Since in this case, there is no mention of any change to the **1972 Act**, the **2011 Act** would not be relevant.

In the instant case, it would seem clear, therefore, that under s 2(4) of the **1972 Act** and in accordance with the doctrine of the primacy of Community law, the 2004 Act should take effect subject to Art 141, assuming that Art 141 is directly applicable in national law. It is clear from the ruling of the ECJ in *Defrenne v Sabena* (1976) that Art 141 is directly effective. Therefore, on this basis, it would appear that the claimant would not be barred from proceeding: s 2 of the 2004 Act would be ineffective due to the doctrine of the primacy of EU law under the 1972 Act.

Of course, under the traditional doctrine of express and implied repeal, the contrary result would be achieved. Since the 2004 Act is the later instrument, s 2(4) of the 1972 Act would be repealed to the extent of its inconsistency with s 2 of the 2004 Act, and Art 141 would take effect subject to s 1(2) of the 1970 Act as amended. However, the UK courts have, with some reluctance, accepted that the traditional understanding of parliamentary sovereignty has had to undergo a modification to deal with the implications of the UK's membership of the EC. When a conflict has arisen between Community law and a subsequent domestic enactment, the UK courts have, where possible, adopted what has been termed a 'purposive' approach. In *Pickstone v Freemans* (1988), the House of Lords determined that the plain meaning of the domestic provision in question would be ignored and an interpretation would be imposed upon it that avoided a conflict with Art 141 of the EC Treaty. A similar approach was taken in *Litster v Forth Dry Dock and Engineering Co Ltd* (1989).

In the instant case, however, the object of s 1(2) of the 1970 Act as amended is clearly incompatible with the object of Art 141, which is to remove pay discrimination. Thus, it would seem impossible to interpret it in any way that could render it compatible with Art 141. Moreover, both *Litster* and *Pickstone* were concerned with inadequate implementation of a directive: the courts could claim to be fulfilling Parliament's will by adopting a purposive as opposed to a literal interpretation in order to ensure that the provision in question did the job it was intended to do. In the instant case, it is clear that the courts could not make such a claim, first, because the 2004 Act was not passed in order to implement a directive and, second, because Parliament's will is clearly expressed to be at variance with Community law in s 2 of the Act.[10]

Had s 2 been omitted from the 2004 Act, dicta of Lord Denning in *Macarthy's v Smith* (1981) might have provided a means of resolving the conflict between s 1(2) of the 1970 Act as amended and Art 141:

> . . . we are entitled to look to the Treaty . . . not only as an aid but as an overriding force. If our legislation . . . is inconsistent with Community law . . . then it is our bounden duty to give priority to Community law.

---

10   While the interpretation approach does not turn out to work in this case, it is important nevertheless to give it some consideration.

However, he added:

> If . . . our Parliament deliberately passes an Act with the intention of repudiating the Treaty or any provision in it – or intentionally acting inconsistently with it – then I should have thought that it would be the duty of our courts to follow the statute.

In other words, the proposition put forward by Lord Denning was to the effect that s 2(4) of the European Communities Act had brought about a variant of the rules of implied repeal but that the rules of express repeal still applied. On this basis, in the instant case, the domestic court would have to apply s 1(2) of the 1970 Act as amended due to the express intention of s 2 of the 2004 Act to legislate contrary to Community law. This receives some support from *Garland v British Rail Engineering Ltd* (1983).

However, in *Secretary of State for Transport ex p Factortame* (1990), the House of Lords and the Court of Appeal may have gone further than Lord Denning in accepting that Community law might impose requirements that would override domestic law. In the Court of Appeal, Bingham LJ said that, where the law of the Community is clear: 'the duty of the national court is to give effect to it in all circumstances . . . To that extent, a UK statute is not as inviolable as it once was.'

Therefore, once a ruling from the European Court had been obtained, Lord Bingham held that the Divisional Court would have to apply it even though this involved 'disapplying' an Act of Parliament. He did not expressly enter the caveat that effect would have to be given to express words used in the Merchant Shipping Act 1988 declaring that its provisions should prevail over those of Community law, although he did state: '. . . any rule of domestic law which prevented the court from giving effect to directly enforceable rights established in Community law would be bad.'

Once the ruling by the ECJ on the issue of interim relief *was* obtained (*Factortame Ltd v Secretary of State for Transport* (1990) (ECJ)), the House of Lords applied it (*ex p Factortame (No 2)* (1991)). Thus, the issue of attempted express repeal of EU law was not clearly determined (any findings would have been obiter in any event), and therefore it is not certain what a UK court would do if faced with a provision such as s 2 of the 2004 Act. In *Secretary of State for Employment ex p EOC* (1994), the House of Lords followed *Factortame* in finding that judicial review was available for the purpose of securing a declaration that UK primary legislation is incompatible with EU law.

However, it is at least arguable after *Factortame* that partial entrenchment of s 2(1) of the 1972 Act has been brought about: if a UK statute is to override Community law, s 2(4) (and, perhaps, s 3(1)) of the European Communities Act must first be repealed – an understanding that would be supported by section 18 of the EUA 2011. On this argument, it seems that the judge in the instant case would ignore the express intention of Parliament and would refuse to give effect to s 2 of the 2004 Act. The claim would therefore be considered under Art 141, as opposed to s 2(1) of the Equal Pay Act as amended by the 2004 Act.

However, the alternative analysis of *Factortame* given in *Thoburn* (2002) must also be considered.[11] The case involved a challenge to EC regulations on the exclusive use of metric measurements by traders and retailers. Laws LJ held that Parliament could not bind itself in any way and had not done so in the 1972 Act. He declared:

> Parliament cannot bind its successors by stipulating against repeal, wholly or partly, of the ECA. It cannot stipulate as to the manner and form of any subsequent legislation. It cannot stipulate against implied repeal any more than it can stipulate against express repeal.

Rather, the explanation for *Factortame* was that the *courts* had recognised the 1972 Act as but one example of what he called 'a constitutional statute', essentially those that affected fundamental rights or the relationship between citizen and State in some general, overarching manner. The legal consequence of recognising a statute as 'constitutional' was simple: 'Ordinary statutes may be impliedly repealed. Constitutional statutes may not.' Under this line of reasoning, all that has happened is that the courts have recognised the 1972 Act as a 'constitutional statute', meaning that it cannot be impliedly repealed. However, it can still therefore be overridden by express words that make Parliament's meaning clear beyond doubt. Such a view would reinforce a court's probable disinclination to embark on the constitutional enormity of ignoring a clear expression of Parliament's will.[12] It is perhaps more likely that a court would instead attempt to distinguish the instant case from *Factortame*. It would be possible to do so on the basis that there was some uncertainty as to compatibility between the Merchant Shipping Act 1988 and provisions of Community law and, therefore, it need not be assumed that Parliament intended to legislate contrary to Community law. The UK courts were therefore merely accepting that an outcome should be avoided that would be contrary to Parliament's presumed intention. In the instant case, where Parliament's intention is completely clear, the court might feel itself bound to give effect to it. Such an outcome would arguably be contrary to Lord Bingham's remarks; however, they would not be binding as they were obiter. On this argument, the court would not allow the claimant to rely on Art 141 and would consider the claim under the 2004 Act (in which case, it would fail). Alternatively, the court might seek a ruling from the ECJ as to how it should respond to such a dilemma.

---

11   It is important for a good essay to recognise the fact that *Factortame* is open to various interpretations, and for these different approaches to be discussed.

12   Answers should recognise this point: courts have never *openly* defied an Act of Parliament, and the *Factortame* case can be seen simply as an example of courts deciding, as a matter of interpretation, whether the Merchant Shipping Act overrode the 1972 Act.

QUESTION 12

Are there any circumstances in which a court can lawfully refuse to obey something that they have recognised as a valid Act of Parliament? Take account of the HRA, the impact of EU law and the recent decision in *Jackson* in your answer.

How to Answer this Question

This is a simply phrased but difficult question. The latter part of the first sentence rules out consideration of the area considered above in Question 8, namely the limited role that the courts have in defining what is a valid Act. It requires the student to consider a number of disparate areas.

Answer Structure

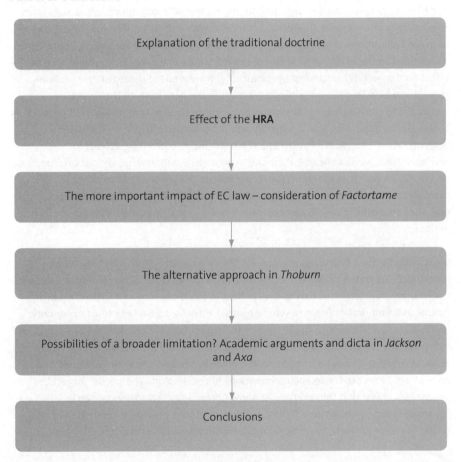

Explanation of the traditional doctrine

Effect of the **HRA**

The more important impact of EC law – consideration of *Factortame*

The alternative approach in *Thoburn*

Possibilities of a broader limitation? Academic arguments and dicta in *Jackson* and *Axa*

Conclusions

ANSWER

The doctrine of parliamentary sovereignty as explained by Dicey means that Parliament has the right to make, unmake or amend any of its Acts and that such power is not open to challenge by any outside body. Since 1688, the doctrine of the supremacy of Parliament has developed to the stage when, in *Pickin v British Railways Board* (1974), it appeared clearly settled that the notion of the courts refusing to obey a valid Act of Parliament could be said to be obsolete. Courts of course will sometimes have to decide which of two Acts of Parliament to obey, if the two conflict. This choice is resolved by the doctrine of implied repeal, which finds that courts should follow the later statute, which is deemed to have impliedly repealed the older one, to the extent of the inconsistency between the two.

The HRA contains no clause purporting to protect the Act from future repeal. But it also emphatically reaffirms the traditional doctrine of sovereignty by allowing the courts only to make declarations of incompatibility if they find statutes incompatible with the rights guaranteed by the ECHR. Section 4(6) of the Act states that such declarations have no effect on the validity, continuing operation or enforcement of the legislative provisions in respect of which they are made. However, s 3(1) of the Act, in which the courts are instructed to construe all legislation compatibly with the Convention rights 'if possible', is such a strong adjuration that it arguably enables courts to blur the line between 'interpretation' of an Act of Parliament and rewriting it, presenting at least a practical challenge to Parliament's ability to enforce its will through legislation. The case of *A* (2001), in which words were read into a statute in such a way as to alter radically its prima facie meaning, is a vivid illustration of this, although it must be conceded that other cases, in particular *Re W and B* (2002), indicate a more cautious approach.

Most importantly, a further qualification to the rule deriving from *Pickin* must be introduced due to the UK's membership of the European Union. Community treaties and Community law capable of having direct effect in the UK were given such effect by the European Communities Act 1972, which, by s 2(1), incorporated all existing Community law into UK law. No express declaration of the supremacy of Community law is contained in the Act; the words intended to achieve this are contained in s 2(4) of the 1972 Act, which reads as follows: '. . . any enactment passed or to be passed . . . shall be construed and have effect subject to the foregoing provisions of this section.' The words 'subject to' appear to suggest that the courts must allow Community law to prevail over a subsequent Act of Parliament. '[T]he foregoing' are those provisions referred to in s 2(1) giving the force of law to 'the enforceable Community rights' there defined.[13]

---

13 Student essays often introduce the qualification to sovereignty deriving from EU law without clearly explaining the provisions of that statute: it is, however, important that they are succinctly but clearly explained.

The problem arises in respect of statutes passed after 1 January 1972. According to the traditional doctrine of parliamentary sovereignty, the later Act should prevail as representing the latest expression of Parliament's will, but the Community doctrine of the primacy of EU law and s 2(4) would require Community law to prevail. In this respect, it has become clear from the Treaty as interpreted by the ECJ (see *Costa v EN EL* (1964) and *Amministrazione delle Finanze dello Stato v Simmenthal SpA* (1978)) that it is an implied Community principle that Community law should prevail over national law.

In *Secretary of State for Transport ex p Factortame Ltd and Ors* (1990), the UK courts had to consider the question of direct conflict between domestic and European Community law. The applicants, who were unable to comply with the conditions imposed on them under the Merchant Shipping (Registration of Fishing Vessels) Regulations 1988 made under the Merchant Shipping Act 1988, sought a ruling by way of judicial review that the Regulations contravened the provisions of the EEC Treaty by depriving them of Community law rights.[14] A ruling on the substantive questions of Community law was requested from the ECJ and, pending that ruling, an order was made by way of interim relief, setting aside the relevant part of the 1988 Regulations.

This order was set aside by the Court of Appeal; Bingham LJ remarked, however, that where the law of the Community is clear:

> whether as a result of a ruling given on an Art 177 [now 234] reference or as a result of previous jurisprudence or on a straightforward interpretation of Community instruments, the duty of the national court is to give effect to it in all circumstances.

To that extent, a UK statute is not as inviolable as it once was. The House of Lords upheld the ruling on the ground that no court had power to make an order conferring rights upon the applicants that were directly contrary to UK legislation. The result of these two rulings was clearly in accord with the traditional doctrine of parliamentary sovereignty as far as English law was concerned. However, their Lordships also accepted that Community law might impose other requirements, which would be overriding. The Lords referred to the ECJ for a preliminary ruling on the question of whether Community law required that a national court should grant the interim relief sought.

The European Court of Justice (ECJ) held (*Secretary of State for Transport ex p Factortame Ltd* (1990)) that the force of Community law would be impaired if, when a judgment of the Court on Community law rights was pending, a national court were unable to grant interim relief that would ensure the full efficacy of the eventual judgment. Therefore, when the only obstacle to granting such relief was a rule of national law, that rule must be disapplied. In view of this judgment (*ex p Factortame Ltd (No 2)* (1991)), the House of

---

14 Although *Factortame* is one of the most important decisions students study in their courses, it is noticeable how infrequently essays are able to explain the factual background clearly and concisely.

Lords granted the relief sought by the vessel owners. The position taken by the House of Lords was reaffirmed in *Secretary of State for Employment ex p EOC* (1994).

It follows from this decision that if it is clear that a statute is inconsistent with EU law, the domestic court would have to 'disapply' it – in other words, refuse to give it effect. However, a different explanation for the result in *Factortame* was given in *Thoburn* (2002), which involved a challenge to EC regulations on the exclusive use of metric measurements by traders and retailers. Laws LJ held that Parliament could not bind itself in any way and had not done so in the 1972 Act. He declared:

> Parliament cannot bind its successors by stipulating against repeal, wholly or partly, of the ECA. It cannot stipulate as to the manner and form of any subsequent legislation. It cannot stipulate against implied repeal any more than it can stipulate against express repeal.

Rather the explanation for *Factortame* was that the *courts* had recognised the 1972 Act as but one example of what Laws LJ called 'a constitutional statute', essentially those that affected fundamental rights or 'the relationship between citizen and State in some general, overarching manner'. The legal consequence of recognising a statute as 'constitutional' was simple: 'Ordinary statutes may be impliedly repealed. Constitutional statutes may not.' It is too early to say whether this revised view of sovereignty has won general acceptance amongst the senior judiciary. If it does, and given our findings on *Factortame*, it is evident that the statement made by Sir Robert Megarry should be modified to read as follows: 'once an instrument is recognised as an Act of Parliament *and is compatible with any enforceable Community law*, no English court can refuse to obey it or question its validity, *although it may refuse to allow it to impliedly repeal a previous, "constitutional statute"*.'

Finally, there is the possibility of a more general limitation upon parliamentary sovereignty, albeit based on tenuous foundations. In *Jackson*, there are a number of dicta that suggest that the courts may no longer accept the orthodox view of parliamentary sovereignty in full. As Lord Steyn remarked (at [102]): 'The classic account given by Dicey of the doctrine of the supremacy of Parliament, pure and absolute as it was, can now be seen to be out of place in the modern United Kingdom.' He went on to say, boldly:

> . . . the supremacy of Parliament is . . . a construct of the common law. The judges created this principle [and] it is not unthinkable that circumstances could arise where the courts may have to qualify a principle established on a different hypothesis of constitutionalism. In exceptional circumstances involving an attempt to abolish judicial review or the ordinary role of the courts, the . . . House of Lords . . . may have to consider whether this is a constitutional fundamental which even a sovereign Parliament acting at the behest of a complaisant House of Commons cannot abolish.

Other dicta suggest such limitations more elusively. Thus Lord Hope remarked (at [104]) that parliamentary sovereignty 'is no longer, if it ever was, absolute', while Lady Hale almost teasingly said (at [159], emphasis added):

> The courts will treat with particular suspicion (*and might even reject*) any attempt to subvert the rule of law by removing governmental action affecting the rights of the individual from all judicial scrutiny.

Similar remarks were made by Lord Hope in *AXA General Insurance v Lord Advocate* [2011] UKSC 46 at [51]; however, his Lordship recognised that, while the rule of law suggested that there must be limits upon Parliament's freedom to reduce or remove the role of the courts in protecting the individual, such limits would be in direct conflict with the traditional doctrine of parliamentary sovereignty; he made no attempt to say how this conflict would be resolved. [15] The possibility that the courts would directly refuse to obey an Act of Parliament would plainly only arise in the most extreme case of an outright attack by Parliament upon the rule of law or basic human rights; it is to be hoped that we will never know what the courts would do in such a case. But the dicta cited above certainly indicate that, to the judges, parliamentary sovereignty is not a fundamental, unalterable principle of the constitution, but one that, like others, is open to evolution over time.

QUESTION 13

By the beginning of 2010, the problem of terrorism in the UK has grown dramatically worse. A series of major attacks have targeted public transport in a number of cities across the UK, resulting in thousands of deaths. The Human Rights Act 1998 has already been (lawfully) repealed and the UK has formally repudiated the European Convention on Human Rights and withdrawn from the Strasbourg system. Despite this, however, the government has become increasingly concerned by the number of defeats it has suffered in the courts on judicial review. Government spokespersons have been vocal in criticising what they call an increasingly activist and 'obstructive' judiciary.

The UK Parliament has recently passed the UK Borders Act 2009, under which border officials may deny entry to any non-British national seeking entry to the UK, without giving reasons. The government has been advised that this Act contravenes directly enforceable principles of EU law guaranteeing freedom of movement.

Assuming that this is the case, advise the government on whether:

(a) the Act will be enforced by the courts.

---

15   While the dicta of Lord Hope were clearly of significance, their indeterminate nature must be acknowledged by good essays.

The UK government also wishes to introduce two further Bills into Parliament. The first of these is the Protection of Democracy Bill, which would extend the life of the current Parliament to eight years. The second is the Justice and Order Bill, under which the Secretary of State for Justice would become exclusively responsible for all judicial appointments to the High Court and above and would be permitted to take into account in making such appointments the extent to which potential appointees would, in his view, be likely or otherwise to frustrate government policies when making judgements. The Bill does not state that it repeals any provisions of the Constitutional Reform Act (CRA) 2005, or any other legislation.

The government believes that the House of Lords, as the Upper Chamber of Parliament, will refuse to pass both of these Bills. It therefore wishes to use the Parliament Acts procedure to pass both Bills and seeks your advice on whether, if this is the case, the courts may refuse to enforce the Bills, because of the use of the Parliament Acts procedure or for any other reason. In light of the above, advise the government on these matters:

(b) in relation to the Protection of Democracy Bill;
      AND
(c) in relation to the Justice and Order Bill.

NB: in relation to (b) and (c) above, do not consider EU law in giving your advice.

How to Answer this Question

This is a long, and initially intimidating and confusing question. Given the recent *Jackson* decision on the use of the Parliament Acts, a question raising an issue under that procedure as at least part of the scenario is very likely to be asked. When tackling a question like this, particularly in exam conditions, it is crucially important (a) to keep calm, and read the question slowly and carefully; (b) to take it bit by bit, breaking it down into its constituent parts; (c) not to do anything that you are not asked to do, or which the facts given in the question preclude. In this scenario, obviously any part of an answer that contained analysis of how the HRA could be used to challenge these Acts/Bills would simply receive no marks.

Applying the Law

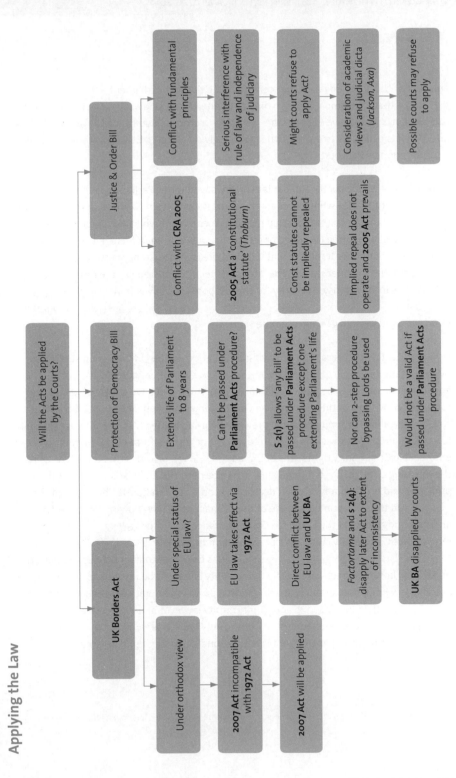

This diagram illustrates the main legislative points to consider in each branch of the question.

ANSWER

(a)

This part of the question raises the scenario of a UK Act of Parliament – the UK Borders Act 2009 – that is incompatible with directly enforceable EU law. The question is whether the UK courts would give effect to the 2009 Act. In order to determine the answer to this question it is necessary to examine the statute giving effect to EU law in the UK, and its interpretation by the courts.[16]

Under the traditional doctrine of parliamentary sovereignty, Parliament is competent to legislate on any matter whatsoever and no court is competent to question the validity of an Act of Parliament. This lack of legal restraint means that while Parliament can legislate on any subject and is free to amend or repeal any previous enactment, it cannot bind successive Parliaments. It follows that where there is inconsistency between a subsequent and a former statute, the later statute impliedly repeals the former to the extent of its inconsistency. Authority for this proposition derives from *Ellen Street Estates Ltd v Minister of Health* (1934) and *Vauxhall Estates Ltd v Liverpool Corp* (1932). Under this view, the courts would give effect to the 2007 Act.

However, EU law that is capable of having direct effect in the UK was given such effect by s 2(1) of the European Communities Act 1972. Section 2(4) provides that: '. . . any enactment passed or to be passed . . . shall be construed and have effect subject to the foregoing provisions of this section.' The words 'subject to' appear to suggest that the courts must allow Community law to prevail over a subsequent Act of Parliament. '[T]he foregoing' are those provisions referred to in s 2(1) giving the force of law to 'the enforceable Community rights' there defined. Section 3(1) provides that questions as to the meaning or effect of Community law are to be determined 'in accordance with the principles laid down by any relevant decision of the European Court'. Thus s 2(4) of the 1972 Act and the Community doctrine of the primacy of EU law flowing from the Treaty and from judgments of the European Court of Justice (ECJ) (see *Costa v ENEL* (1964)) require that Community law should prevail over national law. In *Amministrazione delle Finanze dello Stato v Simmenthal SpA* (1978), it was held that conflict between provisions of national law and directly applicable Community law must be resolved by rendering the national law inapplicable, and that any national provision or practice withholding from a national court the jurisdiction to apply Community law even temporarily was incompatible with the requirements of Community law. Thus, s 2(4) of the 1972 Act appeared to import a departure from the traditional doctrine of parliamentary sovereignty.

---

16 Notice that there is no general introduction to the concept of parliamentary sovereignty – unnecessary in a problem question. Instead, the essay goes straight to the issue raised by part (a) – identifying it precisely.

In cases decided since 1972, the UK courts have, with some reluctance, accepted that the traditional understanding of parliamentary sovereignty has had to undergo a modification to deal with the implications of the UK's membership of the EU. When a conflict has arisen between EU law and a subsequent domestic enactment, the UK courts, after some hesitation, accepted that the relevant domestic legislation, if it cannot be interpreted purposively so as to comply with EU law (as in *Litster v Forth Dry Dock and Engineering Co Ltd* (1989)), should be disapplied, to the extent of its inconsistency. Thus in the *Factortame* litigation, the applicants, who were unable to comply with the conditions imposed on them under the Merchant Shipping (Registration of Fishing Vessels) Regulations 1988 made under the Merchant Shipping Act 1988, sought a ruling by way of judicial review that the Regulations contravened provisions of the EU treaties by depriving them of EU law rights. A ruling on the substantive questions of Community law was requested from the ECJ. The ECJ found the 1988 Act to be incompatible with EU law, and also ruled that domestic courts must be able to provide the appropriate relief in this situation. The result was that in *ex p Factortame (No 2)* (1991), the House of Lords 'disapplied' the 1988 Act, to the extent of its inconsistency with EU law and a like result followed in *Secretary of State for Employment ex p EOC* (1994).

In the instant case, it would seem clear, therefore, that under s 2(4) of the 1972 Act and in accordance with the doctrine of the primacy of Community law, the UK Borders Act should be disapplied to the extent of its inconsistency with the directly effective provisions of EU law referred to in the question. Parliament has asserted that EU law only has the effect that it has in UK law because of the 1972 Act (s 18, European Union Act 2011). Under this analysis, were the 1972 Act to be repealed or amended, parliamentary sovereignty would be reasserted in its traditional form. Since in this case, there is no mention of any change to the 1972 Act, the 2011 Act would not be relevant.

(b)

This scenario is straightforward. The Parliament Acts 1911–49 allow Parliament to pass legislation without the consent of the Lords, in certain circumstances. The House of Lords in *Jackson* found unanimously that such legislation was primary legislation, passed by an alternative route, and that the 1949 Act was valid, despite itself having been passed under the Parliament Acts procedure, even though it modified that very procedure by changing the period that the House of Lords can delay a Bill from two years to one. However, s 2(1) of the 1911 Act, which sets out the basics of the procedure, states clearly that it refers to 'any Bill, other than a Money Bill *or a Bill containing any provision to extend the maximum duration of Parliament beyond five years*'.[17] Moreover, by entertaining the challenge to the Hunting Act 2004 (passed under the Parliament Acts)

---

17 We have read hundreds of student essays on *Jackson* and the **Parliament Acts**; a very common – and irritating error – is for such essays to assert that it is *Jackson* which imposes this limitation, whereas it of course appears in **section 2** of the **1911 Act** itself.

the House of Lords implicitly confirmed that alleged misuses of the Parliament Acts, procedure can be challenged in the courts by way of judicial review. It therefore seems clear that should the Protection of Democracy Bill be passed using the Parliament Acts, procedure, the courts would find it not to be an Act of Parliament and therefore would refuse to enforce it.

(c)

The Justice and Order Bill on its face impliedly repeals the provisions of the Constitutional Reform Act 2005, providing for appointment of the senior judiciary upon recommendation by the Judicial Appointments Committee of candidates to the Lord Chancellor. It also appears to impliedly repeal the provisions in the Act which provide that appointments shall be made solely on the basis of merit, and instead to allow for party-political considerations to be taken into account in appointing judges. This apparent attack upon judicial impartiality would also be seen as contrary to the constitutional principle of the independence of the judiciary, widely seen as central to the rule of law. It is also contrary to s 3(1) of the Constitutional Reform Act, which states:

> The Lord Chancellor, other Ministers of the Crown and all with responsibility for matters relating to the judiciary or otherwise to the administration of justice must uphold the continued independence of the judiciary.

There is little doubt that, applying the analysis of Laws LJ in *Thoburn*, the provisions of the CRA just cited would be seen by the judges as crucial parts of a 'constitutional statute'. These were defined by Laws LJ as those that affected fundamental rights or 'the relationship between citizen and State in some general, overarching manner'. The legal consequence of recognising a statute as 'constitutional' was simple: 'Ordinary statutes may be impliedly repealed. Constitutional statutes may not.' Following that analysis, therefore, such provisions cannot be impliedly repealed, although they remain subject to express repeal. As currently drafted, we are told that the Bill contains no provisions repealing any parts of the CRA, nor any other legislation. If passed as drafted, therefore, it appears that the courts, viewing the resultant Act alongside the CRA, would take the view that the normal rules of implied repeal should be set aside, and the CRA should be applied in preference to the Justice and Order Act.

It is also possible that the courts might refuse to enforce such an Act, regardless of whether it used express repeal or not, on the basis that it is wholly repugnant to the rule of law to allow such blatant political interference with the appointment of judges. Commentators such as T.R.S. Allan (see [1995] PL 614) have long argued that the rule of law must place certain limitations upon the sovereignty of Parliament, and there have been extrajudicial comments by judges suggesting agreement. Lord Woolf, for example, famously said in an academic article that 'If Parliament did the unthinkable then I would say that the courts would also be required to act in a manner which would be unprecedented' (Lord Woolf, [1995] PL 57, at 68–69). More significantly, such comments were made for the first time by members of the House of Lords in *Jackson*. Thus Lord Steyn remarked (at [102]): 'The classic account given by Dicey of the doctrine of the supremacy of Parliament, pure and absolute as it was, can now be seen to be out of place in the modern United Kingdom.' He went on to say, boldly:

> . . . the supremacy of Parliament is . . . a construct of the common law. The judges created this principle [and] it is not unthinkable that circumstances could arise where the courts may have to qualify a principle established on a different hypothesis of constitutionalism. In exceptional circumstances involving an attempt to abolish judicial review or the ordinary role of the courts, the . . . House of Lords . . . may have to consider whether this is a constitutional fundamental which even a sovereign Parliament acting at the behest of a complaisant House of Commons cannot abolish.

Other dicta suggest such limitations more elusively. Thus Lord Hope remarked (at [104]) that 'Parliamentary sovereignty is no longer, if it ever was, absolute', while Lady Hale almost teasingly said (at [159], emphasis added):

> The courts will treat with particular suspicion (*and might even reject*) any attempt to subvert the rule of law by removing governmental action affecting the rights of the individual from all judicial scrutiny.

While ultimately equivocal as to how an ultimate conflict between the rule of law and sovereignty should be resolved, Lord Hope's dicta in *AXA General Insurance v Lord Advocate* [2011] UKSC 46 at [51] appear to amount to further endorsement of at least the possibility of such limitations upon sovereignty. Here, the circumstances are not as extreme, but the judges might consider a direct threat to their independence as a fundamental assault upon the rule of law, requiring their disobedience to an Act of Parliament. However, it must be conceded that, while such considerations would doubtless fuel judicial disinclination to enforce such a statute, the reasoning employed would be far more likely to be that relating to implied repeal and constitutional statutes outlined above.[18]

---

18 Students are often far too quick to consider the 'nuclear' option of judges declaring statutes void or disapplying them on the ground of their conflict with the rule of law; however, other means of resolving issues over Acts of Parliament such as those raised in the current question would be far more likely to be used; since it would undoubtedly precipitate a constitutional crisis, judges would undoubtedly only use the 'nuclear option' as the very last resort.

Common Pitfalls

A common pitfall in problem questions on parliamentary sovereignty is that students do not clearly identify what specific issues are raised by the different factual scenarios in the problem question and consequently fail to discuss and apply only the particular aspects of parliamentary sovereignty that are relevant to those scenarios. Too often the answer degenerates into a general description of parliamentary sovereignty; however accurate the description is, if the law is not applied to the specific issues raised, the answer will not generally get a mark better than a third.

The House of Commons

INTRODUCTION

This chapter brings together a number of rather disparate topics. The three areas commonly examined are parliamentary privilege, scrutiny of legislation and scrutiny of the Executive.

Parliamentary privilege is a reasonably straightforward and discrete topic and most students find it fairly easy to master the basic and clearly established principles. It is, however, an area replete with unresolved questions and students should ensure that they are aware of the conflicting authorities and views on these questions, are able to offer a sensible evaluation of them, and can formulate their own opinions. The proliferation in constitutional law of new areas to study, such as devolution, the Human Rights Act 1998, and the Constitutional Reform Act 2005, has tended to marginalise parliamentary privilege or push it off syllabuses altogether, and to reflect this, we have deleted one question in this chapter on privilege to make way for more topical ones elsewhere. Students need to be familiar with the main thrust of the report of the Nolan Committee on parliamentary regulation of members' outside interests, the rules and mechanisms for their enforcement, including the Commons vote in May 2002 to relax the rules regarding their outside interests. In the area of members' freedom of speech, the Defamation Act 1996 has introduced a significant change. Both of these matters are covered here, as is the possible impact of the Human Rights Act 1998 on both areas of privilege. Finally, students should of course be familiar with the impact of the Parliamentary Standards Act 2009 as amended by the Constitutional Reform and Governance Act 2010. The result of both pieces of legislation has been that only MPs' expenses, not their outside interests, have been subjected to independent regulation; in the end, therefore, they are not of much constitutional significance, since it seems generally agreed that the claiming of expenses is *not* part of 'proceedings in Parliament'; hence the statutory changes do not affect parliamentary privilege at all. The topic lends itself equally well to either essay or problem questions, although the latter seem to be more common in practice.

Scrutiny of legislation and administration is examined by essay questions, which are invariably evaluative in approach. It should be noted that in some syllabuses, particularly on Graduate Diploma in Law (GDL) courses, the House of Lords will probably be examined together with the Commons in one question. If a question requires discussion of 'Parliament', this means, of course, both Houses. The two areas of legislation and administration can be examined separately, as in this chapter, or combined together in one question. Particular note should be taken of the reforms to the select committee system being suggested by various select committees, including the Modernisation, Public Administration and Liaison Committees of the House of Commons, and the ongoing controversy over the system for selecting the membership of select committees, finally resolved by the reforms suggested by the Wright Committee and implemented after the 2010 general election; the establishment of the Back Bench Business Committee should also be noted.

Checklist ✔

Students should be familiar with the following.

Parliamentary privilege:

- a list of all of the privileges, including those that are virtually defunct, with greater awareness of the important ones;

- the area of freedom of speech – the controversy over what amounts to 'proceedings in Parliament'; the status of written accounts and broadcasts of debates, proceedings of committees, etc.;

- the meaning of 'impeached or questioned' as interpreted by the courts and the impact of the **Defamation Act 1996**; the decisions in *Prebble* (1994) and *Hamilton v Al Fayed* (2001) and the possible impact of the **Human Rights Act 1998** through **Art 6** of the **European Convention on Human Rights**, but the difficulties of using the Act against Parliament;

- the recommendations of the Joint Committee on Privileges;

- the right of the House of Commons to regulate its own composition and proceedings, with particular reference to the new rules on registration and declaration of members' interests;

- the impact of the **Parliamentary Standards Act 2009** as amended by the **Constitutional Reform and Governance Act 2010**.

Note that the Joint Committee's Report is HLP 43–41 (1998–99).

QUESTION 14

During a House of Commons debate on a Private Members' Bill to legalise cannabis, Heather MP accuses Laurence MP, an Opposition MP who has spoken in favour of the Bill, of being 'bribed' to speak in favour of, and move an amendment to it, by Stoned UK, a group that campaigns for the legalisation of cannabis. She says that this information was given to her in a letter from one of her constituents, Mrs Spod, and that she has passed the letter on to a group of MPs campaigning for legalisation, known as Members for Free Weed (MFW). Heather also says that Laurence has an agreement with Stoned UK to provide it with advice and information on parliamentary feeling on possible legalisation and any relevant legislative proposals, and that he makes use of a research assistant funded by the group.

Laurence approaches the Speaker after the debate and admits that the second part of Heather's accusation, as to his agreement with Stoned UK and the research assistant, is true. He says that he has received a number of letters from members of the group urging him to do all he can in Parliament to support the current Bill, and saying that they hope he will give the group 'a good return in this respect' for its investment in his research assistant.

▶ Discuss the parliamentary and legal consequences of the above.

How to Answer this Question

This is a fairly typical question in that it requires students to discuss the protection given to verbal and written statements by the privilege of freedom of speech in a wide range of situations, while throwing in a number of possible infringements of the rules relating to members' interests and also a criminal offence committed in the House. (This often appears as an assault by an MP on another member/the Speaker or the damaging of the mace.) The status of the words spoken in the House and the letter from Mrs Spod are fairly uncontroversial, so the answer should devote more time to the letter to MFW and the central problem that it raises of whether such a letter amounts to a 'proceeding in Parliament' – an issue that will virtually always need discussion in answers on this topic. It is important to consider Laurence's possible violation of the rules relating to members' interests from the perspective of possible contempts committed by both him *and* Stoned UK. When dealing with any given event, students must always bear in mind the possibility of both legal *and* parliamentary consequences, and the fact that 'legal consequences' can include both civil and criminal liability.

Applying the Law

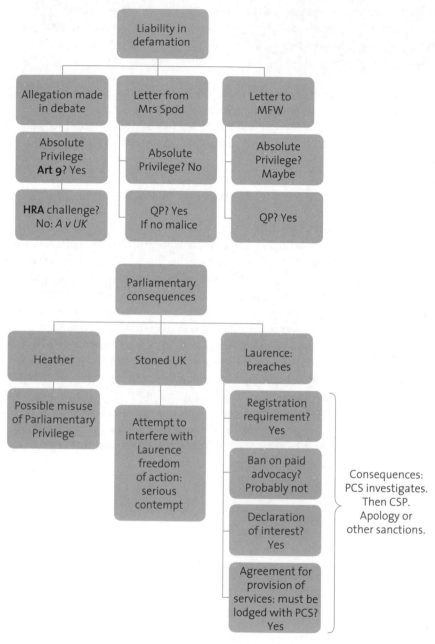

This mind map illustrates the main legal and parliamentary factors to consider in your answer.

ANSWER

This question raises the following broad issues: whether actions by Laurence in defamation against Heather and Mrs Spod would succeed; whether Laurence's association with Stoned UK would be viewed by the House as a contempt of Parliament for breach of registration requirements; and whether they would breach the advocacy rules.[1]

The allegations of Laurence's bribe-taking are prima facie defamatory (any possible defence of justification will not be considered). The words spoken by Heather in debate would be covered by absolute privilege under Art 9 of the Bill of Rights 1688; *Wason v Walter* (1868) confirmed that Art 9 provides complete civil and criminal immunity for members in respect of words spoken by them during proceedings in Parliament, and this position was reaffirmed by the Privy Council in *Prebble v Television New Zealand* (1994). Thus, no cause of action would lie for slander. It is possible that at some future point, the European Court of Human Rights might find this absolute bar a violation of the Art 6 right to a fair trial of those such as Laurence, who have no possible means of having the alleged injury to their reputation adjudicated upon in court. In *A v UK* (2002), the European Court of Human Rights heard a complaint from a woman who claimed to have been defamed during proceedings in the UK Parliament, which had been reported in the press. She argued that her inability to bring proceedings in court violated both her right to privacy under Art 8 and her right to a fair trial under Art 6 and to a remedy under Art 13. The Court found no violation: the privilege that blocked her action was necessary to protect free speech in Parliament and was narrower in scope than the comparable rules existing in other European countries. Whilst Parliament is specifically excluded from the definition of those 'public authorities' that are bound to respect Convention rights (s 6(3) of the HRA), the point could be raised in legal proceedings for defamation, relying on the courts' duty as a public authority itself (s 6(3)) to act compatibly with Convention rights under s 6(1). Nevertheless, given the decision in *A v UK* considered above, it seems highly likely that UK courts would rule against any such claim.

In terms of the parliamentary consequences of this matter, the House might regard Heather's repetition of the accusations as a misuse of privilege and therefore a contempt, particularly if she had made no attempt to verify the contents of the letter.

A libel action against Mrs Spod would have a better chance of success: her letter would not attract absolute privilege, since it clearly does not amount to a proceeding in Parliament. (It may be protected by qualified privilege provided that it is in the public interest and there is an absence of malice (*Rule* (1937)).

---

1   For a problem question like this, the introduction should *not* introduce the topic, as in an essay question. Rather it should be used, as here, to set out briefly but clearly the key issues raised by the question and indicate the order in which they will be tackled.

By sending a copy of the letter to MFW, Heather has republished the libel therein contained. It is uncertain whether the sending of a letter in this way would amount to a proceeding in Parliament and thus be covered by absolute privilege. The case of *GR Strauss* (1958), in which the MP concerned wrote a letter to the Paymaster General on possible misconduct by the London Electricity Board, is applicable but not conclusive. The Committee of Privileges held that the writing of such a letter was a 'proceeding in Parliament', and thus covered by absolute privilege, but the Commons narrowly rejected this finding on a vote. The recent report of the Joint Committee on Parliamentary Privilege in 1999 strongly recommended that such correspondence should *not* attract absolute privilege, the Committee deeming such protection unnecessary, given the effectiveness of the qualified privilege defence in protecting MPs over recent years.[2]

In the case of *Rost v Edwards* (1990), the plaintiff wished to adduce evidence contained in a letter alleging the failure of another member to register an interest from an MP to the Speaker, to be given in court to support a libel action. Popplewell J was of the opinion that the letter added nothing to the evidence in the case but added, obiter, that he had 'no hesitation' in stating that he thought the letter was covered by (absolute) privilege. He cited no authorities in support of this view, but presumably regarded the letter as a 'proceeding in Parliament', which could not be questioned outside Parliament under Art 9 of the Bill of Rights. It is hard to say now whether the weight of authority and expert opinion is still in favour of such letters being afforded absolute privilege. However, in the instant case, since the accusations in the letter were directly relevant to an issue then being debated by the Commons, Heather could perhaps hope for a reversal of the *Strauss* verdict.

If such a decision was made, then any attempt by Laurence to continue the action in respect of Heather's republishing of the libel could amount to a breach of privilege as the Committee of Privileges considered the Electricity Board's action against Strauss to be. If the letter did *not* attract absolute privilege, then following *Beach v Freeson* (1972), it should at least be deemed to enjoy qualified privilege since Heather and the recipients, MFW, have a common, legitimate interest in the contents and there is no evidence of malice.

The possible consequences of Laurence's association with Stoned UK now fall to be considered. Laurence's position raises a number of issues (the possible *responses* of the House will be discussed once Laurence's possible breaches of the rules have been considered). First of all, it is clear that his agreement to provide advice to Stoned UK for which he receives a material benefit, namely, a paid research assistant, is an interest that should have been entered on the register of members' interests. Laurence's association with Stoned UK clearly falls into Category 3 of the register: '... any provision to clients of

---

2   Note the detail given here: for a good 2:1 answer, this is the kind of thing that is needed, rather than a vague assertion that the issue is unclear or contested.

services' which are based on the Member's position as an MP' (*The Guide to the Rules Relating to the Conduct of Members*, hereafter, *The Guide*).

Laurence's obligations go further than mere registration: his agreement with Stoned UK clearly amounts to what a resolution of the House has described as 'an agreement which involves the provision of services in his capacity as a Member of Parliament' (Resolution of 6 November 1995 as amended). Therefore, according to that resolution of the Commons, the agreement must be put into writing and the amount of benefit obtained must be declared by reference to the bands specified in the resolution, unless the amount of the benefit is less than one per cent of the parliamentary salary. The agreement must then be lodged with the Parliamentary Commissioner for Standards (hereafter, 'the Commissioner').

In addition to being placed in formal written form, there is the issue of declaration. The House's Resolution of 22 May 1974 states that: 'In any debate or proceeding of the House or its Committees . . . [each Member] shall disclose any relevant pecuniary interest or benefit . . . he may have.' Plainly, an agreement to provide parliamentary services for a group campaigning for the legalisation of cannabis, in return for a funded research assistant, amounts to a pecuniary benefit relevant to the debate of a Bill to legalise cannabis. Laurence should have declared his interest at the beginning of his remarks in debate. The rules of the House go further than mere disclosure and declaration: Laurence may also have fallen foul of the so-called 'advocacy rule'. The relevant resolution of the Commons states that 'no Member . . . shall, on consideration of any remuneration . . . or reward or benefit in kind . . . advocate or initiate any cause or matter on behalf of any outside body or individual . . . by means of any speech, Question, Motion, introduction of a Bill, or Amendment to a Motion or a Bill' (extract from a Resolution of the House of 15 July 1947, as amended on 6 November 1995). As guidance provided by the Committee on Standards and Privileges, now forming part of *The Guide*, makes clear, this prohibits either initiating or participating in parliamentary proceedings in a way that 'seeks to confer a benefit *exclusively* upon a body' from which the member receives the payment (*The Guide*, para 96). Although Laurence has participated in proceedings, and spoken in favour of a cause that Stoned UK supports, his actions could not be said to have sought to confer a benefit 'exclusively' on Stoned UK. It is suggested that these words would refer to a speech in a debate that, for example, asked for a special tax concession to be given to the particular organisation in question.[3]

In conclusion, therefore, Laurence has failed to register his interest in Stoned UK and has failed to deposit his agreement with the Commissioner as required; in any event, he has

---

3   Note the precision of the analysis here; when dealing with matters of privilege, then the particular wording of the relevant rules of the House needs to be considered and applied with great care and accuracy, just as with a provision in an Act of Parliament.

failed to declare his interest in debate, although he has not breached the advocacy rule. The above omissions would be investigated, if complaint were made, by the Commissioner and, if he found a prima facie case, considered by the Committee on Standards and Privileges. The sanctions that they could demand on finding a breach of the rules range from requiring Laurence to apologise to the House at the lowest end to expulsion from the House at the highest.

In relation to the position of Stoned UK, it is clear that if, as in the *Yorkshire NUM Case* (1975), the sponsoring organisation threatens to withdraw financial support in the event of the MP not voting (or abstaining) as desired, there is no doubt that such threats would be viewed as a serious contempt. Here, the threat is not explicit as in the *NUM* case, but Stoned UK's letters clearly amount to an attempt to apply pressure in respect of a specific matter – the Bill to legalise cannabis – and therefore amount to an attempt to 'control or limit the Member's complete independence and freedom of action' as forbidden by the 1947 Resolution; as such, it would certainly be unacceptable to the House. It is likely that Stoned UK would at the least be required immediately to repudiate the letters, and to make no further attempts to restrict Laurence's freedom of action.

QUESTION 15

'Before the formally dramatic part of the legislative process even begins, almost all the terms of almost all (government) Bills are settled' (Calvert). Would you agree that the House of Commons is redundant as a legislative body?

How to Answer this Question

This question demands a critical assessment of the effectiveness of the House of Commons in its role as a legislative body. This is the type of question that is most commonly asked. It should be emphasised again that, in some examinations, the question will refer to 'Parliament' not 'the Commons', so that any answer would have to include the role of the Lords, which is considered separately in Chapter 4. This answer should confine itself to the Commons' control over legislation; scrutiny of the Executive through, for example, select committees is not relevant here. Students should note that there is an implied presumption behind the question, namely, that if the House cannot often alter government Bills, it may be 'redundant'. This presumption must be challenged by the student because it is of rather more interest to discuss what the House should be aiming to achieve rather than what it actually does achieve, although an analysis of the latter is clearly crucial in the answer.

Answer Structure

A brief discussion of the doctrine of separation of powers and the basic charge against the Commons of the failure to control legislation

Illustrations of government omnipotence and an explanation of how this is achieved – whips and government majority coupled with general control of the government over the legislative process; examples from previous governments

The argument that the Commons' role lies in scrutiny; the issue of publicity

An analysis of effectiveness in this field; the curtailment of scrutiny by guillotine; closure and programming; the effect on the pre-legislative process of the anticipated response of the House

Scrutiny of delegated legislation; the greater recent use of pre-legislative scrutiny

A brief discussion of the ways in which the Commons could improve its current performance, in particular, those suggested by the Modernisation, Liaison and Public Administration Committees relating to Public Bill Committees (formerly Standing Committees)

The reforms brought in by the Wright Committee and their impact thus far

Conclusion – does the Commons perform an important function?

ANSWER

The doctrine of the separation of powers requires, inter alia, that a body separate from the Executive should be vested with legislative power in order to guard against the amassing of disproportionate power in the Executive arm of the State. Parliament has never been a legislative body entirely free from the influence of the Executive, but the increasing dominance of the government of the day through organised political parties has led constitutional observers to view the Commons as having lost its role as legislator, becoming instead a body that merely serves to legitimise government legislation. In what follows, the accuracy of this view will be assessed, alternative views of the role of the Commons will be explored, and a verdict on the continuing importance of the Commons will be offered.

If the role of the Commons is seen as being to provide independent assessment of the merit of government Bills and to make numerous amendments and rejections, then there can be little doubt that it is not fulfilling this role. Throughout the debate, the system of whipping operates to subordinate the judgement of individual MPs to personal ambition and party loyalty. Considerable pressures can be brought to bear on potential rebels, and the efficiency of the party whips, together with the overall majority with which the first-past-the-post system is likely to endow the government, will ensure that the vast majority of government Bills will reach the statute books. In the 1985–86 parliamentary session, out of 50 government Bills, 48 became law. The Blair Government did not lose any Bills in the House of Commons; however, it was defeated on a handful of votes on particular clauses in committee. It lost in its attempt to have overturned certain Lords amendments to the Racial and Religious Hatred Bill 2005 designed to restrict the ambit of the new offence of incitement to religious hatred, and protect free speech; it was also defeated in the Commons on its proposal to extend the time for which terrorism suspects can be held without charge for questioning. The government's proposed 90-day time limit was defeated and a compromise, of an extension to only 28 days, was passed instead. Nevertheless, these were the only legislative defeats inflicted on the Blair Government in its 10 years in power, and this in the context of a government that has passed thousands of pages of legislation a year (3,500 in 2004 alone). The current Coalition Government has not yet lost any votes on legislation in the House of Commons, although it did lose a vote on a motion in December 2011. However, research published in 2012 by Cowley and Stuart shows that this is one of the most rebellious Commons ever; it is just that rebellious Liberal Democrat and Conservative MPs tend to rebel over different issues, while the Government's majority of 76 is substantial.[4] Thus, it remains the case that the general unwillingness of the House of Commons to impose legislative defeats on the government stands in strong contrast to the position in the much more independent

---

4   It is important that current examples are given, to avoid an essay on this topic having a 'dated' feel, and showing that students can themselves update the information and analysis in their textbooks.

House of Lords, which has imposed numerous important legislative reversals on the government. In the 2010-12 session, the Lords inflicted 48 defeats on the Government – a striking contrast.

The committee stage is often perceived as a time in which party loyalties are less strong and more constructive debate may take place. Unfortunately, MPs are often simply lacking in the expertise required to challenge increasingly complex government legislation from a position of sufficient knowledge. Further, partisan debate often appears to be as prevalent in committee stage, a style that is particularly unsuited to examining the factual and technical background to a Bill. Thus, in general, the committee stage results in the acceptance of government amendments only: one study recently found that 'at . . . Committee stage (and indeed at subsequent stages) it is extremely rare – in the case where the government has a majority – for any amendment, other than one moved by the minister, to be accepted' (P. Davis (2007) PL 677, 685). The Hansard Society has commented that the committees 'fail to deliver genuine and analytical scrutiny of [Bills], their political functions are neutered, dominated almost exclusively by government . . ., they fail to engage with the public and the media (in contrast to select committees) and they do not adequately utilise the evidence of experts or interested parties' (quoted in Select Committee on Modernisation of the House of Commons First Report, 1995–06, HC 1097, para 50). In response to such perceptions, the House devised an alternative procedure, allowing Bills to go to special standing committees, which can hold select committee-like meetings at which oral evidence can be taken from expert witnesses and ministers and relevant documentation examined. The committee is thus given the time and resources to build up its expertise on the area covered by the legislation in question, before going on to the usual clause-by-clause examination of the Bill and its amendments. This procedure was followed during the passing of the Criminal Attempts Act 1981 and substantial changes were made during the committee stage. In 2007, the Modernisation Committee made a series of suggestions designed to enhance the scrutiny at committee stage: essentially they advocated adopting this special procedure for all standing committees, which they said should be renamed 'Public Bill Committees'. The Committee's recommendations, including necessary changes to standing orders, were accepted (see Standing Order 84A), and in its review of 2007–08, the Liaison Committee commented very favourably on the new system, finding that 'In the 2007–08 session, 12 PBCs held a total of 35 oral evidence sessions and received 164 pieces of written evidence. While early signs of the impact of this power are promising, it is too soon to judge whether they will really bring about more *independent* scrutiny at Committee Stage (Turpin and Tomkins, at 639).

Should one conclude from the above that the Commons is redundant? It would of course be simply unrealistic to expect the House of Commons to subject government Bills to wholly *independent* scrutiny. The government is the government precisely because it is the party with an overall majority in the Commons. Therefore, by definition, the majority of MPs in the House will be predisposed to support legislation introduced by the government; even if MPs do not personally agree with the legislation, they will generally support it out of party loyalty, and to avoid government defeats, which are seen as damaging to their own party. It is thus built into the nature of parliamentary government that most MPs will not be impartially minded.[5]

If it is accepted, then, that the role of the Commons is not to reverse or drastically amend the government's manifesto programme, then what useful function does it play other than that of a mainly theoretical constitutional safeguard? It is suggested that four main functions may be identified. The first is the education of both government and electorate through the publicising effects of debate in the Commons: the electorate will become aware of the issues surrounding a Bill, whilst the reaction of newspapers, commentators and the public to debates on the proposed legislation will help keep the government informed of the drift of public opinion. The second is the influence on the pre-legislative process that both backbenchers and Opposition MPs may have, and the third is the limited amount of improvement and amendment that, despite the partisan nature of the Commons, still does take place. The fourth is clarification of the meaning of a Bill that may take place as governments explain and defend their legislation during debate. It is clear that, in relation to all of these functions, the amount of time and resources that members have available to them to devote to scrutiny of legislation will be crucial; the importance of the second and third will be closely tied to the size of the government's majority. We take the first and fourth of these to be fairly obvious points. In what follows, we comment briefly on the second and third.

The opportunity for debate in the Commons may also have some effect on the pre-legislative stage. The Commons acts as a forum in which the Opposition can express criticisms of legislation from many sources in society, including pressure groups and those who would be directly affected by the proposals. Government spokesmen will wish to know what these criticisms will be in order to be able to deploy counter-arguments. This desire encourages the government to engage in consultation with these relevant groups; there is a general practice that a department will not introduce a Bill affecting a major organisation without prior consultation with that organisation. Further, the government must take into account the likely response of its own backbenchers to legislation, as ascertained by the whips. If backbenchers are aware of widespread public discontent at proposed legislation, this will be relayed to the government, which will wish to avoid the embarrassment of hearing its own supporters expressing public dissent. The effect of this anticipated response may be to force the government into modifying its proposals: this is of course much more likely to happen where the government in question does not have a very large majority. For example, it was notable, that after the

----

5   This point is very important to make: many student answers (and some academic commentary), in bemoaning the lack of independent scrutiny in the Commons, appears to miss the fact that the combination of the Westminster system and a strong party system makes this a generally unrealistic goal.

2005 election, in which the government's majority was cut to around sixty, it had to engage far more in such pre-legislative negotiation with potential rebels. In 2011, there was widespread opposition both in and outside Parliament to the Government's Health and Social Care Bill, making some important and controversial changes to the NHS in England – including from many Liberal Democrat MPs and the party generally, This forced the Government into a prolonged 'pause' for reconsideration in April 2011 – unusually *after* the legislation had started its parliamentary progress in the Commons. As a result of this, a number of very substantial changes were made to the legislation.

The opportunities of both backbenchers and the Opposition to exert pre-legislative influence on Bills are markedly increased when the government publishes Bills in draft, to allow more detailed comment on them from select committees and other interested bodies. This practice was welcomed by the Modernisation Committee, which commented that such practice would provide 'a real chance for the House to exercise its powers of pre-legislative scrutiny in an effective way' (HC 382, 2000–01, para 19). The practice of publishing Bills in draft is being used more frequently: 18 were treated this way in the five years between 1992 and 1997; 39 between 2000 and 2005.

It is submitted that the influence of the Commons in these areas does give it a useful role to play. It must be noted, however, that the government can, to a certain extent, muzzle the publicising role of the Commons and reduce the Opposition's chance to embarrass it by curtailing the time available for debate. The use of the 'closure' allows debate to be simply cut off at the insistance of government whips (if supported on a vote), while the 'guillotine', in which a set amount of time is allocated by the government for each stage of debate, has been increasingly used in the past 20 years. Both of these devices undoubtedly inhibit the Commons in its scrutinising function. The Blair Government made much greater use of what is known as the 'programming' of Bills: that is, the setting of an agreed timetable, giving reasonable opportunity for debate, in advance, rather than in response to short-term time pressures. However, the experiment has been highly controversial. Many commentators view the result of programming all Bills as simply having been to entrench the reduction in scrutiny and remove from the Opposition its power of delay. Nevertheless, programming of Bills is now standard practice. In this respect, some of the most important reforms to the Commons in decades will probably turn out to be those proposed by the Wright Committee, set up in the wake of the MPs' expenses scandal. Essentially the Committee proposed formally ending the government's control of the House of Commons' timetable, encapsulated in Standing Order 14, which states that 'save as provided in this order, government business shall have precedence at every sitting'. Backbench business would be scheduled by a Backbench Business Committee, from which ministers' influence would be removed. Meanwhile, a House Business Committee, which would compromise backbench and frontbench Members, will agree the overall schedule of business for the week and put a motion before the Commons, which will have to be approved by vote, as in the Scottish Parliament, thus giving the Commons formal control over its own timetable. The first body has been set up, and has resulted in a number of non-legislative debates being scheduled by Parliament itself, rather than the Government. There is as yet no sign of the setting up of the latter body, although the Coalition Agreement promises that it will be established by the third year of the Parliament, shortly to start at the time of writing. If set up, a Business Committee would have great potential for enhancing the ability of the Commons to engage in more systematic scrutiny of government business.

The argument that the Commons plays a valuable role in the scrutiny of legislation is far weaker in relation to delegated legislation. Fundamentally, the problem is that instruments subject to negative affirmation are increasingly becoming law without ever having been debated by the Commons. In practice, it is the government that determines how much time shall be made available for consideration of statutory instruments; it can thus limit scrutiny to negligible proportions. Once again, the Wright reforms, if fully implemented, may help here.[6]

In conclusion, therefore, it has been suggested that the Commons performs a number of useful functions, albeit with varying results, depending on the size of the government's majority. It is thus far from being a redundant body. However, it is clear that it could achieve far more through the use of more varied procedure, particularly in committee, far greater use of pre-legislative scrutiny by expert select committees, something that has already had some impact, the provision of greater resources for members, greater control of its own timetable and a shift away from a culture based heavily on confrontation and defence.

QUESTION 16

How far is it true to say that House of Commons' scrutiny of the government 'illustrates again the unequal struggle between MPs and the Executive' (Hunt, *Open Government*)?

How to Answer this Question

This is a straightforward question, demanding an evaluative description of the various methods deployed by the Commons to scrutinise administration of policy and financial matters. Students should be careful not to stray into the Commons' role in the legislative process except in passing. It is essential for each method to be evaluated in terms of Hunt's quotation – students must not fall into the trap of a mere recitation of methods of scrutiny.

---

6   It is important that answers do deal with delegated primary legislation; although generally more technical in nature than primary legislation, it is extremely important.

Answer Structure

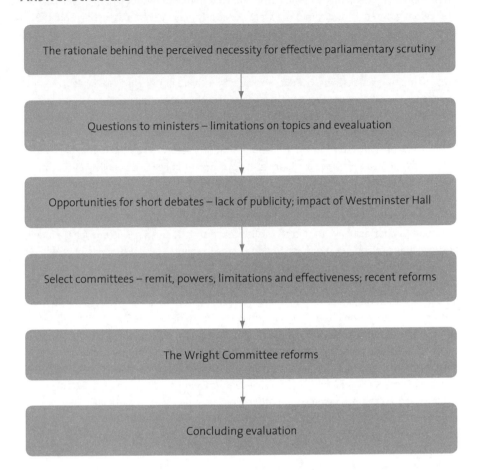

The rationale behind the perceived necessity for effective parliamentary scrutiny

Questions to ministers – limitations on topics and eveavaluation

Opportunities for short debates – lack of publicity; impact of Westminster Hall

Select committees – remit, powers, limitations and effectiveness; recent reforms

The Wright Committee reforms

Concluding evaluation

ANSWER

The concern expressed in Hunt's comment arises from the notion that thorough scrutiny of the Executive arm of the State is vital to a democratic system. It is an important convention, essential to the idea of responsible government, that the Executive should be held accountable to Parliament. The convention owes something to the rationale behind the doctrine of the separation of powers as expounded by Montesquieu, namely, that each organ of the State should act as a check on the powers of the others. The aim of this discussion will be to explore the extent to which Commons' scrutiny of the Executive amounts to effective control over central government.

The most obvious forum for scrutiny is the floor of the House of Commons, although it is here that scrutiny can be at its most ineffective. For example, adjournment debates are often poorly attended, thus achieving little publicity, and requests for emergency debates are seldom granted. Early day motions were previously only rarely debated; however, the setting up of Westminster Hall as a separate chamber of the Commons has improved this position. Far more publicity is given to the questioning of ministers on the floor of the House. Some 45–50 minutes are set aside every day, except Friday, for oral answers to be given to members' questions. Over 60,000 questions were put down by MPs in 2008–09, of which over 56,000 were answered in writing. The oral answering of questions is now often afforded live television coverage. Oral questions and their supplementaries tend to be used as an opportunity to probe ministers' grasp of their portfolios or to attack government policy. They thus have some effect in ensuring that ministers are kept up to the mark and provide an opportunity for weak elements in government policy to be publicly exposed. They are one of the few times in which ordinary backbenchers can raise matters directly with Cabinet ministers. However, the ability of members to put down really probing questions is reduced by the lack of information and support staff available to backbenchers. Ministers, by contrast, have the aid of a skilled team of civil servants who provide them with answers to the tabled questions and undertake research into the questioner's known interests and concerns in an attempt to anticipate and prepare the minister for possible supplementaries. As a method of obtaining information, questions requesting written answers are far more effective. However, as Tomkin has noted, 'An answer to a question cannot be insisted upon if the answer is refused by the minister; the Speaker has refused to allow supplementary questions in these circumstances' ((1996) 16(1) LS 63, p 81). Furthermore, there are a large number of matters on which a minister will refuse to answer, governed now by the Freedom of Information Act 2000 (see the (non-statutory) *Ministerial Code*, Cabinet Office, 2007). However, the Freedom of Information Act 2000 specifies very large areas where information should not be given. In particular, there is a class exemption in s 35 in relation to all information relating to 'the formulation or development of government policy'. The only limitation to this astonishingly broad exemption – which is not subject to any burden on ministers to prove that any harm would be caused by releasing the information in question – is that statistical information relating to a decision is no longer exempted once the decision is made. But, for example, evidence of other policy options considered, and the reasons for rejecting them, would be covered by the exemption. Other excluded areas include: information that would prejudice defence, national security or international relations, or where it would involve disclosing commercial confidences; unreasonable, voluminous or vexatious requests (ss 12 and 14); and information that would harm the 'effective conduct of public affairs' (s 36) – this exception, in particular, being very wide and vague. In addition, a minister may refuse to answer any question that would be likely to cost more than a certain amount (currently £600) to research. Recently answered questions will also be disallowed.[7]

- -

7   Student essays rarely give proper treatment of the important topic of the grounds for refusing answers to PQs. Even if time in an exam does not permit the level of detail given here, at least an outline of the key **FOI** exemptions should be given.

It was precisely to give backbenchers more in-depth knowledge of government departments that the select committees were set up in 1979, covering between them each of the major government departments with the exception of the Law Officers Department and the Lord Chancellor's Department, which were brought within the system in 1991. Regional select committees followed in 2009. The select committees have three main advantages as a method of scrutiny over questions or debate on the floor of the House. First, since MPs tend to commit themselves to a committee for a considerable period, they have time to build up a reasonable level of expertise on their area of concern (an ability enhanced by their power to send for papers and records), which clearly enables them to probe more deeply into departmental affairs. Second, the committees tend to be more non-partisan than almost any other Commons organisation; this should be greatly enhanced now that, following the Wright reforms, members of the committees, and their chairs, are voted on by members of the House, rather than, as before 2010, nominated by a Committee of Selection, whose members were themselves nominated by the whips. There have been many incidents in which governments have sought to keep outspoken and independently minded MPs off the committees, and in particular, sought to prevent them from becoming or remaining committee chairs (as in the attempt in 2001 to keep Gwyneth Dunwoody, previously chair of the Transport Committee, and Donald Anderson, former chair of the Foreign Affairs Committee, from being reappointed to their positions).

The ability of the committees to operate in a non-partisan fashion marks their work out particularly clearly from the general character of proceedings in the House, described by one backbench MP as 'Government and Opposition, locked into a permanent election campaign' (HC Deb, col 1099,13 November 1997). It remains true that most committee reports are unanimous and many are highly critical of government policy. For example, despite its Labour-dominated ranks, the Transport Committee brought out a number of trenchant, critical reports. Its most important was a forensic dissection of the government's Ten-Year Transport Plan – its master plan for tackling the hugely difficult issue of cutting down car usage and improving public transport as an alternative. The Report (HC 558–1, 2001–02) was widely viewed in the media as sounding the death knell for the plan as originally conceived by John Prescott.[8] Recent research published by the Constitution Unit (*Selective Influence*, 2011) found that 40 per cent of Select Committee recommendations are accepted by governments. The overall conclusion was that the committees 'also have an important preventative effect in encouraging more careful consideration of policy within government departments'.

The committees have also recently taken on the new role of engaging in limited, pre-appointment scrutiny of government nominees for major posts such as chair of the

---

8   Concrete examples add colour and conviction to an essay on this topic.

Judicial Appointments Commission, Ofcom, the Charity Commission, Ombudsmen and so on (see *The Governance of Britain*, Cm 7342-I, 2008).

The third advantage of the committees is their ability to send for civil servants and ministers for questioning that is far more systematic and searching than anything that could take place in the Commons Chamber. This power to question members of the Executive is clearly crucial to the efficacy of the committees, and not surprisingly has caused controversy. In 1979, the Leader of the House pledged that 'every minister . . . will do all in his or her power to cooperate with the new system of Committees' (HC Deb, col 425, 25 June 1979). On the whole, this promise and its necessary concomitant of ensuring civil service cooperation has been honoured. However, the committees have sometimes found themselves frustrated when investigating areas of acute sensitivity by the refusal of certain key witnesses to attend. A long-standing problem has been the refusal of ministers in the previous and present governments to allow their special advisers, thought by many to exercise more power than many ministers, to appear before any select committees, despite the revision of the 'Osmotherly rules' in 2005 to provide for their attendance, and assurances given to the Liaison Committee in 2004 that special advisers would now be allowed to give such evidence (Minutes of Evidence, HC 1180–i, Q 26).

To some extent, different problems arise in the case of civil servants. Having secured their attendance, the committee may then find itself hampered by their refusal to divulge certain information on the basis that to do so would contravene the advice given in the so-called 'Osmotherly rules', governing the conduct of civil servants before select committees (now entitled *Departmental Evidence and Response to Select Committees*, which sets out matters about which they should not give evidence); the basic rule is that civil servants should give evidence 'on behalf of the minister and under his instructions'. This applies even to the chief executives of the semi-autonomous 'Next Steps' agencies, who have considerable areas of devolved responsibilities, and is thought to be particularly unsatisfactory in their case. [9]

The record of the committees in obtaining the government records that they require is even less reassuring: in the words of the 1997 Liaison Committee report, 'It is in [this area] that most difficulties have arisen' (para 14). The Committee found that governmental promises to make time for a Commons debate on a refusal to provide requested documentation have not been properly honoured: 'There have been a significant number of cases where Committees have been refused specific documents but the government has not provided time for the subject to be debated.' The Committee recommended that 'the onus should be shifted onto the government to defend in the House its refusal to disclose information to a Select Committee' (para 16). In general, however, it should be

----

9   It is important for students to distinguish clearly between the problems relating to calling ministers and civil servants to give evidence.

conceded that both the restrictions on the divulging of information and the refusal of persons to attend are likely to hamper the committees in exposing major government embarrassments, but interfere little with their day-to-day scrutiny of the relevant departments.

A package of proposals to strengthen select committees was agreed between the Liaison and Modernisation Committees, and most of the key recommendations were accepted by the Commons in May 2002. The key elements include: greater resources for select committees, including making available assistance by the National Audit Office and more support staff; the encouragement of an alternative career structure in select committees, intended to enhance their prestige by payment for their chairpersons; greater coordination between committees and clarification of their tasks, which now include much greater involvement in pre-legislative scrutiny as well as an informal role in scrutinising appointments to Next Steps agencies and other key quangos.[10]

Overall, it is clear that the key to effective scrutiny is undoubtedly sufficient information and sufficient time. Where MPs do not possess sufficient expertise, their questions will often miss the mark. Where, like the Public Accounts Committee, they have access to an abundance of detail, penetrating criticisms can be made – criticisms that can force the government into greater accountability in future. In relation to time, now the Backbench Business Committee timetables non-government business, such as debates of Select Committee reports, Opposition days, and general debates, the House, for the first time, determines the time given to such matters (within limits), rather than having merely to ask the government for it. This should now start to make a significant difference.

QUESTION 17

Discuss the following views of the role of select committees: 'they are intended to redress the balance of power between Parliament and the Executive'; 'they are an institution which is expected to stay on the sidelines'.

How to Answer this Question

This question is quite demanding because it requires detailed knowledge of the operation of select committees. It is also topical due to the growing perception that select committees provide a surer means of scrutinising the Executive than procedures on the floor of the Commons, the package of reforms agreed by the Commons in May 2002 and the increased scope of the committees' work.

10   This 'core tasks' reform was important and must be covered.

Answer Structure

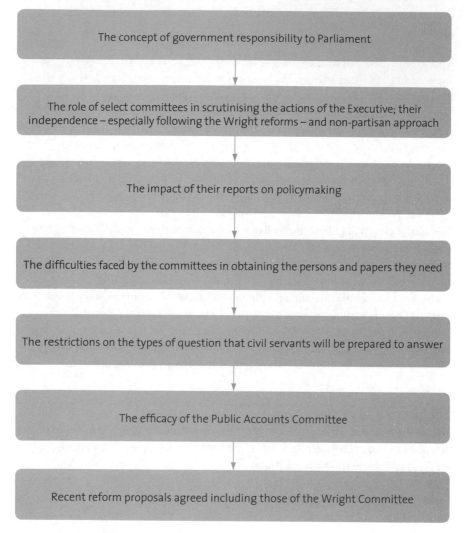

The concept of government responsibility to Parliament

The role of select committees in scrutinising the actions of the Executive; their independence – especially following the Wright reforms – and non-partisan approach

The impact of their reports on policymaking

The difficulties faced by the committees in obtaining the persons and papers they need

The restrictions on the types of question that civil servants will be prepared to answer

The efficacy of the Public Accounts Committee

Recent reform proposals agreed including those of the Wright Committee

Essentially, the areas above should be covered.

ANSWER

The statements taken together imply that expectations of the constitutional change that would be brought about by the select committees were high in some quarters, but that in others, it was always assumed that the new committees were not intended to fulfil them due to various limitations. It should be noted that the phrase 'stay on the sidelines' may be taken to mean both that the input of the committees into the policy-making process is bound to be marginal, and also that the committees' powers, in terms of their ability to gather evidence, are inherently limited and that they are therefore expected to be non-intrusive institutions. Both interpretations will be addressed.[11]

It is clear that the new select committees were set up in 1979 due to widespread dissatisfaction with procedures on the floor of the House of Commons as a means of scrutinising the workings of government, and a consequent perception that the balance of power between the Executive and Parliament was not being maintained under the then current arrangements. While written answers to parliamentary questions are a useful source of information, it is widely accepted that oral questioning of ministers on the floor of the House can never be a very effective scrutinising tool, for two reasons: first, there is simply insufficient time for in-depth scrutiny; second, the *culture* surrounding the institution of Question Time is in general that of an adversarial party system – the key conflict is between the Opposition and the government, rather than between parliamentarians and the Executive. The new committees were intended to provide opportunities for more in-depth and impartial scrutiny and now cover all of the major government departments: regional select committees soon followed in 2009. The committees were better equipped and organised than their predecessors, set up in the 1966–70 Parliament. Their function was expressed to be 'to examine the expenditure, administration and policy of the principal government departments'. The committees allow officials and ministers to be questioned in a systematic and searching manner not possible on the floor of the House of Commons. Furthermore, the members of the committees are well informed and can call on the assistance of expert advisers. The published reports of committees constitute a very significant and valuable source of information about the workings of government.

Perhaps most significantly, the committees show an impartiality remarkable in the contentious atmosphere of the Commons; they conduct their business in an inquisitorial as opposed to an adversarial manner dictated by party lines. This can be partly explained by the fact that the committees' members are chosen from the back benches: no frontbench spokesmen are appointed to them, although former ministers may be. Prior to 2010, MPs were nominated to select committees by the Committee of Selection, the members of which were themselves chosen by the whips. There have been many incidents in which governments have sought to keep outspoken and independently minded MPs off the committees, and in particular, sought to prevent them from becoming or remaining committee chairs, as in the attempt in 2001 to keep Gwyneth Dunwoody, previously chair of the Transport Committee, and Donald Anderson, former chair of the Foreign Affairs Committee, from being reappointed to their positions). This system plainly at least partially compromised the independence of the committees. That

---

11   This is an example of the way in which a good answer will *interrogate* an essay question, breaking it down and providing interpretations of phrases that are capable of more than one meaning.

independence should therefore be greatly enhanced now that, following the Wright reforms, members of the committees, and their chairs are voted on by members of the whole House.

It can be difficult to assess the impact of the committees on departmental policy-making, because committee reports may merely contribute to debate that was already occurring. However, an example of a concrete result flowing from a select committee report can be seen in the positive response of the Labour Government to the report of the Home Affairs Select Committee on police complaints and the disciplinary procedure for officers accused of misconduct (HC 258–1, 1997–98; the government's response appears as HC 683). A large number of the Committee's findings and recommendations were accepted by the government, including the broad thrust of the Committee's findings that the present procedures of the Police Complaints Authority were inadequate and that significant reform was required to strengthen the complaints system. There is no doubt that a number of very recent select committee reports that were critical of government policy have had a marked impact, receiving extensive publicity in the media, thus always forcing government further to explain and defend its policies from the criticisms made and, on occasion, causing it to reconsider its policies. Recent research published by the Constitution Unit (*Selective Influence*, 2011) found that 40 per cent of select committee recommendations are accepted by governments – a figure that was far higher than many would have expected. The overall conclusion was that:

> It is erroneous to assume that select committees are not influential on government policy. They are largely taken seriously in Whitehall, many of their recommendations go on to be implemented (though sometimes not until years later), and they have an important preventative effect in encouraging more careful consideration of policy within government departments (Executive Summary).[12]

This notion of 'preventative effect' related to the phenomena the Committee found whereby ministers and civil servants gave quite strong consideration to the likely reaction of the relevant committee when formulating policy, and were deterred from introducing policies that they thought would result in unanimous, critical reports.

The committees recently acquired a new role, of engaging in limited, pre-appointment scrutiny of government nominees for major posts such as chair of the Judicial Appointments Commission, Ofcom, the Charity Commission, Ombudsmen and so on (see *The Governance of Britain*, Cm 7342-I, 2008).

---

12   Where questions that the answer is grappling with are quite general ('how effective are the Select Committees?') it is important to adduce evidence that is as specific as possible.

Although the role of the Select Committees is significantly more valuable than that played by debate in the Commons as a means of subjecting ministers to scrutiny, the committees are subject to important limitations in terms of time and information available to them (although there has been some marked improvement in some of these areas and further reforms were agreed in May 2002). Committees have the formal power to send for 'persons, papers, and records', but this power is rarely invoked; they prefer to act by invitation. In any event, committees cannot compel MPs or ministers to attend before them: an order would have to made by the House, a largely theoretical possibility only. Committees have experienced difficulty at times in acquiring information or interviewing the minister or official they wish to question. For example, in 1984, the government would not allow the Director of Government Communications Headquarters to give evidence to the Select Committee on Employment, which was inquiring into the trade union ban at GCHQ. A long-standing problem has been the refusal of ministers in the previous and present governments to allow their special advisers, thought by many to exercise more power than many ministers, to appear before any select committees, despite the revision of the 'Osmotherly rules' in 2005 to provide for their attendance, and assurances given to the Liaison Committee in 2004 that special advisers would now be allowed to give such evidence (Minutes of Evidence, HC 1180–118i, Q 26). The Public Administration Select Committee found in 2005 that that there was still a marked reluctance by ministers, notably the then prime minister, to allow the questioning of special advisers by select committees (First Special Report, 2005–06). Moreover, the basic principle remains that it is for ministers to decide which civil servants and advisers should attend on their behalf (evidence to Liaison Committee, ibid).

The record of the committees in obtaining the government records that they require gives rise to more concern: in the words of the 1997 Liaison Committee report, 'It is in [this area] that most difficulties have arisen' (para 14). The Committee found that governmental promises to make time for a Commons debate on a refusal to provide requested documentation have not been honoured: 'There have been a significant number of cases where Committees have been refused specific documents but the government has not provided time for the subject to be debated.' The reference to a debate is to the House's formal power to make a finding that a refusal to supply requested documents – or indeed a refusal to attend a committee at all – represented a contempt of Parliament. Such a finding could only be made after a debate, and the Committee recommended that 'The onus should be shifted onto the government to defend in the House its refusal to disclose information to a Select Committee' (para 16) and that the power of the Privileges Committee 'to require that specific documents or records in the possession of a member relating to its inquiries be laid before the Committee' be extended to all committees. Now the Wright Committee's proposal for a Backbench Business Committee has been implemented, this Committee would schedule the time required for such a debate, rather than it being in the gift of the government – an important change

Not only are the powers of committees to require the attendance of ministers and officials and the production of documents rather weak and uncertain, the areas about which they may interrogate civil servants and the chief executives of 'Next Steps' agencies are subject to quite basic restrictions. Under the so-called 'Osmotherly rules', governing the conduct of civil servants before select committees (now entitled *Departmental Evidence and Response to Select Committees*, 2005), there are a number of matters about which civil servants may not give evidence. The basic rule is that civil servants should give evidence 'on behalf of' the minister and under his or her instructions'. This applies even to the chief executives of the semi-autonomous Next Steps agencies, who have considerable areas of devolved responsibilities, and is thought to be particularly unsatisfactory in their case. As a number of parliamentary and academic commentators have observed, this restriction can hamper the ability of select committees to uncover instances where operational failures attributed by ministers to mistakes by officials or chief executives are in reality the result of ministerial interference, or matters for which the minister is clearly responsible, such as resources or overall policy guidelines.[13] On the whole, however, committees have not found Civil Service recalcitrance a serious handicap: for example, the Select Committee on Trade and Industry stated in its second report of 1985–86, 'In the vast majority of previous . . . Committees, no serious problem has arisen'.

A package of proposals to strengthen select committees was agreed between the Liaison and Modernisation Committees in 2002 and most of the key recommendations were accepted by the Commons in May of that year. The key elements include: greater resources for select committees, including making available assistance by the National Audit Office, and more support staff; the encouragement of an alternative career structure in select committees intended to enhance their prestige by payment for their chairs; greater coordination between committees and clarification of their tasks, which now include much greater involvement in pre-legislative scrutiny, as well as an informal role in scrutinising appointments to Next Steps agencies and other key quangos. While only time will tell how far these reforms – and those of the Wright Committee – will enhance the quality and effectiveness of the work of select committees, in general it is apparent that, certainly at present, the committees are somewhat hampered in their scrutinising function. Therefore, although they can go some of the way towards redressing the balance of power between Parliament and the Executive, their power and influence in this respect are limited. Their contribution to parliamentary accountability, especially in terms of the information they glean and their ability to subject ministers and officials to sustained, non-partisan scrutiny, has, however, undoubtedly improved the ability of the House to investigate and scrutinise government in some depth.

13   Note how the argument here seeks to explain exactly why this limitation may cause a problem in terms of the operation of the doctrine of ministerial responsibility.

Aim Higher ★

The basic arguments in the area are fairly easy to grasp, so in order to produce a better-than-average answer, students should try to marshal original examples for their arguments from cases and materials books, and current events. Examples could include particularly influential recent select committee reports, or questioning by a committee that has been particularly effective – or ineffective – in bringing to light information about government policy or practice.

The House of Lords

INTRODUCTION

This is a reasonably straightforward area that is examined by means of essay questions. Traditionally, questions tended to focus on the paradox of the House of Lords as an anachronism that yet seemed to play a valuable constitutional role. Recently, however, the Lords has become the focus of successive governments' constitutional reform programmes, with the removal of most of the hereditary peers from the House of Lords in 1999, the Wakeham Report on long-term reform, numerous reports since then, including the influential report of the Public Administration Committee, with its counter-proposals for a far more democratic and assertive House, the votes on reform in both Houses held in 2003 and March 2007, and finally, and most importantly, the Coalition Government's 2011 White Paper (House of Lords Reform: Draft Bill (May 2011, Cm 8077) and the 2012 Bill, which was introduced in Parliament in June 2012. The report on the Salisbury and other conventions by the Joint Committee on Conventions (2006) should also be noted, as should the acceptance of its recommendations by both Houses in 2007.

Examination questions are therefore very likely to appear on this highly topical area, and are almost bound to focus on one or more of the above elements of reform.

Checklist ✔

Students should be familiar with the following areas:

- the limits on the powers of the Lords under the **Parliament Acts 1911** and **1949**;
- the conventions on the use of the Lords' powers, including recent examples; the report of the 2006 Joint Committee on Conventions;
- the role of the Lords in relation to legislation emanating in the Commons, including recent examples;
- the scrutiny of delegated legislation of the Executive and of European legislation;
- the Lords' role in initiating legislation; Private Members' Bills emanating in the Lords;

- the composition of the Lords; note that the current composition, including the balance between the different types of peer and the Lords' party make-up, can easily be checked on the Parliament website at www. publications.parliament.uk;

- the removal of the hereditary peers and its consequences;

- further proposals for reform – Wakeham; the Fifth Report of the Public Administration Committee; the Joint Committee's Report in 2002 and the subsequent votes; the Parliamentary votes in March 2007; the 2011 White Paper and **2012 Bill**.

Note the following references: those to the Public Administration Committee are to its Fifth Report (HC 494, 2001–02); those to Wakeham are to the report, *A House for the Future* (Cm 4534); to the Government's 2011 White Paper are to *House of Lords Reform: Draft Bill* (May 2011, Cm 8077); references to the report of the Joint Committee on Conventions are to the 2006 Report, HL Paper 265-I HC 1212-I.

QUESTION 18

'Although the House of Lords has some value, it is an anomaly in a democracy and should be abolished or radically reformed.'

▶ **Discuss. Do not discuss the details of various reform proposals.**

How to Answer this Question

This is quite a straightforward example of a question likely to be asked on the House of Lords, since it asks for an evaluation of the Lords as it still is. Given the wording of the question, only the broad choices for reform should be discussed. The discussion of reform *must* be related to the strengths and weaknesses of the House identified earlier in the essay.

Answer Structure

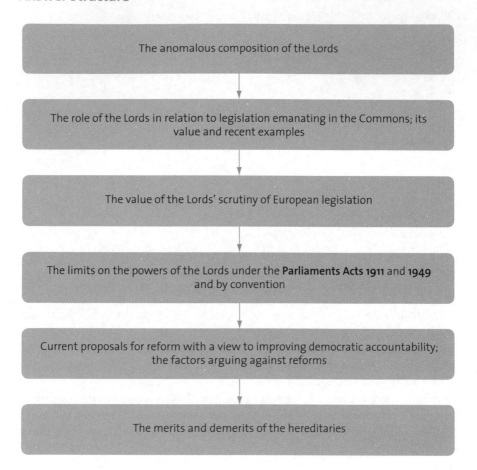

The anomalous composition of the Lords

The role of the Lords in relation to legislation emanating in the Commons; its value and recent examples

The value of the Lords' scrutiny of European legislation

The limits on the powers of the Lords under the **Parliaments Acts 1911** and **1949** and by convention

Current proposals for reform with a view to improving democratic accountability; the factors arguing against reforms

The merits and demerits of the hereditaries

ANSWER

The anomalous position of the House of Lords in a modern democracy is perhaps its most remarkable feature: not one member of the UK Parliament's second chamber is elected. All hold their positions either through birth, appointment or the office they hold. There are still these three main groups in the Lords, although following the House of Lords Act 1999, the balance between the life and hereditary peers has swung dramatically in the former's favour. As at 11 June 2012, the House numbered 775 peers, of whom 660 are life peers and only 89 are hereditary peers, those selected for retention by a vote of the hereditary peers only. The Law Lords have now been removed from the House and make up the membership of the new Supreme Court, under the provisions of the Constitutional Reform Act 2005.

The House's second major affront to democracy formerly lay in the fact that one party, the Conservatives, historically had a permanent strong predominance if not quite an absolute majority. Following the removal of the bulk of the hereditary peers and a deliberate and successful attempt by the Blair and Brown Governments to rebalance the Lords through the appointment of large numbers of life peers, the position has undergone a significant change. As at 12 June 2012, Labour remains the largest single party: it has 231 seats, the Conservatives 213, while the Liberal Democrats have increased their number of seats notably to 90.[1] Despite the fact that David Cameron has appointed a large number of Life Peers, increasing their number by 47 in the last two years, it thus remains the case that Labour, which lost the 2010 general election, remains over-represented in the Lords and the Liberal Democrats under-represented (with only 12% of total Peers). Thus, despite the appointments being made by the Prime Minister, it will take a considerable amount of time to achieve a House reflecting the votes cast at the last general election, illustrating again the way in which the Lords poorly represents the state of the parties. Very importantly, there are now 181 cross-bench peers, so that independent members represent just under a quarter (23%) of the total membership. Peers taking a party whip are appointed by the Queen on the advice of the prime minister; new cross-bench peers are nominated by the (non-statutory) Appointments Commission to the prime minister, who passes those recommendations on to the Queen for appointment.

Despite its undemocratic and unrepresentative nature, most commentators accept that the House of Lords has a valuable part to play in the British constitutional process. Perhaps its most important role lies in scrutinising public Bills passed by the House of Commons, on which it spends around half of its time. The House passes a large amount of amendments to such Bills: in the 1987–90 sessions, the average number of amendments passed was over 2,600. The vast majority of these were subsequently accepted by government (2,038 out of 2,056 in the 1992–93 session), reflecting the fact that most are introduced by government and are technical in nature. But the House is not simply a forum in which government can correct its own mistakes. Barnett's conclusion is that 'the Lords is both very active in relation to legislation, and makes a substantial impact on many legislative proposals' (*Constitutional and Administrative Law*, 4th edn, 2002, p 532). A significant number of its amendments represent changes of principle of a minor or major nature. To an extent, therefore, the Lords can compensate for the inadequate scrutiny bestowed by the Commons and can therefore provide a much-needed check on the government. For example, during the 1980s, due to the nature of the parliamentary process, the Labour Party was helpless in the face of the large Conservative majority. In contrast, the Lords inflicted 173 defeats on the government between 1979 and 1991, some of them relating to important and controversial measures. The Lords also provided often crucial opposition to the last Labour Government, which, with its decisive majorities, could often steamroller opposition in the Commons. For example, in 2000, the Lords inflicted a further major defeat on the Government over its Criminal Justice

---

1   Student essays often refer in general terms to the party composition of the House being quite 'balanced', but rarely give specific figures: these add authority and precision.

(Mode of Trial) Bill, by defeating the Government's proposals to remove the right of defendants to choose jury trial in 'either way' offences, such as theft and burglary. The amendment that the Lords passed, restoring that right, was what is commonly referred to as a 'wrecking amendment', since it altered the fundamental principle of the legislation. The Lords has continued its active role since the Coalition Government came to power: it inflicted 48 defeats during the 2010–12 session alone, including in particular in relation to the numerous cuts to Legal Aid (Legal Aid, Sentencing and Punishment of Offenders Bill 2012); on welfare reform (Welfare Reform Bill 2012) and on the controversial changes to the NHS brought about by the Health and Social Care Bill 2012.

The House of Lords is often seen as having a particularly important role to play in the protection of civil liberties, an issue to which the Commons may often show little sensitivity when both main parties feel obliged to show their 'toughness' on law and order issues. For example, in 2001, their Lordships imposed a series of major defeats on the government, including a record five in one session in relation to its Anti-Terrorism, Crime and Security Bill 2001, which inter alia allowed for the detention without trial for an indefinite period of suspected international terrorists. In the result, the Lords forced some important concessions from the government, a pattern that was repeated in relation to the Prevention of Terrorism Act 2005 and the Racial and Religious Hatred Bill.

Philip Norton (in Jones (ed), *Politics UK*, 1994, p 354) has suggested three main features of the House of Lords that render it 'particularly suitable' for the task of detailed consideration of legislation.[2] First, as an unelected body, it cannot claim legitimacy to reject the principle of measures agreed by the elected House; thus, by default, it has to concentrate on the detail. Second, its membership includes people who have distinguished themselves in particular fields – law, education, industry, industrial relations – so that it can look at relevant legislation from the point of view of practitioners in the field rather than of professional politicians. Third, because the House does not consider money Bills, it has more time than the Commons to debate non-money Bills; furthermore, there is no provision for guillotines or closures to be imposed on debate, so that all amendments are discussed unless withdrawn.

It should be pointed out that two of the positive attributes that Norton identifies arise from the fact that the House is not elected. Its lack of legitimacy means that it cannot reject the principle of Bills; the fact that it does not consider money Bills is also a reflection of its lower, because undemocratic, status. The paradoxical notion that much of the value that commentators perceive in the Lords is attributable to the one characteristic that most lays it open to attack – its unelected status – is a recurring theme in the literature on the subject.

To this can be added the relative political independence of the Lords. First of all, the large contingent of cross-bench peers ensures a strong input of non-party opinion and analysis.

---

2   Essays commonly assert that the Lords has particular strength in the area of scrutiny of legislation, but rarely explain the key reasons why this is so: to do so is vital for a good 2:1 essay.

That just under 25 per cent of peers are now independents compares strikingly to the position in the Commons, in which there are never more than three or four independent MPs. Furthermore, the Lords are not as susceptible to party pressure exerted by the whips as are MPs; most have no political future to safeguard, and so are not as vulnerable to threats or promises. These conclusions are borne out by evidence as to how the Lords behaves in practice, discussed above: defeats of governments of both political complexions are far more frequent than in the Commons, in which, at least if the government has a workable overall majority, they are almost unheard of.

However, while the above factors may facilitate the valuable work the House performs, its unelected and partisan make-up has led it to impose certain conventional restraints on the exercise of its own powers, including the Salisbury Convention, which essentially mean that it is generally unwilling to impose its will upon the government-dominated Commons. Moreover, under the legal restrictions on the powers of the Lords introduced by the Parliament Acts, the Lords may only in the end delay a non-money Bill for one year, provided that it has been passed by the Commons in two successive sessions and twice rejected by the Lords. Again, these limitations reflect the lower status of the unelected House.

Turning to the issue of reform, it is suggested that, in principle, some balance needs to be struck between preserving at least some of those qualities that allow the House to perform its current valuable work – in particular, its expertise across a range of areas, its willingness to examine in detail and a relatively weak degree of party control – and remedying the basic problem of the House's undemocratic and unrepresentative nature. It is the fact that the House's undemocratic nature is strongly linked to the current value of its work that has made the problem of its reform so intractable.

As Brigid Hadfield has pointed out ('Whither or whether the House of Lords' (1984) 35(4) NILQ 313), changing the *composition* of the Lords presents a basic problem. If the members were elected, the chamber could become simply a rival to the Commons, resulting in political impasse. Alternatively, if both chambers were dominated by the same party and the new chamber was as easily dominated by the government as the Commons, it might become redundant. Electing the second chamber might well also jeopardise the current value of its work, since the appointed independent experts who contribute so much to the value of the Lords' work would be lost, replaced by professional politicians. However, a non-elected House would also pose difficulties, both in terms of arguments over the selection procedure (although any system would seem preferable to having the prime minister select peers) and because of the fact that a non-elected senate would have no mandate to assert its will against the elected House of Commons.[3]

---

3   It is important that student essays clearly identify the key problems that lie behind the paradox of Lords reform: in particular the linkage between composition, powers and the likely behaviour of the Lords *must* be brought out.

Clearly, some balance is needed: the Lords must have greater democratic legitimacy or it will continue to be a second-class sidelined body, unwilling to assert its will even when it has a strong argument. On the other hand, making it wholly elected would risk impasse with the Commons, and perhaps more importantly jeopardise precisely those qualities of the Lords – expertise, relative independence from a party – which, it is currently agreed, make its work most worthwhile. It is therefore suggested that the way forward for the Lords is to build on the positive aspects of the Wakeham proposals: an independent statutory Commission to make appointments for the non-elected members, and determine the percentage of party peers nominated, in order to remove the unacceptable patronage of the prime minister of the day; the duty to achieve greater representation in terms of race, sex and regionalism; the retention of a strong independent body of peers, and introducing a strong proportion of elected peers – 50 per cent or 60 per cent as suggested by the Public Administration Committee. The House of Commons voted strongly for a fully elected House in March 2007, with an 80:20 elected/appointed House as the considerably less popular second choice. The last Government accepted this view, while the new Coalition Government, following its 2011 White Paper, brought forward legislation in June 2012 to create a new House that is 80 per cent elected and 20 per cent appointed.

In conclusion, while the House of Lords does valuable work, in particular in providing for an element of non-partisan expert scrutiny of legislation and policy, it is accepted that more radical reform is needed. This should aim to preserve the best features of the existing Lords, whilst giving it the legitimacy to use its powers far more extensively than at present.

Common Pitfalls

There are two common pitfalls when answering on this topic. The first is that students tend to adopt a simplistic stance, either condemning the Lords for its undemocratic nature, or lauding it to the skies for its independent and expert scrutiny. Answers that fail to acknowledge the clear arguments on the other side of the debate will never score very well. The other pitfall is more straightforward: vagueness and generality. Thus we may be told that the House of Lords does valuable work improving legislation – but no examples are given; alternatively, we may be told that it has a different, more balanced distribution of seats between the parties than the Commons, but instead of the precise – or even rough – figures being given, to show how great is the difference, the assertion is left with no evidence and thus lacks both authority and precision.

QUESTION 19

'The valuable legislative function of the House of Lords is impaired because such powers as it possesses are not often used to their full effect.' Do you agree that the House often under-uses its powers?

How to Answer this Question

This is a somewhat tricky version of a typical House of Lords question, because it focuses on quite a narrow aspect of the topic and not the usual 'reform' angle. The issue of the non-legal limits on the powers of the Lords were raised in acute form by the controversy over the Welfare Reform Bill in 2012.

Answer Structure

The formal limits on the powers of the Lords under the **Parliament Acts 1911** and **1949**

The conventions on the use of the Lords' powers; changes in the Salisbury Convention since 1999 and the report of the Joint Committee on Conventions in 2006

The importance of conventions as compared to formal limitations

The issue of the financial privileges of the Commons, as raised during the **Welfare Reform Bill** controversies in 2012

The role of the Lords in scrutinising legislation, particularly legislation affecting civil liberties

The Private Members' Bills emanating from the Lords

The scrutiny of delegated legislation; a convention of restraint?

The impact of the removal of the hereditary peers and rebalancing of the political composition of the Lords on the above; how further reform might affect the behaviour of the Lords

ANSWER

This question implies that the legislative function of the House of Lords is quite severely circumscribed. Before considering the effect of such circumscription, it should first be determined how far the Lords may be said to refrain from full use of its powers and how far it is restrained from doing so by legislation.

The Lords has the same right to initiate and revise legislation as the Commons, subject to the provisions of the Parliament Acts 1911 and 1949. The Acts allow the House of Commons to assert political supremacy over the Lords in two very important instances. First, when a Bill has been passed by the Commons in two successive sessions and it is rejected for a second time by the Lords, it can be presented on its second rejection for the royal assent, provided that a year has elapsed. Second, the Lords may only delay money Bills for one month.

However, the limits on the Lords' power under the Parliament Acts are not as significant as may at first appear, largely because they have been rarely used – only seven times since 1911. This indicates that the *conventional* limitations upon the Lords' power – together with the willingness of governments to accept amendments rather than face delay – on the whole preclude the need for the *legal* assertion of the Commons' supremacy.

Perhaps the most important, and certainly the most clearly established convention of self-restraint has been termed the 'Salisbury Convention', referred to as 'the government Bill convention' by the Joint Committee on Conventions (2006). This doctrine was explained by Lord Salisbury in 1964 as a guiding principle that where legislation had been promised in the governing party's manifesto, the Lords would not block it on the ground that it should be regarded as having been approved by the British people. The Salisbury Convention is taken very seriously by the Lords; there has been no clear instance where the Lords has flatly rejected a manifesto Bill since the Second World War, and it has recently been approved by both Houses in 2007 as having the meaning set out in the Joint Committee report: that the Lords will always give a second reading to any manifesto Bill and will not pass 'wrecking amendments' to it.

However, the application of the Convention to *amendments* to manifesto Bills remains necessarily less clear than the simple principle that no manifesto Bill should be rejected at second reading. The Joint Committee report said that the Convention precludes the Lords from amending a Bill in such a way as to change the government's 'manifesto intention' (para 99).[4] But this has certainly not stopped the Lords amending manifesto Bills in significant ways – the European Parliamentary Elections Bill 1998 was a good example.

---

4   The report of the Joint Committee is very important and should always be cited when discussing issues of Lords–Commons conventions.

In relation to non-manifesto Bills, there is more of a general practice of self-restraint than a clear convention. The Lords very rarely reject government Bills outright; indeed, the rejection of the War Crimes Bill 1990 and the Parliament Bill 1947 represent the only occasions when this happened in fifty years. The House is also often reluctant, in practice, to restore amendments to any Bill that the government has had overturned in the Commons. However, on occasions, the Lords will repeatedly insist upon its amendments. A recent example was the Teaching and Higher Education Bill 1998: a provision in the Bill that waived the payment of fees for the fourth year of a degree taken at a Scottish university for Scottish students, but not those from the rest of the UK, led the Lords to restore on three occasions an amendment rejected by the Commons that equalised the position for students from all parts of the UK. The government was eventually forced to promise an independent review of the system within six months of its establishment, an important concession. A more striking example came with the Parliamentary Voting System and Constituencies Bill, paving the way for the referendum on changing the voting system for general elections, and reducing the size of the Commons by changing some constituency boundaries. Lords and Commons engaged in a marathon struggle, involving a 14-day Committee stage in the Lords – said to be the longest since 1971, while Labour Peers were accused of using filibustering and delaying tactics to hold up the Bill and win concessions.

In 2000, following the reform of the Lords removing most of the hereditary peers, the House rejected the core of the government's Criminal Justice (Mode of Trial) Bill, cl 1, which removed the right of defendants to choose jury trial in 'either way' offences, such as theft and burglary. Where, however, civil liberties clash with the fight against terrorism, historically, the Lords has sometimes fared no better than the Commons in forcing governments to reconsider sometimes draconian measures. Indeed, it has often offered no resistance at all to the rushing through of legislation, often in response to particular atrocities, refusing to exercise even to a small degree its powers to debate legislation at length. Thus, the Lords offered no resistance in 1974 to the first Prevention of Terrorism Bill, passed through both Houses in a single day, following the outrage generated by the Birmingham pub bombings. The Prevention of Terrorism (Additional Powers) Bill 1996 was likewise passed in one day, as was the Criminal Justice (Terrorism and Conspiracy) Bill 1998, which passed through the Lords in a few hours, despite its far-reaching implications for civil liberties. However, the House appears to have become more assertive in recent years, perhaps because of the removal of the hereditary peers. Thus the Lords insisted on amendments to the Terrorism Acts of 2001 and 2005, although giving way on a number of others (see Phillipson (2004) PL 352).

However, an inherent limit to the power of the Lords over legislation – the Common's ability to resolve that the Bill in question is covered by its financial privileges – was highlighted by the controversy over the Government's Welfare Reform Bill in 2012. The privilege, as Jeff King describes it, means that: 'The Commons is entitled to "disagree" with any Lords amendment and ultimately reject it without feeling obliged to provide any reasons other than the existence of the privilege.' By convention, the Lords will accept this determination (though increasingly with protest) (Jeff King 'Welfare Reform and the Financial Privilege', UK Constitutional Law Blog, 3 Feb 2012). Traditionally, the privilege was seen as applying to Bills dealing with supply and taxation, but it was used to summarily reject a large number of Lords' amendments to the controversial Welfare Bill, on the grounds that, by cutting and restricting welfare entitlements, it had important implications for public expenditure. This was highly controversial, since many Bills have such implications. Plainly the scope of this privilege remains unclear, but it is being increasingly used to limit the effect of the Lords' scrutiny of legislation.[5]

The Lords also performs a valuable service by contributing to the scrutiny of delegated legislation. Its powers in this respect are the same as those of the House of Commons, as they were not curbed by the Parliament Acts. For example, on occasion, a point raised in debate in the Lords may lead the government to withdraw the legislation in question with a view to amending it. However, a very clear picture of self-restraint emerges in this area also: up until 2000, the Lords had only once since 1945 thrown out a piece of delegated legislation, and that was the highly controversial Southern Rhodesia Order 1968. Indeed, some observers were of the view that there was in fact a convention that the Lords would not reject delegated legislation at all. The Wakeham Report appeared to act on this assumption, in recommending that the Lords' unused veto power should be replaced by a short power of delay; this was in spite of the fact that when, in 1994, it was suggested to the House that a convention had come into being that the Lords would not vote down items of subordinate legislation, their Lordships' response was bullish: a motion by Lord Simon of Glaisdale to the effect that the House had unfettered freedom to vote on any subordinate legislation before it was overwhelmingly approved in October of that year.

In this area, the removal of the hereditary peers seems to have had a particularly clear effect. The Lords in 2000 was unhappy with the refusal of the government, in its legislation governing the London mayor and assembly, to give candidates a free 'mail shot' to the electorate. The Lords chose to express its discontent on the matter in a novel way: it voted on a piece of secondary legislation – the Greater London Authority (Election Expenses) Order 2000, which dealt with the nuts and bolts of the London mayoral and assembly elections, in particular, the amount of electoral expenditure that candidates would be allowed to incur; the Order required only negative approval, that is, it would go through automatically unless voted against. Erskine May reveals that the House has *never* voted down orders requiring only the negative approval procedure. Nevertheless, the

....

5   The possibly very broad scope of the Common's financial privileges may not be given much coverage in your textbooks; however, following the 2012 Welfare Reform Bill controversy, the issue is clearly of far more importance than many commentators realised. Bringing them into an essay will also impress examiners with the student's ability to integrate examples from current affairs into their work.

Lords, to the consternation of the government, threw the Order out and in so doing, quite clearly relied upon its newly reformed status.

The government's evidence to the Joint Committee on Conventions took the view that it was a breach of convention for the Lords to reject statutory instruments; the Committee in its 2006 report clearly rejected this view, concluding that this was not so, but that the power to reject should be exercised only in exceptional circumstances, including in particular in relation to delegated legislation that altered primary legislation and where the statutory instrument deals with matters normally found in primary legislation, a view accepted by both Houses. Following that report, in March 2007, the Lords again rejected a statutory instrument, in relation to the government's controversial policies on new gambling casinos; the item in question was the Gambling (Geographical Distribution of Casino Premises Licences) Order 2007 – an affirmative instrument. In recent years, the House has made increasing use of 'non-fatal' motions, in which it expresses concern or regret about statutory instruments, while not voting them down.[6]

On the whole, however, the general picture is clear: the House of Lords, which is in a weaker position to resist government Bills (both legally and by convention) than the Commons, in fact utilises its ability to improve Bills in matters of detail, to introduce important changes of principle and to force the government to reconsider far more than the theoretically omnipotent Commons. Thus, the criticism outlined in the question applies in fact less to the second chamber than to the first.

It may therefore be argued that the Lords has managed to create a delicate balance between appearing as a superfluous body that merely rubber stamps the Commons' decisions, and as an undemocratic and anachronistic body that interferes too far in the legislative function of the elected part of Parliament. It is clear that the removal of the hereditary peers has already resulted in a more assertive attitude from their Lordships. The government noted in its 2008 White Paper that 'in the 1997–98, 1998–99 and 1999–2000 sessions, the Government suffered 39, 31 and 36 defeats in the House of Lords, respectively [whereas] from the 2001–02 to the 2006–07 session inclusive, the average number of such defeats in each session was almost 60' – quite a dramatic change.

However, given that the core reason for the House's restraint – its undemocratic status – has not been touched by the removal of the hereditaries, it is unlikely that either the Salisbury Convention or the House's nuanced convention of general restraint will disappear until more comprehensive, democratic reform gives the House unquestionable legitimacy.

....

6   Student essays often miss the issue of delegated legislation; however, it is extremely important, and the issue of what conventions govern the Lords' unfettered legal powers in relation to it remains highly contested.

QUESTION 20

Does the House of Lords Reform Bill 2012 amount to a good solution to the problem of comprehensive Lords Reform? Your answer should consider alternative proposals put forward by Wakeham and others.

How to Answer this Question

This question, or something similar to it, is almost bound to appear on examination papers over the next few years. The current composition and work of the House of Lords needs to be very briefly discussed, in order to show why its work is so valuable and how far different reform proposals might risk jeopardising it in the search for a more legitimate and representative House.

Answer Structure

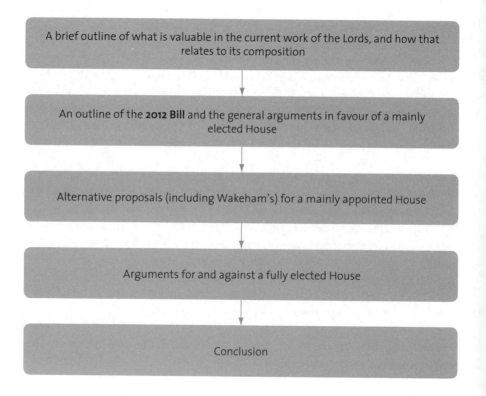

A brief outline of what is valuable in the current work of the Lords, and how that relates to its composition

An outline of the **2012 Bill** and the general arguments in favour of a mainly elected House

Alternative proposals (including Wakeham's) for a mainly appointed House

Arguments for and against a fully elected House

Conclusion

ANSWER

The House of Lords is generally accepted to perform valuable work, particularly in scrutinising and amending legislation, especially that concerning human rights and constitutional matters. Equally, however, it is viewed as being at least partially hamstrung by its lack of legitimacy (reflected in the various powerful conventions of restraint it observes) and (by many) as indefensible in a democracy, given that it exercises considerable political power, but is wholly unelected. This essay will evaluate the reforms embodied in the 2012 Bill in the light of these basic background facts.

The Bill proposes a new House of 450 members, of which some could be part-time (new Peers would be paid per days they attended). Of this 360 members (80%) would be elected and 90 (20%) would be independents, appointed on a non-party basis by a statutory Appointments Commission. The elected members would be gradually phased in: 120 would be elected at each of the 2015, 2020, and 2025 general elections. They would be elected not from constituencies, but eight different regions – a feature thought to avoid the problem of Peers starting to exercise constituency duties and thus treading on the toes of MPs. All members would serve a single non-renewable term of three Parliaments (likely to be 15 years). Twelve Anglican Bishops would remain. The new appointed members would also be phased in, with 30 being appointed after each general election. Members could be expelled for misconduct. The result of the above would make it highly unlikely that any government would command a majority in the House.

In terms of moving towards evaluation of the 2012 Bill proposals, Meg Russell's work is the leading study in this area, in terms of identifying, through comparative analysis, the crucial factors that make for an effective second chamber. As summarised by the Public Administration Select Committee, the reformed Lords should have three key qualities. First, it must have *distinct composition* – it is important that the House maintains a different make-up from the Commons, as at present; otherwise it will not make any distinctive contribution to the legislative process. In particular, it is important to maintain its qualities of *relative* independence and expertise. It is also vital to ensure that the party balance in the chamber is different from and more proportional than that in the Commons, to prevent one-party domination, giving the House an alternative and more broadly based perspective on the development of public policy. Second, a reformed House needs *adequate powers*; thus if the new Upper House is to make a significant impact, it will need to at least maintain its present, moderate powers. Third, a second chamber must have *perceived legitimacy*: in order to use its powers to the full, the new chamber (unlike the existing House of Lords) will need to be seen to have legitimacy, and be able to carry public support.[7]

There appears to be something of a consensus on the issue of the *powers* a reformed second chamber should have. The current powers of the Lords are recognisably at the moderate end of the international spectrum, as Russell finds, although significantly weaker than most second chambers overseas in having no special powers over changes

---

7   It is absolutely crucial in an essay of this sort that such criteria are set out clearly in the answer at the outset.

to the constitution, including fundamental rights. The Wakeham report set the trend by recommending that the powers of a new second chamber should be broadly comparable with those of the present Lords, and this view has not been seriously challenged since, save by academic commentators such as Phillipson (2003 PL). The 2012 Bill provides simply that the Parliament Acts will still apply to the new House (s 2), while the Government's view in the 2011 White Paper was that all the existing conventions would still continue to apply (para 8). It must be noted, however, that most commentators expect a more legitimate Lords to be more assertive and, as the Joint Committee on the Draft Bill observed, the extent of this is hard to predict.

The requirement that the Lords have a distinct composition from the Commons has long been accepted and led successive White Papers, culminating in the 2012 Bill, to propose that members of the second chamber would be elected on a different representative basis from MPs and be able to bring 'independence of judgement' to their work. As noted above, the 2012 Bill proposes that this be achieved primarily by members of the reformed chamber serving long, non-renewable terms of office of 15 years, and by providing for 20 per cent of the members to be appointed. It is of course the case that a House elected by proportional representation (the 2012 Bill proposes a semi-open list system) would have a very different party make-up from the Commons (it would be unlikely that any party would have an overall majority), while the long, non-renewable terms should encourage more independent-mindedness among members, since they could not be subject to threats of deselection where they disobeyed the party line. Moreover, having staggered elections to the second chamber, so that only a third of the members would change at any given election, would also help to minimise domination by one party and ensure a different party make-up from the House of Commons.

The powers of the prime minister in this area would be wholly removed: the Appointments Commission would have sole jurisdiction over appointments and be under no obligation to accept any nominations put to it. Nor would be the prime minister be able to appoint anyone to the House other than persons nominated by the Commission (cl 13(4)).[8]

Essentially then, the 2012 Bill aims in essence to preserve the House's distinctive independence, expertise and different composition from the Commons, but to give it far greater legitimacy by introducing an elected element forming a clear majority of the House's members. Since it also leaves the current moderate powers of the House untouched, on its face it therefore fulfils all three of the criteria set out above. However, in order to see why, as this essay argues, this majority-elected hybrid option is indeed the best out of the possible solutions, it is necessary to consider the main alternatives. These are

---

8   A small but vital point: where new legislation is published that is not covered by textbooks, student essays will gain hugely in credibility where they cite specific provisions.

essentially two: a mainly or fully appointed House on the one hand, or a fully elected one on the other.[9]

The Wakeham Report suggested a mainly appointed House of 550, with a minority of elected members to represent the regions. The remainder of the House would be appointed by a statutory, independent Appointments Committee, which would be under a statutory duty to maintain an independent element of 20 per cent in the House and to ensure that the parties were represented roughly in proportion to the votes cast in the most recent general election, thus removing the historic domination of the House by the Conservative Party. Proposals like Wakeham's, for a mainly appointed House (or a fully appointed one), clearly fulfil the 'distinct composition' criteria discussed above: membership of such a House would be very distinct from that of the Commons, in particular, because of the 20 per cent proportion of independent members and because the party balance would be very different to the position in the Commons. It is in relation to the third factor – *perceived legitimacy* – that proposals like those of Wakeham fall down. The PAC's view was that the public were simply not prepared to support or even tolerate the continuation of such extensive patronage, certainly not from the political parties, but probably not even from an independent Appointments Commission. Moreover opposition from a fully or largely appointed House, based on something like the Wakeham blueprint, could ultimately be brushed aside by governments, on the basis that the House was dominated by party appointees. As Russell observes, the Canadian Senate is ultimately an ineffectual House, despite its very strong formal powers, precisely because of its lack of legitimacy as an appointed body. Keeping the House fully appointed, or injecting only a small elected element, would simply not be enough to give the House enough self-belief to confront the government repeatedly and make it think again.

What then of the opposite alternative – a fully elected second chamber? Such a House clearly commands considerable public support, according to polls, and is the long-standing policy of the Liberal Democrats and currently of the Labour Party. However, it is suggested that calls for such a House are simplistic and misguided. As noted above, most commentators on the current House agree that much of its value flows precisely from the fact that it is *not* elected. Amongst other things, its unelected nature leads to its relative political independence, its freedom from populist pressures, and in particular the presence of experts in various fields, which gives its scrutiny of legislation a mastery of important points of detail generally lacking in the Commons.

---

9   A good essay in this area *must* deal with the arguments for all three of the main options; student essays commonly only contrast e.g. a mainly elected House with a fully appointed one, and thus do not consider the fully elected option.

The most common objection to a wholly elected House is that it would become simply a rival to the Commons, resulting in political impasse. It is suggested that this objection is also somewhat simplistic; it fails to take account of the fact that, as Meg Russell has pointed out, the large majority of second chambers overseas are elected and yet gridlock has rarely arisen. Moreover, the effect of the legal limitations on the House represented by the Parliament Acts and the continuance of the existing conventions would ensure that the House did not challenge the supremacy of the Commons, although it may reasonably be expected to become somewhat more assertive – one of the main reasons to support the reforms.

It is submitted that the real objection to a fully elected chamber is that, as with all elections, it would be practically impossible for anyone, save perhaps a few well-known mavericks, to win a seat without standing as a member of one of the main political parties – although a proportional representation system of some sort would help members of the smaller parties, such as the Greens, to be elected. Thus, the new chamber would be far more dominated than now by whipped party members, reducing considerably its distinctiveness from the Commons. Electing the second chamber might well also jeopardise the current value of its work, in that its expertise and the presence within it of a range of viewpoints beyond party orthodoxies would be wholly lost.

To conclude, then, we have seen that a wholly or mainly appointed House would be hamstrung by its lack of legitimacy. Meanwhile, as argued above, a fully elected House of Lords would be one made up almost exclusively of professional politicians, with very few independents likely – as in the Commons. Thus much of the capacity of the current House for non-partisan, expert scrutiny would inevitably be lost. The only reliable way to ensure that a reformed second chamber retained at least some of this capacity would be to ensure that it had a mixture of elected party politicians and appointed independents within it. Viewed in this light, it is evident that the 2012 Bill proposals look the most attractive of those considered here – although the PAC proposals for a 60/40 split would be arguably better still. The strong elected element would give the House a hugely increased sense of legitimacy and would encourage it to use its powers to make the government think again, particularly where issues of basic human rights, the protection of unpopular minorities and/or constitutional change are at stake, as with the Anti-Terrorism Bill 2001.

For these reasons, it is concluded that the proposals of the PAC would combine the existing strengths of the House with the legitimacy it needs to make it a far more influential voice in the political process, and are thus most worthy of support. The proposals in the 2012 Bill for an 80:20 elected/appointed House are not as satisfactory, it is submitted, because the appointed element would be dominated by the elected members and thus less likely to have much of an impact. A 60:40 split would satisfy the principle of making the House *predominantly* elected while maintaining a strong non-partisan element. Nevertheless, the 2012 proposals would be a huge improvement over the status quo.

Aim Higher ★

When considering what principles should guide reform, students need to place their knowledge of the various reform proposals within the context of a solid base of knowledge about the current composition and powers of the Lords, the conventional restraints upon the House, the party balance and the nature and distinctive value of the work it does. This needs to be backed up by concrete examples — particularly recent ones – in order to show real awareness of the function performed by the House of Lords in the contemporary constitution. Moreover, analysis of the Lords is made far more telling if it is informed by complementary discussion of the characteristics and political behaviour of the Commons. To take analysis of the Lords without consideration of its role as one of the two chambers of Parliament is inevitably to reduce the value of that analysis.

Prerogative Powers

INTRODUCTION

Essay questions, as opposed to problems, tend to be set in this area and will often concentrate on the extent to which courts can control the exercise of prerogative power, particularly given the important recent decision in *Bancoult*. The impact of the Human Rights Act 1998 should also be considered, although at the time of writing, there is little significant case law specifically on its effect on the prerogative. However, we have recently seen two important reforms in this area, governing approval of treaties (Constitutional Reform and Governance Act 2010) and replacing the prerogative power of dissolution of Parliament by the Fixed Term Parliaments Act 2011; examiners are therefore highly likely to focus on these. Meanwhile, the development of a possible convention governing the need to consult Parliament before committing the armed forces to action remains highly topical, given the Libya example, as does the possibility of a Commons resolution to concretise the possible convention. Two questions here therefore focus on these recent developments.

Checklist ✔

Students should be familiar with the following areas:

- the nature of prerogative powers;
- the more important prerogatives – to use armed force, make treaties, recognise states, appoint a prime minister, dismiss and appoint ministers; the personal prerogative of the monarch – various immunities such as the Queen's personal immunity from suit or prosecution and property rights;
- the matters that the courts have traditionally considered in relation to the prerogative – its existence and extent, its relationship with statute and the duty of the Crown to compensate citizens affected by prerogative powers;
- *Council of Civil Service Unions v Minister for the Civil Service* (1984) (the *GCHQ* case) – powers exercised under the prerogative may be open to review; excluded categories of prerogative power and how they have been cut down since *GCHQ*; the impact of the **Human Rights Act 1998** on review of the prerogative;

- reforms introduced and proposed re current near-absence of parliamentary controls over the exercise of the prerogative, particularly in relation to the use of armed force; proposals for reform in the government's 2008 White Paper *The Governance of Britain*, Cm 7342-I) and the **2010 Act**;

- the **Fixed Term Parliament Act 2011**.

QUESTION 21

How far do you think it is true to say that the role of judges in relation to the exercise of the royal prerogative may now prevent arbitrary Executive action? Do not consider the interrelationship of prerogative and statute.

How to Answer this Question

This question is often asked in one form or another and is reasonably straightforward. Students should not spend much of their essay rehearsing legal history by outlining the 'old' position; rather, the emphasis should be on the *GCHQ* case and how the 'excluded categories' have fared since then. Discussion of the impact of the Human Rights Act 1998 (HRA) will also gain marks.

Answer Structure

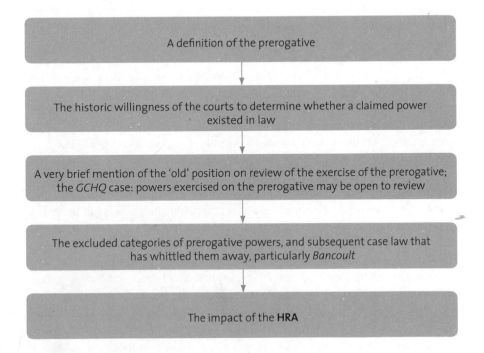

A definition of the prerogative

The historic willingness of the courts to determine whether a claimed power existed in law

A very brief mention of the 'old' position on review of the exercise of the prerogative; the *GCHQ* case: powers exercised on the prerogative may be open to review

The excluded categories of prerogative powers, and subsequent case law that has whittled them away, particularly *Bancoult*

The impact of the **HRA**

ANSWER

The term 'prerogative' refers to residual powers that the sovereign has as opposed to those granted by statute. The vast majority of such powers are, in practice, exercised by the prime minister, the Cabinet or individual ministers. The prerogative includes most key powers relating to foreign affairs, such as the making of treaties, recognition of states and the use of force, and, on the domestic front, the power to dissolve Parliament, to assent to Bills, award honours, pardon criminals, establish universities, and to dismiss and appoint ministers. As to judicial control of the prerogative, two broad questions arise. First, who has the power to determine whether a claimed prerogative power exists in law? Second, are the courts prepared to review the manner in which a prerogative, recognised to exist, has been exercised and if so, what are the limitations upon this review?[1]

The courts have long asserted that it is for them to determine whether a particular prerogative power actually exists and whether the decision taken falls within its scope. The famous *Case of Proclamations* (1611) made the seminal declaration that 'the King hath no prerogative, but that which the law of the land allows him'. The courts will not allow new prerogatives to be created by Executive fiat. In *BBC v Johns* (1965), the courts held that the limits of the prerogative powers 'are now well settled and incapable of extension'. However, the courts have, on occasions, been prepared to allow a recognised prerogative to broaden in adapting itself to new situations: in *Malone v Metropolitan Police Commissioner* (1979), the assertion that a prerogative power existed to authorise telephone tapping was based on the argument that no new power was being created, although an old one was being extended to a new situation.

Also disturbing in this respect was the decision in *Secretary of State for the Home Department ex p Northumbria Police Authority* (1989), in which one key issue was whether there was a hitherto largely unrecognised prerogative power to keep the peace, under which the Home Secretary could lawfully offer to supply CS gas and plastic baton rounds to any Chief Constable whose police authority would not supply him with such equipment. The court found that there was a general prerogative to keep the Queen's peace; while the judges conceded that there was virtually no authority for such a power existing, they used the perhaps perverse argument that the 'scarcity of references in the books to the prerogative of keeping the peace within the realm does not disprove that it exists. Rather, it may point to an unspoken assumption that it does.' It was further said that there was no need to demonstrate the existence of a prerogative to equip or supply the police force. Rather, the power under which the Home Secretary wished to act in supplying CS gas and plastic bullets could be brought under the general umbrella of the prerogative to do all that was reasonably necessary to keep the peace. This rather accommodating approach by the courts to the existence and scope of prerogative powers

---

1   It is very important that these two issues are clearly distinguished; otherwise the legal analysis will remain confused.

seems plainly incompatible with the basic notion, derived from *Entick v Carrington* (1765), that any act infringing on liberty must be justified by some positive piece of law.

Turning to the issue of the propriety of the exercise of prerogatives admitted to exist, one may broadly track an increased determination of the judiciary to ensure that the legal accountability of the Executive may be discerned. Lord Denning's view that the prerogative was as open to judicial scrutiny as any other governmental power (in *Laker Airways v Department of Trade* (1977)) was approved in the landmark case of *Council of Civil Service Unions v Minister for the Civil Service* (1984) (the *GCHQ* case). The House of Lords determined that the mere fact of the power deriving from the prerogative as opposed to statute was not a sufficient reason to exclude it from review. However, Lord Roskill suggested a number of prerogative powers that, by virtue of their nature and subject matter, were not amenable to the judicial process; these included the making of treaties, the disposal of the armed forces, the defence of the realm, the dissolution of Parliament, the prerogative of mercy, the granting of honours and the appointment of ministers.

In a number of cases since *GCHQ*, the courts have begun to whittle away Lord Roskill's excluded categories, suggesting a readiness in principle to review all prerogatives other than those that relate to matters at the heart of the political process, such as the dissolution of Parliament, the appointment and dismissal of ministers and matters of high foreign policy or defence: *Secretary of State for the Foreign Office ex p Rees Mogg* (1994) confirmed that the courts would not entertain challenges to the prerogative power to conclude treaties, in this case, the **Treaty of Maastricht**. It should be noted, of course, that Lord Roskill's list of excluded categories does not and never did represent an authoritative statement of the law; it was an obiter suggestion only.

Thus, in *Secretary of State for Foreign and Commonwealth Affairs ex p Everett* (1989), it was held that the courts were competent to review the exercise of the prerogative power of the Secretary of State to issue passports, although the power was related to foreign affairs and had traditionally been regarded as unreviewable. A further inroad into the excluded areas – in this case into the prerogative of mercy – was made by the decisions in *Secretary of State for the Home Department ex p Bentley* (1993), and *R (On the application of Page) v Secretary of State for Justice* (2007). A more generalised attack on the scope of the excluded categories was made in the case of *Ministry of Defence ex p Smith and Ors* (1996), which concerned a challenge to the previous policy of the British government to exclude homosexuals from the armed services. The government argued that the case involved governmental policy in relation to the armed forces, and hence amounted to a challenge to 'the exercise of a prerogative in an area – the defence of the realm – recognised by the courts to be unsuitable for judicial review'. Both the High Court and the Court of Appeal firmly rejected this argument and held the decision to be susceptible to review, although, on the facts, the challenge did not succeed. Smith LJ took the opportunity to put down a more general pointer, commenting that, in his view, 'only the rarest cases' would be non-justiciable, those that involved 'national security properly so called and where in addition, the courts really do lack the expertise or material to form a judgment on the point at issue'. The remark was not confirmed by the Court of Appeal, but was not repudiated by it either.[2]

The most recent cases are *Abbasi* (2002), *(Al Rawi)* (2007), *CND* (2002) and *Bancoult* (2008). All confirm the courts' continued strong disinclination to engage in a searching review of powers exercised in relation to foreign affairs and the use of armed force. In *Abbasi*, a British national detained at Guantanamo Bay argued that, since he was being subject, in effect, to arbitrary detention, in violation of habeas corpus, the Foreign Office had a duty either to make representations on his behalf to the US Government, or, at the least, to explain why it had in fact taken no action in relation to his case. The Court's finding was that the mere fact that the prerogative power in relation to foreign affairs was in issue was not enough to oust the jurisdiction of the court – it was the particular subject matter that was determinative. Moreover, in an extreme case where the Foreign Office appeared to be refusing even to consider making representations to the US Government about someone in the position of the applicant, judicial review would lie; however, such consideration had been given in this case, and there was no question of the court ordering the government to make representations. *Al Rawi* took a similar approach in relation to a non-British national detained at Guantanamo, who had been granted permanent leave to remain.

In the *CND* case, the court refused to give a ruling on whether **UNSC Resolution 1441**, which gave Iraq a final chance to comply with previous resolutions as to disarmament and threatened serious consequences if it did not, gave the UK the right in international law to use force against Iraq .The key reason for the refusal was that any declaration by the court would be damaging to the UK's national interest in terms of international relations and defence, since it could embarrass or tie the hands of the UK Government. It was therefore non-justiciable. This finding was unsurprising, since it would have involved the court entering directly into a highly sensitive issue of international relations. The *Abbasi* decision is more interesting: it exemplifies the contemporary approach of the courts that it is not the broad area under consideration that determines justiciability, but rather whether the particular issues raised by the challenge involve questions unsuited to judicial determination. To that extent, the relatively crude 'list' approach of Lord Roskill in *GCHQ* has been quite substantially modified.

This impression is partially heightened by consideration of the most dramatic decision, *Bancoult*. The government had, in 2004, forbidden the return home of the native inhabitants of the Chagos Islands, ruled as a colony. The inhabitants had been removed from the islands, mainly to Mauritius, by a 1971 Ordinance because Diego Garcia, the principal island, was required for use as a US military base. In 2000, the 1971 Ordinance was quashed by the Divisional Court on the ground that the exclusion of an entire population from its homeland

---

2   It is often not noted that what Lord Roskill said in *GCHQ* was plainly obiter: hence his list of excluded areas has no binding force on lower courts; the approach taken in *Smith* is radically different, rejecting the notion of broad areas of non-justiciable powers.

lay outside the purposes of the 1965 Order under which the Ordinance had been made. At the time, the government stated that it accepted the Court's ruling. However, it later decided that the territory was still wanted for defence purposes and made two fresh Orders in Council, which had the effect of preventing the Chagossians from returning home. The Court of Appeal quashed the Orders in Council on the grounds that the government had not had sufficient regard to the legitimate expectations of the islanders, created by the government statement in 2000 that they would be allowed to return: the decision was therefore an abuse of power. When the case came to the House of Lords, their Lordships unanimously confirmed that Orders in Council were fully subject to judicial review – a finding that the government had contested. However, the finding that the particular orders had been unlawful was overturned by the House of Lords in a controversial 3–2 decision. The majority stressed the sensitivity of the area, involving foreign policy, and relations with the UK's, most importantly the USA. The majority also refused to imply limitations into the power to make rules by Orders in Council for ceded territories, save for the (largely theoretical) possibility of *Wednesbury* challenge. While formally advancing judicial review of the prerogative to cover the vires of Orders in Council therefore, the judgment remained highly deferential to the Executive, confirming the pattern of *Abassi*, *CND* and *Al Rawi*.[3]

In conclusion, with the exception of a few doubtful decisions such as *Northumbria*, a general movement first of all to bring the exercise of the prerogative within the remit of judicial review, and then gradually to extend the remit of that review to cover areas previously thought to be immune can be discerned. While a number of important areas remain largely immune from review, overall there has been a significant extension of the scope of the legal accountability of the Executive and hence a sharp restriction on the capacity of government for arbitrary action.

Common Pitfalls

The most common problem in these kinds of questions is a simple one: insufficient knowledge of the case law. At its worst this leads a script simply to fail, when, for example, no decision is cited save for *GCHQ* (a sadly not uncommon occurrence). Mediocre (as opposed to failing) answers tend to have a general, rather vague knowledge of some recent cases but are not able to analyse them with any precision. In particular, *Bancoult* is a long and complicated decision: students need carefully to pick out the 'progressive' points (the finding that Orders in Council are open to review) with the more Executive-friendly findings, in particular the refusal of the majority to read limitations based on international human rights law into the power to make rules for ceded territories by Order in Council.

---

3   While detailed knowledge of the case law is obviously essential, a really good answer will not simply treat each case separately but note the *broad trends* represented by a sequence of cases.

QUESTION 22

There has been long-standing and widespread dissatisfaction with the absence of effective parliamentary controls over the exercise of the prerogative. In light of this, critically assess the reforms to parliamentary control over treaty-making and the former prerogative of the dissolution of Parliament.

▶ Do not discuss judicial review of the prerogative in your answer.

How to Answer this Question

This question is quite specific: students must have good knowledge of the relevant provisions of the Constitutional Reform and Governance Act 2010 and the Fixed Term Parliaments Act 2011.

Answer Structure

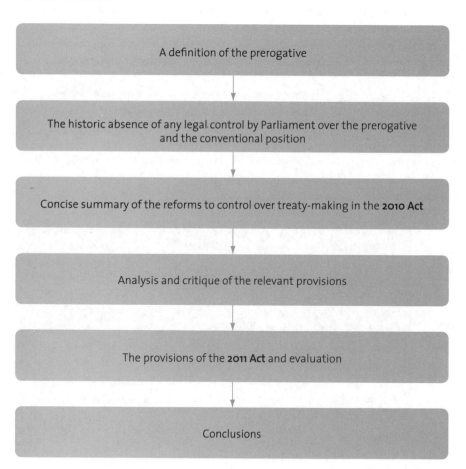

A definition of the prerogative

The historic absence of any legal control by Parliament over the prerogative and the conventional position

Concise summary of the reforms to control over treaty-making in the **2010 Act**

Analysis and critique of the relevant provisions

The provisions of the **2011 Act** and evaluation

Conclusions

ANSWER

The term 'prerogative' refers to residual powers that the sovereign has as opposed to those granted by statute. The vast majority of such powers are, in practice, exercised by the prime minister, the Cabinet or individual ministers. The prerogative includes most key matters relating to foreign affairs, such as the making of treaties, recognition of states and the use of force, and, on the domestic front, to assent to Bills, award honours, pardon criminals, establish universities, appoint a government, and to dismiss and appoint ministers. Up until the Fixed Term Parliaments Act 2011, it also included the very important power to dissolve Parliament. The concern lying at the heart of the statement in this question is that, by means of this historical relic, the UK Constitution allows powers of great breadth, magnitude and importance to be wielded by the Executive alone. This area, which greatly concerned Labour in opposition, remained entirely untouched by the great wave of constitutional reform enacted by the Blair administration from 1997 on; it was not until the dying days of the Brown Government that some cautious reform in the area of parliamentary approval of treaties was introduced via the Constitutional Reform and Governance Act 2010; reform of the long-criticised power to dissolve Parliament, wielded by the prime minister of the day, had to await the Coalition Government and the 2011 Act. This essay will critically analyse how far the two statutes introduce effective parliamentary controls. A crucial distinction between the two should be noted at the outset: whereas the first simply gave legal effect to an existing convention of parliamentary scrutiny of a prerogative power, but left the power itself in place, the second *abolished* the prerogative in question and *replaced* it with a power vested in the House of Commons, rather than in the Executive.[4] It was thus a far more bold and comprehensive reform.

The courts in the last 20 years have made great strides in bringing many areas of the prerogative under legal control; however, in relation to parliamentary accountability it is only very recently that any control has been established and then only of the most cautious kind. One of the most remarkable features of the prerogative, to foreign observers, must be the way in which it has traditionally allowed 'almost the whole terrain of foreign policy in the UK [to be] carried on by the government . . . [without] the need to secure any formal [parliamentary] approval to its diplomatic agreements and executive decisions' (Blackburn, 'The House of Lords', in Blackburn and Plant (eds), *Constitutional Reform: The Labour Government's Constitutional Reform Agenda*, 1999, p 33). This included a complete absence of any formal parliamentary control over two of the most important types of decision that government may make: the signing of treaties, and the decision to dissolve Parliament early, thus triggering a general election – a power, that, by convention, was exercised by the prime minister alone, and used openly to secure maximum political advantage.

As to the former, Blackburn (*ibid*) noted in 1999 that:

---

4   This is a fundamental distinction between the two statutes, and any good essay *must* note it.

The UK now has the only Parliament in the European Union that lacks any formal mechanism for securing scrutiny and approval to treaties. The 1924 Ponsonby 'Rule' – now a Foreign Office circular – is clearly inadequate as a basis for effective scrutiny. It involves the voluntary practice of governments laying treaties signed by the UK before Parliament as Command Papers after their entry into force, and in the case of treaties requiring legal ratification a copy being placed on the Table of the House 21 days beforehand.

The Constitutional Reform and Governance Act 2010, which implemented proposals put forward in the *Governance of Britain* reform package, lays on government a statutory requirement to follow the Ponsonby procedure, with the stipulation that treaties will not be deemed ratified until this has been done (see ss 20–25).

However, numerous aspects of the scheme dilute this prima facie requirement considerably. First of all, as the Public Administration Select Committee (PAC) pointed out (10th Report of 2007–08), the proposals do not require there to be a debate or vote: 'It would be for Members to demand a vote, and for the Government, if willing, to find the opportunity for this vote to take place.' Now that the Back Bench Business Committee can schedule a limited amount of parliamentary time, at least this first obstacle could be overcome. More importantly, however, even if there is such a vote, and the government loses it, the Act provides in s 20(6) that the government may bring the treaty back before the House at a later date and seek another vote. As the PAC points out, this could presumably take place repeatedly, until one side or the other gives way.[5] Furthermore, per s 22, there is a very broad exception to the requirement to lay the treaty before Parliament: s 22(1) states simply that the laying requirement does not apply 'if a Minister of the Crown is of the opinion that, exceptionally, the treaty should be ratified' without it. The government seemed to envisage that such circumstances could include situations in which a treaty needs to be ratified during a parliamentary recess or 'In circumstances where [in the opinion of the Secretary of State] delay would be detrimental to the national interest'. 'Other cases of urgency' may occur. In such cases, under s 22(3) the government is obliged only to lay before Parliament a copy of the treaty and an explanatory memorandum after the fact. As the PAC report remarked, this allows 'the Government alone to decide whether to circumvent its obligations to Parliament'. In short, the statutory provisions, while a small advance on the previous position, represent a very weak reform, shot through with exceptions.

The prerogative of dissolution has been subject to equal criticism. By convention exercised by the prime minister alone, it has long been used quite openly simply to gain maximum political advantage for the PM's party. Moreover, Parliament has no role at all

5   This is one of the key holes in the provision, in terms of accountability; note the use of a Parliamentary Committee report to cite clear and authoritative criticism of it.

in even scrutinising this decision. As the Deputy Prime Minister said, 'it is simply not right that general elections can be called according to a Prime Minister's whims'(HC Deb col.23, July 5, 2010). While this prerogative, and the manner of its exercise, had long been criticised, successive governments had simply found it too advantageous to give up. The Fixed Terms Parliaments Act 2011 (based on similar provisions in the Scotland Act 1998) is therefore a reform of major significance. It abolishes the royal prerogative of dissolution and provides that general elections will be fixed at five-year intervals; the next election will be on May 7, 2015 (s 1(2) and (3)). The prime minister has power to delay an election by up to two months, a provision intended to allow for the delaying of an election where there is some national crisis, such as the nationwide outbreak of foot-and-mouth disease before the 2001 general election, but even this limited power is to be exercised by statutory instrument subject to the approval of both Houses (s 1(6)).

It is generally recognised that there is a need to have some way of triggering an early general election, particularly in the instance where a government loses the confidence of the House of Commons and cannot therefore effectively govern any more. By convention, a government defeated in a motion of no confidence must resign; however, in a rigidly fixed system, there would be no means of resolving what could sometimes be a political impasse by holding fresh elections. Hence the Act contains two 'triggers' for an earlier general election. First, Parliament may dissolve itself early if the Commons so votes by a two-thirds majority (s 2(2)). Second, if the government is defeated on a formal motion of no confidence and resigns, the parties have 14 days to form a new government that is able to command the confidence of the House – affirmed by a formal motion of confidence (s 2(5)). If no such motion of confidence is passed within the 14 days, Parliament is automatically dissolved (ss 2(3) and (4)). Polling day follows 17 working days after dissolution (s 3(1)). By providing in s 3(2) that Parliament cannot be dissolved other than under the provisions of the Act, the prerogative of dissolution is formally abolished.

The key advantage of the Act is that it removes from the prime minister 'the inbuilt partisan advantage of determining the date of the next general election' (M Ryan, 'The Fixed-term Parliaments Act 2011' (2011 PL 213, 215). Ryan also notes that the reform should lead to more coherent planning of policy and legislation and remove the unsatisfactory mess and rush of the 'wash-up' – the attempt to deal with all outstanding Bills in the very short time left after what may be a snap decision by a prime minister to call a general election. The only real argument *against* the reform – made by the Constitution Committee (*Fixed-term Parliaments Bill*, HL Paper 69 (2010), para. 38) – is that democratic accountability may in some circumstances call for an early general election and that the Act may frustrate this. However, at present, a deeply unpopular government can cling to power for several years, simply because its MPs will vote down any motion of confidence for fear of losing their seats at the subsequent general election. It is submitted that the advantages of the Act clearly outweigh its disadvantages and that the two 'triggers' are both sensible and allow for early elections when really needed, to cater for events such as a grave national crisis, such as war or other emergency, or where a government falls and the parliamentary arithmetic precludes the formation of an alternative. In light of these provisions, it is submitted that the 'undemocratic' critique is wholly unconvincing; parliamentary opposition to the Bill in reality rested almost entirely on small 'c' conservatism. [6]

In conclusion, both Acts advance parliamentary control over executive power; but whereas the 2010 Act did so in a meagre and stingy way, the 2011 Act did so boldly and in a manner that was both sensible and principled. It is to be hoped that future reform of the prerogative will use the latter, not the former, as a model.

Aim Higher ★

There is a simple way in which students aiming higher can achieve better marks in problems involving new statutes: proper citation of particular statutory provisions. This sounds like an obvious point, but examiners encounter it repeatedly, particularly amongst first years. Many law students seem to be allergic to the idea of actually reading and working out statutes for themselves (something they will certainly have to do in practice!) and this seems to feed through into a reluctance to cite particular provisions in essays and exams. In most cases a broad-brush approach is preferred, which, while it may put across the broad thrust of the provisions, fails to gain the higher marks that may be obtained by specific citation of authority.

QUESTION 23

'The royal prerogative amounts to a substantially uncontrolled power in the hands of the Executive, particularly in relation to the crucial power to take military action: urgent reform is needed.'

▶ In light of the above, discuss the options for reform in this area.

How to Answer this Question

This is a demanding but topical question. Students need to have a good knowledge of the reforms proposed by the Brown Government in its paper *The Governance of Britain*, Cm 7342-I and of the various reports of parliamentary committees in the last Parliament and this one.

---

6   Note how both sides of the argument are considered, but both arguments are *evaluated* and a clear conclusion reached.

Answer Structure

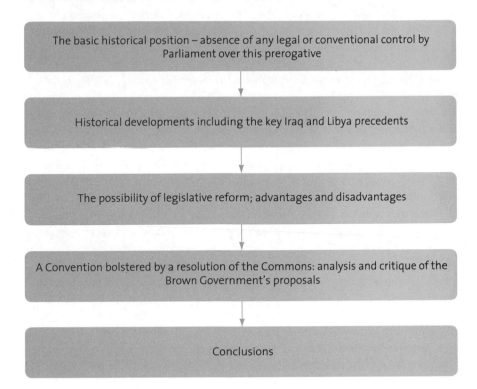

The basic historical position – absence of any legal or conventional control by Parliament over this prerogative

Historical developments including the key Iraq and Libya precedents

The possibility of legislative reform; advantages and disadvantages

A Convention bolstered by a resolution of the Commons: analysis and critique of the Brown Government's proposals

Conclusions

ANSWER

The term 'prerogative' refers to the very significant residual powers that the sovereign has, as opposed to those granted by statute. The vast majority of such powers are, in practice, exercised by the prime minister, the Cabinet or individual ministers. The concern lying at the heart of the statement in this question is that, by means of this historical relic, the UK Constitution allows powers of great breadth, magnitude and importance to be wielded by the Executive alone, with no effective oversight, let alone control, by Parliament. Plainly one of the most important of the prerogatives is the power to use armed force, exercised by ministers, on behalf of the Crown. Unlike some other countries, which have War Powers Acts, the UK Parliament has no formal role in the decision to use armed force. This lack of any necessity to seek approval from, or even consult with Parliament before committing the country's armed forces to conflict abroad, whether in a formal state of war or not, is perhaps the other most remarkable feature of the use of the prerogative. As Brazier comments (R Brazier, *Constitutional Reform*, 2nd edn, 1999, p 123):

How odd – perhaps bizarre – it is that the approval of both Houses of Parliament is required for pieces of technical, and often trivial, subordinate legislation, whereas it is not needed at all before men and women can be committed to the possibility of disfigurement or death.[7]

Despite the absence of any *legal* requirement to consult Parliament, has there been a practice of doing so, or a convention that this should occur? Surprisingly, again, the historical answer is no, although recent developments indicate a possible change. Brazier notes that in the cases of the Suez crisis, the Falklands Conflict, and the Gulf War of 1991, no attempt was made to seek formal parliamentary approval before committing forces to war. To these can be added the deployment and use of the RAF in Bosnia in the 1990s by the Major Government, and the prolonged campaign of air strikes against the targets in Kosovo and Serbia authorised by the Blair Government, neither of which were the subject of formal parliamentary approval. It was in fact not until the Iraq war in 2003 that the Government decided that a formal vote should be held in Parliament before committing troops to battle, and this was done more as a matter of political necessity than out of a sense of constitutional *obligation*. Nevertheless, this dramatic parliamentary debate, which saw the resignation of Robin Cook from the Government, and a massive Labour rebellion, rapidly came to be seen as a possible model for the future.

The British armed forces have been deployed in Afghanistan now for over a decade, and no vote was held before military operations commenced in October 2001 as a response to the 9/11 attacks on the USA. The newly formed Backbench Business Committee timetable a debate and a vote on a substantive motion on the presence of British forces in Afghanistan, but not for until 9 September 2010. The debate was on the substantive motion 'That this House supports the continued deployment of UK Armed Forces in Afghanistan' and was agreed on division by 310 to 14. Since this took place so long after troops were initially deployed, it cannot be seen as setting any meaningful precedent for consulting Parliament *before* or even *shortly after* military action is taken.

It was however, the Libya conflict in 2011 that saw the most significant progress toward the establishment of at least a basic convention of consultation.[8] While the option of imposing a 'no fly zone' in Libya via NATO air assets was under active consideration, Sir George Young for the Government stated in the House of Commons on 10 March 2011:

A convention has developed in the House that before troops are committed, the House should have an opportunity to debate the matter. We propose to observe that convention except when there is an emergency and such action would not be

....

7   A good example of the use of a striking quotation by a senior academic to reinforce an important point.
8   The following paragraph is a good example of the use of recent history – something that may be too recent to be covered in a textbook – to evidence an important constitutional development.

appropriate. As with the Iraq war and other events, we propose to give the House the opportunity to debate the matter before troops are committed.

The promised debate duly took place on 21 March 2011. The motion, a substantive one, approving the use of UK armed forces to enforce UN Security Council Resolution 1973, by protecting civilians and enforce the No Fly Zone, was approved by a vote of 557 to 13. Notably also, the Government's belief in the existence of such a convention was confirmed by the Cabinet Secretary, Sir Gus O' Donnell, who wrote to the Commons Political and Constitutional Reform Committee in March 2011, stating:

> the Government believes that it is apparent that since the events leading up to the deployment of troops in Iraq, a convention exists that Parliament will be given the opportunity to debate the decision to commit troops to armed conflict and, except in emergency situations, that debate would take place before they are committed. (House of Commons Political and Constitutional Reform Committee, *Parliament's Role in Conflict decisions* (8th Report of 2010–12) (para 3).

Somewhat surprisingly, during the Libya debate, the Foreign Secretary also said: 'We will *enshrine in law* for the future the necessity of consulting Parliament on military action' (HC Deb, 21 March 2011, col. 799, emphasis added). However, since then, exchanges between the Commons Political and Constitutional Reform Committee and the Government in 2011 made clear that there is no immediate prospect of bringing forward any legislation, while the Government, in two responses to the Committee, remained reluctant to commit to any timetable for drafting and introducing a resolution for debate and adoption by the Commons. The Committee's original report found that its academic witnesses did not agree that there was a clear convention in existence. Noting this, the Committee stated:

> There is an urgent need for greater clarity on Parliament's role in decisions to commit British forces to armed conflict abroad. We therefore recommend that the Government should as a first step bring forward a draft detailed parliamentary resolution, for consultation with us among others, and for debate and decision by the end of 2011 (8th Report of 2010–12, para 6).

However, in its responses to the Committee, the Government refused to set what it said would be an 'artificial' timetable for adopting a resolution. It did, however, agree with the Committee's suggestion that the newly published Cabinet Manual should reference the convention. The relevant paragraph now reads:

> In 2011, the Government acknowledged that a convention had developed in Parliament that before troops were committed the House of Commons should have an opportunity to debate the matter and said that it proposed to observe that convention except when there was an emergency and such action would not be appropriate (Cabinet Office, 2011, 1st edn, para 5.38).

There are three basic options for reform. First, and most radically, the prerogative could be abolished and replaced by legislation, a War Powers Act, setting out the lawful powers of the government to use armed force, and the procedures to be followed whereby Parliament may authorise it in specific cases. Second, the prerogative could be retained, but supplemented by a legal obligation to *consult* Parliament on the use of force. (The Foreign Secretary's surprising pledge would appear to refer to the second of these options.) Third, the current doubtful convention could be placed on a firm basis and concretised by means of a House of Commons resolution, setting out in a definitive and authoritative text the terms of the relevant convention. These options will be taken in turn.

A War Powers Act could include a requirement that a vote be held in Parliament prior to the commencement of hostilities, unless necessity precluded it, in which case such a vote would have to be held within a fixed period, for example, seven days. There have been a number of attempts to achieve such reform by Private Member's Bill, most recently in one put forward by Lord Lester. However, the Select Committee on the Constitution (15th Report of 2005–06) took a different stance, arguing that the fear of exposing members of the armed forces to prosecution for taking part in what could be found to be an illegal war and the possibility of judicial review, once the power to use force was placed on a statutory footing, both pointed strongly away from a statutory solution. The Committee argued instead for a parliamentary convention whereby governments would be required to seek parliamentary approval before committing forces to actual or potential armed conflict. However, the concerns of the Constitution Committee were, it is suggested, overstated. First of all, there is already the possibility of legal consequences for waging unlawful war under the jurisdiction of the International Criminal Court. Second, if in future the UK Government were only to use armed force when it was certain that it could justify such action as lawful, many would see this, following the Iraq war, as a positive rather than a negative result. It is suggested, therefore, that a strong case can be made for legislative reform in this area.[9]

At present, therefore, it appears that only option 3 – a convention to be concretised by way of a parliamentary resolution – is currently a realistic proposition. This is in itself disappointing, but the details of the way forward, as proposed by the Brown Government in *The Governance of Britain* (2008, Cm 7342-I), appeared to be designed to allow for maximum governmental control over the process. The proposal was for the approval of the House of Commons to be sought by way of debate and vote before committing the armed forces to conflict. However, there were numerous important caveats. First of all, as is generally agreed to be necessary, the government could decide to waive the requirement in cases of urgency or where surprise military action was required. This is only sensible; however, there was no requirement for retrospective approval of a decision to use armed force in such cases: the government would simply inform the House without, seemingly, permitting either debate or vote. Second, it would be entirely for the prime minister to decide (a) *when* in the process of the build-up to conflict to seek approval from Parliament and (b) what *information* to give Parliament on the background to the situation and the government's reasons for wishing to use armed force. In relation to the former, it is, of course, far harder, politically, for Parliament to vote against such a proposal when troops have already been deployed in a neighbouring country and war is imminent, as in the case of Iraq. Such a vote would be likely to force the prime minister to resign, as Tony Blair was prepared to do had he lost the vote on the Iraq war, something that is likely to deter a negative vote by MPs from the governing party.

As to the latter, given the controversy over the completeness and accuracy of the information given to Parliament in the run-up to the Iraq war, retaining this matter entirely within the prime minister's discretion is hardly reassuring. In particular, the Government proposed that the Attorney General's advice on the legality of the proposed use of force would *not* be revealed – despite the huge controversy over this point in relation to the Iraq war and calls for such advice to be revealed in full on future occasions. Moreover, it was proposed that the prime minister could decide not to provide *any* information, if to do so would, in his or her opinion, 'prejudice ... the United Kingdom's international relations'. In short, the prime minister, in deciding how to present the case for war to Parliament, would be left entirely as judge in his own case, as the Public Administration Select Committee pointed out (10th Report of 2007–08) remarks: there was to be no independent element at all in the process. Hence the proposed reform, while welcome in principle, is of the most timid and executive-friendly nature.

It remains to be seen whether the Cameron Government will bring forward more radical proposals, or whether the House of Commons will itself seize the initiative and bring forward its own resolution. Now that the Back Bench Business Committee could schedule time for a debate and vote, there is no need for the Commons simply to await action from the government: it can bring forward its own resolution and hold its own debate on it.

The Executive

INTRODUCTION

The Executive includes the government, the monarchy, the Civil Service, local government, the armed forces and the police. The areas examined within this topic tend to vary, and students should be guided in their revision by their own courses. For example, some courses include material on local government and central–local government relationships; others look at the issue of regulation and quangos in some detail. The royal prerogative is a major part of any study of the Executive; it is considered in the previous chapter. This chapter will concentrate on the operation of central government, which includes a consideration of the role of the Cabinet and the relationship between ministers, their departments and civil servants. In relation to the latter, the placing of the Civil Service on a statutory basis for the first time in the Constitutional Reform and Governance Act 2010, Part I is a reform of some significance. Questions in this area tend to concern the relationship between the prime minister and the Cabinet and the extent to which individual ministers and government in general are responsible to Parliament. The latter topic took on greater importance following the Scott Report and the continuing concern about ministerial responsibility and accountability thrown up by the information given to Parliament about Iraq, currently still under investigation by the Chilcot Inquiry. Questions on the difficulties and confusions thrown up by the new approach to responsibility and, in particular, the issues raised by the Next Steps agencies are very likely to be set. Clearly, government and Parliament are closely interlocked: government is part of the Executive but also dominates the legislative body – Parliament – and therefore there is some overlap between this area and Chapter 3 on the House of Commons. Chapter 3 is, however, concerned with the efficacy of scrutinising procedures in the House of Commons whereas, although such matters are touched on in this chapter, its emphasis is on the principle of ministerial responsibility.

Checklist ✔

Students should be familiar with the following areas:

- conventions relating to Cabinet government – collective Cabinet decision-making; the concept of collective government responsibility to Parliament and the effect on the latter of the current Coalition Government;

- the placing of the Civil Service on a statutory basis by the **Constitutional Reform and Governance Act 2010, Part I**;

- the basic concept of individual ministerial responsibility to Parliament; the distinction between 'accountability' and 'responsibility'; the difficulties with the distinction;

- the differing types of accountability of civil servants, chief executives of Next Steps agencies and ministers;

- the obligation on ministers to accept blame/resign for mistakes of 'policy';

- ministerial resignation in practice including recent examples;

- the extent of the obligation to account to Parliament; the Ministerial Code; the limitations on the types of question that must be answered as set out in the **Freedom of Information Act 2000**;

- the findings of the Scott Report; the giving of incomplete information; the concept of 'knowingly' misleading Parliament; the absence of resignations over information given to Parliament over weapons of mass destruction (WMD) and Iraq; official inquiries by Butler, Hutton and Chilcot (ongoing at the time of writing);

- the **Freedom of Information Act 2000**, particularly the exemption in **s 35** covering information relating to the development of government policy.

Note that references to Woodhouse are to D Woodhouse, 'Ministerial responsibility: something old, something new' [1997] PL 262; references to 'the Scott Report' are to Sir Richard Scott, *Inquiry into Exports of Defence Equipment and Dual-Use Goods to Iraq and Related Prosecutions* (HC 115–1, 1995–96); and references to the Public Service Committee are to its second Report (HC 231, 1995–96), unless otherwise stated. The 2007 London School of Economics Study may be found online at http://www2.lse.ac.uk/newsAndMedia/news/archives/2007/MinisterialResignations.aspx. References to the Butler Report are to *Review of Intelligence on Weapons of Mass Destruction* HC 898 (2003–04); to Chilcot are to the Inquiry established in 2009 and ongoing: http://www.iraqinquiry.org.uk.

QUESTION 24

'The conventions of collective Cabinet decision-making and collective ministerial responsibility are more honoured in the breach than in the observance; the result has been a movement towards prime ministerial government.'

▶ Discuss.

How to Answer this Question

A question concerning the conventions and the reality of Cabinet government is commonly set and is reasonably straightforward. It is, however, a very wide-ranging question and it will not be possible to cover one area in depth if a proper essay structure is to be maintained.

Answer Structure

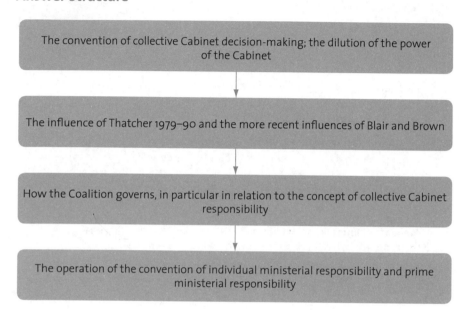

The convention of collective Cabinet decision-making; the dilution of the power of the Cabinet

The influence of Thatcher 1979–90 and the more recent influences of Blair and Brown

How the Coalition governs, in particular in relation to the concept of collective Cabinet responsibility

The operation of the convention of individual ministerial responsibility and prime ministerial responsibility

ANSWER

Bagehot, writing in 1867, called the Cabinet 'the most powerful body in the nation' (*The English Constitution*, 1963) and considered that collective responsibility meant that every member of the Cabinet had the right to take part in Cabinet discussion but was bound by the decision eventually reached. In contrast, in 1977, John Mackintosh (*The British Cabinet*, 1977) wrote: '. . . the principal policies of a government may not be and often are not originated in Cabinet.' Michael Heseltine, in the aftermath of the Westland affair in 1986, said that there had been a 'breakdown of constitutional government', in that the prime minister had frustrated collective consideration of the Westland issue and many saw Blair's administration as exemplifying a system of presidential, rather than Cabinet, or collegial government.

These suggestions that conventions governing Cabinet government are in decline bear out the statement to be considered. The convention of collective decision-making clearly underpins collective responsibility: the obligation placed upon ministers by the convention of collective responsibility is most readily justified if government decisions are reached collectively. Thus, it will first be considered whether there has indeed been a diminution in the importance of collective decision-making.[1]

The Cabinet is composed of around 22 ministers who agree to pursue a common policy; some ministers will be outside the Cabinet and it may include some whose offices involve few or no departmental responsibilities. The function of the Cabinet is, in theory, to determine finally the policy to be submitted to Parliament and to coordinate and control administrative action. However, a number of writers, including Richard Crossman, have considered that Cabinet government is developing into prime ministerial government and that therefore collective decision-making has suffered. Crossman wrote that the power of the prime minister to sack ministers, to determine the Cabinet agenda and the existence and membership of Cabinet committees meant that his control over the Cabinet was the most important force within it. Under Mrs Thatcher, who was prime minister between 1979 and 1990, the importance of this force became more apparent, not because she increased the power of the prime minister, but because she used the available power to the full. In particular, she displaced important decision-making to small informal groups of ministers convened by herself, and exercised the prime minister's exclusive right to appoint and reshuffle ministers in order to reshape the Cabinet in accordance with her own ideological outlook. For example, she managed, during the first two years of her administration, to move no less than five out of the seven 'moderates' or 'wets' out of the Cabinet.

It is now apparent that, in general, Mr Blair made little use of full Cabinet; key decisions were taken by Cabinet committees or small groups of ministers. For example, the crucial decision in May 1997 to give the Bank of England independence and the power to set interest rates was apparently taken by the Prime Minister and the Chancellor of the Exchequer alone, in consultation with their special advisers. Other members of the Cabinet were not even consulted. Many commentators saw a marked centralisation of power under Mr Blair, with himself and Gordon Brown, then Chancellor, exerting great influence over the decisions and priorities of other departments. Richard Butler, the former Cabinet Secretary, who conducted a review on the intelligence used to justify the decision to launch the invasion of Iraq, was highly critical of the Blair Government's style of decision-making. Butler commented that 'the government reaches conclusions in rather small groups of people who are not necessarily representative of all the groups of interests in government' and that 'the Cabinet now . . . does not make decisions' (*Guardian*, 10 December 2004).[2]

---

1   Note how the argument here is built up of logical steps, which are explained in advance.
2   It is important, when making assertions about a general style of government under a particular administration, to give examples that are as authoritative as possible.

However, in diluting and fragmenting the power of the Cabinet in this fashion, it might be argued that Thatcher and Blair were merely taking further a process that had already begun. The use of gatherings other than Cabinet to make decisions – inner Cabinets, Cabinet committees, ministerial meetings – had been growing for the last 30 years, and had arguably undermined the Cabinet as a decision-making body. The general view of constitutional writers seems to be (see Peter Hennessey, *Cabinet*, 1986) that although Mrs Thatcher flouted the spirit of Cabinet government, she did not destroy it. However, the Blair style of governing seemed to take the process of marginalising Cabinet even further than did Thatcher. It seemed clear that Mr Blair sought to increase central control over the actions of government departments. It seems plausible to suggest that Gordon Brown's administration may have seen a return to a more collegiate style of decision-making; however, even if this did occur, it was perhaps more a symptom simply of Brown's relative political weakness, rather than a principled change in direction.

It is too early to assess significance of the current Coalition Government for these matters. Simply because it is a coalition, however, it is clear that prime ministerial power is somewhat reduced. Most importantly, the Prime Minister did not appoint the Liberal Democrat members of the Cabinet – these appointments were made by the Deputy Prime Minister, Nick Clegg; by the same token it would politically difficult if not impossible for the PM to sack such members without the agreement of the Deputy PM. From these factors, Vernon Bogdanor concludes that the Coalition entailed 'a very significant reduction in the power of the Prime Minister' (*The Coalition and the Constitution* (2011) at p 49). Moreover, the fact that decisions made by the Government have to be broadly agreed by both Liberal Democrat and Conservative ministers seems to favour a more formal style of decision-making, through Cabinet Committees and full Cabinet (Bogdanor, at p 51).

If the Cabinet as an institution has in general terms suffered a decline along with the doctrine of *primus inter pares*, it might appear that the basis of the doctrine of collective ministerial responsibility will also have been undermined. It could also be argued that it has been undermined by the failure of accountability of the Cabinet to Parliament. Theoretically, a check is kept on the Executive through the operation of the convention of collective ministerial responsibility to Parliament. The convention means that ministers are collectively responsible to Parliament for their actions in governing the country, and therefore should be in accord on any major question. As all ministers are accountable to Parliament for government policy, no minister can disclaim his responsibility on the basis of disagreement with it (exceptions come where the government comes to a formal 'agreement to differ', as the current Government did over the referendum on changing the voting system for general elections to the Alternative Vote). Ministers should resign if in disagreement with the policy of the Cabinet on any major question. Examples of such resignations include Sir Anthony Eden's in 1938 over Chamberlain's policy towards Mussolini and, arguably, Michael Heseltine's in 1986 due to disagreement with government policy in respect of Westland plc and the requirement to submit statements on the subject to the Cabinet Office for prior clearance. Robin Cook's resignation, on the eve of the Iraq war in 2003, on the grounds that he could not agree with the decision to take military action, is a particularly clear and principled example; Clare Short's was also a resignation on these grounds, although with much less impact due its bungled timing.

Gordon Brown's Government lost a great many ministers, and at times there appeared to be an intent by ministers to use their resignations to signal not just their disagreement with particular policies, but with the whole direction of government, and in particular the premiership of Gordon Brown. The clearest example of this is the resignation of James Purnell as Work and Pensions Secretary in June 2009; Purnell left the Cabinet and called on Brown to step aside in the interests of the Government and the Labour party. But if there was a concerted 'plot' it was botched, and Brown managed to survive the departure of five cabinet ministers in a week. Hazel Blears resigned as Communities Secretary shortly before Purnell, in a move that seemed clearly designed to destabilise the Government; however, she was by then deeply unpopular as a result of her part in the MPs' expenses scandal; moreover, it seemed that she may merely have resigned to avoid the humiliation of being sacked or demoted. In the same week, John Hutton resigned as Defence Secretary, but claimed it was for family reasons, lessening the impact of his departure, while Geoff Hoon resigned as Transport Secretary, again, seemingly due to criticisms of his expenses claims. Jacqui Smith's resignation of the post of Home Secretary was seemingly also due to the expenses scandal.

It follows from the broad convention of responsible government that a government should resign after being defeated on a vote of no confidence in the House. On the face of it, unless Parliament can express its disapproval of government decisions and policy in this way, it might seem that it can have little impact on government action. However, only two governments, both in a minority in the Commons, have lost the confidence of the House since 1924. In 1924, Ramsay MacDonald's first Labour Government was deserted by its Liberal allies, while in 1976, the Labour Government lost its small majority, partly through by-election defeats, and was defeated on a Conservative vote of no confidence in 1979. Apart from these examples, governments that lose in the House on particular issues have managed to muster their majorities and procure a reversal of the vote. For example, in July 1992, the Major Government suffered a defeat due to a backbench rebellion in a vote relating to the Maastricht Treaty. However, the prime minister put down a motion of confidence the following day, and secured a majority. Similarly, Gordon Brown recently managed partially to reverse Tony Blair's Commons defeat in November 2005 on extending the period of pre-charge detention for terrorism suspects. While Blair was defeated on plans to increase the period to 90 days, Brown managed in June 2008 to persuade MPs to vote for an increase to 42 days, albeit only after extensive pressure was applied by the whips and he suffered a major backbench rebellion.[3]

---

3   Note the importance in essays of this sort of specific examples from recent political history.

It may be concluded that the current arrangements at the centre of government can, at their worst, merely provide a cloak for prime ministerial power, or the power of the PM and Chancellor together (as under Blair). The prime minister can present policies as though they were the product of Cabinet discussion, and can expect ministers who have not participated in such discussion to defend them. If such policies miscarry, ministers may be able to disclaim responsibility, perhaps on the basis that officials have erred, but eventually, if the only alternative is a demand for the resignation of the prime minister, an individual minister may be prepared to resign and the prime minister may be able to distance himself from what has occurred. While the position is different under the current Government, this appears to be the direct result of the fact that it is a coalition; the next time a strong party leader is elected with a large majority, we may expect to see the trends noted under Blair and Thatcher revive.

QUESTION 25

'The doctrine of individual ministerial responsibility as currently understood fails to provide a clear and satisfactory framework for the division of responsibility and accountability as between ministers, civil servants and, in particular, the chief executives of Next Steps Agencies; consequently, it allows ministers to evade and displace responsibility for departmental failings and thus fails to provide a firm basis for accountable government.'

▶ Discuss.

How to Answer this Question

This is a focused question that requires more detailed knowledge of the subject area, in particular, the problems thrown up by the creation of the Next Steps agencies. The subject of the question is not the extent of the obligation to give an account (for example, areas excluded from questioning), but rather the issue of responsibility for departmental errors and the allocation of accountability between ministers and officials. Recent examples should be used where possible to illustrate the student's ability to apply the general principles discussed to contemporary political activity.

Answer Structure

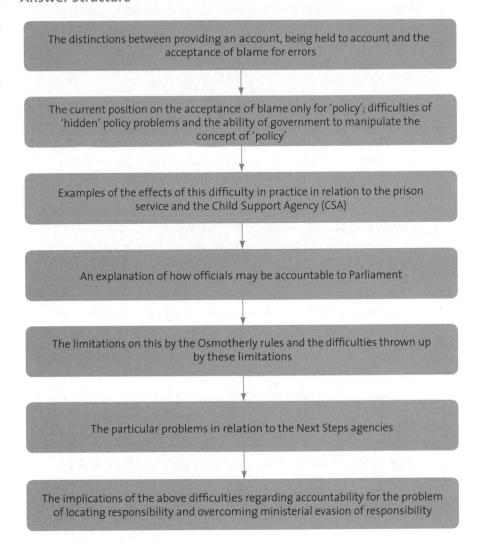

The distinctions between providing an account, being held to account and the acceptance of blame for errors

The current position on the acceptance of blame only for 'policy'; difficulties of 'hidden' policy problems and the ability of government to manipulate the concept of 'policy'

Examples of the effects of this difficulty in practice in relation to the prison service and the Child Support Agency (CSA)

An explanation of how officials may be accountable to Parliament

The limitations on this by the Osmotherly rules and the difficulties thrown up by these limitations

The particular problems in relation to the Next Steps agencies

The implications of the above difficulties regarding accountability for the problem of locating responsibility and overcoming ministerial evasion of responsibility

ANSWER

The doctrine of individual ministerial responsibility has recently been the subject of much controversy: the doctrine itself and its efficacy were subject to a rigorous analysis in the Scott Report and the analysis continued, in the light of Scott's findings, by the Public Service Committee's inquiry into ministerial responsibility and accountability. The at least partial misleading of Parliament that took place in relation to the intelligence on Iraq and weapons of mass destruction (WMD) has kept the controversy alive, as ministers and others are questioned by the ongoing Chilcot Inquiry. The question suggests that the above review has not resulted in satisfactory solutions to the problems of dividing responsibility and accountability between ministers and officials. In what follows, the particular criticisms contained in the question will be addressed and an assessment made as to whether the charges of ministerial evasion and lack of proper accountability are made out.

It should be asked, first of all, what the notion of responsibility entails. Broadly speaking, two notions are involved: first, that for every area of government policy, there should be a minister who is prepared to explain and justify government policy either personally or via his officials; second, that in the case of failings within the department, someone will be prepared to take responsibility for that failure. The doctrine therefore requires both that there be some obligation on ministers to *give an account* of their actions and policies to Parliament, and that if fault is revealed, there must be some means for Parliament to exact some kind of redress. This can broadly be of two types: punitive, in the sense that the minister is 'punished' by being forced to resign; and rectificatory, or amendatory, whereby a minister must promise and execute action to correct the problems and then report back to Parliament on the success of that action, a response that may be more important in practice than whether any resignations are produced.[4] Formally, Parliament does possess the power effectively to get rid of ministers by passing motions of no confidence or censure; it may also pass motions calling for changes in existing policy. In practice, as we shall see, this penal power is virtually never used, although the threat of its use can be important.

This basic distinction between the provision of an account and the reaction to it seems clear enough. However, the terminology that has been suggested and which appears to have been accepted by governments of both political persuasions is somewhat different, although it deploys the same basic concept. Here, a distinction is drawn between the duty to provide an account ('accountability') and the obligation to accept personal responsibility when things go wrong ('responsibility'). In this version, the duty to provide an account extends to answering criticisms, to defending the record of the department in question, even to what was termed above 'rectificatory' redress, namely, promising investigation and remedial action if necessary. So, 'accountability' goes far beyond the mere transmission of information: it means not only 'giving an account', but also 'being held to account', with the proviso that this does not include the acceptance of personal fault by the minister. Acceptance of such fault means acceptance of 'responsibility' and resignation may become an issue.[5] The distinction may be illustrated by the example of a

---

4   Note here the careful distinction first drawn between two different kinds of accountability – explanatory and amendatory. The whole issue of ministerial responsibility rests upon such distinctions and essays on this topic *must* make them clearly – before going on to interrogate them.

5   This is the second key distinction – a considerably more controversial one, as the essay-writer must make clear!

complaint about the poor quality of food in Brixton Prison. The Home Secretary may be asked questions about this, may have to put in hand an investigation as to what has gone wrong and report back to Parliament on remedial action and whether this has worked. However, no one would realistically expect that the minister should be seen as personally at fault for this problem. As Jack Straw said when he became Home Secretary in 1997, he could not be blamed every time a prison officer accidentally left a cell door open.

Therefore, the first issue to be addressed is whether this distinction between 'responsibility' and 'accountability' works satisfactorily, or whether it provides a means for ministers to avoid accepting responsibility when they should. There are two possible problems with the responsibility/accountability distinction: first, it has been suggested that the distinction between policy on the one hand and its implementation on the other is not a coherent one, and that drawing a sharp distinction simply obscures ministerial responsibility for the overall record of the department. This is because, as Professor Hennessey pointed out in evidence before the Public Service Committee: 'There is not actually a proper division between [policy and operations] . . . These are seamless garments. If, operationally, you hit real trouble, it is usually because the policy is flawed.' In other words, the day-to-day problems that occur in a department may in actuality be attributable to overall – but hidden – policy problems, such as insufficient funding. So, policy mistakes may be *inferred* from widespread operational difficulties. Government has, however, tended to take the opposite line, relying on a 'bright line' distinction between the two that serves in practice to exonerate ministers from blame after departmental failings have come to light. In fact, save for the resignation of Lord Carrington following the invasion of the Falkland Islands, it is virtually impossible to find any example of ministers admitting that responsibility for major departmental errors or failings lies with them. For example, when the highly critical Learmont Report on the state of Britain's prisons came out, Michael Howard found that all of the problems identified were due not to his policies, but to the way they had been put into practice by the head of the prison service, Derek Lewis, who he promptly sacked. Similarly, Robin Cook, in relation to the Sandline affair in 1998, and Straw, in relation to the passports crisis of 1999, both stated that essentially operational decisions were to blame for the problems that arose in their departments, assertions that to be fair to them have been largely accepted by independent commentators (see, for example, Woodhouse [2002] PL 73). Cook did recognise systemic and cultural problems with the Foreign Office, but given that he had been Foreign Secretary for less than a year, could not reasonably be expected to take personal responsibility for these. A 2007 study by academics at the LSE found no clear instances of resignations from the Blair Government on issues of departmental policy, although 14 calls for such resignations were made. While the current Government has seen the resignations of David Laws, Liam Fox and Chris Huhne, all these relate to issues of their own personal conduct (in Fox's case, his professional relationship with a friend, Adam Werrity) and none to departmental policy.

The second related problem is that not only may operational problems really be attributable to hidden policy mistakes, but the notion of 'policy' itself is vague and subject to manipulation by government. Ministers in the Conservative administrations of the 1980s and 1990s showed a tendency to narrow down the areas definable as 'policy', thus making the minister responsible – in the sense of having to take the blame – for an ever-shrinking area. Thus, as Woodhouse points out ('Ministerial responsibility', pp 268–269), after the Brixton Prison escapes in 1991, the Home Secretary, when called upon to resign, announced that 'policy' was confined to matters of overall strategy or high government policy, whilst departmental policies, which gave effect to the political preferences, were absorbed into 'administration'; a viewpoint also relied upon by Michael Howard following the Learmont Report in 1995, and described by him as having been accepted for 'years, even generations'.

The focus thus far has been on how well the division between responsibility and accountability works; the above analysis would appear to suggest that not only is the distinction unclear and unsatisfactory, but that the charge in the question that it allows ministerial evasion of responsibilities appears to have some substance. We will now examine the operation of accountability, whether it enables Parliament to gain the information it needs or whether it contributes to the problems outlined above.

As a matter of common sense, clearly, a minister will not be able to give an account of everything going on within a large and complex government department in which hundreds of decisions may be taken every day. In practice, the minister will often either have to find out what has happened and report back to Parliament, or Parliament will have to question civil servants about the matter directly. The ability of select committees to subject civil servants and the heads of Next Steps agencies ('agencies') to sustained questioning, in order to obtain first-hand information on the workings of the departments under their remit, is generally seen as being one of their main strengths. Additionally, it may be noted that heads of agencies – with the exception of the head of the Prison Service – also give written answers to parliamentary questions on operational matters, which appear in Hansard. Thus the system does allow first-hand questioning of officials, an important ingredient in effective information-gathering and hence in ensuring accountability.

However, there are two major restrictions on this ability to engage in first-hand questioning. First, ministers continue to assert the right – contested by select committees – to choose which particular civil servants appear in front of the committees, although in practice they have usually acceded to committee requests in this respect, save in relation to special advisers. Perhaps more importantly, the basic principle of the Osmotherly rules is that both heads of agencies and civil servants answer questions 'on behalf of ministers' (para 40); that is, they remain under ministerial instructions as to how to answer questions at all times. The Blair Government gave this doctrine its full backing.

In practical terms, this restriction means that while an official may give his own account of factual matters, when it comes to providing explanations and justifications of departmental policy, he will provide only the government's view, without criticising it in any way, or suggesting alternatives – a restriction said to be justified by the need to retain Civil Service neutrality. Thus, in giving factual information, civil servants will have to avoid any suggestion that government policy may be flawed in any way. They will therefore give only a limited account. The application of this rule to the chief executives of agencies is seen as particularly problematic, because it does not match the fact that the executives have full responsibility for operational matters delegated to them under their framework documents with an ability to give to Parliament a full account of the areas *within* that responsibility. The ability of the chief executives to manage their agencies properly will, of course, be heavily dependent upon policy decisions on which they are forbidden to comment. This is unsatisfactory both for the chief executive and for Parliament. In effect, by instructing civil servants to take a particular line with a committee, a minister can, to an extent, control the flow of information about the very incident in relation to which he or she stands accused of possible fault.[6]

In conclusion, it may be argued that the present understanding of ministerial responsibility relies upon a series of distinctions that are open to manipulation and abuse by government, and that Parliament appears to be currently deprived of the ability to challenge such manipulation and make its own determination as to where responsibility should be located from a position of comprehensive knowledge, due to the restrictions represented by the Osmotherly rules. It may be further contended that the dogmatic application of these rules to chief executives and the continued accountability of ministers for the workings of the Next Steps agencies seems illogical and likely to undermine the demarcation of duties between ministers and officials, which the agencies are supposed to follow and uphold.

Common Pitfalls

There are two common pitfalls seen in exam answers in this area. First, the answers are simply lacking in detail, particularly in relation to contemporary examples of ministerial responsibility, such as, for example, resignations under the Cameron Government. Second, and notoriously, students tend to focus, often to the exclusion of all else, on ministerial *resignation* as the only aspect of ministerial responsibility they discuss. (To be fair, in this respect, students are merely reflecting the media approach to these matters.) The much more subtle and important issues of explanatory and rectificatory accountability often go almost entirely undiscussed, resulting in poor grades, in the 40s at best.

6   The issue of the application of the ministerial responsibility doctrine to civil servants is a core one, and yet seldom is it properly discussed in student essays, still less in a way that *clearly explains* what problems it throws up in terms of accountability to Parliament.

QUESTION 26 ---

'The obligation on ministers to give a full and frank account to Parliament of the actions of their departments is limited, uncertain and unsatisfactory in scope and does not in practice prevent Parliament from being misled or, at the least, under-informed.'

▶ Discuss.

How to Answer this Question

This is a fairly straightforward question on the scope of the duty to give an account to Parliament and one that is likely to be popular with examiners, given the findings of the Scott Report and the continued academic and parliamentary interest in accountability. Students should make sure that their answer includes practical examples – the findings of Scott provide the best source – of apparently unsatisfactory answers to parliamentary questions or letters. Answers should also briefly indicate the impact of the Freedom of Information Act 2000 in this area.

Answer Structure

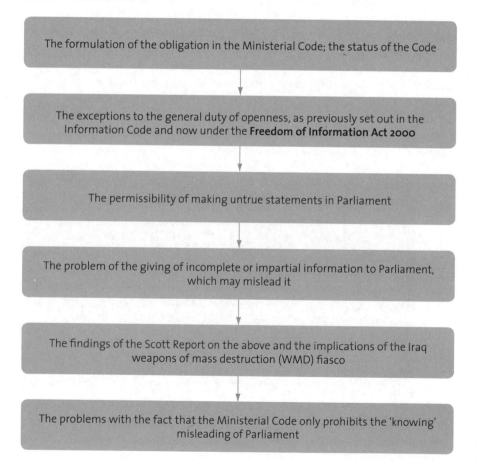

The formulation of the obligation in the Ministerial Code; the status of the Code

The exceptions to the general duty of openness, as previously set out in the Information Code and now under the **Freedom of Information Act 2000**

The permissibility of making untrue statements in Parliament

The problem of the giving of incomplete or impartial information to Parliament, which may mislead it

The findings of the Scott Report on the above and the implications of the Iraq weapons of mass destruction (WMD) fiasco

The problems with the fact that the Ministerial Code only prohibits the 'knowing' misleading of Parliament

ANSWER

While Parliament finally passed a Freedom of Information Act (FOI) in 2000, it only came into force quite recently, and its impact upon ministerial accountability to Parliament remains unclear at present. The obligation of ministers to account to Parliament for the actions and decisions of their departments is a core principle of the British constitution and remains one of the most important guarantees of a reasonable degree of accountability and transparency in government. The obligation has received unprecedented attention in the last 20 years; Lord Justice Scott made a series of findings on how far ministers had satisfactorily discharged their duty of 'explanatory accountability' (to use Marshall's phrase) in the particular context of the 'arms to Iraq affair', although he also made some more general findings. The Public Service Committee undertook a comprehensive review of this area in 1995–97; one of the last actions of the Parliament of 1992–97 was to pass a resolution on ministerial accountability (on 20 March 1997), which became the basis of the governmental view of the extent of the obligation of accountability, set out in the Ministerial Code. The at-least-partial misleading of Parliament that took place in relation to intelligence on Iraq's alleged WMD in the run-up to the Iraq war has kept this subject firmly in the forefront of political debate. The question suggests that the convention is still unsatisfactory in formulation and not properly adhered to in practice. Both these assertions will be tested in order to arrive at a considered conclusion.

The obligation, as formulated by the Blair Government, and reappearing in the revised version introduced by the Coalition Government in 2010, reads:

> It is of paramount importance that Ministers give accurate and truthful information to Parliament, correcting any inadvertent error at the earliest opportunity. Ministers who knowingly mislead Parliament will be expected to offer their resignation to the Prime Minister. Ministers should be as open as possible with Parliament and the public, refusing to provide information only when disclosure would not be in the public interest, which should be decided in accordance with the relevant statutes and the Freedom of Information Act 2000.
>
> (Para 1.2 c and d, Ministerial Code, Cabinet Office, 2010)[7]

This formulation follows more or less word for word the version put forward by the previous government, which was approved by the House of Commons on 20 March 1997, although it has been updated to take account of the advent of the FOI 2000. The wording of the obligation in the Code is important because the experience of the previous administrations suggests that it is this, the only authoritative formulation of the obligation that we have, that will be relied upon by ministers accused of misleading Parliament, and so will set the parameters for debate.

7   In this area of the constitution, as the essay argues, the Ministerial Code has become the authoritative rule-book. It is essential, therefore, that it is quoted – accurately!

The exceptions to the general duty to give information set out in the Ministerial Code itself must first be examined. The excluded categories of information still include all of those set out in the Official Secrets legislation and, more significantly, the very broad exemptions set out in the FOI 2000. These include law enforcement and legal proceedings (ss 30 and 31), information that might harm national security, defence, the economy, international affairs or relations between UK administrations, information relating to the formulation or development of government policy (s 35) and information that would harm the 'effective conduct of public affairs' (s 36) – this exception, in particular, being very wide and vague. It should be noted that some of the most significant of these exclusionary categories do not require a harm test: that is, in these categories, it does not even have to be shown that release of the information would cause any harm before the minister can refuse to supply it. This is the case in relation to the astonishingly broad exemption in s 35 noted above. The only limitation to this exemption is that statistical information relating to a decision is no longer exempted once the decision is made. But, for example, evidence of other policy options considered, and the reasons for rejecting them, would be covered by the exemption. The Information Commissioner can order release of the information concerned if satisfied (per s 2) that the public interest in withholding information does not outweigh the interest in its reception; however, because the information relates to a central government department, its release can ultimately be vetoed by a Cabinet minister (s 53). The veto has now been used four times: the first related to the release of Cabinet Minutes in which the decision to invade Iraq was formally approved; the most recent vetoed the release of the risk register on the Government's highly controversial reforms to the NHS in England.

While the Ministerial Code sets out areas in which answers may be refused, it also makes it clear that ministers must always be truthful with Parliament, 'correcting any inadvertent errors at the earliest opportunity'. Are there then any circumstances in which it is permissible to tell a direct lie to Parliament? The answer appears to be that this would be acceptable only in the most extreme circumstances, such as concealing an imminent devaluation of the currency, where disclosure would be economically catastrophic, or where an untruth was necessary in order to save the life of British citizens.

The more problematic question is whether, and if so when, it is legitimate to give incomplete answers to Parliament. The version of the obligation that appears in the Ministerial Code does not use phrases such as 'full' or 'comprehensive' information. This appears to leave the door open to the view that giving incomplete information is not necessarily misleading – the 'half a picture can be true' thesis put forward by two very senior civil servants, Sir Gore Booth and Sir Robin Butler, and a minister, William Waldegrave, during the Scott Inquiry.

The objection to the 'half the picture' thesis is obvious, and was expressed forcefully in the Scott Report: the problem, Scott commented, is that the person getting the information will not know that the information is only partial. They are therefore 'almost bound ... to be misled' (Scott Report, para D4.55). Scott suggested that the information given should, in the absence of compelling public interest reasons, be at the least a 'fair summary of the full picture'. There is nothing in the Ministerial Code that expressly deals with this institutionalised problem. This failure may be seen to be a further unsatisfactory aspect of the convention of accountability.

The fear that these deficiencies in the convention itself may lead to the misleading, or at least the under-informing of Parliament is, to an extent, substantiated by the quotes noted above. Further evidence may be found in the Scott Report. For present purposes, Scott's overall conclusion may be cited (para D4.63):

> Government statements made in 1989 and 1990 about policy on defence exports to Iraq consistently failed ... to comply with the standard set by [the earlier version of the Ministerial Code (QPM)] and, more importantly, failed to discharge the obligations imposed by the constitutional principle of ministerial accountability.[8]

No such finding has been authoritatively made in relation to what has arguably been one of the gravest foreign policy disasters of recent times – the invasion of Iraq. In essence, Parliament was given information – that Iraq had WMD, in particular strategic weapons that could be used within 45 minutes of the order to launch being given – which turned out to be comprehensively false. Despite the widespread popular perception that the government, in particular Mr Blair, simply lied about the issue, it appears that the more accurate view is that the evidence rather was heavily 'spun' and that much of the fault lay with the intelligence services, and the failure of the Joint Intelligence Committee to scrutinise the raw data more sceptically and rigorously. In terms of presentation, Sir Robin Butler's Report found that at times caveats and doubts over specific claims were not passed onto Parliament. Thus the impression was given that the intelligence supporting the claims about Iraq's WMD threat was 'firmer and fuller' than it actually was. But Butler – to widespread scepticism – found that there had been 'no deliberate distortion' of the available information. This allowed Blair and his Government largely to escape parliamentary censure for misleading it, although there is overwhelming evidence that the public has rejected Butler's findings and believes that Blair was disingenuous.

This was also partly because Blair and others could rely on the defence that, although they gave Parliament information that turned out to be incorrect, they did not 'knowingly' mislead Parliament. This formulation allows ministers to escape resignation where they have, perhaps through negligence, or oversight, misled Parliament. Conversely, it can be very hard to prove a deliberate intention to mislead, as the Scott Report showed in relation to William Waldegrave and others, when they maintained that guidelines over arms exports to

---

8   Let it be said again – use specific examples! In this area in particular, student essays often descend into vague generalities; to counter this, use the Ministerial Code, Scott Report and concrete examples to give your essay authority and precision!

Iran and Iraq had not changed, but were merely being more flexibly interpreted. Scott described this viewpoint as one 'that does not seem to me to correspond with reality' and added, 'The description of [the new policy] as merely a flexible interpretation of the guidelines … [was] bound to be misleading.' Nevertheless, he also said, 'I did not receive any impression of any insincerity on Mr Waldegrave's part' and suggested that 'Mr Waldegrave … did not have any duplicitous intent' in putting forward this explanation. It is suggested that the duty on ministers ought, in cases where the matter is arguable, to be not just to give their view – for example, 'the guidelines have not changed' – but to give full factual information as to what has occurred, and allow Parliament to draw its own conclusions. The convention, as set out in the Code, does not appear to require this at present.[9]

In conclusion, it has been argued that insofar as the convention of accountability is for all practical purposes expressed by the formulation set out in the Ministerial Code, the charges made in the question are largely substantiated. There are still very broad and vaguely defined areas where information may be withheld: the Code does not appear to tackle the culture of giving only partial information, and it allows ministers to deny that they have misled Parliament by reference to their own subjective and possibly eccentric interpretations, instead of requiring adherence to a more objective standard. It is therefore submitted that while the present position does represent a small advance upon that which existed pre-Scott, the accountability regime requires both greater strength and greater clarity.

Aim Higher ★

Students could make the broader point that that the passage of a resolution by Parliament, which forms the basis of the obligations set out in the Ministerial Code, is a significant advance on the previous position, whereby the obligation as set out in Questions of Procedure for Ministers (the forerunner of the Ministerial Code) was produced simply as a unilateral act of government, thus allowing government to determine the extent of its own accountability. As Tomkins puts it, 'The government acting on its own cannot now change the terms on ministers' responsibility to Parliament in the way that the Conservative Government did throughout its period in office' (*The Constitution after Scott: Government Unwrapped* (1998), p 62). The new statement of the obligation was at least approved by Parliament. However, it should be noted that the wording of the obligation was suggested by the Government for approval by Parliament, and that the Government had rejected a more radically worded version produced by the Public Service Committee.

---

9   Students should of course feel free to challenge the provisions of the Code itself: a number of commentators are critical of some of its provisions.

Judicial Review

INTRODUCTION

This topic is very extensive and is often taught as a separate course on administrative law in the second or third year of degree courses. However, on constitutional law courses, it is of a manageable size and sometimes attracts two questions in exams – which can make it a good return for your revision (check your past papers). In this area, extensive knowledge of case law is clearly necessary, but must be bound together and informed by a grasp of basic principle. Questions can appear as either essays or problems and quite often both appear in one paper. Essays will generally demand an evaluation of the effectiveness of judicial review in one form or other. If a problem question asks the student to advise clients, it is important to remember standing, amenability, procedure and remedies, bearing in mind the changes introduced by the Civil Procedure Rules (CPR). Some papers treat natural justice as a separate topic, and this has been reflected in the questions given below. In theory, a problem could combine traditional judicial review issues with questions arising under the Human Rights Act 1998 (HRA). However, the textbooks and most courses treat the HRA separately and examiners seem generally to be setting questions that test the student's knowledge of the English principles of judicial review, without confusing this with possible claims brought under the HRA – although again, you should check past papers on this. In addition, answering a problem question on the HRA would generally require knowledge of the European Convention on Human Rights (ECHR) case law, particularly in relation to Art 6, which first-year students would not generally be expected to have. There is, in particular, a very complex legal issue as to how far judicial review of a decision taken by a body that does not itself satisfy the requirements of Art 6 of the ECHR can provide a level of protection such that, overall, Art 6 is satisfied. Therefore, the answers given to the problem questions here do not include possible HRA points, except in one important area. The HRA has already had the effect of changing the ordinary English law on bias, with the courts accepting that Art 6 of the ECHR requires a modification of the previous *Gough* test. This is therefore included. Additionally, essay questions on judicial review may well ask for an analysis of how the HRA has changed the standard of substantive review in human rights cases. Such a question is included here.

Checklist ✔

Students should be familiar with the following areas:

- the public/private law boundary – **r54** of the **CPR**, *locus standi*, time limits and amenability of bodies to review;

- procedural impropriety other than natural justice; mandatory/directory express requirements, for example, consultation;

- tests for the applicability of natural justice, including 'legitimate expectation';

- the *audi* rule – what it will demand in different situations; when are legal representation, witnesses, cross-examination or an oral hearing required?

- the rule against bias – direct interests (*Pinochet*) and indirect interest; how the test for the latter has been changed by the **HRA** (*Porter v Magill* (2002));

- illegality – fettering by policy, delegation, improper purpose, inferred purpose or plurality of purposes; irrelevant considerations and concept of error of law; the effect of rulings that all such errors are reviewable; substantive legitimate expectations;

- irrationality – is this the same concept as '*Wednesbury* unreasonableness'?; critiques of the notion;

- remedies – basic knowledge, discretion to refuse, instances when certain remedies are inappropriate or will not lie;

- the impact of the **HRA**; the possible development of proportionality as a ground of review.

QUESTION 27

Blankshire County Council is empowered by s 3 of the (fictitious) Street Traders Act to grant licences to street traders and withdraw them for, inter alia, misconduct. It has been the custom of the Council to grant hearings to consider the case against proposed revocation of licences, provided that a written request is received within 14 days of the decision being announced. Under the Cautious Party, previously in control of the Council, such licences were granted sparingly. The Enterprise Party, now in power, has announced that in six months' time, 50 new licences are to be granted over a six-week period.

The following events occur.

Doreen, a current licence-holder, is disgruntled by the decision to grant new licences, fearing such a massive increase in competition; she requests a hearing from the Council. She receives a letter in reply stating that, normally, only revocation of a licence gives rise to a hearing and that, in any event, unprecedentedly low Council funds forbid a hearing.

She is also told that the detailed statement of her reasons for opposing the new licences will not be considered, as the decision has already been made.

Vic and William receive notification that their licences are to be revoked for misconduct, subject to their right to put their case against the revocation. William is given a fair chance to state his case at a meeting of the Licensing Board. However, he recognises one of the five members of the Board, Bert, as the former husband of Alison; Alison recently left Bert for William in an episode that generated much publicity. The Board orders revocation. After the hearings are over, it emerges for the first time that Bert covertly encouraged Alison to have the affair with William so that he could divorce her and marry his secret, long-standing mistress, with whom he is now blissfully happy.

Vic is unhappy because it was only at his hearing that he was told full details of the case against him: that there was evidence that specific products sold from his stall were unsafe. Previously he had only been told that his licence was being revoked 'on health and safety grounds'. The Board orders revocation. Vic is indignant because he claims he has detailed evidence of the safety of his products, which he could have raised in evidence in the hearing, had he known the true grounds of the Council's case.

Jane applies for a licence to run a stall but is refused. She is indignant, because the Council has provided no reasons for the refusal.

▶ Discuss the issues of 'procedural impropriety' raised by the above.

How to Answer this Question

This is a long and initially rather confusing question. On analysis, however, it can be seen to break down into a number of fairly distinct issues surrounding fair procedure. Students must take care to work out the application of all of the given facts to all of the applicants before starting to answer the question: for example, the fact that persons whose licences have been revoked have been customarily granted a hearing is primarily relevant not to Vic and William, but to Doreen. Note that discussion of remedies and procedure is *not* required, as the question calls for a discussion of the issues of procedural impropriety, not for advice to be given to possible applicants for judicial review.

Essentially, the following areas should be covered:

❖ whether the rules of natural justice require a hearing for Doreen or at least an opportunity for her to make representations; the argument for 'legitimate expectation' by analogy from existing custom with respect to revocation;

❖ whether there is an infringement of the *nemo judex* rule regarding William's hearing; the test for bias is now *Porter v Magill* (2002); the effect of facts pointing to bias at the time of the hearing, but not subsequently;

❖ Vic – failure to give a person full notice of the case against them;

❖ Jane – failure to give reasons for an administrative decision.

Applying the Law

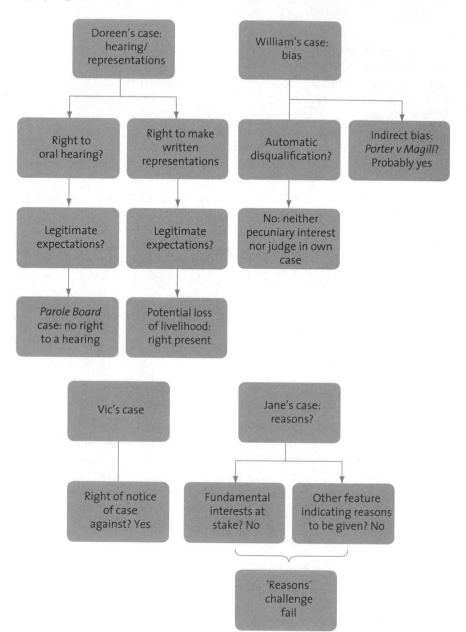

ANSWER

Blankshire Council may have been guilty of procedural impropriety during the revocation of licences, the refusal of Jane's licence, and in the taking of the decision to grant new licences. In what follows, the claims of each of the possible applicants will be considered in turn.[1]

The question of Doreen's possible entitlement to a hearing will be considered first. One of the two rules of natural justice is *audi alteram partem*, which, at its most basic level, denotes that both sides should be heard in making certain decisions. In *Ridge v Baldwin* (1963), Lord Reid, in the course of his judgment, stated (strictly obiter) that the crucial characteristic of a hearing or decision that would render it subject to the rules of natural justice is that a person's rights would be affected by the outcome; he disposed of the fallacy that the proceedings had to have the further characteristic of being quasi-judicial. In the instant case, Doreen could claim that her right to trade granted by her licence would be affected to her detriment by a massive increase in competition.

Further, it can be argued that Doreen has a 'legitimate expectation' of a hearing. This notion was first formulated by Lord Denning MR in *Schmidt v Home Secretary* (1969) and its principles were clarified in *Council of Civil Service Unions v Minister for the Civil Service* (1984). Lord Fraser stated that a legitimate expectation 'may arise either from an express promise or from the existence of a regular practice which the claimant can reasonably expect to continue'. Doreen may be able to argue that she has a legitimate expectation based on the Council's 'custom' of consultation over revocation of licences. It is arguable that if it is legitimate to expect consultation over revocation of licences – an expectation particularly strong where economic loss may be caused by the revocation – then it would also be reasonable to expect consultation over a decision that would greatly devalue licences in existence and similarly cause economic loss. Lord Denning put forward this line of reasoning (obiter) in *Liverpool Corp ex p Liverpool Taxi Fleet, etc* (1972) (a decision approved in *Devon County Council ex p Baker; Durham County Council ex p Curtis* (1995)), in which it was held that taxi drivers were entitled to be consulted over a proposal to increase the number of taxi cabs; however, in that case, an express promise had been given of full consultation with existing taxi drivers, so it is not directly applicable to the instant situation.

However, the Council would argue that Doreen is not entitled to a hearing, especially in light of its unprecedented shortage of funds: Doreen is not being deprived of a benefit but merely subject to increased competition. *R (West) v Parole Board* (2006) strongly suggests that an oral hearing would not be considered necessary in such a marginal case.

---

1   Note that answers to problem questions do not need to start with an introduction to the *topic*: instead, they should *briefly* indicate the issues raised by the question and the way in which they will be answered.

The court would then, probably take the view that while Doreen is not entitled to a full hearing, she should have had an opportunity to make full representations to the Council: the court is likely to take this view if it believes that the opportunity to make representations in writing will give Doreen a proper opportunity to put her case (*Lloyd v McMahon* (1987)). The Council, then, will almost certainly not be obliged to give Doreen an oral hearing – the consequences for her in this case are far less grave than those in *Lloyd*, which involved a massive surcharge on negligent councillors. However, its failure to grant Doreen a right to make written representations is probably in breach of the *audi* rule.[2]

Vic appears to have a relatively clear case. The right to full notice of the case against a person is the lowest level of procedural protection; if you have no notice of the case against you, then clearly you cannot make any effective representations on your own behalf. In *R v Governing Body of Dunraven School & Anor, ex p B (by his Mother & Next Friend)* (1999), a 15-year-old boy was excluded from school. He successfully applied for judicial review on the basis that he had not been informed of the main evidence against him (provided by another boy). Therefore the right to notice is only likely to be denied either for particular reasons of public policy (e.g. national security) or where the applicant is very much in the position of merely applying for a benefit, for example, applying for a licence. Neither is the case here and it is clear that holding a hearing, at which one side cannot, through the other's failure to inform them properly, present their side of the argument properly, is a breach of the duty to act fairly.

The fact that Bert sits on the Board that hears William's case fails to be considered. Clearly, the perception of his probable hostility towards William raises questions about the fairness of William's hearing. The second main rule of natural justice, *nemo judex in causa sua*, is commonly expressed to forbid bias on the part of the decision-maker. It must initially be established whether personal animosity towards the applicant by the decision-maker can amount to bias for the purposes of natural justice. The persuasive authority of *Re Elliott* (1959) suggests that it can, and in the recent decision of *Locabail* (2000), Lord Woolf expressly mentioned 'personal animosity' as a circumstance that could found a legitimate claim of bias. However, in cases where the decision-maker has neither a pecuniary interest in the outcome, nor is actually involved with an organisation that is a party to a case – the further category added by the *Pinochet* decision (*Bow Street Stipendiary Magistrates ex p Pinochet Ugarte (No 2)* (2000)) – it is not enough simply to establish the facts pointing to bias, without more. In other words, the automatic disqualification rule does not apply in such cases. Instead, the test, following the House of

---

2   Note the careful distinction here between an oral hearing and written representations and the clear conclusion that only the latter would be found to be required. In our long joint experience, students generally tend greatly to overestimate the extent of procedural protection a claimant would be granted by a court.

Lords' decision in *Porter v Magill* (2002), is that the decision will be quashed where 'the fair-minded and informed observer, having considered the [relevant] facts would conclude that there was a real possibility that the tribunal was biased'.[3] Thus, the court is concerned not to ascertain whether there was *in fact* 'a real danger of bias' (the old test under *Gough* (1993)). It is concerned with whether a fair-minded observer would so conclude, in recognition of the fact that the appearance of the matter is just as important as the reality (as Lord Nolan observed in *Pinochet*). Such an observer would not have to think that it was more probable than not that there was bias, merely that it was a real, and not a fanciful possibility. On the facts of the present case, a perception of bias might well have arisen at the time of the hearing, since observers would know that Bert's wife had left him for William – presumably common knowledge in view of the widespread 'publicity' that the affair created – and would therefore be very likely to apprehend bias on the part of Bert. A court would probably therefore find that a fair-minded observer would inevitably have suspected bias at the time. If this were the case, the decision relating to William would be quashed.

Jane's only ground of complaint is that she has not been given reasons for her decision. There is no general duty to give reasons for administrative decisions, but the courts are rapidly developing broad categories of cases in which reasons must be given. Unfortunately for Jane, she does not appear to fall within any of them and *R v Lancashire CC ex p Huddleston* (1986) is authority for the proposition that reasons do not have to be given for the refusal of a discretionary benefit. Jane has not suffered an interference with her legal rights or other 'highly regarded interests' (*R v Secretary of State for the Home Department ex p Doody and Ors* (1994)), and nor is there any particular feature of the decision, such as its being inexplicable (*Sinclair* (1992)) or against her legitimate expectations (*R v Criminal Injuries Compensation Board ex p Cunningham* (1991)) that might require reasons to be given. Further examples of instances in which reasons have to be given include cases that are particularly 'judicial' in character (*Stefan v General Medical Council* (1999)) and instances in which there is a conflict of factual evidence, and it is unclear what view of the facts the decision-maker took (*R v Criminal Injuries Compensation Board ex p Cummins* (1992)). Neither of these are applicable to Jane. Jane is a 'bare applicant' for a benefit, and as such is most unlikely to be held to be entitled to anything more than that the decision-maker is unbiased and the decision not perverse (*McInnes v Onslow Fane* (1978)). Her claim that she should have been given the reasons for the decision against her will almost certainly fail.[4]

....

3 This distinction is clearly fundamental to the rule against bias; however, even quite good students routinely fail to make it clear, especially in exam answers. Failure to draw such a distinction, however, is exactly the kind of weakness that should preclude the award of a 2:1 mark.

4 As with the 'oral hearing' issue, note the clear conclusion *against* the claimant's possible argument here; student answers typically assume that reasons must be given, rather than carefully analysing the case law to decide whether in the particular case, a court would find that there was a duty to give them.

QUESTION 28

The Opticians' Regulatory Body (ORB), established by statute, is empowered to designate certain opticians' practices as being 'ORB approved', if it appears to the ORB that the practice concerned is 'a credit to the profession'. Upon such a designation being made, a central government grant will be made to the practice. The ORB may also publicly designate opticians it considers to be 'negligently run' as 'not recommended'. The following events occur in Dansfield Town.

(a) Edward's practice is designated 'not approved'; at his hearing, the Dansfield Town branch of the ORB tells him that it considers his practice 'too small to provide an efficient service'. Edward is very unhappy with this decision, but puts off seeking legal advice for some time because of his fear of going to court.

(b) Thirty practices, making up the 'I Can See Clearly' conglomerate, are given block approval by the Dansfield Town branch of the ORB. In response, Julia, the chair of the national Citizens Against Government Waste (CAGW) group, points out that many of the ORB members sit on the Dansfield local council, which is very concerned about unemployment among secretaries in the area; she admits, however, that all of the practices concerned are meritorious.

(c) Three months after the announcement of the block approval, Fanny, who has been running a practice for two months that has been lauded as a model of efficiency in letters to the *Dansfield Herald*, requests a favourable designation from the Dansfield Town branch of the ORB. At her hearing, she is told that the body has a policy of refusing to approve practices that are less than one year old. Her practice is not approved.

You may assume that all of the hearings given are in accordance with the principles of natural justice.

▶ Advise Edward and Fanny, who wish to challenge the decisions about their practices, and Julia, who wishes to question the legality of the block approval of 30 practices.

How to Answer this Question

This is a fairly typical problem question, which includes decisions that may be open to attack under various heads of judicial review. Students should note that, unlike in the last question, they are asked to advise possible claimants, rather than to 'discuss issues'. Consequently, matters of standing, procedure and remedies *must* be covered. Natural justice should obviously not be discussed here; it should be noted, however, that one issue of natural justice is sometimes thrown into a question that is otherwise mainly concerned with illegality and irrationality.

Applying the Law

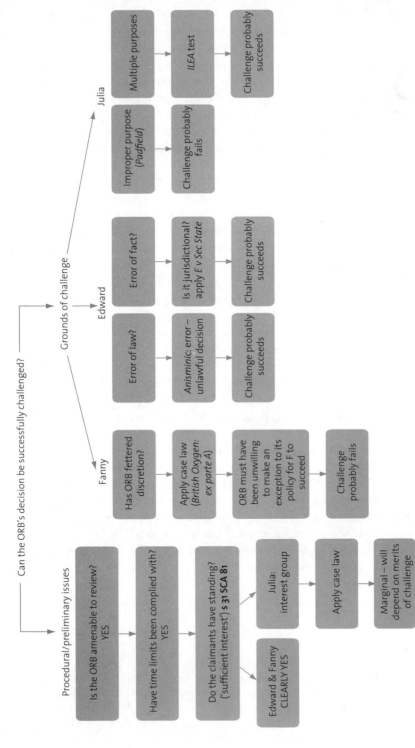

This mind map shows the main issues to consider when forming your answer.

ANSWER

The Opticians' Regulatory Body is a public body, established by statute; its decisions will therefore be subject to the supervisory review jurisdiction of the High Court on the basis that it clearly exercises a 'public function' as r54.1(2) of the Civil Procedure Rules (CPR) requires.[5] It is clear moreover that judicial review is the appropriate mode of challenge to such decisions. Under r54.4 of the CPR, applicants must initially seek the courts' permission to apply for judicial review; this must be done 'promptly, and in any event not later than three months after the grounds to make the claim first arose' (r54.5 of the CPR). It will be assumed that all three potential claimants are within this basic time limit.[6]

Applicants must show that they have a sufficient interest in the matter to which the application relates (s31(3) of the Supreme Court Act 1981). Clearly, Edward and Fanny have sufficient interest, as the decisions by the ORB have given them an individual grievance. Julia, however, may have more difficulty establishing standing, since she is not personally affected by the decision. Cases such as *ex p National Federation* appear to show some reluctance to allow challenges by interested groups, although that case in reality may have been more about protecting the confidentiality of taxpayers' affairs. The decision in *Secretary of State for the Environment ex p Rose Theatre Trust Co* (1990), which indicates that pressure groups whose only interest in a decision is concern about the issues involved will not in general have *locus standi* to challenge the decision, represents a further difficulty. However, since the *Rose Theatre* decision, the courts have begun to take a much more flexible and accommodating approach to the question of standing when a sufficiently important issue is raised by the application, such that the case is now generally regarded as being out of line with the general thrust of judicial policy. Thus, in *Secretary of State for Foreign and Commonwealth Affairs ex p Rees-Mogg* (1994), it was found that the applicant had standing 'because of his sincere concern for constitutional issues'. In *Secretary of State for Foreign Affairs ex p the World Development Movement* (1995), the WDM was granted *locus standi* on the basis of a number of factors, including the importance of the issue raised (the possibly illegal use of the government's overseas aid budget), the absence of any other challenger and the prominence and expertise of the applicant pressure group in relation to the issues raised by the case. In other cases, the courts have stressed the importance of pressure groups representing people living in the area affected by the contested decision: see *Inspectorate of Pollution ex p Greenpeace* (1994). Applying these criteria to Julia and the CAGW, her claim for standing appears rather weak. The challenge is mainly one of local interest, so the pure public interest

----

5   This is a good example of a straightforward point, that must be disposed of rapidly, but nevertheless *precisely*, with citation and application of the relevant legal authority. A common weakness in student answers – particularly in exam answers – is that far too much time is spent on such simple points, leaving insufficient time for the more complex ones that carry nearly all of the marks.

6   See the point above!

approach is not really applicable; applying the *Greenpeace* case cited, the courts will probably inquire whether Julia or the group have any local connection, as the general public interest in the issue appears quite weak. On the other hand, the CAGW may have some expertise in the area of government waste, a point that would count in its favour. Probably, the issue of standing would ultimately therefore turn upon whether the courts considered that Julia's challenge raised serious issues of possible unlawful action, a matter that will be considered below.[7]

The substantive merits of each of the applicants' challenges will now be considered, starting with the decision to designate Edward's practice as 'not approved'. Such a designation may be made only if the ORB considers a practice to be 'negligently run'. There is, it is submitted, a clear argument that the ORB has made an error of law by misinterpreting the word 'negligent'. The word would probably be treated as a legal term of art like the words 'successor in title' in *Anisminic Ltd v Foreign Compensation Commission* (1969) and, as such, its interpretation would be a matter for the court to decide upon if necessary, substituting its own judgment for that of the ORB (as confirmed in *O'Reilly v Mackman* (1982)). An error in interpreting such a word would mean, as *Anisminic Ltd v Foreign Compensation Commission* (1969) established, that the decision-making body would have 'asked itself the wrong questions ... thereby stepping outside its jurisdiction'.

It is apparent from the reasons given to Edward that the ORB has taken the word 'negligently' to mean 'not sufficiently efficient'. This may conceivably connote an ordinary usage of the word 'negligently', but it is not the legal understanding. Assuming that the courts would view the word as a term of legal art, it is submitted that the question that should have been asked was: 'Is Edward's practice run with a lack of reasonable care for those who might foreseeably be harmed by lack of such care on his part?' It is apparent that the answer to that question would be in the negative, as the only complaint against Edward is that the practice is small, not that it is run with lack of reasonable care. If it is accepted that the ORB has asked itself the wrong question, the result would be, per Lord Diplock in *Re Racal Communications Ltd* (1981), 'that the decision they reached would be a nullity', as it would have decided a matter that it was not empowered to decide and thus exceeded its vires. Therefore, a quashing order will lie to quash the decision.

The ORB might argue in its defence that the decision as to whether a practice is 'negligently run' is, rightly construed, one of fact and that errors of fact are not generally a ground of challenge on judicial review. However, an important exception relates to what are known as 'jurisdictional facts'. This exception refers to instances where the decision-maker is only entitled to enter upon his inquiry if a particular fact exists. Here,

----

7   Note here the balanced survey of the legal arguments, the final resolution being deferred to the resolution of a further set of substantive legal arguments.

'the exercise of power, or jurisdiction, depends on the precedent establishment of an objective fact. In such a case, it is for the court to decide whether that precedent requirement has been satisfied' (*Khawaja v Secretary of State for the Home Department* (1983)). Since the ORB may only take the decisive action of designating a business as 'not approved' should it be 'negligently run', it would seem possible to characterise the existence of such negligence as a precedent fact, and therefore a matter for the court. The ORB might, however, argue that to make the court the assessor of whether a given business is 'negligently run' is to deprive it of the exercise of judgment in its area of expertise – a freedom that Parliament intended to give it under the statute. In other words, it could contend that the finding of negligence is not a precedent fact that entitles it to enter upon the real inquiry, but rather one of the principal roles it is given under the statute. Recent developments, however, indicate that the courts are becoming more willing to strike decisions down on the basis of error of fact, even if that fact is not jurisdictional. In *Criminal Injuries Compensation Commission ex p A* (1999), four of their Lordships accepted that a decision on a 'crucial matter' that was tainted with a material error of fact could be quashed. *Adan v Newham BC* (2002) made it clear, however, that the courts will not attempt to investigate complex factual disagreements but only intervene in clear cases, an approach confirmed in *E v Secretary of State for the Home Department* (2004). Clearly, the finding that Edward's business is 'negligently run' is the crux of the matter. Provided that the error is clear and unarguable, rather than a contested matter of opinion on which the court would consider itself bound to defer to the expertise of the ORB, Edward should succeed on this ground.[8]

The decision not to approve Fanny's practice because of the ORB's policy with respect to recently established practices now falls to be considered. There can be, as Lord Reid observed in *British Oxygen Co Ltd v Board of Trade* (1971), 'no objection' to a body evolving even a fairly precise policy with respect to its area of remit. What it must not do is apply this policy rigidly in every case; it must still decide each case on its merits and consider whether an exception to the policy should be made. Thus, in the *British Oxygen* case, the Board had a policy of not giving grants for items costing less than £25, but their Lordships found that it was willing to hear reasons from any applicant as to why the policy should not be applied in his case. Similarly in *R v Secretary of State for the Home Department ex p Hindley* (2000), the setting of a 'whole life' tariff for a murderer was lawful provided that it was kept under review. By contrast, in *Secretary of State for the Environment ex p Brent LBC* (1982), the minister refused to hear representations from the authority before applying his policy; consequently, his decision was unlawful. In the instant case, the ORB granted Fanny a hearing; if it could show that it knew the age of Fanny's practice before it held the hearing, there would be a strong inference that it was prepared to consider making an exception, since otherwise the hearing would have been a waste of time. This argument would be hard to refute; it could be claimed that the ORB only held the hearing

---

8   Note how a complex argument, taking in numerous cases, culminates with a clear conclusion.

to avoid falling foul of the rules of natural justice, and if Fanny could convince the court that the apparent preparedness to consider exceptions was only a sham, *North West Lancashire Health Authority ex p A and Ors* (2000) is authority for the proposition that the policy would therefore be considered as truly rigid and thus unlawful. However, without actual evidence of this, it would be hard to destroy the inference that the ORB must have been holding the possibility open of making an exception to its policy, and therefore made a lawful decision.[9]

Julia's grounds of complaint will now be considered. It is well established that where an authority is endowed with power to achieve one goal, and uses it to achieve another, that exercise of power is unlawful (*Hanson v Radcliffe* (1922)). In the instant case, no purpose is stated in the parent Act, but the courts have been prepared on a number of occasions to infer a purpose (as in *Padfield's* case) and then hold a decision ultra vires for not conforming with that purpose. It could be sensibly inferred here that the statute creating the ORB had the purpose of raising standards amongst opticians by providing performance incentives through grants to meritorious practices. If the block approval was made with the purpose of decreasing unemployment (the hope being that the practices receiving the grants would expand and employ more staff), or even if the ORB was influenced by that consideration, then the decision will be a nullity for illegality or possibly for unreasonableness.

The situation is, however, complicated by the fact that all of the practices approved are, as Julia concedes, meritorious and therefore could properly be approved within the purposes of the Act. Where a decision has been taken with both a proper and an improper purpose in mind, the approach of the courts has been to ask whether it would have been taken in the absence of the improper consideration. If it would not (as in *ILEA ex p Westminster City Council* (1986)), then the decision is unlawful. If the same decision would have been taken without the improper motive, as in *Brighton Corp ex p Shoosmith* (1907), then it will be allowed to stand. In the instant case, the motives behind the ORB's decision would be a matter for evidence, but prima facie it would seem unlikely that a block approval of 30 practices would have taken place without the additional motive of the councillors. Moreover, the *ILEA* case also suggested that the test of whether the improper purpose 'materially' affected the decision could be used: a test that would clearly be easier to satisfy. Assuming that the ORB was materially influenced by the desire to address the problem of unemployment, Julia would have a reasonable chance of demonstrating the decision to be unlawful. If so, as discussed in relation to Edward, a quashing order would lie to quash it.

....

9   Students typically misstate the 'no fetter' argument; it does *not* preclude public authorities adopting strong policies, but only the application of them that refuses to consider the possibility of making an exception. The analysis here states the principle accurately and then goes on to apply it carefully to the facts. Failing to do the latter is probably the most common weakness in answers to problem questions.

Common Pitfalls ✗

The most common problem in questions on judicial review is a very simple one, which the authors have noted, with bafflement, year after year, particularly in exam scripts. This is the absence of case law cited and used in answers. Aside from failing to spot the relevant grounds, this is probably the commonest reasons for scripts failing (no case law cited) or being awarded only a low grade (only one or two cases cited). It is important to grasp the fact that judicial review, just like tort or contract, is essentially made up of decided cases: just as in a tort problem question, therefore, answers should make *detailed reference* to a wide variety of cases.

QUESTION 29

'It is often said that judicial review is intolerably uncertain and amounts to little more than a licence for judges to interfere arbitrarily with the machinery of government and administration' (Emery and Smythe).

▶ Consider whether this amounts to a fair criticism in relation to the grounds of the duty to act fairly and 'irrationality'.

How to Answer this Question

This is a fairly typical essay question on judicial review, in that it demands an evaluative approach. Essays in this area are often concerned with the efficacy of judicial review. In this case, the focus is narrowed to a discussion of the charge of uncertainty, but this still leaves a very large area that could be discussed. However, students would not be expected to assess every subhead of judicial review for certainty. A sensible solution, therefore, would be to focus on the controversial, ambiguous areas, while indicating briefly what are the more settled grounds. The answer below selects certain of these areas; it would be perfectly legitimate, however, to use other examples, such as the uncertain scope of the duty to give reasons or the issue of when legitimate expectations may receive substantive protection.

Answer Structure

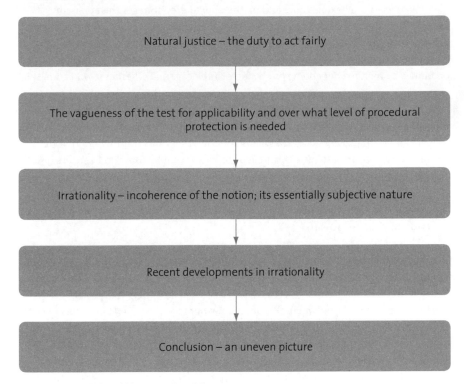

The areas above should be considered for your answer.

ANSWER

A comprehensive discussion of the above criticism of judicial review will clearly be impossible in this context if any depth of discussion is to be maintained. Accordingly, in what follows, discussion will focus on aspects of the specified heads that are the subject of particular debate and controversy. An effort will be made to ascertain how fixed the principles governing intervention are, and to reveal whether, in certain cases, apparent principles are merely a cloak to allow improper intervention.

Procedural impropriety is one of the three main grounds of review identified by Lord Diplock in *Council of Civil Service Unions v Minister for the Civil Service* (1984). There are perhaps two main questions to be considered. One is the issue as to when the rules will apply, the other the controversy concerning what will satisfy the rules in a given situation. In their treatment of the second of these areas, the courts have again taken the flexible approach – in this case, by allowing compliance with the *audi* rule to be fulfilled by widely differing conduct in different situations.

The growth of the notion of the 'duty to act fairly' (perhaps originating from *Re HK* (1967)), an even more flexible concept than the *audi* rule, epitomises the apparent determination of the judiciary to avoid laying down rigid rules or to force administrative decision-makers into adopting a more judicial approach. For example, the House of Lords in a recent 2005 ruling was only able to give us general guidance that an oral hearing will sometimes be required depending on the facts of the case and whether it would assist in the just disposition of the matter (*R (West) v Parole Board* (2006)), although it is fairly well settled that cases involving interferences with legal rights or 'highly regarded interests' will give rise to a higher level of procedural protection than those in which the applicant is a mere applicant (*Doody* (1994)). Rawlings, among others, has commented that from the point of view of an administrator anxious to know what he must do to ensure his decision is correct, this notion is 'hopelessly imprecise', for 'all [the administrator] knows is that he must be "fair" – and what fairness requires in the particular circumstances he can only find out when the court . . . tells him that he has or has not been fair' ((1986) 64 Public Administration 140–141).

It is arguable that Rawlings is somewhat overstating the case:[10] for example, an administrator *does* know that a person must be informed of the substance of the case against him (*Secretary of State, etc ex p Philippine Airlines Inc* (1984), confirmed by the Court of Appeal to be a fundamental common law right in *W (Algeria) v Secretary of State for the Home Department* [2010] EWCA Civ 898); however, his argument that flexibility has been taken too far is certainly attractive. It is, however, difficult to see how a degree of uncertainty could have been avoided, given the huge range of situations to which natural justice applies. A greater rigidity in the rules might create the risk that either low-level administrative decisions would be shackled with inappropriately stringent procedural requirements, with a consequent loss of efficiency and speed, or that disciplinary hearings would give insufficient procedural safeguards to those whose cases they were trying.

The accusation of intolerable uncertainty can, it is submitted, have more applicability to the head of irrationality. The head seems to be expressed in two different ways, both of which reveal muddled judicial thinking. Lord Diplock's definition of irrationality in the *GCHQ* case seems essentially redundant; it is hard to visualise circumstances in which a decision that is outrageously immoral or illogical would not in any event be seen by the judiciary as being outside the purposes of the governing statute and therefore ultra vires. The head of irrationality is alternatively expressed as referring to decisions that are so unreasonable that no reasonable person could come to them. Two comments can be made about this definition. First, such decisions would again surely be outside the purpose of the parent Act; second, as Jowell and Lester argue, the definition is

---

10 Note how a key commentator's views are not only accurately cited, but then *evaluated* – the mark of a First Class answer.

tautologous (a decision is unreasonable if a reasonable man could not have made it). For these reasons, it is submitted that the doctrine of unreasonableness as traditionally understood adds nothing to the law of judicial review and should be abandoned as its subjective nature inevitably renders it uncertain. In that respect, Lord Cooke's recent comment in *Secretary of State for the Home Department ex p Daly* (2001), 'I think that the day will come when it will be more widely recognised that [*Wednesbury*] was an unfortunately retrogressive decision in English administrative law', is a welcome harbinger of possible future change. However, in going on to say only that it 'may be that the law can never be satisfied' merely by finding that a decision was not absurd, Lord Cooke adds further uncertainty to the law. Moreover, the decision in *Association of British Civilian Internees Far Eastern Region v SS for Defence* (2003) seems to row back from Lord Cooke's comments: it confirms that where no Convention rights are in play under the **Human Rights Act 1998**, the proper standard for review remains *Wednesbury*.

However, it appears that the courts may be in the process of rendering this head more sophisticated. Clayton has pointed out that 'The full rigour of the *Wednesbury* test has been softened recently, and reformulated into a test which asks whether the decision is "within the range of reasonable responses" under the relevant power. In some cases, the focus is on whether the reasoning process was "logically flawed" ' (R Clayton and K Ghaly, 'Shifting Standards of Review' (2007) JR 210, 211). The head is certainly not moribund. Recent examples of successful challenges include courts holding that there has been: an unreasonable refusal of interim housing (*Paul-Coker* (2006)), an unreasonable decision against a residential care assessment (*LH* (2006)) and an unreasonable refusal of a cancer drug (*Rogers* (2006)). In the last-named case, the court found that the claimant fell within the group who were eligible to be given treatment with the drug but that the health authority had a policy of withholding assistance save in unstated exceptional circumstances. It found that such a policy would be rational in the legal sense, provided that it was possible to envisage, and the decision-maker did envisage, what the exceptional circumstances might be. But if it was not possible to envisage any such circumstances, the policy would be in practice a complete refusal to fund the drug treatment, and as such would be irrational, in the sense of being illogical, or not rationally justified. This was first of all because the reasoning given by the authority was incomplete, in that it relied on the notion of exceptional circumstances but was unable to give an indication of what these might be and how the authority would justify refusing the drug to one patient and granting it to another; and second because it purported to be a policy of allowing treatment in exceptional circumstances but in practice was a policy of always refusing treatment.[11]

Such cases indicate a more structured and certain form of review; however, overall it must be conceded that the head, with its variable standard (the so-called 'sub' and 'super'

---

11   Note the *detailed* treatment of this case, indicating a clear understanding of the court's specific reasons for finding against the health authority.

Wednesbury tests, allowing for more 'anxious scrutiny' where human rights are at stake (see e.g. *R v Lord Saville ex p. A* (2002)) and an even more hands-off approach than normal in cases concerning economic policy (*Nottinghamshire County Council v Secretary of State for the Environment* (1986)) is still far from predictable in operation. Further judicial work is required to clarify it; better still, it could be replaced with a general doctrine of proportionality.

It is clear that, overall, a mixed picture has emerged. In some cases, doctrines that have been insufficiently worked out have left judges open to charges of unwarranted interference. However, workable principles have been developed, and uncertainty can be due to the range of situations to which review applies, or to Parliament's failure to legislate clearly on the subject in hand. The charge of *intolerable* uncertainty is therefore concluded to be overstated.[12]

QUESTION 30

'The law of judicial review before the Human Rights Act 1998 provided uncertain and unsatisfactory levels of protection for civil rights and freedoms.'

▶ Consider how far you agree with this statement, and how far the Human Rights Act has changed this situation. Take into account decided cases under the Act.

How to Answer this Question

This question is a popular subject with examiners, given the current dynamic state of the law in this area.

---

12   Note how the conclusion returns to the question asked and seeks to provide a clear answer to it.

Answer Structure

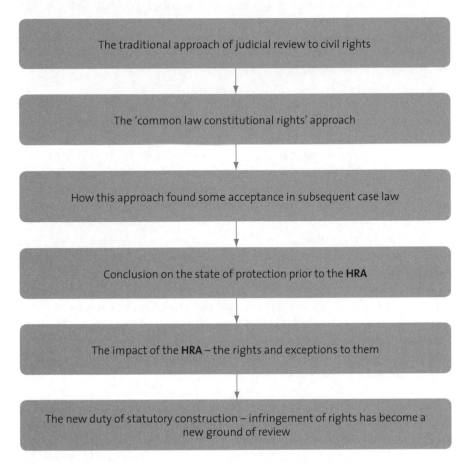

The traditional approach of judicial review to civil rights

The 'common law constitutional rights' approach

How this approach found some acceptance in subsequent case law

Conclusion on the state of protection prior to the **HRA**

The impact of the **HRA** – the rights and exceptions to them

The new duty of statutory construction – infringement of rights has become a new ground of review

The areas above should be considered for your answer.

ANSWER

Historically, judicial review has not been greatly concerned with the protection of human rights per se. Since its traditional basis has been the ultra vires doctrine, and since liberties have been mainly residual rather than being granted positively by statutes, this is perhaps not surprising. Cases such as *GCHQ* (1984) showed some recognition of the importance of civil rights – in that case, freedom of association – but up until quite recently, they have generally played a marginal role in public law. This essay will examine how much impact the more rights-orientated approach of recent years has had, the limitations inherent in this approach, and the change brought about by the Human Rights Act 1998 (HRA).

Calls for a more rights-based approach to judicial review had multiplied in the years before the HRA. Jowell and Lester, in a well-known article ([1987] PL 368), made the concrete proposal that the courts, when reviewing decisions taken under statute, could perfectly legitimately apply a presumption – displaceable only by clear statutory language – that Parliament did not intend to authorise actions incompatible with the UK's obligations under the European Convention on Human Rights (ECHR).

Such an approach was roundly rejected by the House of Lords in the *Brind* case (*Secretary of State for the Home Department ex p Brind* (1991)), on the basis that the imposition of such a presumption would amount to de facto incorporation of the Convention 'by the back door', since the effect would be to render all administrative decisions violating the Convention unlawful, even if the statute had granted a broad discretion that on its face encompassed rights-violating action. This, the Lords thought, would be a usurpation of judicial power, given Parliament's persistent refusal to introduce the Convention through legislation.

Partly in response to this decision, which rejected the proposal to develop judicial review principles by reference to the then unincorporated Convention, Laws J [1993] PL 59 argued that the correct approach was to view the norms implicit in the ECHR as already reflected in the common law – an approach that gained some support from the House of Lords' decision in *Derbyshire CC v Times Newspapers* (1993) – and to argue that it is the importance that the common law consequently attaches to fundamental rights that makes a presumption that statutes do not intend to facilitate infringement of such rights a permissible, indeed, legitimate one.

This approach was demonstrated in some notable cases, an early example being *Lord Chancellor ex p Witham* (1997). It then gained acceptance from the House of Lords in two important decisions. Lord Hoffmann remarked in *Secretary of State for the Home Department ex p Simms* (2000) that 'fundamental rights cannot be overridden by general or ambiguous words'. The House of Lords found that general words in a statute were not sufficient to warrant a rule laid down by the Home Secretary that prevented a prisoner from contacting journalists with a view to starting a campaign that his own conviction amounted to a miscarriage of justice. Freedom of expression was held to be a common law right, to be ousted only by express words or necessary implication, a principle accepted also in *Secretary of State for the Home Department ex p Pierson* (1998) by Lord Browne-Wilkinson.

These decisions show how far the basic doctrine of ultra vires, coupled with a readiness to impose strong presumptions as to legislative intent on Parliament, can go. Indeed, in stating that express words would be required to remove the right of access to the courts, Laws J in *Witham* effectively gave notice that there were certain rights in defence of which the judiciary would be prepared to suspend the doctrine of implied repeal, an approach that, as we shall see, is actually more radical than that of the HRA itself. The essential problem with this situation was that, with the exception of certain established categories, it was very difficult to know when a judge would decide that a given right was sufficiently firmly 'embedded' in the common law to justify the imposition of such strong legislative presumptions. Privacy, for example, was clearly not such a right, at least according to earlier decisions like *Malone* (1979).

Moreover, where the ultra vires approach used in *Simms* and *Witham* could not plausibly be used, and the approach had to be framed in terms of *Wednesbury*, the attempt to utilise judicial review to provide a strong defence of rights outside the context of freedom of expression and access to a court met with flat rejection from the higher judiciary, which continued to take the view that the *weight* to be afforded to competing interests, including any human rights, was primarily for the decision-maker, although the courts would scrutinise the decision with somewhat greater care where human rights were at stake (*Ministry of Defence ex p Smith* (1996)). The rejection of Laws J's approach at first instance in *Cambridge Health Authority ex p B* (1995) by the Court of Appeal was a stark example.

Thus, the pre-HRA position revealed great potential in the law of judicial review for greater rights protection and some manifestation of that potential. But, it also revealed divisions within the judiciary, uncertainty as to which rights will merit strong protection and disagreement as to how strong that protection should be. In some cases, such as *ex p Smith*, the rhetoric of rights yielded barely any greater protection in practice than the old *Wednesbury* approach. Moreover, there are cases on the books in which may be found refusals even to recognise the existence of the claimed right (privacy in *Malone* (1979)) or, less extremely, denials of any duty to modify the traditional grounds of review to ensure rights protection (*Secretary of State for the Environment ex p Nalgo* (1993)). Consistency and coherence were conspicuously lacking.[13]

How far then was this situation remedied by the introduction of the HRA? It is suggested that six key changes have been brought about. These are considered in turn, with discussion of relevant case law where necessary.

First of all, the Act, by incorporating the ECHR, has made it clear which rights are recognised as fundamental; this is no longer left to the views of individual judges. Second, the Convention spells out the permissible grounds for derogating from the rights. Although the exceptions to Arts 8–11 are expressed in very broad and general terms, Arts 3 and 6 have no express exceptions, whilst Arts 2, 4 and 5 permit only tightly defined and narrow exceptions. Moreover, even in relation to the rights with generalised exceptions (Arts 8–11), at least some of the detailed work in elucidating the appropriate

---

13 Note, in relation to the common pitfall noted above, how the answer has already authoritatively summarised the key relevant point to be derived from nine decided cases.

balance between particular rights and particular exceptions has been done by the ECHR; such jurisprudence has to be taken into account by UK judges (s 2 of the HRA). Moreover, dicta in *Alconbury* (2001) instruct the courts that they should follow the 'clear and settled' case law of the ECHR, save in exceptional circumstances, still the basic approach to the Strasbourg case law in 2012.

Third, and perhaps most importantly of all, s 6(1) of the HRA makes it clear beyond doubt that infringement of a Convention right will, per se, render an administrative decision or provision in delegated legislation unlawful, unless the enabling legislation clearly allows for or mandates the infringement (s 6(2)). Thus, there is now no uncertainty as to whether Convention rights are restraints upon broad discretions, mandatory considerations or even optional considerations, although as we shall see in a moment, that straightforward provision has given rise to a surprising amount of difficulty for the judiciary.

Fourth, the pre-HRA doubts as to whether legislation can be presumed not to give power to infringe rights has been dispelled: in accordance with s 3(1) of the HRA, past and future legislation has to be read and given effect in a way that is compatible with Convention rights, if this is possible, although incompatible legislation remains valid and of full effect (s 3(2) and s 4). The decisions in *A* (2001) and *AF (No 3)* (2009) has made it clear that this very powerful rule of construction is to be applied rigorously, and may allow for the implication of words into statutory provisions, as well as strained readings of statutory language. *Re W and B (Children) (Care Order)* (2002) has tempered the strongly activist stance taken in *A* by clarifying that the courts may not effectively read entirely new provisions into statutes. It is fair to say that decisions on s 3(1) have not removed all uncertainty as to its scope (cf e.g. *Ghaidan v Mendoza* (2004) with *Bellinger v Bellinger* (2003)). How far s 3(1) allows the judiciary to go has not therefore been wholly settled. But the position is still far clearer than before the HRA.

The fifth effect of the Act is that it is no longer necessary to 'tag' human rights arguments onto existing grounds, such as ultra vires or *Wednesbury*, as in the cases discussed above. Section 7 of the HRA provides for proceedings against public authorities simply on the basis that they have infringed Convention rights.[14]

The final effect of the HRA is not as clear-cut. On the face of it, the wording of s 6(1), 'It is unlawful for a public authority to act in a way that is inconsistent with a Convention right,' meant that questions of whether rights have been violated become a matter of statutory construction of the Convention and its case law: thus, so it appeared, the question would be a hard-edged legal one, for determination by judges. There would be no more division between a primary decision by the decision-maker and a secondary review of it by the courts: the issue of infringement would be one in relation to which the

---

14   This simple but key point is often missed by students when discussing the significance of the HRA.

courts must substitute their judgment of the matter for that of the decision-maker. So, at least, one would think from a straightforward reading of s 6(1) (see, for example, Leigh [2002] PL 265). However, the position, it turns out, is more muddy than that, and a great deal of case law has followed on the tricky issue of judicial deference when applying the proportionality test required by many of the **Convention** rights. Some early judgments seemed intent on watering down s 6(1) into merely a modified *Wednesbury* test (e.g. *Mahmood* (2001). However, in *Daly* (2001), Lord Bingham said clearly that 'domestic courts must *themselves* form a judgment whether a Convention right has been breached', while Lord Steyn stressed that under the **Convention** proportionality test, the courts were required to assess the balance struck by the decision-maker between the primary right and the competing interests, looking at the previously forbidden territory of the *weight* assigned by the decision-maker to the various factors in the balance. *Daly* therefore seemed to have scotched any attempt to equate the protection given under the ECHR with the heightened *Wednesbury* test used in *Smith* (above).

In conclusion, the **HRA** has forcibly plunged the judiciary into the task of interpreting a series of broadly worded guarantees, around which a formidable and complex jurisprudence has already been generated. This has created some inevitable uncertainty as to the detailed accommodation to be made between the rights and their inbuilt exceptions, particularly when further latitude – of as yet uncertain scope – has to be given to the views of the original decision-maker. However, the advent of the **HRA** has firmly dispelled the quite fundamental uncertainties as to the place fundamental rights hold in public law that pertained before its coming into force.[15]

Aim Higher   ★

In questions such as this one, or others on the **HRA**, students aiming for the top marks will venture into the tricky area of judicial deference, or the 'area of discretionary judgment'. Essentially, when the court is deciding whether a given decision, which impacted on a **Convention** right, was proportionate to the aim pursued, it will extend an area of latitude to the body it is reviewing, thus abjuring a rigorous inquiry into proportionality, in deference to the 'area of judgment' or 'discretion' of another body. *DPP ex p Kebilene* (1999) provided an early endorsement of this doctrine, and it has been deployed in many cases since: *Brown v Stott* (2001) was an early important example; it was seen in perhaps its most marked form in *ProLife Alliance* (2003). Effectively, the court affords great weight to the view of the decision-making body itself on the question of proportionality; this can lead it to intervene

---

15 Note how the essay has analysed uncertainties under the common law, and those under the **HRA** *and then* compared the two with each other, reaching a clear evaluative conclusion as between the two.

only where that body has manifestly got the question wrong. This can lead straight back to the approach in *Mahmood* and a dilution of the **Convention** protection. On the other hand, in some cases, it would seem undesirable for the court to rush to substitute its judgment where the matter was primarily one of real expertise, or of a considered social policy choice made by the legislature. Conversely, in cases concerning grave invasions of the core of rights held dear by the judiciary, a rigorous approach towards assessing proportionality has been taken. The outstanding example is *A v Secretary of State* (2004), in which, in the context of the detention without charge of suspected terrorists, the House of Lords firmly rejected the submission of the Attorney General that because national security was in play, the courts should largely defer to the view of the Executive as to what was required to protect it, on democratic grounds. Lord Bingham said, trenchantly, that 'the function of independent judges charged to interpret and apply the law is universally recognised as a cardinal feature of the modern democratic State, a cornerstone of the rule of law itself'. The trouble at present is that some uncertainty has been imported into the application of the **HRA**, in that the courts have made only limited progress in indicating when it is appropriate to apply a wide area of discretion, and when a narrow, or no area; as Lord Steyn observed in *Daly*: 'In law, context is everything.'

Ombudsmen

INTRODUCTION

Questions about the Ombudsman system tend to concentrate on the Parliamentary Commissioner for Administration (referred to here as the Parliamentary Ombudsman or PO), but the Ombudsman system has been extended into a number of areas, including in Scotland and Wales, and, as explained below, does not operate in the same way in each. Therefore, it is necessary to be aware of other Ombudsmen. A knowledge of parliamentary procedures and of the scope of judicial review is valuable in tackling this area, because a typical question might concern the extent to which the Ombudsman system provides remedies for the aggrieved citizen not available by those means. The question most commonly asked concerns the efficacy of the Ombudsman despite the limitations of the system.

Checklist ✔

Students should be familiar with the following areas:

- the provisions of the **Parliamentary Commissioner Act 1967** and the setting up of the Ombudsman system – in particular, the nature of 'maladministration' under **s 10(3)**;

- matters excluded from the scrutiny of the Ombudsman under **Scheds 2** and **3** to the Act;

- the extension of the system – Local Commissioners; Health Service Commissioners; the Parliamentary Commissioner for Northern Ireland; the Scottish and Welsh Ombudsmen;

- the characteristics of the system (which do not apply equally to all Ombudsmen) – lack of direct access, informal procedures, lack of formal remedies, the ability to persuade bodies to make widespread changes in administrative practices;

- the efficacy of the Ombudsman – governmental compliance with recommendations;

- the reforms suggested by the Cabinet Office Review (2000) and the limited government response in Cabinet Office, *Reform of the Public Sector Ombudsmen in England* (2005); the limited reforms made by the Regulatory Reform Order;
- the use of parliamentary procedures as a means of providing redress for maladministration;
- the decision in *R (on the application of Bradley) v Secretary of State for Work and Pensions* (2007).

QUESTION 31

'The constraints on the Parliamentary Commissioner which appear to limit her power are actually a source of strength; if they were lifted, her role would, paradoxically, be less valuable.'

▶ Discuss.

How to Answer this Question

A question concerning the extent to which the Parliamentary Commissioner, or Ombudsman, is effective despite several factors impairing her efficiency is commonly set and is quite straightforward. This question introduces a variation on that theme, as it suggests that the Ombudsman is effective because of the restrictions rather than despite them. However, the issues to be discussed are the same in either case: what are the restrictions and what effect do they have? The further issue that this particular question raises concerns the extent to which the restrictions are beneficial and probably inherent in her role. A distinction could be drawn between such restrictions (if any) and those that are arguably not a necessary concomitant of her role.

Answer Structure

The aim in setting up the Ombudsman system

The nature of 'maladministration'

The matters excluded from scrutiny

The detriment caused by the lack of direct access to the Parliamentary Commissioner for Administration (PO)

The informal procedure adopted by the PO

The lack of coercive remedies available to the PO and the beneficial and detrimental impacts of this

The decision in *R (on the application of Bradley) v Secretary of State for Work and Pensions* (2007)

The impact of reforms suggested by the Cabinet Office Review (2000) – the limited governmental response

ANSWER

In addressing this question, a distinction will be drawn between two types of constraint on the PO: first, those that appear to be a necessary concomitant of her role as presently conceived and which, if removed, would arguably create not only a completely different body but also a less effective one; second, those that, it will be argued, are *not* a necessary concomitant of her office and that impair her efficacy. The thrust of the argument will be that on the whole, contrary to the statement to be discussed, constraints on the PO weaken her efficacy, although it will be agreed that some are indeed a source of strength.

It will first be necessary to consider the role the PO was set up to fulfil. The system was set up under the **Parliamentary Commissioner Act 1967** as a result of the perception that arose after the Crichel Down affair in 1954 that pre-existing judicial and parliamentary remedies did not provide adequate redress for members of the public who had suffered as a result of maladministration in central government. The PO was given the ability to investigate a wider range of complaints than could be investigated in a court and given greater investigative powers than those available to MPs. She is empowered to consider 'maladministration' (under s 10(3) of the Act) as opposed to illegality. 'Maladministration' was described by Richard Crossman as 'bias, neglect, inattention, delay, incompetence, ineptitude, perversity, turpitude, arbitrariness and so on'. Although these words are wide, they suggest a limitation of the role in that the PO is, on the whole, concerned with procedural defects rather than with the merits of a decision. This distinction is contained in s 12(3) of the **1967 Act**, which provides that the PO may not investigate the merits of a decision taken without maladministration.

It must not be forgotten that once maladministration is found, it must be shown that it caused 'injustice' (s 10(3)). It was recently clarified in the case of *Parliamentary Commissioner for Administration ex p Balchin (No 2)* (2000) that 'injustice' is specifically *not* limited to identifiable loss or damage, but includes 'a sense of outrage caused by unfair or incompetent administration'.[1]

However, there are a number of limitations on the powers of the PO that, it will be argued, are *not* inherent in the nature of her office and *do* impair her efficacy. She is unable to investigate at all in certain areas. The bodies affected by the Act, which are set out in **Sched 2**, do not include public corporations, tribunals, the Criminal Injuries Compensation Board or, crucially, the police (although the Independent Police Complaints Commission now provides a robust mechanism for police complaints). The system has been expanded to cover the National Health Service and local authorities – Local Commissioners were established in 1974. Prior to 1987, the PO's jurisdiction was limited

---

1   It is important to remember that both maladministration *and* injustice must be shown.

to central government departments and agencies, but the **Parliamentary and Health Service Commissioners Act 1987** amended the **1967 Act** in order to add about fifty non-departmental public bodies (NDPBs) such as the Arts Council and the Equal Opportunities Commission to its remit. In 2006 the PO acquired a new area of work, in hearing complaints from victims of crime in relation to the criminal justice system under the new Victims Code (2006).

The **Scotland Act 1998** requires the Scottish Parliament to legislate for the creation of an Ombudsman to investigate actions of the Scottish Executive (s 91), and the **Scottish Public Services Ombudsman Act 2002** created an Ombudsman with a much broader remit than the PO, encompassing the devolved institutions, local government and the Scottish NHS. In relation to Northern Ireland, an Assembly Ombudsman was established under the **Northern Ireland Act 1998** (see SI 1996/1298 (NI 8)) and one for Wales in the **Public Services Ombudsman (Wales) Act 2005**. In relation to the UK PO, certain matters, set out in Sched 3 to the Act, are excluded from investigation. These include extradition and fugitive offenders, the investigation of crime by or on behalf of the Home Office, security of the State, action in matters relating to contractual or commercial activities, court proceedings and personnel matters of the armed forces, teachers, the Civil Service or police. The government has always resisted the extension of the Ombudsman system into these areas.

Of these restrictions, those attracting the most criticism have been the exclusion of contractual and commercial matters and of public service personnel matters, although, as Seneviratne notes (*Ombudsmen in the Public Sector*, 1994), in practice, this exception 'has accounted for few rejections [of complaints to the PO], perhaps because its scope has been limited by successive POs who have decided that a service does not become commercial [merely] because a charge is made for it' (p 23). A further important limitation, the system of making the complaint through a Member of Parliament, has been much criticised: it is thought that this 'screening' of complaints does not serve the best interests of complainants. The screening of complaints by MPs either before or after the PO receives them could arguably undermine the importance of the PO as a means of making up for the inefficacy of some parliamentary procedures. The involvement of MPs in the process may mean that complaints which should lead to investigation in the department in question are dealt with through inadequate parliamentary procedures. This system does not, moreover, encourage citizens to complain directly to the PO and, due to her low profile, many will in any event be unaware that a complaint is possible. The Cabinet Review (2000), the PO herself and the Public Administration Committee in 2000 and its 4th and 10th Reports of 2009–10 all recently agreed that the MP filter has outlived its usefulness and that its removal was long overdue. It is noteworthy that there is no equivalent filter in the **Scottish Public Services Ombudsman Act 2002**, nor in the equivalent legislation for Wales (above). But no government has so far found time to remove it – no pledge to do so appears in the Coalition Agreement.

A further limitation on the role of the PO arises due to the lack of power to award a remedy. The PO can neither order compensation nor apply to a court to enforce her findings (although see below on judicial review); compliance is therefore voluntary. The remedies recommended vary: *ex gratia* payments to individuals adversely affected by maladministration appear to be made in roughly half the cases in which the PO makes a finding against the department concerned (in 92 out of 177 cases in 1992, and in 108 cases out of 236 in 1995). However, although this inability to award compulsory remedies might appear to weaken the PO severely, it is arguable that the need for such a limitation is inherent in the role. If the PO could award remedies, it would be hard to avoid making the investigative proceedings more formalised so as to give the body complained of a full opportunity to answer the allegations made. Probably, some of the procedures would have to be conducted in public. The fact that the PO operates informally and privately has been thought to enhance her powers of persuasion.[2]

Furthermore, research indicates that the influence of the PO is far greater in practice than her limited formal powers might suggest. Writing in 1994, Rodney Austin noted that 'Whitehall's record of compliance with the nonbinding recommendations of the Ombudsman is actually outstanding: on only two occasions have government departments refused to accept the PO's findings and, in both cases, the PO's recommendations were [nevertheless] complied with' ('Freedom of information: the constitutional impact', in Jowell and Oliver (eds), *The Changing Constitution*, 1994, p 443). Since this was written, the government rejected the adverse findings of the PO's report on the blight caused by the Channel Tunnel Rail Link (HC 193, 1994–95); although faced with unanimous Select Committee backing for the PO's findings (HC 270, 1994–95), the relevant department did eventually agree to award some *ex gratia* compensation to some of those affected, although without admitting any fault. However, one may note three further recent rejections by the government of PO findings. The first related to a report entitled *A Debt of Honour* (July 2005), dealing with *ex gratia* payments to former British civilian internees in the Far East. However, while initially rejecting the PO's findings, the government eventually relented, and by the time the PO produced her annual report for 2006, she was able to report that the MOD had agreed to expand the eligibility criteria for compensation. The second instance related to a systemic problem with occupational pensions, in which 125,000 people lost significant parts of their pensions, due, the PO found, to government maladministration (Select Committee on Public Administration, 6th Report, 2005–06). Her recommendation that the government consider restoring benefits to those affected, was at first brusquely rejected by the government, but by the end of December 2007, the government relented and put in place compensatory measures that the PO described as amounting to full compliance with her report. The

---

2   Points like this are key in responding directly to the 'paradox' posed in the Introduction.

collapse of Equitable Life provoked a major conflict with the PO: the previous government rejected many of the PO's findings of maladministration and refused to implement her suggested compensation scheme. In this case the impasse was broken by a change of government: the Coalition Government accepted all 10 of the PO's findings of maladministration and established an independent commission to allocate compensation, although a group set up by those who had lost their pensions contested the £1.5 billion made available as compensation. However, the decision in *R (on the application of Bradley) v Secretary of State for Work and Pensions* (2008) adds teeth to findings of the PO. It concerned the PO report on pensions mentioned above. The Secretary of State's rejection of her findings was challenged by a number of individuals by way of judicial review. The Court of Appeal found that the Secretary of State had been wrong to reject some of the PO's findings and must reconsider. It put forward the test that where a minister rejected a PO finding, he or she must do so for 'cogent reasons'. It was just before the Department's appeal to the Court of Appeal that it agreed to implement the PO's findings, indicating that the legal proceedings acted as an effective means of indirect enforcement: moreover, the general finding that PO findings may only be rejected for good reason will make it far harder for departments simply to disregard compelling findings of maladministration in future.[3]

It may be said that accepting the need to appear reasonably emollient is endemic in the PO system and even desirable, as being more likely to allow its persuasive powers to take effect. Probably, the need to do so is inherent in the role of the PO as currently conceived, but it is arguable that it is not a necessary part of it. If, for example, members of the public could contact the PO directly, and if her role were publicised, she might feel more able to incur the displeasure of government departments because she would be supported by public opinion.

Thus, although the PO at present has arguably evolved a limited role for herself as a gentle instrument of change that may represent a departure from the role it was hoped she would fulfil, it is submitted that this was not inevitable but occurred due to some of the constraints that were imposed externally. In this respect, a distinction should be drawn between allotting the PO formal powers to award coercive remedies that, as argued above, might well detract from her efficacy, and removing certain of the limitations on her, particularly as regards direct public access. The removal of such limitations would, it is submitted, lead to a bolder approach and would benefit the people she is expected to serve.

---

3   This important case should always be mentioned in answers dealing with the effectiveness of the PO.

Common Pitfalls

Generally, the problem with answers on the Ombudsman is simply that they are too general. Since this topic is quite straightforward, and it is hard to make conceptually more sophisticated points, as an examiner you often find yourself reading a series of essays or exam answers that are very similar to each other. A poor essay simply describes the system, setting out its basic features but without giving any real examples to back up the points made.

Aim Higher

This is an example of the use of such detail. In relation to the restricted access to the PO, students could give some comparative figures on the numbers of people who make complaints. The current lack of direct access to the PO may account for the very small number of complaints received in comparison with the number of administrative decisions taken. The Select Committee on the PO, in its 1994 Report (HC 64, 1993–94), noted the far greater volume of complaints received in a sample year, 1991, by Ombudsmen in countries with far smaller populations than the UK: the Danish Ombudsmen, catering for a population of five million, received 2,000 complaints; the Swedish Ombudsmen, 4,000 complaints (population eight million); while the UK Ombudsmen, from a population of 55 million, received at that time only 766 complaints. These figures are striking. Moreover, the majority of complaints are rejected as being outside the jurisdiction of the PO, or for some other reason. The caseload of the PO has only been one sixth of what was anticipated, although it continues to rise quite sharply, climbing to 1,933 in 1996 and levelling out at 1,721 in 2001 and 1,853 in 2005 (parliamentary cases only).

QUESTION 32

'In a number of respects, the Parliamentary Ombudsman has proved more effective as a means of providing redress for the citizen mistreated by government authorities than have judicial and parliamentary remedies.'

▶ Discuss.

How to Answer this Question

This is a more straightforward question than the last. It again raises the question of whether the Ombudsman system is effective, but it is of wider scope as it: (a) includes a comparison with two other means of redress; and (b) concerns the whole of the Ombudsman system, not just the Parliamentary Commissioner for Administration (PO). It must be remembered that, in some respects, certain Ombudsmen may be more effective than others in comparison with other available remedies.

Answer Structure

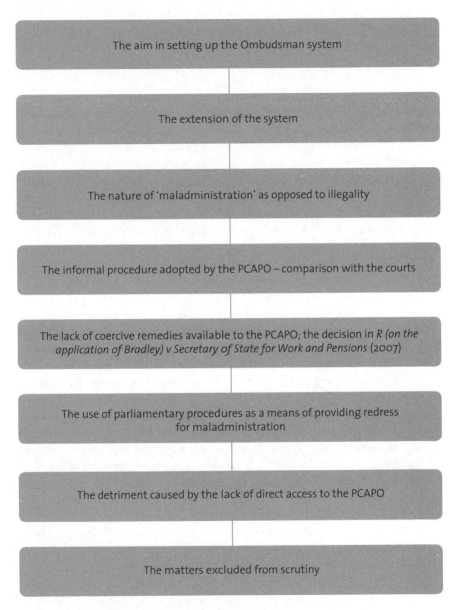

The aim in setting up the Ombudsman system

The extension of the system

The nature of 'maladministration' as opposed to illegality

The informal procedure adopted by the PCAPO – comparison with the courts

The lack of coercive remedies available to the PCAPO; the decision in *R (on the application of Bradley) v Secretary of State for Work and Pensions* (2007)

The use of parliamentary procedures as a means of providing redress for maladministration

The detriment caused by the lack of direct access to the PCAPO

The matters excluded from scrutiny

The matters above should be considered in your answer.

ANSWER

In addressing this question, it should be borne in mind that the Ombudsman system was not set up as a replacement for other remedies, but in order to remedy their deficiencies and to fill gaps they created. It will be argued that although the system does have advantages over pre-existing judicial and parliamentary remedies, its limitations mean that it is hampered in fulfilling its aims. As the statement applies to the whole of the Ombudsman system, it will be argued that in some respects, certain Ombudsmen may be more effective than others in comparison with other available remedies.

The PO was set up under the **Parliamentary Commissioner Act 1967** as a result of the perception that arose after the Crichel Down affair in 1954 that pre-existing judicial and parliamentary remedies did not provide adequate redress for members of the public who had suffered as a result of maladministration in central government. Thus, defective administrative action was going unremedied either because it fell outside the jurisdiction of the courts or because MPs did not have sufficient powers to investigate it satisfactorily. In providing a further means of investigating complaints, the intention was that the PO would not only uncover maladministration, but would also enable civil servants wrongly accused of maladministration to clear their names. The Ombudsman system has been extended to the NHS, to Northern Ireland and to Scotland and Wales, under devolution. In being required to consider 'maladministration' (under s 10(3) of the 1967 Act) as opposed to illegality, Ombudsmen are empowered to investigate a wider range of complaints than could be investigated by a court. A court can intervene in judicial review proceedings only where a decision is ultra vires, or where it is considered *Wednesbury* unreasonable, or where there has been a breach of natural justice or a breach of rights protected under the **European Convention on Human Rights (ECHR)**, as incorporated into UK law via the **Human Rights Act 1998 (HRA)** (s 6(1)). Alternatively, in some instances, there may be a statutory right of appeal to a tribunal. 'Maladministration' may cover some instances that would give rise to redress in a court or tribunal, but it goes further than that. It has been described as 'bias, neglect, inattention, delay, incompetence, ineptitude, perversity, turpitude, arbitrariness and so on' (Richard Crossman in the debate on the **Parliamentary Commissioner Bill 1967**). Where a court or tribunal could consider such defective administration, the PO will not investigate the matter unless it would not be reasonable to expect the complainant to seek redress in litigation.

Although maladministration is a wide concept, it does mean that the PO is broadly concerned with procedural defects rather than with the merits of a decision. This distinction is contained in s 12(3) of the 1967 Act, which provides that the PO may not investigate the merits of a decision taken without maladministration.

Procedurally, the Ombudsman system may have advantages over a court hearing: its informality in investigation may be more effective at times in discovering the truth than the adversarial system in the courts. It is also, of course, free to use. Moreover, in court, the Crown may plead public interest immunity to avoid disclosing documents; in contrast, the PO can look at all departmental files. Such flexibility is also reflected in the fact that the Ombudsman procedure is not circumscribed by rules as regards time limits, and therefore may provide a remedy in instances which cannot be considered by a court.[4]

On the other hand, unlike a court, the PO lacks the power to award a remedy, although *ex gratia* payments to individuals may at times be made. In some situations, this lack might be said to amount to a weakness in the PO system. However, although the lack of formal power to award a remedy might appear to weaken the PO severely, it is arguable that the need for such a limitation is inherent in the role. If the PO could award remedies, it would be hard to avoid making the investigative proceedings more formalised, so as to give the body complained of a full opportunity to answer the allegations made. Probably, some of the procedure would have to be conducted in public. The fact that the PO operates informally and privately has been thought to enhance her powers of persuasion. Moreover, the decision in *R (on the application of Bradley) v Secretary of State for Work and Pensions* (2007) adds teeth to findings of the PO. It concerned the PO report finding maladministration by the Department for Work and Pensions in relation to people who had lost benefits through the winding up of final salary pensions schemes, partly, it was found, because of misinformation provided by the Department. The Secretary of State's rejection of the PO's findings was challenged by a number of individuals by way of judicial review. The Court of Appeal found that the Secretary of State had been wrong to reject some of the PO's findings and must reconsider. It put forward the test that where a minister rejected a PO finding, he or she must do so for 'cogent reasons'. It was just before the Department's appeal to the Court of Appeal that it agreed to implement the PO's findings, indicating that the legal proceedings acted as an effective means of indirect enforcement; moreover, the general finding that PO findings may only be rejected for good reason will make it far harder for departments simply to disregard compelling findings of maladministration in future.

When the Commissioner for Complaints in Northern Ireland finds that an individual has sustained injustice as a result of maladministration, the individual concerned can apply to the county court under s 7(2) of the **Commissioner for Complaints Act (Northern Ireland) 1969**, which may award damages at its discretion. The new Welsh Ombudsman (above) may, if he or she is satisfied that a public authority has disregarded a report served on it without lawful excuse, issue a certificate to that effect to the High Court (s 20).[5] It has been suggested by Birkinshaw and Lewis (*When Citizens Complain*, 1993) that giving the Local Government Ombudsman (LGO) powers to enforce their findings would imperil their relationship with local authorities which, they fear, would become defensive and 'minimalist' in their responses to LGO recommendations; the current practice of negotiating the response of the authorities in a consensual and informal way

---

4 It is important to set out clearly and with sufficient detail the advantages of the PO system over court remedies.

5 These form cogent counter-examples to the argument that it is inherent in the role of the PO that her recommendations are *not* enforceable.

would be placed in jeopardy (p 39). In response to this, it may be argued that even if the LGO were given enforcement powers, consensual methods would still be used; that they would still be, and would be presented as being very much the norm; that court action would be kept largely out of mind, seen as an exceptional and rare last resort. Overall, however, the Cabinet Office Review (2000) drew favourable conclusions as to the work of the LGO (para 1.5): 'Stage II of the Financial Management and Policy Review of the CLA in 1996, which drew on polls by MORI in 1995, concluded that the work of the LGO was generally well respected by complainants, their advisers and local authorities; although there was widespread concern about delays. A survey by MORI of complainants to the LGO in 1999 reported "a broadly encouraging improvement from the 1995 survey".'

It may be concluded that where a body is susceptible to informal persuasion, this method has advantages over litigation as a means of improving administrative procedures. Otherwise, it is arguably desirable to make the Ombudsman's recommendations enforceable in the courts, on the basis that it would be worth the risk of damaging the relationship between her and the body in question in order to bring about such enhancement of her power; the *Bradley* decision appears to bring this position closer to reality. It is worth noting in this respect that the Cabinet Office review recommended that the Ombudsman should continue to work by persuasion, rather than having the power to award compulsory remedies. Aside from the reasons canvassed above, it was feared that if the Commissioner had such a power, it could become subject to Art 6 of the ECHR, thus imposing a more formal, court-like procedure.[6]

Thus, the statement that the Ombudsman system offers advantages that litigation does not, has some substance but needs qualification. On the other hand, there are clear advantages for the aggrieved citizen in using the Ombudsman service rather than relying on an MP to resolve the problem. Although MPs are of course able to hear a wide range of complaints, their powers of investigation are limited. The PO in contrast has wide powers of investigation. Under s 7 of the 1967 Act, she may examine all documents relevant to the investigation, and the duty to assist her overrides the duty to maintain secrecy under the Official Secrets Acts. Furthermore, MPs may be hampered or may appear to be hampered by their political allegiance, in contrast to the Ombudsman, who is independent. Although MPs may not know the political allegiance of a constituent who makes a complaint regarding the activities of central government and might, in any event, be uninfluenced by it, the constituent might assume that the complaint would be more forcibly pursued by an Opposition MP.

Parliamentary procedures such as questions and select committees are plainly less efficacious than the Ombudsman. Such procedures operate within the doctrine of ministerial responsibility; in other words, the expectation is that the minister in question

---

6   Here, as in other places, the Cabinet Office Review is important, and should be cited in essays of this sort.

will remedy matters. The PO, on the other hand, looks behind that expectation and considers the workings of the administrative body itself. The PO's procedure can be more flexible than that of a select committee due to its informal, private nature and may get closer to the root of a problem.

However, although the Ombudsman system may offer an effective means of redress to citizens who manage to invoke it, many citizens who need to do so cannot get access to it either because they do not know of its existence or because, having contacted an MP with a complaint, the MP decides not to refer the complaint on to the PO. The PO cannot be contacted directly by a citizen, because it is thought that to allow such contact would be to undermine the constitutional principle that an MP should defend the citizen against the Executive.

Even if a complaint is referred to the PO, it may be rejected as being outside her jurisdiction. The PO cannot investigate bodies that are not ultimately under ministerial control. Moreover, certain matters, set out in Sched 3 to the 1967 Act, are excluded from investigation. These include extradition and fugitive offenders, the investigation of crime by or on behalf of the Office, security of the State, action in matters relating to contractual or commercial activities, court proceedings and personnel matters of the armed forces, teachers, the Civil Service or police (although the Independent Police Complaints Commission now provides a robust mechanism for police complaints).

Therefore, as a system, the Ombudsman has many limitations; its informal procedures can be effective in securing change, but at the same time, in comparison with litigation, may lead to problems of enforcement. It certainly provides a valuable rectificatory alternative to the aggrieved citizen.

Protection for Human Rights: the Human Rights Act

INTRODUCTION

The Human Rights Act 1998 (HRA) does not provide the only means of protecting human rights and liberties in the UK, but it is the central piece of legislation in the field. The Act has now been in force for thirteen years (it came into force in 2000), so it is possible to make an interim assessment as to its efficacy in protecting human rights and freedoms in the UK. It affords further effect to a number of the rights protected under the European Convention on Human Rights (ECHR). It remains a controversial piece of legislation; for example, in 2006, in a distorted and misleading fashion, parts of the media blamed it for weakening the UK in its 'war' against terrorism, and for the early release of criminals. Prior to the 2010 general election the Conservative Party stated that its policy was to repeal the Act if a Conservative government was elected, and to replace it with a 'British Bill of Rights'. Once the current Coalition Government was in place, this policy became problematic since the Liberal Democrats were pledged to retain the HRA. An independent Commission was appointed to examine the possibility of repealing the HRA and introducing a Bill of Rights in its place. The intention appears to be to ensure that a new Bill of Rights provides as much protection for human rights as the HRA does. It is likely that there will be a long period of consultation before such a Bill of Rights is put in place, and it is unlikely that this will occur before the 2015 general election. If – which remains a matter of doubt – eventually a Bill of Rights is enacted, it would presumably protect the Convention rights that are currently protected under the HRA, so the respect in which it would sharply differ from the HRA is currently unclear. It might be made weaker than the HRA in certain respects – for example, s 3 HRA might be reproduced in the new statute, but modified to discourage judges from taking a radical approach to rendering statutory provisions compatible with Convention rights through creative interpretation. It is also possible that s 2 HRA might undergo 'weakening' to allow the UK courts to depart from Strasbourg rulings more readily.

In this forensic climate, in which the HRA remains controversial, it is important to examine the background to the Human Rights Act and to look carefully at what it can and cannot do. Its effects in fields ranging well beyond those of criminal justice or terrorism may need to be considered.

The very first edition of this book dealt in considerable detail with the Bill of Rights debate pre-1998, the advantages and disadvantages of a written human rights guarantee and the deficiencies of the European Convention on Human Rights (ECHR). It also considered the various human rights enforcement mechanisms. The reception of the Convention into UK law via the Human Rights Act 1998 has rendered that debate partly defunct, but knowledge of the history of the Convention in the UK remains essential to an understanding of the background to the HRA, and the legal context that it should be placed in. Political and public support for some form of Bill of Rights grew overwhelming by the mid-1990s, but the resulting statute, the HRA, bears the marks of several compromises. Further, the Bill of Rights debate has been resurrected by the Conservative pledge on repeal of the HRA just mentioned, and the whole issue of possible repeal of the HRA may begin to appear on exam papers in 2013 and beyond.

Essay questions tend to centre mainly upon the status of the ECHR in UK law, its effectiveness as a human rights guarantee and the improvements in domestic human rights protection, which had already resulted from it and will be likely to result from its introduction. Questions are likely to ask you to consider the way in which the courts have dealt with the interpretation over the first 10 years of its life of the key sections of the Act – ss 3 and 6; they are also likely to focus on gaps and inadequacies in both the Convention and the 1998 Act. Now that the HRA has been fully in force for 12 years, commentary on the relevant case law will be expected. The role of the judges has now come under fresh scrutiny, since they hold an important and enhanced role as human rights watchdogs, yet under the HRA lack the ultimate power of striking down legislation that breaches the Convention. Questions may ask you to consider whether they should have been granted that power. Many different styles of essay question are possible on this large and wide-ranging topic; the following questions cover most of the debate at the time of writing. Certain relevant issues are also touched on in other chapters.

Checklist ✔

Students must be familiar with the following areas and their interrelationships:

- the legal protection for civil liberties before the introduction of the **HRA** and the former difficulties of relying on the **ECHR** in UK courts;

- the drive towards incorporation of the **Convention (ECHR)** and the reasons for introducing the **HRA**;

- the doctrine of parliamentary sovereignty;

- the key provisions of the **HRA** and the **Convention**, especially **ss 2, 3, 4, 6, 10, 12,** and **Arts 3, 5, 6, 8, 10,** and **11**;

- key case law on the **Convention**;

- key **HRA** cases, especially on **ss 3** and **6**;

- the current possibility of favoured by Cameron, of repealing the **HRA** and replacing it with a Bill of Rights.

QUESTION 33

Critically examine the implications of introducing the Human Rights Act 1998, in terms of providing an effective protection for human rights, emphasising the interpretations of ss 3 and 6 in recent cases.

How to Answer this Question

This is a reasonably straightforward essay question, which is commonly set. However, it is important that the answer should not degenerate into a list of advantages and disadvantages of the Human Rights Act 1998 (HRA) and the European Convention on Human Rights (ECHR). The implications include: a comparison with the previous situation; the changed role of judges; the impact on public authorities; the change that may be caused by s 3 in relation to interpretation of statutory provisions that raise human rights issues. A number of the significant decisions on ss 3 and 6 must be examined, indicating how far the HRA's protection for the ECHR rights has been enhanced or diminished by them. One further implication, which should be touched on briefly, is the choice of the HRA mechanism as opposed to the introduction of a Bill of Rights on the US model.

Answer Structure

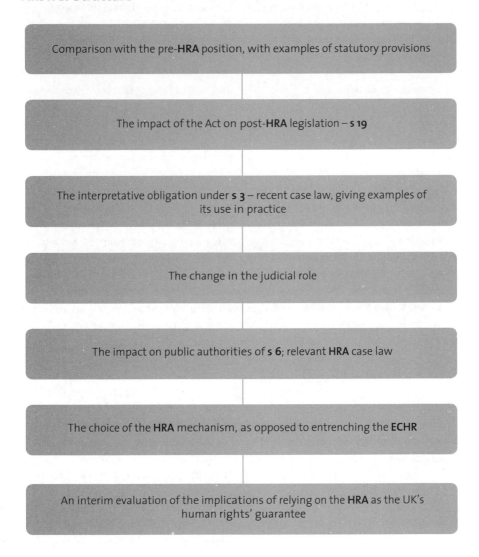

Comparison with the pre-**HRA** position, with examples of statutory provisions

The impact of the Act on post-**HRA** legislation – **s 19**

The interpretative obligation under **s 3** – recent case law, giving examples of its use in practice

The change in the judicial role

The impact on public authorities of **s 6**; relevant **HRA** case law

The choice of the **HRA** mechanism, as opposed to entrenching the **ECHR**

An interim evaluation of the implications of relying on the **HRA** as the UK's human rights' guarantee

ANSWER

Until 1998, the precarious and disorderly state of civil liberties and human rights in the UK created a strong argument in favour of the adoption of some form of Bill of Rights. The law sought to protect certain values, such as the need to maintain public order but, in doing so, curtailed the exercise of certain freedoms because nothing prevented it from disregarding them. Thus, human rights (recognised as 'liberties' in the UK) had a precarious status, in that they only existed, by deduction, in the interstices of the law. For example, the Public Order Act 1986 contains extensive provisions in ss 12 and 14 that allow stringent conditions to be imposed on marches and assemblies. They are not balanced by any provision in the 1986 Act that takes account of the need to protect freedom of assembly.

This essay will argue that the ECHR, as afforded further effect in domestic law by the Human Rights Act 1998 (HRA), appears to provide a better safeguard than the previous reliance placed upon executive reluctance to use rights-infringing provisions to the full, with Parliament's consent. In contrast to the previous situation, the HRA now represents a minimum guarantee of freedom. The HRA allows Parliament to pass legislation incompatible with the Convention rights (see s 19(1)(b), s 6(2) and s 3(2)), but it is notable that so far in the first decade of the HRA only one Bill has been presented to Parliament unaccompanied by a statement of its compatibility with the rights – the Bill that became the Communications Act 2003. Formally speaking, citizens of the UK post- HRA no longer have to rely upon the ruling party to ensure that its own legislation does not infringe freedoms. They can at least be sure that the government has made some effort to ensure that a Bill is Convention-compliant before it becomes an Act of Parliament. If, despite the statement of compatibility under s 19 HRA, statutory provisions are passed that conflict with some fundamental Convention guarantee, courts now have to interpret such provisions in order to bring them into compliance with the Convention if at all possible under s 3 of the HRA (see R v A (No 2) (2001)). They must also do so in respect of pre-HRA statutes.

In satisfying the obligation under s 3 they must take account of ECHR jurisprudence under s 2, to determine to what extent, if at all, the rights may justifiably be curtailed and decide whether the provision in question goes further in curtailing a right than can be justified. Section 3 goes well beyond resolving ambiguity in legislation in favour of the Convention-compliant interpretation and has received a fairly generous interpretation in the courts (see Ghaidan v Mendoza (2004); AF No 3 (2009)). Under s 3 HRA, words can even be read into a statute in order to achieve Convention-compliance (Ghaidan and R v A), so long as the changes do not oppose a pervasive feature of the statute (R (on the application of Anderson) v Secretary of State for the Home Dept (2002)). This stance was taken in Re S and Re W (2002); as Kavanagh argues, the courts demonstrated that although they are prepared to read words into statutes, as in R v A, they will not do so, 'as a way of radically reforming a whole statute'. The position under s 3 is in strong contrast to the prior situation, where the courts had no choice but to apply a provision of an Act of Parliament, no matter how much it might breach the Convention if it unambiguously expressed Parliament's intention to allow such a breach.

If, having striven to achieve compatibility under s 3, it is found to be impossible, a court of sufficient seniority can issue a declaration of incompatibility (s 4), although it will merely have to go on to apply the law in question (see H v Mental Health Tribunal, North and East London Region and Another (2001)). If a court does issue a declaration of incompatibility, the government has so far accepted that it should act promptly to take remedial action – although it does not have to do so (s 10).[1]

Apart from its implications for legislation, public authorities have been greatly affected by the inception of the HRA due to the requirements of s 6. Under s 6, it is unlawful for a public authority to act in a way that is incompatible with a Convention right. This is the main provision giving effect to the Convention rights; rather than full 'incorporation' of the Convention , it is made binding against public authorities. In stark contrast to the previous situation, such bodies act illegally if they fail to abide by the Convention rights. Previously, unless forced impliedly to adhere to a particular right legislatively (for example, under s 58 of the Police and Criminal Evidence Act 1984, imposing on the police, in effect, a duty to abide by one of the implied rights within Art 6(1)), or under the common law, they could disregard the rights in their day-to-day operations with impunity.

Under s 6, public authorities are either 'core' or 'functional'; if the latter, they are only bound by the Convention in relation to their public, not their private, functions.[2] The division between functional public authorities and purely private bodies remains one of the most controversial and difficult matters under the HRA. Obviously its resolution has very strong human rights implications since a person affected by a rights-infringing action of a private body has no cause of action under the HRA, s 7. One of the early leading decisions on this matter was *Poplar Housing & Regeneration Community Association Ltd v Donoghue* (2001). Poplar was set up by Tower Hamlets as a registered social landlord specifically for the purpose of receiving its housing stock. Poplar claimed, inter alia, that it was neither a standard public authority (which the Court of Appeal accepted) nor a body performing a function of a public nature. As to this latter point, Lord Woolf said that an act can be 'public' for HRA purposes where a combination of features is present. Statutory authority for what is done can help to mark the act as being public; so can the extent of control over the function exercised by another body that is a public authority. The Court found that Poplar *was* exercising a public function in relation to the management of the social housing it had taken over from Tower Hamlets because it was so closely associated with Tower Hamlets, a core public authority.

Where no public function has been transferred, the question appears to be whether the function in question should be viewed as inherently private or public, not whether the body in question is a private or public institution (*Parochial Council of the Parish of Aston* (2003)). Focusing on the function rather than the institution is a more generous means of

---

1   Examiners would give credit for candidates who consider other sections of the HRA (especially s 2) as well as ss 3 and 6.

2   Credit would be given for an answer that gives broadly equal time to both ss 3 and 6.

delimiting the concept of a public authority, and therefore may allow for a wider protection for the Convention rights.

A functional approach was adopted in *YL v Birmingham CC* (2007) in relation to the question whether a private care home was a functional public authority. The majority in the Lords noted that the local authority's activities are carried out pursuant to statutory duties and responsibilities imposed by public law and the costs of doing so are met by public funds. In the case of a privately owned care home, it was noted, the manager's duties to its residents are, whether contractual or tortious, duties governed by private law. In relation to those residents who are publicly funded, the local and health authorities become liable to pay charges agreed under private law contracts and for the recovery of which the care home has private law remedies. The recovery by the local authority of a means-tested contribution from the resident is a matter of public law, but is no concern of the care home. On this basis, the House of Lords held, by a 3:2 majority, that private care homes are not discharging a public function and so are not bound by the European Convention on Human Rights, even when they look after clients on behalf of a local authority. That was the view of Lords Scott, Mance and Neuberger. Lord Bingham and Baroness Hale dissented. Thus the *YL* case, now the leading authority, gave a restricted meaning to the term 'public function' under the HRA, meaning that a number of people cannot rely on Convention rights directly against a range of bodies (although as far as private care homes themselves are concerned, *YL* was overturned via statute).

Despite this limitation, the HRA has created a far more active judicial role in protecting basic rights and freedoms. The open-ended nature of the terms of the Convention means that its interpretation is likely to continue to evolve in accordance with the UK's changing needs and social values as it is interpreted and applied by domestic judges (see *Campbell v MGN* (2004)). Incorporation of the Convention under the HRA has already had a number of advantages. Citizens may obtain redress for human rights breaches without needing, except as a last resort, to apply to the European Court of Human Rights (ECtHR) in Strasbourg. This saves a great deal of time and money for the citizen and thus greatly improves access to human rights protection. The range of remedies available under the HRA is the same as in any ordinary UK court case (apart from criminal sanctions), and so includes injunctions and specific performance where appropriate, rather than simply damages. British judges are already making a contribution to the development of a domestic Convention rights jurisprudence (see, for example, *Lambert* (2001), *Offen* (2001), *A and others* (2004), *AF No3* (2009)).

However, the interpretations given by judges to the ECHR have at times diluted its impact greatly. The watering down of Art 6 that occurred in *Brown v Stott* (2001) and of Art 5 in *Gillan* (2006) exemplified this problem. On the other hand, the judges have also shown themselves willing to take an activist stance in protecting the right to liberty: key provisions of the Anti-Terrorism, Crime and Security Act 2001 Pt 4 were declared incompatible with Arts 5 and 14 of the ECHR (protecting the rights to liberty and to freedom from discrimination) by the House of Lords in *A and Ors v Secretary of State for the Home Dept* (2005), in a constitutionally significant, and human rights-oriented decision. So far, this essay has indicated that the HRA is having an impact on the interpretation of legislation and on the operations of a large number of bodies in the UK. But there are limitations on its impact which the *YL* case has exacerbated. Citizens cannot always be certain of being able to rely on their Convention rights domestically.

In conclusion, the HRA is allowing for the incremental improvement of the UK's recognition and enforcement of domestic human rights. Certain weaknesses are identifiable within the HRA 1998 and the Convention, but the method chosen is creating, it is argued, a reasonable compromise between protection for human rights and parliamentary sovereignty. Prior to the inception of the HRA, Parliament was free, at the domestic level, to disregard the ECHR, although it was unlikely to state openly that it was doing so. Under the HRA, failure to adhere to the ECHR is more likely to be drawn to Parliament's attention under s 4 HRA, and the courts, although unable to wield a strike down power as is possible in the USA, can use s 3 to bring legislative provisions into compliance with the ECHR.[3]

Common Pitfalls

Failing to discuss both s 3 and s 6 in detail with reliance on key cases; failing to make some comparison with the pre-**HRA** situation; failing to examine both weaknesses and strengths of the **HRA**.

Aim Higher

It could also be noted that citizens have still at times had to seek a remedy for breach of the **ECHR** at Strasbourg (compare *Gillan* (2006) with *Gillan v UK* (2010)), the very problem that the **HRA** was supposed to address.

QUESTION 34

In terms of enhanced human rights protection, are there arguments in favour of introducing a tailor-made Bill of Rights for the UK as proposed by senior Conservatives prior to and after the 2010 general election, as opposed to relying on the Human Rights Act 1998?

How to Answer this Question

This is a fairly demanding question that requires quite detailed knowledge of the European Convention on Human Rights (ECHR), the Human Rights Act 1998 (HRA), decisions on it and key Convention decisions. It is also necessary to say something about

---

3   Credit would be given for a conclusion that refers back to the title and introduction to the essay.

the possible differences between a Bill of Rights and the HRA in terms of enhanced human rights protection. This is a pertinent question at the present time, as the question indicates, given David Cameron's (Prime Minister) expressed predilection for a 'British Bill of Rights', possibly to be introduced in 2015. You are not expected to discuss specific current plans for a Bill of Rights as these have not yet emerged, but you can refer to the preference to avoid increasing judicial power. This essay asks a straightforward question, and therefore you must come down on one side or the other in principle, albeit while acknowledging the force of the arguments on the other side. The essay below answers the question posed in the negative, but an affirmative answer would be entirely arguable. Further, since the detail of the plans for a Bill of Rights is not available, you should acknowledge that in practice protection for rights might be weakened under it.

Answer Structure

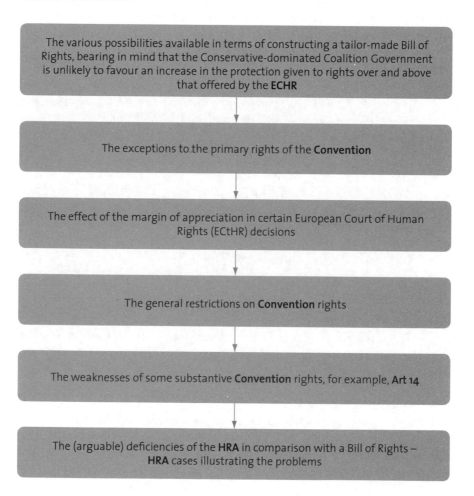

The various possibilities available in terms of constructing a tailor-made Bill of Rights, bearing in mind that the Conservative-dominated Coalition Government is unlikely to favour an increase in the protection given to rights over and above that offered by the ECHR

The exceptions to the primary rights of the Convention

The effect of the margin of appreciation in certain European Court of Human Rights (ECtHR) decisions

The general restrictions on Convention rights

The weaknesses of some substantive Convention rights, for example, Art 14

The (arguable) deficiencies of the HRA in comparison with a Bill of Rights – HRA cases illustrating the problems

ANSWER

The HRA gave the European Convention on Human Rights and Fundamental Freedoms further effect in UK law, as will be discussed, using the mechanism of an ordinary Act of Parliament. It did not seek to entrench its own provisions or the Convention, and it has not introduced any new rights other than those of the Convention. (It may be noted that not all of the Convention rights were included in Sched 1 HRA; Art 1, Art 13 and the Protocols, apart from the First and Sixth ones, were excluded.) The possibility of introducing a tailor-made Bill of Rights was considered but rejected in 1997. This essay will argue that there are arguments in favour of introducing a Bill of Rights that would be unique to the UK, as proposed by the Conservative Party.

The ECHR is a cautious document: it is not as open-textured as the US Bill of Rights and it contains long lists of exceptions to most of the primary rights – exceptions that suggest a strong respect for the institutions of the State. These exceptions have at times received a broad interpretation in the ECtHR and such interpretations are having a strong influence on domestic courts as they apply the rights directly in the domestic arena under the HRA. For example, Art 10, which protects freedom of expression, contains an exception in respect of the protection of morals. This was invoked in the *Handyside* case (1976) in respect of a booklet aimed at schoolchildren that was circulating freely in the rest of Europe. It was held that the UK Government was best placed to determine what was needed in its own country in order to protect morals (application of the margin of appreciation doctrine), and so no breach of Art 10 had occurred.

Since the HRA has now been in force for 12 years, it is possible to come to some conclusions about the response of UK judges under the HRA to interpretations of the Convention rights at Strasbourg. The judges are failing to take the view that they should not apply a particular decision because it has been affected by the margin of appreciation doctrine. Arguably, this stance was taken in the post-HRA cases of *Alconbury* (2001), *Pro-life Alliance* (2002) and *Animal Defenders* (2008). Thus, the watering-down effect at Strasbourg of this doctrine may also be occurring under the HRA. The judges are also giving full weight to the express exceptions under Arts 8–11 of the Convention, even where possibly Strasbourg might have decided on a different outcome. This may be said of *Interbrew SA v Financial Times Ltd* (2002), where the Court of Appeal found that on the facts of the case no protection for a media source need be given. In *R(on the application of Gillan) v Commissioner of Metropolitan Police* (2006), the House of Lords found that, assuming that Arts 8 and 10 were applicable, the exceptions under them were satisfied, without engaging in any proportionality analysis. The Strasbourg Court in contrast found a breach of Art 8 when the case of *Gillan* reached it – *Gillan v UK* (2010).[4]

---

4 It is important to consider instances in which, despite the **HRA**, challenges have succeeded at Strasbourg.

Apart from the express exceptions to Arts 8–11, Strasbourg's interpretation of the reach of the guarantee may leave gaps or uncertainties as to the protection it offers. Now that the ECHR has been incorporated and the interpretative jurisprudence of the ECtHR is being used in domestic cases as a guide (s 2 of the HRA), such exceptions or gaps are tending to offer judges a means of avoiding a controversial conflict with the government, especially in the national security sphere (see, for example, the case of *Secretary of State for the Home Dept v MB* (2007)). Lord Bingham has made it clear that Convention rights should be interpreted domestically to offer as much as the Strasbourg jurisprudence accepts (*Ullah* (2004)). The domestic courts have succeeded in finding exceptions even to rights that appear to be largely unqualified, such as Art 6(1): this was evident in *Brown v Stott* (2001) and in *Alconbury* (2001). They have done so by relying on a case at Strasbourg, *Sporrong and Lonnroth v Sweden* (1982), in which it was said that the search for a balance between individual rights and societal concerns is fundamental to the whole Convention. Thus, it may be argued that the domestic judiciary has explored methods of watering down the rights, which arguably would not be so readily available under a tailor-made Bill of Rights, if the provision appearing to 'anchor' the judges to Strasbourg, s 2 HRA, was weakened.

However, the judges do have an important function under the HRA in giving primacy to the rights, even if, eventually, an exception to a particular right is allowed to prevail. The Strasbourg jurisprudence and the rights themselves make it clear that the exceptions are to be narrowly construed and that the starting point is always the primary right. This is in contrast to the previous position, in which the judges in some instances merely applied the statute in question (e.g. the Public Order Act 1986) without affording much or any recognition to the freedoms it affected. For instance, Art 14 has had an impact on the forms of discrimination that are unlawful in situations where another Convention right or freedom is engaged (*Ghaidan v Mendoza* (2004), *A and Ors v Secretary of State for the Home Dept* (2004)). Strasbourg gave a lead to the UK judges in *A v UK* (2009), granting greater protection for fair trial rights than the domestic judges had done. Thus, curbing the impact of the Strasbourg jurisprudence in a new Bill of Rights would not necessarily lead to enhanced protection for rights since the judges might revert to their traditional deferential stance.

A tailor-made Bill of Rights could contain a more extensive list of rights, including social and economic rights, although it is unlikely that such rights would appeal to a Conservative-dominated government. In particular, it could include a free-standing anti-discrimination guarantee. Art 14 of the ECHR prohibits discrimination on 'any ground such as sex, race, colour, language, religion', but only in relation to any other Convention right or freedom. It has been determined in a string of Strasbourg cases since *X v Federal Republic of Germany* (1970) that Art 14 has no separate existence, but that, nevertheless, a measure that is, in itself, in conformity with the requirement of the Convention right governing its field of law may, however, infringe that Article when it is read in conjunction with Art 14, for the reason that it is discriminatory in nature.

The HRA itself has limitations in terms of enhanced human rights protection. The choice of the HRA as the enforcement mechanism for the ECHR means that the Convention is incorporated into domestic law, but not entrenched on the US model; thus, it could be removed by the simple method of repeal of the HRA, as argued for currently by the Conservative Party. Moreover, the judiciary cannot strike down incompatible legislation. Entrenchment was rejected in order to maintain parliamentary sovereignty and to avoid handing over too much power to the unelected judiciary.[5] This means that Parliament can deliberately legislate in breach of the Convention (ss 19 and 3(2)), and the incompatible legislation will be effective (s 6(2)). It also means that if prior or subsequent legislation is found to breach the Convention in the courts and cannot be rescued from doing so by a creative interpretation under s 3, it must simply be applied (see *H v Mental Health Tribunal, North and East London Region and Anor* (2001)), although a declaration of the incompatibility can be made under s 4, as it was in that instance. In *R(M) v Secretary of State for Health* (2003), a declaration of incompatibility was made in relation to ss 26 and 29 Mental Health Act 1983, but by 2007, the government had failed to introduce remedial legislation.

The key provisions of the Anti-Terrorism, Crime and Security Act 2001 Pt 4 were declared incompatible with Arts 5 and 14 of the ECHR (protecting the rights to liberty and to freedom from discrimination) by the House of Lords in *A and Ors v Secretary of State for the Home Dept* (2004) in relation to persons detained under Pt 4. The government bowed to the pressure and repealed Pt 4. However, as Ewing points out, the decision of the Lords did not lead to the opening of the gates of Belmarsh; the government continued for a time to rely on the incompatible legislative provisions to imprison the detainees. There was no guarantee that the government would act to repeal the provisions. It is clear that citizens cannot always be certain of being able to rely on their Convention rights domestically. An entrenched Bill of Rights (BoR) accompanied by a strike-down power on the US model could provide them with that certainty and, at the sacrifice of parliamentary sovereignty as traditionally understood in the UK, could therefore deliver an enhanced degree of rights protection. However, a Bill of Rights need not be entrenched and it is clearly unlikely that the Coalition Government would adopt this more radical model in relation to a new Bill of Rights since senior Conservatives have made it clear that they do not favour an increase in judicial power under a BoR.

The use of ss 3 and 6 HRA as the means of affording the Convention further effect in domestic law means that there are inherent limitations to the rights protection that the HRA offers. If no statute is applicable in a particular instance, and the rights-infringing body does not have a 'public function' under s 6, a citizen cannot obtain legal protection for his or her Convention right, unless there is an existing common law cause of action

---

5   It is important to indicate that the HRA was always intended to be limited in effect due to the doctrine of parliamentary sovereignty.

that can be utilised via the doctrine of indirect horizontal effect (*Campbell* (2004)) – so far, breach of confidence. Further, even if the citizen could probably obtain redress at Strasbourg in the particular circumstances (see *Kay v Lambeth London Borough Council; Leeds City Council v Price* (2006)), redress can be denied domestically if a House of Lords precedent stands in the way.

In reaching a conclusion on the question posed, it should be borne in mind that the ECHR was never intended to be used as a domestic Bill of Rights, although Klug has argued that the HRA has become In effect a BoR. If a new Bill of Rights was introduced in the UK, then it would be brought into line with the experience of most of the other European signatories. These states already possess codes of rights enshrined in their constitutions, but the majority also adhere to a general practice of incorporation of the ECHR into domestic law, either automatically, as in Switzerland, or upon ratification, as in Luxembourg. A domestic Bill of Rights intended to enshrine the Convention rights, but including certain rights of a specifically UK character, such as a right of jury trial, could potentially cure some of the gaps, defects and inadequacies of the ECHR and the HRA. However, given the unpopularity of the ECHR as far as the Conservative Party is concerned, it may be more likely that ultimately, depending on the detail of the new Bill of Rights, protection for rights is somewhat weakened, rather than enhanced.

Common Pitfalls

Allowing the answer to degenerate into a list of advantages and disadvantages of the **Human Rights Act 1998 (HRA)** and the **European Convention on Human Rights (ECHR)**, without answering the question.

Aim Higher

The relationship between a new BoR and Strasbourg could be explored further, given that the Coalition Government has not proposed withdrawing from the **ECHR**, although the **Brighton Declaration (2012)** may give member states a degree of greater autonomy in human rights' matters.

Consideration could be given to **s 2 HRA**; senior Conservatives (in particular Dominic Grieve in 2011) have proposed that in a BoR the **s 2** equivalent should allow judges to depart from Strasbourg.

QUESTION 35

The Eastern European democratic State of Mandislavia is considering how best to guarantee the human rights of its citizens. Mandislavia is already a signatory to the European Convention on Human Rights (ECHR) but it has not incorporated the

Convention into its law. You have been employed by the Mandislavian Law Commission to draft a consultation paper detailing the options available to the Government in this matter. Drawing on the experience of the UK in relation to the ECHR, compare and contrast the main relevant methods of ensuring human rights in Mandislavia.

How to Answer this Question
This is a new take on a standard question, which requires consideration of a wide range of options in guaranteeing human rights.

Answer Structure

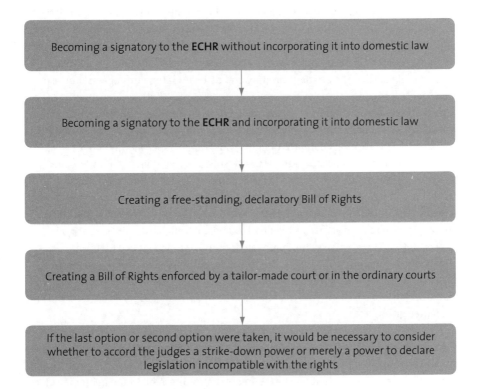

Becoming a signatory to the **ECHR** without incorporating it into domestic law

Becoming a signatory to the **ECHR** and incorporating it into domestic law

Creating a free-standing, declaratory Bill of Rights

Creating a Bill of Rights enforced by a tailor-made court or in the ordinary courts

If the last option or second option were taken, it would be necessary to consider whether to accord the judges a strike-down power or merely a power to declare legislation incompatible with the rights

ANSWER
The Mandislavian Government needs to decide to what extent it wishes to guarantee human rights within its jurisdiction and, hence, to what extent it needs to amend or overrule its existing law and legal system. Some of the available options are little more than window dressing, and would merely provide an additional legal remedy for a citizen who believes that his rights have been infringed; others would have a dramatic effect

upon Mandislavian law and would override all existing and future contradictory provisions. There are essentially four main options available:

(1)   becoming a signatory to the Convention without incorporating it into domestic law;
(2)   becoming a signatory to the Convention and incorporating it into domestic law;
(3)   creating a free-standing Bill of Rights to perform a declaratory function; or
(4)   creating a Bill of Rights with a court to supervise and enforce it or allowing it to be enforced in the ordinary courts.

Each of these options will be evaluated in turn.

The first option would put Mandislavia into broadly the same position as that held by the UK until the Human Rights Act 1998 (HRA) came into force on 2 October 2000. Until 1998, the precarious and disorderly state of civil liberties and human rights in the UK was a strong argument in favour of the adoption of some form of Bill of Rights. In certain areas of civil liberties, the existing statutory and case law safeguards against abuse of power were less comprehensive and arguably less effective than in many other democratic countries. Citizens of the UK did enjoy a reasonable level of tolerance of individual behaviour, but there were serious gaps and the tolerance itself, because it was not bolstered by a formal guarantee of rights, was fragile, especially in times of crisis. The law sought to protect certain values such as the need to maintain public order but, in doing so, curtailed the exercise of certain freedoms because nothing prevented it from disregarding them. Thus, human rights had a precarious status, in that they only existed, by deduction, in the interstices of the law. Individual citizens who believed that their human rights had been violated, either had to find an available domestic action and remedy or try to take a case to the European Court of Human Rights (ECtHR) in Strasbourg. Although the Eleventh Protocol has recently speeded up the Strasbourg system, it is still a slow and expensive process with a high chance of failure; average Mandislavian citizens might find their rights little more than illusory if this were the only guarantee given.

If the second option were to be taken, Mandislavia would find itself in a situation remarkably similar to that currently at play in the UK since the HRA came into force. In contrast to the previous situation, the HRA now represents a minimum guarantee of freedom. When laws are passed that conflict with some fundamental freedom, courts now have to interpret such laws in the light of the ECHR under s 3 HRA. The HRA has therefore created a far more active judicial role in protecting basic rights and freedoms. If a senior court considers that a statutory provision, which is under its consideration, infringes the Convention rights or freedoms, then it may issue a declaration of incompatibility (s 4 of the HRA), upon which it is hoped the government will act promptly (s 10). The use of s 3(1) of the HRA is more significant, since it demands that legislation should be construed compatibly with the Convention rights if it is possible to do so. The judges have been – in certain contexts – very proactive in using s 3 (see, for example, *R v A*

(2001), *Ghaidan* (2004), *AF No 3* (2009)). The HRA is also providing the impetus to create a far more comprehensive right to respect for private and family life (see *Douglas v Hello!* (2001), *Campbell v Mirror Group Newspapers* (2004) and *McKennitt v Ash* (2006)) than the patchy and piecemeal one previously protected under various other causes of action in domestic law.

But in the first 13 years of the operation of the HRA, it was, however, not apparent that the senior judiciary were determined – in general – to take a dynamic approach to the Convention rights (see e.g. *AG v Punch* (2003), the *ProLife Alliance* case (2003), *Gillan* (2006) – all in the House of Lords). The British judiciary are in general highly regarded, but they are an elite group, drawn mainly from a certain stratum of society and therefore, to varying degrees, out of touch with the working class. They have been trained in techniques of legal analysis, which include deciding cases without the responsibility of considering their social repercussions. The interpretations given by judges to the Convention can dilute its impact (compare *Gillan* (2006) with *Gillan v UK* (2010)).

Thus, it may be said that in the UK – which had already protected human rights within the common law – some resistance to the Convention as a 'foreign' instrument is apparent. However, depending upon its political and legal systems, this option might be an attractive one for Mandislavia, albeit perhaps as a first step towards a Bill of Rights tailored to the needs and mores of that State.

As in the UK, incorporation of the ECHR would be likely to have a number of advantages. Citizens could obtain redress for human rights breaches without needing, except as a last resort, to apply to the ECtHR in Strasbourg. The range of remedies available under the HRA is the same as in any ordinary UK court case, and so includes injunctions and specific performance where appropriate, rather than simply damages. This should save a great deal of time and money for the citizen and thus greatly improves access to justice.

At present, in the UK the Convention has been afforded further effect in domestic law, but not entrenched; thus, it could be removed by the simple method of repeal of the HRA. It is submitted that this creates a reasonable compromise at present, both in terms of the maintenance of parliamentary sovereignty and to avoid handing over too much power to the unelected judiciary. Whether it is similarly sensible for Mandislavia depends upon information that is not provided in the question as to the independence of the judiciary, the political system and the current status of human rights in that State.[6] In summary,

---

6   This is an important point to make in comparing the **HRA** with a potential similar instrument in Mandislavia.

this scheme should allow for the relatively fast, but incremental improvement of Mandislavia's recognition and enforcement of domestic human rights. Certain weaknesses are identifiable within the HRA and the ECHR, but the method chosen is a reasonable compromise or first step towards a rights-based culture in UK law and society, and could serve the same function in another State. It has been argued by Klug that the HRA, via judicial interpretation, has come to serve the purposes of a BoR.

The third option would be to create a Bill of Rights specific to Mandislavian needs, but making it merely declaratory. The UK has repeatedly rejected this option. The House of Lords Select Committee, as long ago as 1978, was unanimous on this issue: 'To attempt to incorporate *de novo* a set of fundamental rights would be a fruitless exercise.' Starting from scratch and developing a Bill of Rights for Mandislavia would inevitably be a burdensome task, because the political parties (and the various pressure groups) would have enormous difficulty in reaching agreement on it, while the process of hearing and considering all of the representations made by interested parties would be extremely lengthy. This is suggested by the experience of Austria, where a Commission was set up to draw up a code of fundamental rights. After 12 years, it had produced only alternative drafts of two rights. Apart from the cumbersome nature of the process, a Bill of Rights might take too much account of the interests of the government in power at the time when it was passed. Even if agreement could be reached as to the content of the Bill of Rights, if it were merely declaratory it would provide a very weak guarantee for citizens. However, those, such as Ewing, who would prefer the legislative body to make determinations as to rights protection, due to its democratic mandate which unelected judges do not share, might see this option as having advantages.

The final, and by far the strongest and most radical solution for Mandislavia, would be to create a domestic Bill of Rights tailor-made to Mandislavian needs and mores, and supervised and enforced by a specific domestic court. Although producing a tailor-made Bill of Rights would certainly be difficult, it can be argued that Mandislavia should nevertheless attempt it rather than incorporating the ready-made ECHR, which is arguably defective in content. The Convention was never intended to be used as a domestic Bill of Rights.

It is a cautious compromise document: it is not as open-textured as the US Bill of Rights and it contains long lists of exceptions to most of the primary rights, exceptions that suggest a strong respect for the institutions of the State.[7] These exceptions have, at times, received a broad interpretation in the ECtHR and it would be likely that the

---

7   It is important that the candidate examines the deficiencies of the **ECHR**, with examples, and compares them with the possibilities presented by a new BoR.

resulting cases would have a great influence on domestic courts when they came to apply the rights directly in the domestic arena for the first time. For example, Art 10, which protects freedom of expression, contains an exception in respect of the protection of morals. This was invoked in the *Handyside* case (1976) in respect of a booklet aimed at schoolchildren, which was circulating freely in the rest of Europe. It was held that the UK Government was best placed to determine what was needed in its own country in order to protect morals and so no breach of Art 10 had occurred. Adoption of an entrenched Bill of Rights, offering a rights-protection going beyond that offered by the ECHR, would follow the model of many other European states. The very comprehensive South African Bill of Rights could be considered as a model. This option would be particularly apt if Mandislavia either already has a written constitution and a constitutional court or, alternatively, is willing to create both. The judges could also be given a strike-down power, on the US model. This option has the advantages, inter alia, of clarity, supremacy of human rights over conflicting law and ease of access by citizens to their rights. Nevertheless, much depends on the method of appointment of judges to the court, since the American experience has demonstrated that political divisions can impede justice and that political neutrality may be difficult to maintain. However, the existence of such a strong declaration of rights, combined with a court empowered to strike down legislation and overrule executive actions that infringe those rights, is a high ideal for which to aim and one that might well be apt for Mandislavia in future, if not under present conditions.

If a Mandislavian Bill of Rights were developed, it would be brought into line with the experience of most of the other European signatories. These states already possess codes of rights enshrined in their constitutions, but the majority also adhere to a general practice of incorporation of treaties into domestic law, either automatically, as in the case of Switzerland, or upon ratification, as in the case of Luxembourg. In Mandislavia, the Mandislavian equivalent of the HRA could be viewed as an interim measure to secure the further protection of the rights provided by the ECHR, in the hope that a domestic Bill of Rights would later cure the gaps, defects and inadequacies of the Convention. Thus, the Convention and the HRA, which incorporates it, represent positive steps towards the greater priority and recognition of rights in the UK, particularly in courts, and could be adapted to suit Mandislavian needs and culture.

Common Pitfall ✗

Assuming that the question is largely focused on the **HRA** possibility and affording little time to exploring the other options.

Aim Higher ★

Re Option 2 – it could be pointed out that there are advantages in incorporating the **Convention** as opposed to introducing a domestic instrument if Mandislavia has ratified the **ECHR**. In particular, if a right was violated there, and primary legislation mandated the violation, the possibility of recourse to Strasbourg would be available. That would encourage the legislative body to adhere to the **ECHR**.

Re Option 4 – further examples could be given of more comprehensive Bills of Rights and of the rights that could be included, such as specific rights for children and certain socio-economic rights.

Freedom of Expression and Freedom of Information

INTRODUCTION

Freedom of expression is a key area in the protection of human rights element of constitutional law courses. Examiners tend to set general essays in this area; the emphasis is usually on the degree to which a balance is struck between freedom of expression and a variety of other interests. It is essential in your answers to take the European Convention on Human Rights (ECHR) into account, especially Art 10, which provides a guarantee of freedom of expression. The Convention was received into UK law when the Human Rights Act 1998 (HRA) came fully into force in October 2000. Until that time, Art 10 and other Convention Articles relevant in this area were not directly applicable in UK courts, but the judiciary referred to the Convention more and more in resolving ambiguity in statutes in the run-up to the inception of the HRA. The HRA has now been in force for over twelve years and a number of significant cases in the field of freedom of expression (such as *Prolife Alliance* (2003), *Ashworth* (2002), *Interbrew SA v Financial Times Ltd* (2002), *Punch* (2003) and *Shayler* (2002)) have been decided under the HRA. Whether any particular case is relevant will depend of course on the essay title.

Section 3 HRA requires that: 'So far as it is possible to do so, primary and subordinate legislation must be read and given effect in a way which is compatible with the Convention rights.' Section 3(2)(b) reads: '. . . this section does not affect the validity, continuing operation or enforcement of any incompatible primary legislation.' This goes beyond the *current* obligation to resolve ambiguity in statutes. All statutes affecting freedom of expression and media freedom therefore have to be interpreted so as to be in harmony with the ECHR if that is at all possible. Under s 6 of the HRA, Convention guarantees are binding only against public authorities. These are core or functional public authorities (defined as bodies that have a public function – see Chapter 9). The definition is therefore quite wide, but means that private bodies, including media bodies/regulators (apart from the bodies that are public authorities or have a 'public' function, such as Ofcom, the BBC (probably), and the Press Complaints Commission) can violate Convention rights, unless a part of the common law, which also should be interpreted in conformity with the Convention, bears on the matter. Thus, exam questions currently reflect the demands of the HRA in this extremely significant area and will expect an awareness of the Art 10 jurisprudence and of the impact of the HRA on freedom of expression.

This chapter considers other values that often oppose freedom of expression, such as the administration of justice or official secrecy. One of the main concerns of certain of the questions in this chapter is with the methods employed by governments to ensure that official information cannot fall into the hands of those who might place it in the public domain, and with methods of preventing or deterring persons from publication when such information has been obtained. The balance between what may be termed State interests, such as defence or national security, and the individual entitlement to freedom of expression and information is largely struck by the **Official Secrets Act 1989** and various common law provisions. However, the interpretation of the **1989 Act** and the application of those provisions may be affected by the **Convention** rights as applied under the **HRA**.

Freedom of information, in contrast to freedom of expression, concerns the ability of the citizen to gain access to State information even from an unwilling speaker. The most important value associated with freedom of information is the need for the citizen to understand as fully as possible the working of government, in order to render it accountable. This chapter therefore places a strong emphasis on the choices that were made as to the release of information relating to public authorities – not only to central government – in the **Freedom of Information Act 2000** (in force 2005).

Examiners tend to set general essays rather than problem questions in relation to freedom of information; the emphasis is usually on the degree to which a balance is struck between the interest of the individual in acquiring government information and the interests of public authorities in withholding it. Where information held by central government or by other public authorities is not covered by the **1989 Act**, the citizen may be able to obtain access to it under the **Freedom of Information Act 2000**. The **2000 Act** is a significant development that is highly likely to feature on exam papers.

Checklist ✔

Students should be familiar with the following areas:

- key aspects of the **Official Secrets Act 1989**;
- the basic aspects of the **Public Records Act 1958** and very basic key aspects of the **Data Protection Act 1998**;
- very basic aspects of freedom of information measures in other countries, particularly Canada and the USA;
- the doctrine of breach of confidence as used by the government;
- the key aspects of the **Freedom of Information Act 2000**; aspects of the work of the Information Commissioner and Tribunal;

- **Art 10** of the **ECHR**; other relevant rights such as **Art 6**; **Art 10** jurisprudence;
- the **Human Rights Act 1998**, especially **ss 3, 4, 6, 12**;
- post-2000 domestic freedom of expression decisions taking account of the **HRA** and **Art 10**, such as *Prolife Alliance* (2003), *Ashworth* (2002), *Interbrew SA v Financial Times Ltd* (2002), *Campbell* (2004), *Shayler* (2002), *Animal Defenders* (2009).

QUESTION 36

'The Freedom of Information Act 2000 is a grave disappointment to those who are genuinely committed to the principle of freedom of information.' Do you agree?

How to Answer this Question

This is a very specific essay question that requires a detailed and critical evaluation of the 2000 Act. It should not be attempted unless the student has quite detailed knowledge (with references to sections) of this complex Act. In a form similar to that taken here, this question is highly likely to appear on exam papers at the present time.

Answer Structure

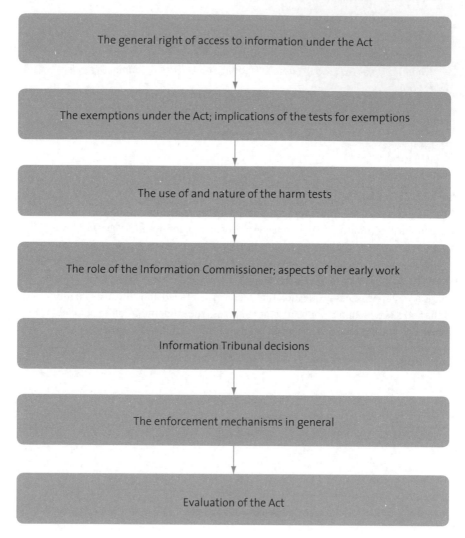

The general right of access to information under the Act

↓

The exemptions under the Act; implications of the tests for exemptions

↓

The use of and nature of the harm tests

↓

The role of the Information Commissioner; aspects of her early work

↓

Information Tribunal decisions

↓

The enforcement mechanisms in general

↓

Evaluation of the Act

The above matters should be discussed in your answer.

ANSWER

The Freedom of Information Act 2000 provides a general right of access to the information held by a range of public bodies. The Act covers 'public authorities' and s 3 sets out the various ways in which a body can be a public authority. Under s 5, private organisations may be designated as public authorities insofar as they carry out statutory functions, as may the privatised utilities and private bodies working on contracted-out functions.

Section 1(1) provides that any person making a request for information under the 2000 Act to a public authority is entitled to be informed of whether it holds information of the description specified in the request and if it holds the information it must communicate it. From 2005 onwards, when the Act came into force, individuals were able to gain access to information relating to them personally, such as tax and medical records. They also now have the right to obtain information on other, general matters from the departments and bodies covered.

As indicated, the Act begins with an apparently broad and generous statement of the rights it confers; it is also generous in its coverage. However, the rights are subject to a wide range of exceptions and exemptions. The harm-based exemptions under the Act are similar to those indicated in the White Paper: they require the public authority to show that the release of the information requested would (or would be likely to) cause prejudice to the interest specified in the exemption. However, this test for harm is of course less restrictive than that proposed under the White Paper. Further, a number of exemptions are class-based, meaning that in order to refuse the request, the authority only has to show that the information falls into the class of information covered by the exemption, not that its release would cause or be likely to cause harm or prejudice.

However, the Act provides a public interest test in relation to some, but not all, of the class exemptions, and almost all of the 'harm exemptions'. The authority, having decided that the information is prima facie exempt (either because the information falls into the requisite class exemption or because the relevant harm test is satisfied, as the case may be), must still then go on to consider whether it should be released under the public interest test set out in s 2. This requires the authority to release the information unless 'in all the circumstances of the case, the public interest in maintaining the exemption outweighs the public interest in disclosing the information'.

The discussion in this essay cannot cover all of the freedom of information class exemptions, but will consider some of the more controversial ones. Section 23(1) covers information supplied by, or which relates to, the intelligence and security services. The bodies mentioned in this exemption are not themselves covered by the Act at all. This exemption therefore applies to information that is held by *another public authority*, but which has been supplied by one of these bodies. Because it is a class exemption, it applies to information that has no conceivable security implications, such as evidence of a massive overspend on MI5 or MI6's headquarters. Bearing in mind the complete exclusion of the security and intelligence services from the Act, the use of this class exemption, unaccompanied by a harm test and not subject to the public interest test, means that sensitive matters of great political significance will remain undisclosed, even if their disclosure would ultimately benefit those services or national security. Section 32 covers information *that is only held* by virtue of being contained in a document or record served on a public authority in proceedings, or made by a court or tribunal or party in any proceedings, or contained in a document lodged with or created by a person conducting an inquiry or arbitration, for the purposes of the inquiry or arbitration. The public interest test does not apply.

Certain class exemptions are subject to the public interest test. In relation to these exemptions, in practice, while the Information Commissioner always has the last word on whether the information falls into the class in question, he/she will not always be able to enforce a finding that it should nevertheless be released on public interest grounds if the information is held by certain governmental bodies, since the ministerial veto may be used (see below). Section 30(1) provides a sweeping exemption, covering all information, whenever obtained, which relates to investigations that may lead to criminal proceedings. It represents a specific rejection of the recommendation of the Macpherson Report that there should be no class exemption for information relating to police investigations. It overlaps with the law enforcement exemption of s 31, which does include a harm test. There are certain aspects of information relating to investigations that would appear to require disclosure in order to be in accord with the principle of openness enshrined in the Act. For example, a citizen might suspect that his telephone had been tapped without authorisation or that he had been unlawfully placed under surveillance by other means. Under the Act, no satisfactory method of discovering information relating to such a possibility will exist. It is therefore unfortunate that telephone tapping and electronic surveillance were not subjected to a substantial harm or even a simple harm test.

The s 30(1) exemption extends beyond protecting the police and the Crown Prosecution Service (CPS). Other bodies are also protected: it covers all information obtained by safety agencies investigating accidents. It covers routine inspections as well as specific investigations, since both can lead to criminal prosecution. It is particularly hard to understand the need for such a sweeping class exemption when s 31 specifically exempts information that could prejudice the prevention or detection of crime, or legal proceedings brought by a public authority arising from various forms of investigation. That exemption ensures that no information is released that could damage law enforcement and crime detection.

The other major class exemption in this category, under s 35, has been equally criticised. It amounts to a very broad exemption covering virtually all information relating to the formation of government policy. Section 36 contains a harm-based exemption that covers almost exactly the same ground. Since it covers all information the release of which might cause damage to the working of government – and is framed in very broad terms – it appears to be unnecessary to have a sweeping class exemption covering the same ground. Moreover, this exemption is not restricted to Civil Service advice; it covers also the background information used in preparing policy, including the underlying facts and their analysis.

While information in this category under the Act is subject to a public interest test, if the Commissioner orders disclosure on public interest grounds, the ministerial veto is usually available to override him or her. (This occurred in the 2012 case involving the Department of Health, discussed below, after the Department had attempted to rely on s 35.) However, the Commissioner has issued important guidance on this provision that all but changes it into a 'harm-based' test. There must be some clear, specific and credible evidence that the formulation or development of policy would be materially altered for the worse by the threat of disclosure under the Act.

The Information Commissioner has issued a series of guidance notes on the interpretation and operation of the Act, one of which deals with the 'prejudice' test. As to the meaning of 'prejudice', the Commissioner indicates that the term is to be interpreted, in general terms as meaning that the prejudice need not be substantial, but the Commissioner expects that it will be more than trivial. The phrase 'likely to prejudice' has been considered by the courts in the case of *R (on the application of Alan Lord) and The Secretary of State for the Home Department* (2003). Although this case concerns the Data Protection Act 1998, the Commissioner regards this interpretation as persuasive. Following this judgment the probability of prejudice occurring need not be 'more likely than not', but there should certainly be substantially more than a remote possibility.

The enforcement review mechanism under the Act is clearly crucial, but it is also open to criticism in certain key respects. The rights granted under the Act are enforceable by the Data Protection Commissioner, now known as the Information Commissioner. Section 50 provides that any person can apply to the Commissioner for a decision as to whether a request for information made by the complainant to a public authority has been dealt with in accordance with the Act. In response, the Commissioner has the power to serve a 'decision notice' on the authority, stating what it must do to satisfy the Act. The Commissioner may ultimately force a recalcitrant authority to act by serving upon it an 'enforcement notice' (s 52(1)) requiring it to take the steps specified in the notice. If a public authority fails to comply with a decision, enforcement or information notice, the Commissioner can notify the High Court, which (s 52(2)) can deal with the authority as if it had committed a contempt of court.

The Commissioner's decisions are themselves subject to appeal to the Information Tribunal, and this power of appeal is exercisable upon the broadest possible grounds. The Act provides that either party may appeal to the Tribunal against a decision notice and a public authority against an enforcement or information notice (s 57(2) and (3)) either on the basis that the notice is 'not in accordance with the law', or 'to the extent that the notice involved an exercise of discretion by the Commissioner, that he ought to have exercised his discretion differently' (s 58(1)). The Tribunal is also empowered to review any finding of fact on which the notice was based. There is a further appeal from the Tribunal to the High Court, but on a 'point of law' only (s 59). The Convention rights under the Human Rights Act 1998 could be invoked at this point. As an example of the controversial nature of its decisions – in 2012 the Tribunal ruled that extracts of a phone conversation between Tony Blair and George Bush a few days before the invasion of Iraq must be disclosed, after a freedom of information request was made by a private individual as to the conversation.

Enforcement can be affected by the ministerial veto, which is another highly controversial aspect of the Act. The veto can be exercised if two conditions are satisfied under s 53(1) : first, the notice that the veto will operate to quash must have been served on a government department, the Welsh Assembly or 'any public authority designated for the purposes of this section by an order made by the Secretary of State'; second, the notice must order the release of information that is prima facie exempt but which the Commissioner has decided should nevertheless be released under the public interest test in s 2. Such a veto clearly dilutes the basic freedom of information principle that a body independent from government should enforce the rights to information. In 2012 there was an example of the operation of the veto: a freedom of information request by a Labour MP regarding the risk of patient care suffering while NHS managers were distracted by restructuring and financial failures. The Department refused. Two investigations by the Information Commissioner rejected the Department's refusal to publish the information. The Information Tribunal ordered the Department of Health to publish the document (*Dept of Health v Information Commissioner, Healey* (2012)). But the Department relied on the ministerial veto. The Health Secretary, Andrew Lansley, then made a formal statement to the House of Commons explaining the Cabinet's decision to veto the ruling, but accepting that a limited amount of the relevant information would be released.[1]

In conclusion, it is suggested that the Act is indeed disappointing. It creates so many restrictions on the basic right of access that, depending upon its interpretation, much information of any conceivable interest can still be withheld. Nevertheless, the Act does represent a turning point in British democracy since, for the first time in its history, the decision to release many classes of information has been removed from government and from other public authorities and placed in the hands of an independent agency, the Information Commissioner. Most importantly, for the first time a statutory 'right' to information, enforceable if necessary through the courts, has been established.[2]

Aim Higher ★

The issue of exemptions could be considered further and it could be pointed out that the Act, through amendments to the **Public Records Act 1958**, provides that some of the exemptions will cease to apply after a certain number of years, although these limitations are hardly generous.

---

1   It is important to use up-to-date examples of rulings to illustrate the working of the key sections of the Act.
2   Examiners will give credit to students taking a balanced view in relation to the question.

Common Pitfall

Students sometimes fail to discuss specific sections of the Act and make the discussion too general; it is essential to focus closely on specific exceptions where the information can be withheld.

QUESTION 37

The government has various means of preventing the disclosure of information. But taking account of relevant developments, including the introduction of the Freedom of Information Act 2000, it is clear that the tradition of government secrecy has been breaking down over the last 25–30 years.

▶ Critically evaluate this statement.

How to Answer the Question

This is clearly a general and wide-ranging essay that requires knowledge of a number of different areas. It is concerned with restrictions on access to State information, methods of ensuring that information cannot fall into the hands of those who might place it in the public domain, and with methods of preventing or deterring persons from publication when a leak has occurred. The latter two issues are both aspects of freedom of expression, but the first is given greater prominence here. The question asks you, in essence, to present a critical analysis of the current scheme preventing disclosure of certain State information, and to consider whether the right of access to information introduced in the 2000 Act is dramatically improving the public's access to information. Since the essay is so wide-ranging, you are not expected to engage in a detailed analysis of the 2000 Act.

Answer Structure

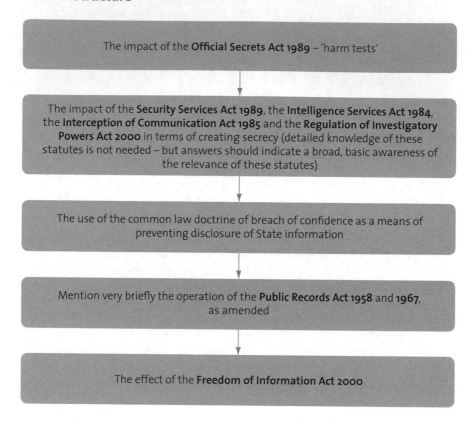

The impact of the **Official Secrets Act 1989** – 'harm tests'

The impact of the **Security Services Act 1989**, the **Intelligence Services Act 1984**, the **Interception of Communication Act 1985** and the **Regulation of Investigatory Powers Act 2000** in terms of creating secrecy (detailed knowledge of these statutes is not needed – but answers should indicate a broad, basic awareness of the relevance of these statutes)

The use of the common law doctrine of breach of confidence as a means of preventing disclosure of State information

Mention very briefly the operation of the **Public Records Act 1958** and **1967**, as amended

The effect of the **Freedom of Information Act 2000**

ANSWER

It has often been said that the UK is more obsessed with keeping government information secret than any other Western democracy. The Official Secrets Act 1989, which decriminalised disclosure of some official information, was heralded as amounting to a move away from obsessive secrecy. However, since it was in no sense a freedom of information measure, it did not allow the release of any official documents into the public domain, although it does mean that if certain information is disclosed outside the categories it covers, the official concerned will not face criminal sanctions. (He/she might, of course, face an action for breach of confidence as well as disciplinary proceedings.)

The narrowing down of the official information covered by the 1989 Act was supposed to be achieved by introducing 'harm tests', which took into account the substance of the information. However, there is no test for harm at all in the category of information covered by s 1(1) of the 1989 Act, which prevents members or former members of the security services from disclosing anything at all about the operation of those services (see *Shayler* (2003)). Equally, there is no test for harm under s 4(3) of the Act, which covers information obtained by or relating to the issue of a warrant under the **Interception of Communications Act 1985** or the **Security Service Act 1989**. Thus, the Act was always unlikely to have a liberalising impact on the publication of information allowing the public to scrutinise the workings of government.

The **Official Secrets Act 1989** works in tandem with other measures designed to ensure secrecy. **Sections 1 and 4(3)** work in conjunction with the provisions of the **Security Service Act 1989** to prevent almost all scrutiny of the operation of the security service. In a similar manner, s 4(3) of the **Official Secrets Act**, which prevents disclosure of information about telephone tapping, works in tandem with the **Regulation of Investigatory Powers Act 2000**, which does, however, place a number of surveillance powers on a statutory basis. Under the **2000 Act**, complaints can be made only to a tribunal (set up under the Act), with no possibility of scrutiny by a court.

Developments in the use of the common law doctrine of confidence as a means of preventing disclosure of information provide a further method of ensuring secrecy where information falls outside the categories covered by the **Official Secrets Act**, or where it falls within one of them, but a prosecution is not undertaken. *AG v Guardian Newspapers* (1987), which concerned the publication of material from *Spycatcher* by Peter Wright, demonstrated that temporary injunctions could be obtained to prevent disclosure of official information, even where prior publication has ensured that there is little confidentiality left to be protected. However, the House of Lords eventually rejected the claim for permanent injunctions on the basis that the interest in maintaining confidentiality was outweighed by the public interest in knowing of the allegations in *Spycatcher*. Moreover, it was impossible to sustain a restriction based on confidentiality when the worldwide publication of the book meant that the information it contained was clearly in the 'public domain'.

A restraint over obtaining an injunction or damages for breach of confidence is now to be found in s 12 of the **Human Rights Act 1998 (HRA)**. This requires any court considering such relief not to grant any interim injunctions unless it is satisfied that the claimant is likely to be successful at trial. Courts must apply existing statutory and common law rules with a far greater focus upon the public right to know. In this respect, the case of *AG v Times* (2001) is significant. A former MI6 officer wrote a book, *The Big Breach*, about his experiences in MI6 that *The Sunday Times* intended to serialise. There had been a small amount of publication of the material in Russia. The Attorney General sought an injunction to restrain publication. It was found that he had failed to demonstrate why there was a public interest in restricting publication; therefore, no injunction was granted. The requirement to seek clearance should not, it was found, be imposed: the editor had to form his own judgment as to whether the material could be said to be already in the public domain. That position was, the court found, most consonant with the requirements of Art 10 and s 12. This decision suggests that bearing in mind the requirements of the HRA, an injunction is unlikely to be granted where even a very small amount of prior publication has already taken place.

The position was affected by the decision of the House of Lords in *Cream Holdings Ltd and Ors v Banerjee* (2004). This decision gives the definitive interpretation of the meaning of s 12(3) HRA, which provides, inter alia, that no relief affecting the Convention right to freedom of expression 'is to be granted so as to restrain publication before trial unless the court is satisfied that the applicant is likely to establish that publication should not be allowed'. The effect of the decision of the House of Lords is that, in nearly all cases – absent the claim of immediate and serious danger to life, limb, or presumably national security – the party seeking the injunction, that is the government in these kinds of cases, must show not only an arguable case, as previously, but that it is 'more likely than not' that they will succeed at final trial. This approach, assuming it is applied consistently to *Spycatcher*-type cases, should make it significantly harder for future governments to obtain gagging injunctions against the media. But the general principle that publishing material covered by a temporary Injunction against another media body will create liability for contempt at common law was reaffirmed by the House of Lords in *A-G v Punch* (2002).

It is clear from the discussion so far that the government has a range of measures available to it to prevent publication of forms of State information, but that the measures have recently become more liberal. The 1989 Act is a narrower measure than its predecessor and the action for breach of confidence has a narrower application due to the impact of the HRA. However, the narrowing down of the measures available to the State to prevent disclosure of information does not in itself mean that access to official information is available.

Information of historical interest may be obtainable via the UK Public Records Act 1958, as amended by the Public Records Act 1967 and the Freedom of Information Act 2000. However, under the 1958 Act, public records in the Public Records Office are not available for inspection until the expiration of 30 years, and longer periods can be prescribed for sensitive information. Some information can be withheld for 100 years or forever and there is no means of challenging such decisions. For example, at the end of 1987, a great deal of information about the Windscale fire in 1957 was disclosed, although some items were still held back. Thus, the 1958 Act, even after amendment, could hardly be viewed as being equivalent to a statutory right of access to current information.

However, there was a slow but progressive movement towards freedom of information legislation for the UK prior to 2000, culminating in the Freedom of Information Act 2000, which came into force in 2005. The Act has a number of important consequences. Primarily, it places a general right of access to information on a statutory basis for the first time, in s 1. The right allows the public access to information held by a very wide range of public authorities, including local government, the NHS, schools and colleges, and the police. An Information Commissioner supervises the scheme and the public can contact him directly. Public authorities must, on request, indicate whether they hold information required by an individual and, if so, communicate that information to him within 20 working days.

It may be noted that the 2000 Act is not the only freedom of information measure available, and different bodies may be affected by other measures even though they are not public authorities for the purposes of the 2000 Act. For example, the Information Commissioner has issued a decision notice that provides that Network Rail is caught by the definition of 'public authority' under the Environmental Information Regulations 2004. This decision indicates that a 'public authority' under the Regulations encapsulates a different group of organisations to those caught by the Freedom of Information (FoI) Act 2000 and, unlike the Act, includes some private companies such as Network Rail, which had argued previously that as a 'private company' it was not bound by the Regulations.

Under the 2000 Act, a number of forms of information are exempt, including that relating to security matters or which might affect national security, defence or the economy. The harm-based exemptions under the Act require the public authority to show that the release of the information requested would or would be likely to cause prejudice to the interest specified in the exemption. However, this test for harm is less restrictive than that proposed under the White Paper preceding the FoI Act. Further, a number of exemptions are class-based, meaning that in order to refuse the request, the authority only has to show that the information falls into the class of information covered by the exemption, not that its release would cause or be likely to cause harm or prejudice.

However, the Act provides a public interest test in relation to some, but not all, of the class exemptions and almost all of the 'harm exemptions'. This requires the authority to release the information unless 'in all the circumstances of the case, the public interest in maintaining the exemption outweighs the public interest in disclosing the information'.

Section 32 provides a particularly controversial class exemption: it covers information *that is only held* by virtue of being contained in a document or record served on a public authority in proceedings, or made by a court or tribunal or party in any proceedings. The public interest test does not apply. The other major class exemption, under s 35, has been equally criticised. It amounts to a very broad exemption covering virtually all information relating to the formation of government policy. Section 36 contains a harm-based exemption that covers almost exactly the same ground.

The imprecise terms used to indicate the exempted information and the introduction of class exemptions may be allowing the government to exempt from the disclosure provisions much information that is merely embarrassing or damaging to its reputation. Some such information may also be subject to the ministerial veto, where it relates to central government, which means that it cannot be disclosed even if it is not exempt. Birkinshaw argues that the use of the veto means that government scandals, such as that of Matrix Churchill which underpinned the decision to introduce the **FoI Act**, might not be prevented due to its use, because the veto still allows for cover-ups. In 2012 there was an Important example of the operation of the veto: a freedom of information request by a Labour MP regarding the risk of patient care suffering while NHS managers were distracted by restructuring and financial failures. The Department refused. Two investigations by the Information Commissioner rejected the Department's refusal to publish the information. The Information Tribunal ordered the Department of Health to publish the document (*Dept of Health v Information Commissioner, Healey* 2012). But the Department relied on the ministerial veto in refusing to publish all the information requested; partial information was published eventually.

A right to appeal to the Information Tribunal is granted by the Act to complainants and much depends upon the interpretations of the statute by the Commissioner and the courts. The Act has proved an irritant to government, attracting strong criticism from both Tony Blair and David Cameron. The Ministry of Justice released figures in 2012 showing that FoI requests went up 7 per cent in 2011.[3] This suggests that the Act is working, but also that It may be under threat, as senior ministers compare its operation with the previous situation in which secrecy could be much more readily maintained.

It is concluded that the developments described here do suggest that a movement away from the tradition of government secrecy has been occurring over the last three decades, culminating in the 2000 Act (which played a part in revealing abuse of expenses by MPs in 2009). Nevertheless, the existence of class exemptions in the Act and of the ministerial veto suggest that some aspects of that tradition are reflected, ironically, in that Act.[4]

QUESTION 38 -

'Over the last 30 years, there has been a significant movement towards more open government which is largely, but not wholly, attributable to decisions under the European Convention on Human Rights, whether at Strasbourg or under the Human Rights Act.' Critically evaluate this statement.

How to Answer this Question

This is clearly a fairly narrowly focused question, since the need to consider recent developments limits its scope. It should be borne in mind that the statement makes a

3   Credit will be given for the use of up-to-date examples and mention of figures indicating usage of the Act.
4   Credit will be given where examinees refer back to the title in the conclusion and provide a balanced answer to the question posed.

number of separate assertions, each of which must be evaluated. The assertions need not be accepted as correct.

Answer Structure

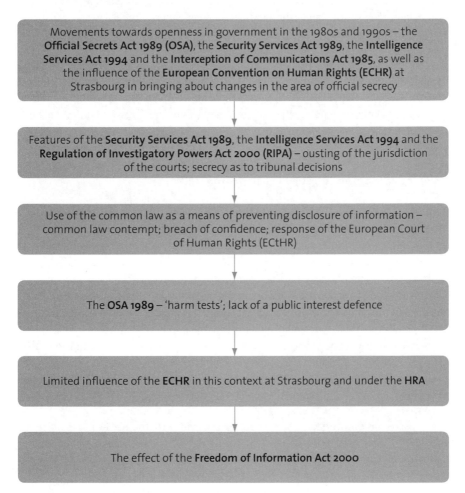

Movements towards openness in government in the 1980s and 1990s – the **Official Secrets Act 1989 (OSA)**, the **Security Services Act 1989**, the **Intelligence Services Act 1994** and the **Interception of Communications Act 1985**, as well as the influence of the **European Convention on Human Rights (ECHR)** at Strasbourg in bringing about changes in the area of official secrecy

Features of the **Security Services Act 1989**, the **Intelligence Services Act 1994** and the **Regulation of Investigatory Powers Act 2000 (RIPA)** – ousting of the jurisdiction of the courts; secrecy as to tribunal decisions

Use of the common law as a means of preventing disclosure of information – common law contempt; breach of confidence; response of the European Court of Human Rights (ECtHR)

The **OSA 1989** – 'harm tests'; lack of a public interest defence

Limited influence of the **ECHR** in this context at Strasbourg and under the **HRA**

The effect of the **Freedom of Information Act 2000**

ANSWER
A general survey of certain recent developments might indeed suggest that a movement towards more open government has been taking place over the last 25 years. Disclosure of a range of information was decriminalised under the Official Secrets Act 1989 (OSA); MI6 and GCHQ were placed on a statutory basis by the Intelligence Services Act 1994, which also set up a parliamentary committee to oversee the work of the security and

intelligence services. The Freedom of Information (FoI) Act 2000 (in force 2005) represented a further and very significant step in that direction. But a closer look at some of these developments reveals, it will be argued, that they were often not imposed due to decisions of the ECtHR, although such decisions have had quite a significant impact in this context. In particular, the ECHR did not provide the driving force behind the introduction of the most significant measure aiding openness – the FoI Act.[5] It will further be argued that, in general, in any event, these changes, apart from the introduction of FoI, have not had a very clear or significant liberalising impact.

The Interception of Communications Act 1985 came into being after the decision of the ECtHR in the *Malone* case (1984), but the decision only required the UK Government to introduce legislation to regulate the circumstances in which the power to tap could be used, rather than giving guidance as to what would be acceptable limits on the right to privacy. The limits of the Act (not applying to private telephone systems, for example – see *Halford v UK* (1997)) and massive technological development led to its replacement by the Regulation of Investigatory Powers Act 2000 (RIPA).

The limits to open government, found in the 1985 Act, are continued by the RIPA, and information about authorised (let alone unauthorised) phone taps remains hard to obtain. Complaints, including allegations of human rights violations, can be made only to a tribunal set up under the Act, with no possibility of scrutiny by a court. Similarly, the Security Service Act 1989 came into being largely as a response to the finding of the ECtHR that a complaint against MI5 was admissible (*Harman and Hewitt v UK* (1989)). The Security Service Act places MI5 on a statutory basis, but prevents almost all effective scrutiny of its operation. Even where a member of the public has a grievance concerning its operation, it will not be possible to use a court action as a means of scrutinising such operation. Complaints, including those involving the HRA, can only be made to the tribunal established under s 65 of the RIPA. The proceedings of this tribunal are not open and its decisions are not questionable in any court of law.

This measure was not introduced solely due to the operation of the ECtHR. Its inception was probably also influenced by the challenge to the legality of the tapping of the phones of Campaign for Nuclear Disarmament (CND) members mentioned above, in *Secretary of State for the Home Department ex p Ruddock*, which proved embarrassing to the government, although it failed. In any event, the effect of these statutes has not been to open up the workings of internal security to greater scrutiny. They suggest a perception that no breach of the Convention will occur so long as a mechanism is in place that is able to consider the claims of aggrieved citizens, however ineffective that mechanism might be.

The two statutes mentioned work in tandem with the OSA 1989, which was not brought into being in response to pressure from Europe, but largely due to pressure from other

---

5   Examinees gain credit for examining the claims made in the essay title closely and making it clear in the introduction how they will be addressed.

sources. In particular, the failure of the government to secure a conviction under s 2 of the OSA 1911 in *Ponting* (1985) probably had a significant effect. It had been recognised for some time even before the *Ponting* case that s 2 was becoming discredited due to its width. Obviously, the criminal law is brought into disrepute if liability is possible in respect of extremely trivial actions. The 1911 Act had no test of substance and although obtaining a conviction should therefore have been relatively straightforward, the decisions in *Aitken* (1971) and *Ponting* suggested that the very width of the section was undermining its credibility.

It was made clear from the outset that the 1989 Act was unconcerned with freedom of information. Thus, one must be cautious in viewing the OSA 1989 as amounting to a move away from obsessive secrecy; it does not allow the release of any official documents into the public domain, although it does mean that if certain pieces of information are released, the official concerned will not face criminal sanctions. (He or she might, of course, face an action for breach of confidence as well as disciplinary proceedings.)

It is, however, fair to accept that the 1989 Act covers much less information than its predecessor, due to its introduction of a 'harm test', which takes into account the substance of the information. Clearly, such a test is to be preferred to the width of s 2 of the OSA 1911, which covered all official information, however trivial. However, there is no test for harm at all under s 1(1), which prevents members or former members of the security services disclosing anything at all about the operation of those services. All such members come under a lifelong duty to keep silent, even though their information might reveal serious abuse of power in the security services or some operational weakness. These provisions also apply to anyone who is notified that he or she is subject to the provisions of the subsection. Equally, there is no test for harm under s 4(3), which covers information obtained by, or relating to, the issue of a warrant under the RIPA or the Intelligence Services Act 1994.

The Act contains no explicit public interest defence and it follows from the nature of the harm test that one cannot be implied into it: any good flowing from disclosure of the information cannot be considered; merely any harm that might be caused. This was confirmed by the House of Lords in *R v Shayler* (2002) and was said to be compatible with Art 10 of the ECHR. Moreover, no express defence of prior publication is provided. Prior publication can be an issue, however, since the prosecution could find it hard to establish the appropriate type of harm where there had been a great deal of prior publication. Thus, although it may be said that some features of the Act suggest a move towards some liberalisation of official secrecy law, it was clearly intended that this move should not be fully carried through.

The doctrine of breach of confidence was largely uninfluenced domestically by Art 10 ECHR pre-HRA. In relation to the publication of the book *Spycatcher* in the USA in 1987, the House of Lords decided (relying on *American Cyanamid Co v Ethicon Ltd* (1975)) to continue the temporary injunctions against the newspapers on the basis that the

Attorney General still had an arguable case for permanent injunctions (*AG v Guardian Newspapers Ltd* (1987)). The injunctions continued until, in the hearing of the permanent injunctions, the House of Lords found that it was impossible to sustain a restriction based on confidentiality when the worldwide publication of the book meant that the information it contained was clearly in the 'public domain'.

When the ECtHR considered the case (*The Observer and The Guardian v UK* (1991); *The Sunday Times v UK* (1991)), it found that, given the extent of publication in the USA, the temporary injunctions, although for a legitimate purpose, were disproportionate and a violation of Art 10. The injunctions obtained before publication in the USA were not found to breach Art 10; therefore, this ruling did little to discourage use of such injunctions in many instances where a disclosure of official information is threatened – although s 12(3) HRA has created some liberalisation in this respect.

The *Spycatcher* cases (*AG v Newspaper Publishing plc* (1990), as approved by the House of Lords in *Times Newspapers and Anor v AG* (1991)) had confirmed the principle that once an interlocutory injunction has been obtained restraining one organ of the media from publication of allegedly confidential material, the rest of the media may be in contempt if they publish that material, even if their intention in doing so is to bring alleged iniquity to public attention. In *AG v Punch* (2003), a magazine published articles written by an ex-security services officer in breach of an injunction restraining the officer from publishing. The magazine could only have the *mens rea* for contempt if, by publication, it intended to destroy the purpose of the injunction. The Court of Appeal's view, that the purpose of such an injunction was to prevent damaging confidential material from being published, was rejected by the House of Lords, despite Art 10 ECHR scheduled in the HRA, for whom the point of the injunction was to protect the interest of the court as the effective tribunal in which the issue of confidentiality should be determined. This decision makes it easier for the State to prove that the media are in contempt if they publish in breach of a temporary injunction imposed on others.

A much more significant development is the passing of the Freedom of Information (FoI) Act 2000, which was brought fully into force in 2005. It requires public bodies to publish information and to disclose information on request. The Act is a major step forward in that, under it, access to information is now a statutory right rather than a discretionary privilege depending on the attitude of the Information Commissioner and Tribunal to enforcing it. The findings of the Tribunal in January 2009, regarding the requirement of disclosure of the Cabinet minutes relating to the decision to engage in military action in Iraq, is obviously of great significance due to the importance of the decision.

There are, however, many exceptions and the success of the Act depends on how these exceptions are interpreted. A particularly worrying exception is that, under s 53, a government department can substitute its view for that of the Commissioner on whether the public interest does or does not require disclosure of information on a wide range of policy matters involving the department. There is also a right of ministerial veto. Birkinshaw argues that the use of the veto means that government scandals, such as that of Matrix Churchill which underpinned the decision to introduce the FoI Act, might not be prevented due to its use, because the veto still allows for cover-ups.[6] In 2012 there was an important example of the operation of the veto: a freedom of information request by a Labour MP regarding the risk of patient care suffering while NHS managers were distracted by restructuring and financial failures. The Department of Health refused. Two investigations by the Information Commissioner rejected the department's refusal to publish the information. The Information Tribunal ordered the Department of Health to publish the document (*Dept of Health v Information Commissioner, Healey* 2012). But the Department relied on the ministerial veto in refusing to publish all the information requested; partial information was published eventually.

It may be concluded that claims under the Convention have led to some breaking down of the tradition of secrecy in government. The failings of the Security Service Act, the RIPA and the caution of the European Court judgment in the *Spycatcher* case do not, however, support the suggestion that radical change has occurred, or can occur, by this means. This is also true in respect of freedom of information where the ECtHR has only fairly recently found that Art 10 provides a right to receive information that others, including the State, wish not to give (*Matky v Czech Republic* (2006)). British courts had adopted the view that Art 10 does not provide such a right in *R (Persey) v SSEFRA* (2002), in denying a legal challenge to the government's refusal to hold a public inquiry into the foot-and-mouth epidemic. The FoI was not introduced as a result of a decision at Strasbourg but rather as a response to a general pressure to come into line with most democracies on this matter. Thus, if greater openness in government has been achieved – a claim that, as indicated, is itself debatable – it is fair to say that the ECHR at Strasbourg or under the HRA can claim only a small part of the credit for it.[7]

Common Pitfall

Some candidates only give a general survey of the area and fail to address the question posed.

QUESTION 39

The statutory provisions governing official secrecy, the administration of justice and protection for journalistic sources fail to ensure compatibility with Article 10 of the European Convention on Human Rights or other Articles. Reform is therefore needed.

▶ Discuss.

6   It is important to refer to academic writing in essay answers.
7   Examinees will gain credit for examining a claim made in the title closely, and then deciding that it is not correct, supporting their conclusion with evidence.

How to Answer this Question

This is clearly a fairly narrowly focused essay. Note that only *statutory* developments in the areas in question need be considered, although of course that means that case law on the statutes in question must also be considered. Also, unless the answer is not to become unmanageably long, it would be wise to interpret the question as unconcerned with other aspects of freedom of expression, such as freedom of information – which is linked to media freedom of expression. If a question expects those aspects to be discussed, it will make that clear. Notice that Article 10 Is not the only Article that could be considered. Also media freedom Is not always synonymous with freedom of expression – this point should be highlighted.

Answer Structure

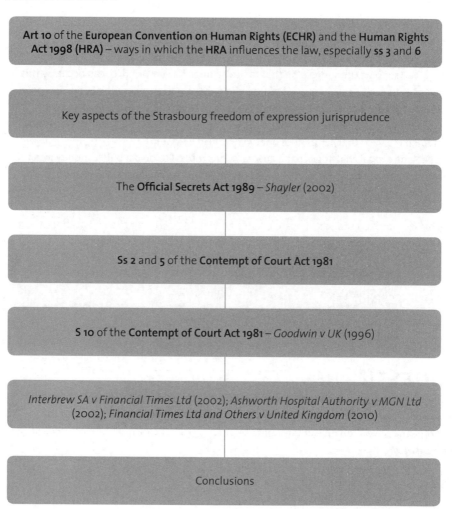

Art 10 of the **European Convention on Human Rights (ECHR)** and the **Human Rights Act 1998 (HRA)** – ways in which the **HRA** influences the law, especially **ss 3** and **6**

Key aspects of the Strasbourg freedom of expression jurisprudence

The **Official Secrets Act 1989** – *Shayler* (2002)

Ss 2 and 5 of the **Contempt of Court Act 1981**

S 10 of the **Contempt of Court Act 1981** – *Goodwin v UK* (1996)

Interbrew SA v Financial Times Ltd (2002); *Ashworth Hospital Authority v MGN Ltd* (2002); *Financial Times Ltd and Others v United Kingdom* (2010)

Conclusions

ANSWER

The HRA received the ECHR, including the guarantee of freedom of expression under Art 10, into domestic law. Thus public authorities and the courts became bound under s 6 HRA by Art 10. Legislation must be read by the courts in a manner that gives effect, so far as is possible, to the Convention rights (s 3 of the HRA); if this is not possible, a declaration of incompatibility may be issued (s 4), and remedial action may be taken as a result (s 10). Further, the HRA gives special regard to the importance of freedom of expression and forbids restraint of publication before a full trial of an injunction, unless the court is satisfied that the applicant is more likely than not to win at trial (s 12).

The Strasbourg freedom of expression jurisprudence demonstrates that Art 10 is one of the most significant Articles of the Convention, as far as *political* expression is concerned. The Court has repeatedly asserted that freedom of expression 'constitutes one of the essential foundations of a democratic society' (*The Observer and The Guardian v UK* (1991)) and that it is applicable not only to 'information' or 'ideas' that are regarded as inoffensive, but also to those that 'offend, shock or disturb' (*Thorgeirson v Iceland* (1992)). Particular stress has been laid upon 'the preeminent role of the press', which, in its vital role of 'public watchdog', has a duty 'to impart information and ideas on matters of public interest' that the public 'has a right to receive' (*Castells v Spain* (1992)). However, it is a marked feature of the Strasbourg jurisprudence that clearly political speech receives a much more robust degree of protection than other types of expression. Thus, the 'political' speech cases of *Sunday Times* (1979), *Jersild v Denmark* (1994), *Lingens v Austria* (1986) and *Thorgeirson v Iceland* (1992) all resulted in findings that Art 10 had been violated and all were marked by an intensive review of the restriction in question in which the margin of appreciation was narrowed almost to vanishing point. By contrast, in cases involving artistic speech, an exactly opposite pattern emerges: applicants have tended to be unsuccessful and a deferential approach to the judgments of the national authorities as to its obscene or blasphemous nature has been adopted (*Müller v Switzerland* (1991) ; *Handyside v UK* (1976) ; *Otto-Preminger Institut v Austria* (1994) ; *Gay News v UK* (1982)). Where artistic speech, however, is viewed as having a political element, the Court does adopt a strict stance (*VBK v Austria* (2010)) in holding the national authorities to account under Art 10.

Thus, it is submitted that the statutory developments to be considered in this essay are undergoing, and will undergo, fresh scrutiny under the HRA, creating further possible changes in the balance that they create between protecting freedom of expression and protecting other interests, such as the need for official secrecy and the administration of justice. This is especially the case where the statutes in question restrict political speech, broadly defined. Article 10, unlike domestic law, provides a clear means of attempting to consider the extent to which the 'balance' in question is maintained, since its starting point is the primacy of freedom of expression, and Art 10(2) provides a number of tests that must be satisfied before a restriction of expression can be justified. However, this essay will argue that, as Fenwick and Phillipson (2006) find, Article 10 as applied via the

HRA, has not on the whole had a dramatic impact in this area. It has tended to change the process of reasoning, but not the outcome.[8]

The Official Secrets Act 1989 represented a highly significant development that was arguably likely to prove more effective in preventing disclosure and publication of information than its predecessor. The Act was supposed to bring about an increase in the information that could be disclosed to the public without incurring criminal liability, by introducing a test that took into account the substance of the information. However, it is apparent that there is no test for harm at all in certain of the categories of information covered, including s 1, which prevents members of the security services disclosing anything, however trivial, about the operation of those services. In the categories covered by s 3(1)(b), although there appears to be a test for harm, it may in fact be satisfied merely by establishing the nature of the information. Thus, the Act was always unlikely to have a liberalising impact on the publication of information, allowing the public to scrutinise the workings of government. It might therefore have been expected that the HRA could have a liberalising effect on it, that s 3 could be used to impose an Art 10-friendly interpretation on the statutory provisions, especially as they affect political expression. The provisions prevent civil servants divulging relevant information to journalists, and journalists themselves are also threatened with sanctions if they publish material covered by the 1989 Act (s 5).

However, the Shayler case (2002) put paid to the expectations that the HRA would have a liberalising effect on ss 1 and 4 of the 1989 Act. In 2002, David Shayler was tried under the 1989 Act on the basis that he had infringed ss 1 and 4 by divulging MI6 secrets. Since s 1 of the 1989 Act provides no means of balancing any harm to the security and intelligence services against the interests of freedom of expression, it might have been expected that it would be found to be incompatible with Art 10.

This argument was rejected by the House of Lords (Shayler (2002)) on the basis that avenues of complaint were available to Shayler. There were various persons to whom the disclosure could be made, including those identified in s 12. Further, significantly, under s 7(3) of the 1989 Act, a disclosure can be made to others if authorised; those empowered to afford authorisation are identified in s 12. Thus while a truly blanket ban on disclosure of the information in question could not have been viewed as proportionate to the aim sought to be achieved, under Art 10(2), the ban was not absolute, and therefore proportionality was achieved. Thus Art 10 has had no impact on ss 1(1) and 4(1) since, according to this ruling, there is no incompatibility between Art 10 and the two provisions. One of the most important principles recognised at Strasbourg is that rights must be real, not tokenistic or illusory. It is argued that the right to freedom of

---

8   Candidates will gain credit for demonstrating their appreciation of cautious, nuanced developments in the law, rather than jumping to the conclusion that **Art 10** under the **HRA** has ushered in, or will usher in, dramatic changes.

expression – one of the central rights of the ECHR – is rendered illusory by ss 1(1) and 4(1) of the 1989 Act in relation to reporting on or communications about allegedly unlawful activities of the security services – a matter of great significance in a democracy.

If ss 1 and 4 of the 1989 Act make little effort to balance national security and the protection for use of covert surveillance against freedom of expression, the Contempt of Court Act 1981 in contrast does make an overt effort to create a balance between protecting the administration of justice and media freedom of expression. In particular, it introduced stricter time limits (s 2(3)), a more precise test for the *actus reus* (s 2(2)) and allowed some articles on matters of public interest to escape liability even though prejudice to proceedings was created (s 5). Section 5 reflects the guarantee under Art 10. It affords a high value to political speech, broadly defined, and therefore reflects the value placed upon such speech at Strasbourg. *AG v English* (1983) is the leading case on s 5 and is generally considered to provide a good example of the kind of case for which s 5 was framed. The ruling gave an emphasis to freedom of speech that tended to bring the strict liability rule into harmony with Art 10 as interpreted by the European Court's ruling in the *Sunday Times* case. Due to the interpretation afforded to s 5, it is probable that the 1981 Act is already in harmony with the demands of Art 10. However the inception of the HRA appears to have had an indirect impact in changing the balance that it strikes between the two interests in question (*A-G v Guardian* (1999)), and in effect media freedom has been given greater protection, since the hurdle represented by s 2(2) has become higher, not necessarily to the benefit of protection for freedom of expression. These changes, however, are those of interpretation and do not necessarily require reform of the Act to protect fair trials under Article 6 ECHR.[9]

In other respects, it might have been expected that the 1981 Act would require reform or at least reinterpretation due to the inception of the HRA. Section 10 of the 1981 Act provides some protection for media sources, unless a court finds that disclosure is necessary in the interests of justice or national security or for the prevention of disorder or crime. Thus, s 10 creates a presumption in favour of journalists who wish to protect their sources, which is, however, subject to four wide exceptions, of which the widest arises where the interests of justice require that disclosure should be made. In *Goodwin v UK* (1996), the European Court found that Art 10 had been infringed in the *X v Morgan Grampian Publishers* decision, as insufficient weight had been given to the need of journalists to protect their sources. It might have appeared, therefore, that s 10 would require reinterpretation under s 3 once the HRA was in force, in order to take the *Goodwin* decision into account.

However, in *Interbrew SA v Financial Times Ltd* (2002) and *Ashworth Hospital Authority v MGN Ltd* (2002), the Court of Appeal and House of Lords, respectively, considered that the

---

9   This point picks up on the mention of other Articles of the **ECHR** as well as **Art 10** in the title.

journalists in question had to reveal the source of the information in the interests of justice, interpreting that phrase very widely. The House of Lords in *Ashworth* and *Interbrew* purported to do what the ECtHR did in *Goodwin*, but, it is argued, misweighed both the harm done to the privacy interest and the value of the speech. In the context the privacy interest in secrecy was less pressing since some of the patients at Ashworth appeared to want to bring malpractice to the attention of the authorities and so appeared to be content with disclosure of the medical records. Both of these decisions took account of the effect of the HRA and the courts considered that the outcomes were consistent with the demands of **Art 10** of the **Convention**. In the *Interbrew* case – *Financial Times Ltd and Others v United Kingdom* (2010) the Strasbourg Court found a breach of **Art 10** on the basis that the House of Lords had not given enough weight to **Art 10**, thus requiring further reform via interpretation in this context. The ECtHR held unanimously that an order requiring various media organisations to disclose original leaked documents which might have led to the revelation of a journalistic source constituted an unjustified interference with **Article 10 ECHR** (the right to freedom of expression).[10]

In conclusion, it appears that while the HRA may not have ensured that protection of freedom of speech is enhanced where it comes into conflict with the interests of the State, especially the interest of national security, the judiciary does show an awareness of the need to afford such protection. The HRA requires judges to weigh the interest claimed against the demands of freedom of expression under **Art 10(2)**, giving primacy to the latter right. It is possible that eventually **Art 10** will be used to create clearer, fairer boundaries to restrictions on freedom of expression, outside matters relating to the security and intelligence services. However, judicial determination to create a proper balance between freedom of speech and other interests may find expression only where it is not countered by judicial reluctance to allow the needs (or apparent needs) of such other Interests, especially national security, to be abrogated. It would appear that the UK statutory provisions in question do not require reform in Parliament in order to ensure compatibility with **Art 10** of the **ECHR** under the HRA, but this does not necessarily mean that freedom of expression is receiving the degree of protection that it would receive at Strasbourg – as the *Interbrew* case demonstrated.

Common Pitfall ✗

Giving a general survey only and then ending with a brief sentence, unsupported by the evidence, that the **HRA** Is likely to have a dramatic effect in raising free expression standards.

---

10 Candidates will gain credit for Indicating that despite the **HRA**, domestic findings on freedom of expression may still be found not to have upheld a satisfactory free speech standard at Strasbourg.

Aim Higher

The points about the *Interbrew* case at Strasbourg could have been developd further. The point could be made that due to the impact of **s 2 HRA** the case is likely to lead to a change in the interpretation of **s 10** domestically.

The Individual and the State: Police Powers and Counter-Terrorist Measures

INTRODUCTION

This chapter concerns the balance struck by the law between 'ordinary' powers conferred on the police, counter-terrorist measures, and the maintenance of individual freedom and of due process.

Examiners often set problem questions in the area of 'ordinary' (as opposed to counter-terror) police powers, since the detailed rules of the Police and Criminal Evidence Act 1984 (PACE), as amended, and the Codes of Practice (revision of Codes C, G and H occurred in 2012) made under it lend themselves to such a format. (Note also the power to stop and search arising under the Misuse of Drugs Act 1971, s 23(2).) The questions usually concern a number of stages from first contact between police and suspect in the street up to the charge. This allows consideration of the rules governing stop and search, arrest, searching of premises, seizure of articles, detention, treatment in the police station and interviewing. (It must be borne in mind that interviews do not invariably take place in the police station; an important area in the question may concern an interview of the suspect that takes place in the street or in the police car.) Depending on the areas covered in your particular course, you need to be aware of the most important changes made between 2005–2012 to the PACE Codes. In particular, an arrest Code, Code G, and a special Code, Code H (covering police detention of terrorist suspects) were introduced in 2006. The Codes, especially Code C, are very long and detailed; you only need, however, to be aware of the key provisions – the ones mentioned in the questions below. You also need to be aware of ss 34–37 of the Criminal Justice and Public Order Act 1994, as amended, which curtail the right to silence and therefore affect police interviewing. (In freedom of assembly questions involving police powers, covered in Chapter 12, you also need to be aware of the extension of police powers in the public order context, contained in Pt V of the 1994 Act.) The common law power to arrest to prevent a breach of the peace is still extensively used and may need to be considered. It is considered in Chapter 12.

The rules governing obstruction and assault on a police officer in the execution of his duty under s 89 of the Police Act 1996 may be relevant as necessitating analysis of the legality of police conduct, in order to determine whether or not a police officer was in the execution of his duty. Finally, the question may call for an analysis of the forms of redress available to the suspect in respect of any misuse of police power. If essay questions are set, they often tend to place an emphasis on the balance struck by PACE between the suspect's rights and police powers.

Police powers to deal with 'ordinary' suspects differ from those available to deal with terrorist suspects; in general the level of due process available in relation to terrorist suspects is lower. Also, post-9/11 special measures were introduced to deal with terrorist suspects outside the normal criminal justice process – these were and are proactive measures, including detention without trial, designed to deal with terrorist activity before it occurs. So this chapter deals with a range of police powers applicable to 'ordinary' suspects and also aspects of the current counter-terrorist scheme. The Codes of Practice made under the Police and Criminal Evidence Act 1984 reflect the differences between terrorist suspects and non-terrorist suspects since terrorist suspects are no longer covered by Code C (the Code covering interviews and police detention) but by Code H. Police powers in relation to terrorist suspects, special terrorism offences and sanctions operating outside the criminal justice system are contained in the Terrorism Act 2000, as amended, especially by the Terrorism Act 2006, and the Terrorism Prevention and Investigation Measures Act 2011, which came into force in 2012. Part 4 of the Anti-Terrorism, Crime and Security Act 2001 – the key UK counter-terrorist response to 9/11 – has been repealed, as has the Prevention of Terrorism Act 2005, which governed the control orders regime. However, this chapter takes account of both sets of provisions in order to place the 2011 Act in its proper context. The provisions of the 2000 and 2006 Acts were added to by the Counter-Terrorism Act 2008. Counter-terrorism powers are most likely to be discussed in essay format. It should be noted that some public law courses may not cover counter-terrorism powers, or may cover only the 'police powers' aspects.

Articles 5 and 6 of the European Convention on Human Rights (ECHR), which provide guarantees of liberty and security of the person and of a fair trial respectively, were received into UK law once the Human Rights Act 1998 (HRA) came fully into force in 2000. It should be noted that Art 6 protects a fair hearing in the civil and criminal contexts, but our concern is with the criminal context, and in particular with pre-trial procedures that may affect the fairness of the trial and which, therefore, may need to be considered under Art 6 (*Teixeira v Portugal* (1998); *Khan v UK* (2000)). Under the HRA, Arts 5 and 6 and other Convention Articles relevant in this area, such as Art 8 (which provides a right to respect for private life and for the home), are directly applicable in UK courts since the courts are bound by them (s 6 HRA). The police and other public authorities involved in the criminal justice process are also so bound.

The rights should also be taken into account in relation to interpreting and applying common law and statutory provisions affecting the powers of State agents, including the police, and counter-terrorist powers. Section 3 of the HRA requires that: 'So far as it is possible to do so, primary and subordinate legislation must be read and given effect in a way which is compatible with the Convention rights.' Section 3(2)(b) reads: 'this section does not affect the validity, continuing operation or enforcement of any incompatible primary legislation.' This goes well beyond the previous obligation to resolve ambiguity in statutes by reference to the ECHR. All statutes affecting this area, in particular, PACE, the Terrorism Act 2000 and the (now repealed) Prevention of Terrorism Act 2005, therefore must be interpreted so as to be in harmony with the Convention, if that is at all possible.

So the application of the powers under all of these statutes, in specific instances, should be in harmony with all of the Convention rights, since those applying the powers, including the courts, are bound by those rights, under s 6 HRA. As Chapter 9 explained, under s 6, Convention guarantees are binding only against public authorities. In this context, if the police or other State agents use powers deriving from any legal source in order to interfere with the liberty or privacy of the citizen, this means not only that the rights should be adhered to, but that the citizen may be able to bring an action against them under Arts 5, 6 or 8 (and/or any other relevant Article). Within the criminal process, citizens can rely on Art 6 in order to ensure the fairness of the procedure, under s 7(1)(b) of the HRA. Also, in a hearing relating to interference with the liberty of terrorist suspects *outside* the normal criminal process, Art 6 will be applicable. Exam questions therefore demand awareness of the Arts 5, 6 and 8 jurisprudence and of the impact of the HRA in this area. It is not good practice merely to refer to the HRA in answers; you should refer to specific sections of the HRA, usually ss 3 or 6 and to the relevant Convention right. Reference should also be made to the ECHR jurisprudence and to the domestic use of the Convention in relevant post-HRA cases.

Checklist ✔

Students must be familiar with the following areas:

- the key provisions under **PACE**, as amended, in particular by **s 110** of the **Serious and Organised Crime Act 2005**, the **PACE Codes of Practice (2008)** affecting the areas mentioned above, especially **Codes A** and **C**, and **ss 1, 2, 17, 18, 24, 28, 32, 58, 76**, and **78** of **PACE**;

- **s 23(2)** of the **Misuse of Drugs Act 1971**;

- key cases on **PACE** and related provisions, especially *R v Samuel* (1988), *R v Loosely* (2001), *R v Khan* (1996), *Osman* (1999), *DPP v Hawkins* (1988), *R v Beckles* (2004), *R v Condron* (1997), *R v Delaney* (1988), *R v Paris* (1993) and *Gillan* (2006);

- the provisions under the **Criminal Justice and Public Order Act 1994 (CJPOA)**, as amended, relevant to police powers, especially **ss 34, 36, 37** and **60**;

- **s 58** of the **Youth Justice and Criminal Evidence Act 1999**, which inserts **34(2A)** into the **CJPOA**;

- the offences of obstruction and assault on a police officer in the execution of his duty under **s 89** of the **Police Act 1996**;

- the issues raised by the revisions of the **Codes of Practice** made under **PACE**; latest revisions; new arrest Code, **Code G**, introduced in 2006;

- the **PACE** rules governing exclusion of evidence, particularly **s 78**;

- the relevant tortious remedies;

- the police complaints mechanism under **Police Reform Act 2002 Pt 2** and **Sched 3**;

- police powers contained in the **Terrorism Act 2000**, as amended, especially by the **Terrorism Act 2006**; **PACE Code H (2006)**;

- counter-terrorist offences under the **Terrorism Act 2000**, as amended;

- counter-terrorist measures under the **Prevention of Terrorism Act 2005**;

- **Pt 4** of the **Anti-Terrorism, Crime and Security Act 2001**; the **Terrorism Prevention and Investigation Measures Act 2011** – key provisions;

- **Arts 3, 5, 6** and **8** of the **Convention**; relevant **ECHR** case law, especially *Khan v UK* (2000), *Condron v UK* (2001), *Beckles v UK* (2003);

- the **HRA**, especially **ss 2, 3**, and **6**.

QUESTION 40

Albert and Bill, two policemen in uniform and driving a police car, see Colin outside a factory gate at 11.30 pm on a Saturday. Albert and Bill know that Colin has a conviction for burglary. Colin looks nervous and is looking repeatedly at his watch. Bearing in mind a spate of burglaries in the area, Albert and Bill ask Colin what he is doing. Colin replies that he is waiting for a friend. Dissatisfied with this response, Bill tells Colin to turn out his pockets, which he does. Bill seizes a bunch of keys that Colin produces and, still suspicious, tells Colin to accompany them to the police station. Colin then becomes abusive; Bill takes hold of him to restrain him, and Colin tries to push Bill away. Albert and Bill then bundle Colin into the police car, telling him that he is under arrest. Colin does not resist them. They proceed to Colin's flat and search it, discovering a small amount of cannabis, which they seize.

Albert and Bill then take Colin to the police station, arriving at 12.20 am. He is cautioned under Code C, informed of his rights under Code C by the custody officer, and told that he is suspected of dealing in cannabis. Colin asks if he can see a solicitor, but his request is refused 'for the time being'. Colin is then questioned and eventually admits to supplying cannabis. The interview is tape-recorded. He is then charged with supplying cannabis and with assaulting a police officer in the execution of his duty.

▶ Advise Colin.

How to Answer this Question

This is a reasonably straightforward question, but it does cover a very wide range of issues. The most significant and difficult issue is that of the arguably unlawful arrest(s) –

so that should form a large part of the answer. The most straightforward approach is to consider the legality of the police conduct at every point. Once this has been done, the applicability of the possible forms of redress can be considered. It should be noted that the examinee is merely asked to 'advise Colin'; therefore, all relevant possibilities should be discussed – albeit briefly due to the time constraint. European Court of Human Rights (ECtHR) cases should be considered in relation to the relevant Articles of the ECHR, contained in Sched 1 to the HRA, and the effects of ss 3 and 6 of the HRA should be mentioned where relevant.

Applying the Law

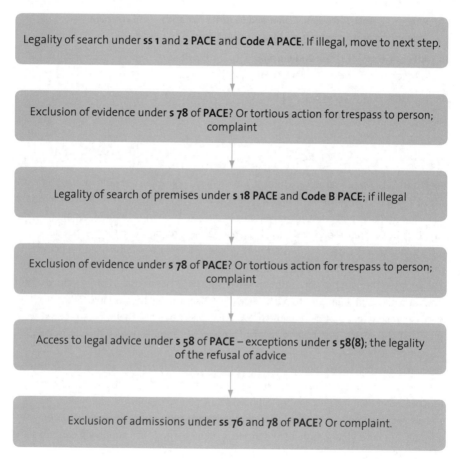

Legality of search under **ss 1** and **2 PACE** and **Code A PACE**. If illegal, move to next step.

Exclusion of evidence under **s 78** of **PACE**? Or tortious action for trespass to person; complaint

Legality of search of premises under **s 18 PACE** and **Code B PACE**; if illegal

Exclusion of evidence under **s 78** of **PACE**? Or tortious action for trespass to person; complaint

Access to legal advice under **s 58** of **PACE** – exceptions under **s 58(8)**; the legality of the refusal of advice

Exclusion of admissions under **ss 76** and **78** of **PACE**? Or complaint.

This diagram shows the main issues relating to **PACE** *that should be discussed in your answer.*

ANSWER

The legality of the police conduct in this instance will be considered first; any possible forms of redress open to Colin will then be examined. The impact of the Human Rights Act 1998 (HRA), which affords the European Convention on Human Rights (ECHR) further effect in domestic law, will be taken into account at a number of significant points. The police are bound by s 6 HRA to abide by the ECHR. Articles 5 and 6 are of particular significance in this context.

When Colin is asked to turn out his pockets, this appears to be part of a voluntary search. However, such searches are now forbidden under Code A. Thus the search and seizure of the keys should be part of a lawful stop and search. Thus, it must be shown that the police officers complied with the provisions of ss 1 and 2 of PACE and of Code A. Under s 1(2), a police officer may search for stolen or prohibited articles if he has reasonable grounds (s 1(3)) for believing that he will find such articles.

The necessary reasonable suspicion is defined in s 2 of Code A. There must be some objective basis for it that will relate to the nature of the article suspected of being carried. Various factors could be taken into account, including the time and place, the behaviour or demeanour of the person concerned (see *Slade* (1996)) and the carrying of certain articles in an area that has recently experienced a number of burglaries. In the instant situation, the lateness of the hour and the fact that Colin is outside a factory in an area that has recently experienced burglaries, coupled with his nervous behaviour, might give rise to a generalised suspicion, but it could be argued that the suspicion does not relate specifically enough to a particular article, since there is very little to suggest that Colin is carrying any particular article (this was found in *Black v DPP* (1995) and in *Francis* (1992)). Following this argument, it is doubtful whether a power to stop and search arises. But in any event, even if it could be established that reasonable suspicion is present, the search is unlawful, since the procedural requirements of s 2 of PACE are breached (*Osman* (1999)); the seizure of the keys is therefore also unlawful.

After Colin becomes abusive, Bill takes hold of him to restrain him. If this restraining is not part of a lawful arrest and therefore lawful under s 117 of PACE, it could be characterised as an assault on Colin. Even if s 24 PACE is satisfied on the basis that reasonable suspicion of burglary may be present, s 28 is not, since no reason is given for the arrest and the fact of the arrest is not stated, although it is later. At this point, before Colin becomes abusive, it would be practicable to state the fact of and reason for the arrest as required by s 28 since Colin has been cooperative so far; therefore the arrest becomes unlawful at that point (*DPP v Hawkins* (1988)). Therefore, since no power to arrest arises, the restraint of Colin is unlawful. Under s 2 Code A, officers need to inform the suspect of the fact of the arrest even if it is obvious; they also need to inform of the reason for the arrest. A strict approach to s 28 PACE also accords with the demands of Art 5(2), under the HRA.

The arrest may be for simple assault or for assault on a police officer in the execution of his duty, an offence arising under s 89(1) of the Police Act 1996, but this reason is not given. If it is to arise under s 24, two tests must be satisfied. First, it must be shown that one of the general arrest conditions under s 24 arises: the police need to show that the arrest is needed to allow the prompt and effective investigation of the suspected offence in question or to prevent prosecution of the offence from being hindered by Colin's disappearance (s 24(5)(e) and (f)). It is probable that one of these conditions will be found to be satisfied in relation to most arrests, and an offence has already occurred.

Second, Albert and Bill must be able to show that Colin is suspected of an offence – that the assault has been perpetrated or that they have reasonable suspicion that he is guilty of the offence (s 24(2)(3)). It may be argued, following *Marsden* (1868) and *Fennell* (1970), that since Bill had exceeded his authority in restraining Colin, Colin was entitled to resist by way of reasonable force; any such resistance would be lawful and therefore could not amount to an assault on an officer in the execution of his duty, so on this argument the offence under s 89 Police Act is not made out. Simple assault would not be made out either since he was entitled to resist. Even assuming that reasonable suspicion is present of assault or burglary, no reason is given for the arrest.

Thus, it is arguable that the arrest was therefore unlawful for a period of time, before Colin pushed Bill. It arguably became lawful for a period of time, but then again became unlawful when the point came and passed at which Colin could have been given the reason (under s 28 and Code G) – in the police car. On this argument, when Colin is bundled into the car, Albert and Bill are entitled to use reasonable force under s 117, as they are in the exercise of an arrest power. But they are not entitled to use force before Colin pushes Bill. The subsequent detention – after the point when they could have informed Colin of the reason for the arrest – is also unlawful. These findings as to the arrest would appear to accord with the demands of Art 5(1) and (2) ECHR, received into UK law under the HRA. The police are bound 'by the HRA to obide by the Convention rights, as a public authority'.

The search of Colin's flat also appears to be unlawful. Under s 18, a power to enter and search premises after arrest arises in instances covered by s 24. Since the arrest appears to be unlawful at this point, this condition is not satisfied. It follows from this that the power of seizure under s 19(2) does not arise, as it may only be exercised under s 19(1) by a constable lawfully on the premises. The seizure of the cannabis is therefore unlawful. The search of the home also appears to breach Art 8 under the HRA and gives rise to an action in trespass. The search should also comply with Code B, but Colin is not given a notice of powers and rights as the Code requires. Section 30(1) PACE requires that Colin should be taken to the police station as soon as practicable after arrest; since there is no basis for the search, it appears that s 30(1) has not been complied with.

At the police station, Colin is denied access to legal advice. Delay in affording such access will only be lawful if one of the contingencies envisaged under s 58(8) of PACE will arise if

THE INDIVIDUAL AND THE STATE 239

a solicitor is contacted. Following *Samuel* (1988), the police must have a clear basis for this belief. In this instance, the police made no effort to invoke one of the exceptions and have therefore breached s 58 and para 6 of Code C, which provides that once a suspect has requested advice, he must not be interviewed until he has received it.

Having identified a series of illegal acts on the part of the police, it will now be necessary to consider the redress, if any, available to Colin in respect of them. The first such act was the unlawful seizure of the keys. The appropriate tortious cause of action in this instance will be trespass to goods; damages will, however, be minimal.

In taking hold of and then detaining Colin outside the context of a lawful arrest, Bill commits assault and battery and breaches Art 5 of the ECHR. The facts of the instant case closely resemble those of *Collins v Willcock* (1984) or *Kenlin v Gardner* (1967), which established this principle. Further, the unlawful arrest and the subsequent unlawful detention in the car and police station will support a claim of false imprisonment. The search of the home, based on an unlawful arrest, will give rise to an action in trespass to land. The seizure of the keys was part of an unlawful search; Colin could therefore sue the police authority for trespass to land and to goods.

Colin may hope that the keys and cannabis will be excluded from evidence under s 78 of PACE, as found during the course of unlawful searches. However, according to *Thomas* (1990) and *Effick* (1992), and confirmed in *Khan* (1997) and *Loosely* (2001), physical evidence is admissible subject to a very narrow discretion to exclude it. It appears that no strong argument for exclusion of the cannabis or keys from evidence arises, and this outcome appears to be in accordance with the demands of Art 6 under s 3 of the HRA. Section 78 must be interpreted in accordance with Art 6, under s 3 HRA, but no change in the current interpretation appears to be required due to the findings in *Khan v UK* (2000).[1]

Can a reasonable argument be advanced that Colin's admissions in the police station interview should be excluded from evidence under s 76? Following *Alladice* (1988) and *Hughes* (1988), unless it can be shown that the custody officer acted in bad faith in failing to allow Colin access to a solicitor, it seems that s 76(2)(a) will not apply. Following *Delaney* (1989), it is necessary to show under s 76(2)(b) that the defendant was in some particularly difficult or vulnerable position, making the breach of PACE of special significance. Since this does not appear to be the case here, it seems that s 76(2)(b) cannot be invoked.

....

1   It is important for candidates to remember to refer to the **ECHR**, received into UK law under the **HRA**. It is not enough just to consider police powers. That is the case even if referring to the **ECHR** would not affect the outcome of the answer.

On the other hand, Colin's admissions may be excluded from evidence under s 78 on the basis that the police breached s 58.[2] Following *Samuel* (1988), it must be shown that the breach of s 58 was causally related to the admissions made in the second interview. (It should be noted that the wrong caution was given; the caution should have been that of Annex C para 2 Code C since the restriction on drawing adverse inferences from silence applied as he had been denied access to legal advice.) Since he was not afforded an opportunity to have legal advice (s 34(2A) Criminal Justice and Public Order Act 1994), the adviser could have warned him that there was probably no risk involved in staying silent under s 34 CJPOA. On this analysis, it is possible that the requisite causal relationship exists and the admissions might, therefore, be excluded from evidence under s 78. A further possibility is that the actions of the police in breaching the PACE Codes and PACE itself could be the subject of a complaint, as could the other unlawful actions mentioned, under the Police Reform Act 2002.[3]

Finally, Colin may want to know whether the charge of assaulting a police officer in the execution of his duty will succeed. Clearly, it will fail on the argument that Colin's actions did not amount to an assault, as he was entitled to resist Bill. Moreover, it has been determined that Bill was outside the execution of his duty since he was in the course of perpetrating an unlawful arrest.

Common Pitfalls

Some students concentrate on the police powers provisions and fail to mention the **HRA**. The Introduction in weaker answers refers only to **PACE**.

Aim Higher

The approach to exclusion of the admissions is given additional weight by the importance attached to access to legal advice by the European Court of Human Rights under **Art 6** (received into UK law under the **HRA**) in cases such as *Murray (John) v UK* (1996) and *Averill v UK* (2000). Under **ss 6 and 2** of the **HRA**, those decisions need to be taken into account in considering whether the evidence should be excluded; they would be likely to tip the balance in favour of exclusion.

---

2   Candidates will gain credit for remembering to discuss **s 78** in relation to exclusion of evidence (any type of evidence) as well as **s 76**.

3   When considering means of redress, candidates will gain credit for bearing in mind the possibility of making a complaint.

QUESTION 41

Toby, who has a history of mental disorder and has two convictions for possessing cannabis, is standing on a street corner at 2 am on Sunday when he is seen by two police officers in uniform, Andy and Beryl. Andy says: 'What are you up to now, Toby? Let's have a look in your pockets.' Toby does not reply, but turns out his pockets and produces a small quantity of Ecstasy. Andy and Beryl then ask Toby to come to the police station; he agrees to do so.

They arrive at the police station at 2.20 am. Toby is cautioned, informed of his rights under Code C by the custody officer and told that he is suspected of dealing in Ecstasy. He asks if he can see a solicitor, but his request is refused by Superintendent Smith, on the ground that this will lead to the alerting of others whom the police suspect are involved. Toby is then questioned for two hours, but makes no reply to the questions. He then has a short break; when the interview recommences, he is recautioned and reminded of his right to legal advice although he is again told that he cannot yet exercise the right. After another hour, he admits to supplying Ecstasy. The interviews are tape-recorded. He is then charged with supplying Ecstasy.

Toby now says that he only confessed because he thought he had to in order to get home.

▶ Advise Toby as to any means of redress available to him.

How to Answer the Question

This question is fairly demanding and quite tricky, since it covers the problem of apparently voluntary compliance with police requests and the particular difficulties created when the police are dealing with a mentally disordered person. The most straightforward approach is probably to consider the legality of the police conduct at every point. Once this has been done, the applicability of the possible forms of redress in respect of each possible breach can be considered. As special problems arise in respect of each, they should be looked at separately. It should be noted that the examinee is merely asked to 'advise Toby as to any means of redress'; therefore, all relevant possibilities should be discussed. It is important to remember to consider whether adverse inferences are likely to be drawn at trial from Toby's silence under ss 34 and 36 of the Criminal Justice and Public Order Act 1994 (CJPOA), as amended.

Applying the Law

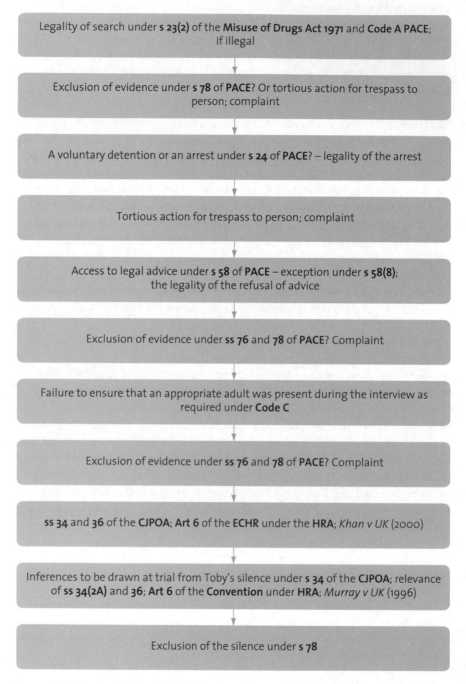

Legality of search under s 23(2) of the **Misuse of Drugs Act 1971** and **Code A PACE**; if illegal

Exclusion of evidence under **s 78** of **PACE**? Or tortious action for trespass to person; complaint

A voluntary detention or an arrest under **s 24** of **PACE**? – legality of the arrest

Tortious action for trespass to person; complaint

Access to legal advice under **s 58** of **PACE** – exception under **s 58(8)**; the legality of the refusal of advice

Exclusion of evidence under **ss 76** and **78** of **PACE**? Complaint

Failure to ensure that an appropriate adult was present during the interview as required under **Code C**

Exclusion of evidence under **ss 76** and **78** of **PACE**? Complaint

ss 34 and **36** of the **CJPOA**; **Art 6** of the **ECHR** under the **HRA**; *Khan v UK (2000)*

Inferences to be drawn at trial from Toby's silence under **s 34** of the **CJPOA**; relevance of **ss 34(2A)** and **36**; **Art 6** of the **Convention** under HRA; *Murray v UK (1996)*

Exclusion of the silence under **s 78**

The main legal principles to apply in this scenario are outlined here.

ANSWER

The legality of the police conduct in this instance will be considered first; any possible forms of redress open to Toby will then be examined. In both instances, the impact of the Human Rights Act 1998 (HRA) will be taken into account.

When Toby is asked to turn out his pockets, this appears to be a request. He cannot be subject to a voluntary search under s 1.5 Code A (2008). Thus, the search should not have taken place unless the police officers can show reasonable suspicion as the basis for the exercise of the power. In order to do so, it must be shown that the police officers complied with the provisions of s 23(2) of the Misuse of Drugs Act 1971 and of Code A. Under s 23(2), a police officer may search for controlled drugs if he has reasonable grounds for believing that he will find such articles. The necessary reasonable suspicion is defined in s 2 of Code A. There must be some objective basis for it, which might include various objective factors. In the instant situation, the lateness of the hour might give rise to some suspicion, but it is apparent that the suspicion does not relate specifically enough to the possibility that Toby is in possession of drugs (*Black v DPP* (1995)). In *Slade* (1996), the suspect's demeanour gave rise to suspicion; here, Toby has done nothing that might arouse suspicion since he is merely standing on a corner. Following this argument, no power to stop and search arises; the search itself and the seizure of the Ecstasy are therefore unlawful. It should further be noted that the procedural requirements of s 2 PACE are breached since the officers do not identify themselves or give the other required information (see *Osman v DPP* (1999), in which it was found that s 2 is mandatory). There are therefore two bases on which to find that the search is unlawful.[4]

The request made to come to the police station appears to assume that Toby will come on a voluntary basis. When he is cautioned, he must also be told that he is free to leave if he is not under arrest (Code C). It is not clear that this is done. Arguably, since the police must abide by Art 5 of the ECHR under s 6 of the HRA, the better view is that he has not given a true consent to the detention, on the ground that where there is a doubt as to consent to a deprivation of liberty, a strict view should be taken giving the emphasis to the primary right (*Murray v UK* (1994)).

If this assumption is correct, it is necessary to consider whether a power to arrest arises. Toby is presumably arrested for possessing Ecstasy, an offence arising under s 5(3) of the Misuse of Drugs Act 1971. In order to arrest under s 24 PACE, it is necessary to show that Andy and Beryl had reasonable grounds for suspecting that Toby was in possession of the Ecstasy. Clearly, this is the case. Nevertheless, even assuming that reasonable suspicion is present, the 'arrest' (if it may be characterised as such) is clearly unlawful due to the failure

---

4   Even if a candidate decided that the search might be lawful it would still be important to consider forms of redress on the basis that illegality might be found – i.e. as an alternative argument.

to state the fact of the arrest and the reason for it as required under s 28 of PACE and Art 5(2) of the Convention (see *Wilson v Chief Constable of Lancashire Constabulary* (2000)).

At the police station, Toby is not afforded access to legal advice. Delay in affording such access will be lawful only if it is the case that one of the contingencies envisaged under s 58(8) will arise if a solicitor is contacted. In this instance, the police will wish to rely on the exception under s 58(8)(b), allowing delay where contacting the solicitor will lead to the alerting of others suspected of the offence. It will be necessary for the police to show, following *Samuel* (1988), that some quality about the particular solicitor in question could found a reasonable belief that he or she would bring about one of the contingencies envisaged if contacted. There is nothing to suggest that the police officers have any basis for this belief, especially as Toby has not specified the solicitor he wishes to contact. He may well wish to contact the duty solicitor. A further condition for the operation of s 58(8) is that Toby is being detained in respect of an indictable offence. He is in detention at this point in respect of possession of Ecstasy. So, as supplying Ecstasy is an indictable offence, this condition is fulfilled. However, the lack of any basis for the necessary reasonable belief under s 58(8) means that there has been a breach of s 58. This strict approach to s 58 is supported by *Samuel* (1988) and by the approach of the European Court of Human Rights to the right of access to legal advice under Art 6. It has placed considerable importance on the right in cases such as *Murray (John) v UK* (1996) and *Averill v UK* (2000).

Since Toby is mentally disordered, he should not have been interviewed except in the presence of an 'appropriate adult' as required under Code C. Under Code C, if an officer has any suspicion that a person may be mentally disordered or mentally vulnerable, then he should be treated as such for the purposes of the Code. Therefore, a further breach of PACE has occurred, unless it could be argued that the officers were not aware of the disorder; if so, following *Raymond Maurice Clarke* (1989), no breach of the Code provision occurred. The behaviour of Andy suggests, however, that the officers were aware of Toby's condition.

Having identified a series of breaches of PACE and the Codes on the part of the police, it will now be necessary to consider any redress available to Toby in respect of them. The first such act was the unlawful seizure of the Ecstasy. The appropriate cause of action in this instance will be trespass to goods; damages will, however, be minimal.

Will the Ecstasy be excluded from evidence under s 78?[5] According to the analysis above, the stop and search was unlawful. It would be possible to argue, following *Edward Fennelly* (1989), that the products of the search should be excluded from evidence on the basis that there was no power to search in the circumstances. According to *Thomas* (1990) and *Effick* (1992), however, physical evidence will be excluded only if obtained with deliberate

---

5   Candidates will gain credit for considering **s 78** in some detail in relation to the physical evidence.

illegality; the pre-PACE ruling of the House of Lords in *Fox* (1986) would also lend support to this contention. Following the decision of the House of Lords in *Khan* (1997), evidence other than involuntary confessions obtained improperly is nevertheless admissible, subject to a narrow discretion to exclude it. The House of Lords took Art 6 of the ECHR into account in reaching this conclusion, basing this finding on *Schenk v Switzerland* (1988). In *Khan* itself, it was found that the trial judge had properly exercised his discretion to include the improperly obtained evidence under s 78. This position has been unaffected by the reception of Art 6 into domestic law under the HRA (*AG's Reference (No 3 of 1999)* (2001) and *Loosely* (2001)). The courts have therefore taken the view that the position that has developed under s 78 regarding exclusion of non-confession evidence need not be modified. It may be concluded that the Ecstasy would not be excluded from evidence.

Toby could make a complaint under the provisions of the Police Reform Act 2002 in respect of the illegal seizure of the Ecstasy since it can be characterised as resulting from an unlawful search in breach of s 23(2) of the Misuse of Drugs Act 1971 and of s 2 PACE and Code A. Assuming that the arrest was unlawful (which cannot be determined with certainty), Toby could bring an action for false imprisonment for the whole period of his detention. A further option might be to make a complaint in respect of the failure to observe the provisions of s 28 of PACE.

Can a reasonable argument be advanced that the admissions made by Toby will be excluded from evidence under s 76? Following *Alladice and Hughes* (1988), unless it can be shown that the custody officer acted in bad faith in failing to allow Toby access to a solicitor, it seems that s 76(2)(a) will not apply. However, following *Delaney* (1989), which was concerned with the operation of s 76(2)(b), if the defendant was in some particularly difficult or vulnerable position, the breach of PACE may be of special significance. Toby may be said to be in such a position due to the fact that he is mentally disordered. On this basis, it seems that s 76(2)(b) may be invoked to exclude the admissions from evidence.

The admissions may also be excluded from evidence under s 78, on the basis that the police breached s 58. If so, following *Samuel* (1988) and *Alladice* (1988), it must be shown that the breach of s 58 was causally related to the admissions made in the second interview. The adviser might have considered that the risk involved in remaining silent should be taken, especially as it could probably be established that the wrong caution had been used; the correct caution is in Code C and the adviser might have been aware of this. This seems the stronger argument, bearing in mind Toby's mental disorder. It appears that Toby may have needed such advice. Given his mental condition, it is unlikely that he would fully understand the implications of silence; he was obviously more vulnerable than the appellant in *Dunford*. On this analysis, the requisite causal relationship exists and the admissions may also be excluded from evidence under s 78.

It has further been argued that a breach of Code C occurred, in that Toby was interviewed, although no appropriate adult was present. Following *DPP v Blake* (1989), the judge would therefore be likely to use his discretion to exclude the interview under s 78 on the basis that it may be unreliable or because Toby would not have made the admissions at all had the adult been present.

The breach of s 58 could also be the subject of a complaint, as could the breach of Code C.[6]

It follows from the above analysis that the first interview, which may be said to be causally related to the breach of Code C and s 58, may be excluded from evidence under s 78, since had Toby had legal advice, he might *not* have decided to remain silent. Exclusion of the first interview under s 78 would appear to accord with the duty of the court under s 6 of the HRA since the European Court of Human Rights has, as indicated above, held that delay in access where the defendant faces the possibility that adverse inferences may be drawn from silence is likely to amount to a breach of Art 6 of the ECHR. Such a breach could be avoided by excluding the interview. On the other hand, the courts, as indicated, are very reluctant to use the discretion under s 78 to exclude non-confession evidence (*Khan*).

Since there is a strong possibility that the interview will not be excluded, it must be considered whether adverse inferences would be likely to be drawn from Toby's silence during it. Section 34(2A) of the CJPOA, introduced in order to satisfy Art 6 of the Convention under the HRA, applies (see *Murray v UK*). Under s 34(2A), inferences cannot be drawn if the defendant has not had the opportunity of having legal advice. Thus, no adverse inferences can be drawn.

Common Pitfalls

Some students fail to mention the **HRA** at all, and/or fail to mention exclusion of evidence.

Aim Higher ★

The approach to exclusion of the admissions is given additional weight by the importance attached to access to legal advice by the European Court in cases such as *Murray (John) v UK* (1996) and *Averill v UK* (2000). Under **ss 6 and 2** of the **HRA**, those decisions need to be taken into account in considering whether the evidence should be excluded; they would be likely to tip the balance in favour of exclusion.

---

6   It is important to remember to consider this remedy as well as that of exclusion of evidence.

QUESTION 42

It is now nearly thirty years since the Police and Criminal Evidence Act 1984 (PACE) was enacted. PACE and the Codes of Practice made under it were supposed to strike a fair balance between increased police powers and greater safeguards for the suspect. Taking the effect of the Human Rights Act 1998 (HRA), amendments to PACE and to the Codes, ss 34–37 of the Criminal Justice and Public Order Act 1994 (CJPOA), and relevant aspects of the Police Reform Act 2002, into account, how far would it be fair to say that such a balance is still evident?

How to Answer the Question

This is a reasonably straightforward essay question, a version of which is commonly set on PACE. It is clearly very wide-ranging and therefore needs care in planning in order to cover provisions relating to the key stages in the investigation. Note that it does not ask you to comment on the treatment of terrorist suspects in the pre-trial investigation governed by the Terrorism Act 2000 as amended. It is clearly necessary to be selective in your answer.

Answer Structure

> The arrest provision under **s 24** of **PACE**, as amended in 2005; **Art 5** of the **ECHR**; **Code G** (2006)

> The stop and search provision under **s 1 PACE** and **Code of Practice A** (2006) and the efficacy of the procedural safeguards; **s 60** of the **Criminal Justice and Public Order Act 1994 (CJPOA)**

> The detention provisions under **Pt IV PACE**; **Art 5** of the **Convention**

> The safeguards for interviews under **Pt V** and **Codes C** and **E** (2006) – relevance of **ss 34–37** under the **CJPOA**, as amended; **Art 6** of the **Convention** under the **HRA**

> A brief overview of the redress available for breaches of these provisions – tortious remedies; the police complaints mechanism (**Police Reform Act 2002**); exclusion of evidence; the impact of the **HRA**, especially **Art 6** of the **Convention**

Essentially, the above points should be considered, mentioning relevant case law, including post-HRA cases.

ANSWER

It will be argued that although the Police and Criminal Evidence Act 1984 (PACE) and the Codes of Practice contain provisions capable of achieving a reasonable balance between increasing the power of the police to detain and question and providing safeguards for the suspect, that balance is not maintained in practice. Moreover, it has changed significantly since PACE came into force. PACE has been amended, most significantly by s 110 of the Serious and Organised Crime Act 2005; the Codes have gone through a number of revisions, most recently in 2012; new Codes have been introduced, including Code G, the Arrest Code. Other provisions, including in particular s 34 of the Criminal Justice and Public Order Act 1994 (CJPOA), and the Police Reform Act 2002, have been introduced. The safeguards in the Codes have been increased, but those in PACE itself have diminished while the powers have increased. The curtailing of the right to silence had a significant impact on the balance that was originally created under PACE.

In s 1 PACE, a general power to stop and search persons is conferred on the police if reasonable suspicion arises that stolen goods or prohibited articles may be found. This general power is balanced in two ways. First, the concept of reasonable suspicion, which is defined in s 2 of Code A, appears to allow it to be exercised only when quite a high level of suspicion exists. However, the level of reasonable suspicion needed is not very high in practice (see Slade (1996)). Second, the police must give the person to be searched certain information.

It now appears unlikely that the HRA will tend to encourage a stricter adherence to the rules providing safeguards for suspects who are stopped and searched. Art 5, contained in Sched 1 to the HRA, provides a guarantee of liberty and security of person. Deprivation of liberty can occur only on a basis of law and in certain specified circumstances, including, under Art 5(1)(b), the detention of a person in order to secure the fulfilment of any obligation prescribed by law and, under Art 5(1)(c), the 'lawful detention of a person effected for the purpose of bringing him before the competent legal authority on reasonable suspicion of having committed an offence'. The House of Lords decided in Gillan (2006) that Art 5(1) does not cover temporary detention for the purposes of a search. In Gillan v UK (2010), however, the Strasbourg Court came closer to finding a breach of Art 5, while deciding the case under Art 8. This may lead to a stricter stance towards stop and search.

Originally, the police also acquired a general power of arrest under s 25. This power did not merely allow an officer to arrest for any offence so long as reasonable suspicion can be shown. It was balanced by what were known as the general arrest conditions, which also had to be fulfilled. The inclusion of those provisions implied that the infringement of civil liberties represented by an arrest should be resorted to only where no alternative exists. However, s 25 was repealed in 2005 by s 110 of the Serious and Organised Crime Act 2005 and s 24 of PACE was amended, making the arrest powers available much broader. Under s 24, a person can be arrested on reasonable suspicion of having committed or being about to commit an offence – any offence. The arrest conditions originally under s 25 also have to be satisfied under s 24 but, crucially, two new ones have been added. The police can also show that the arrest is needed to allow the prompt and effective investigation of the suspected offence in question or to prevent prosecution of the offence from being hindered by the suspect's disappearance (s 24(5)(e) and (f)). It is highly probable that one of these conditions will be found to be satisfied in relation to most arrests. Thus the police now have the broad power of arrest that would have been viewed as too draconian had it been introduced in 1984. Some attempt at balancing this power with increased safeguards for arrestees was made by the introduction of Code G, the Arrest Code, in 2006.

The concept of reasonable suspicion, which should ensure that the arrest takes place al quite a late stage in the investigation, limits the use of the s 24 power, although the concept tends to be flexibly interpreted. This can be found if the leading post-PACE case on the meaning of the concept, *Castorina v Chief Constable of Surrey* (1988), is compared with the findings of the Strasbourg Court in *Fox, Campbell and Hartley v UK* (1990).

It is debatable whether the UK courts are in general applying a test of reasonable suspicion under PACE or other provisions for arrest that reaches the standards that the European Court had in mind in *Fox, Campbell* (1990), especially where terrorism is not in question. The departure that the HRA brings about is to encourage stricter judicial scrutiny of decisions to arrest.

Detention under PACE can be for up to 24 hours. In the case of a person in police custody for a serious arrestable offence (defined in s 116), it can extend to 36 hours with the permission of a police officer of the rank of superintendent or above, and may extend to 96 hours under s 44 after an application to a magistrates' court. These are very significant powers. However, they are supposed to be balanced by all of the safeguards created by Pt V of PACE and by Codes C and E. The most important safeguards available inside the police station include contemporaneous recording under s 11.7 of Code C, tape recording under s 3 of Code E, the ability to read over, verify and sign the notes of the interview as a correct record under s 11.9 and 11 Code C, notification of the right to legal advice under s 58 and s 3.1 of Code C, the option of having the adviser present under s 6.6 of Code C and, where appropriate, the presence of an appropriate adult under s 11.15 of Code C.

The right of access to legal advice was intended to bolster the right to silence. That right, originally included in the PACE scheme since it was reflected in the Code C caution, was severely curtailed by ss 34–37 of the CJPOA, thereby disturbing the 'balance' that was originally created. However, s 34(2A) was inserted into the CJPOA by s 58 of the Youth Justice and Criminal Evidence Act 1999. The amendments provide that if the defendant was at an authorised place of detention and had not had an opportunity of consulting a solicitor at the time of the failure to mention the fact in question, inferences cannot be drawn. This is a very significant change to the interviewing scheme, which was introduced as a direct response to the findings of the European Court of Human Rights in

Murray v UK (1996). Had this change not been made, ss 34–37 might have been found to be incompatible with Art 6 under s 4 of the HRA.

Damages will be available at common law in respect of some breaches of PACE. For example, if a police officer arrests a citizen where no reasonable suspicion arises under s 24 of PACE, an action for false imprisonment arises. Equally, such a remedy would be available if the provisions governing time limits on detention were breached.

However, tortious remedies are inapplicable to the provisions of the Codes under s 67(10) and seem to be inapplicable to the most significant statutory interviewing provision, the entitlement to legal advice. There is no tort of denial of access to legal advice: the only possible tortious action is for breach of statutory duty. Whether this tort lies is a question of policy in relation to any particular statutory provision, and so the application of this remedy was purely conjectural. Under s 7(1)(a) of the HRA, it is possible to bring an action against the police for breach of the Convention rights. However, it is probable that this remedy is not available in relation to breaches of Art 6 (which would cover the legal advice scheme), on the basis that Art 6 is concerned with the trial as a whole and therefore potential breaches of it should be addressed within the trial itself.

The police complaints mechanism covers any breaches of PACE, including breaches of the Codes under s 67(8), but it is generally agreed that it is defective as a means of redress. It does not allow for compensation to the victim or for the victim to attend any disciplinary proceedings. In any event, most complaints do not result in disciplinary proceedings and it appears that none have been brought in respect of breaches of the Codes. Furthermore, despite the involvement (albeit limited) of the Independent Police Complaints Commission, introduced by the Police Reform Act 2002, with a view to creating a stronger independent element in the system, the complaints procedure is still largely administered by the police themselves.

The context in which many breaches of PACE have been considered is that of exclusion of evidence. In *Samuel* (1988), the police unlawfully denied the appellant access to legal advice; the court took the view that if a breach of s 58 had taken place that was causally linked to the confession, s 78 should be invoked. However, the provisions of ss 34–37 of the CJPOA, reflected in the caution introduced under the 1995 revision of Code C, and continued in the 2006 version (unless the detainee has had no 'opportunity' to have legal advice, in which case the 'old' caution should be used) make it less likely that advisers will advise silence, since adverse inferences may be drawn at trial from silence. Thus, it may be more difficult to establish the causal relationship in question relying on the method used in *Samuel*.[7] Section 78 may become less effective as a means of maintaining the balance between police powers and suspects' rights.

....

7   Credit would be given for explaining this complex point clearly.

Following the decision of the House of Lords in *Khan* (1997), evidence other than involuntary confessions obtained improperly is nevertheless admissible, subject to a narrow discretion to exclude it. This position has been unaffected by the reception of Art 6 into domestic law under the HRA (*AG's Reference (No 3 of 1999)* (2001); *Loosely* (2001)) on the basis that the assessment of evidence is largely a matter for the national courts. The courts have therefore taken the view that the position that has developed under s 78 regarding exclusion of non-confession evidence need not be modified under the HRA.

The relevant decisions so far under the HRA do not indicate that the HRA is having or is likely to have a significant impact in this context. This is particularly the case in relation to the decisions in *Gillan* (2006) and *Beckles* (2004), although the earlier decisions in *Osman* (1999) (in relation to adopting a strict view of the identification requirement of s 2 PACE) and *R v Chief Constable of Kent* (2000) (demanding that to accord with Art 5 reviews of detention should be in person, not by video link; the decision was reversed by s 73 Criminal Justice and Police Act 2001) suggested otherwise.[8]

In conclusion, it is therefore argued that the balance originally struck is no longer being maintained. This failure arguably arises partly due to the changes that have occurred since 1984, partly because many of the safeguards can be evaded quite readily, and partly because there is no effective sanction available for their breach. It is contended that while the relevant Articles of the Convention, afforded further effect in domestic law under the Human Rights Act 1998 (HRA), are having some impact in encouraging adherence to the rules intended to secure suspects' rights, they are not having a radical effect, especially in terms of encouraging the exclusion of evidence where the rules have not been adhered to.

Common Pitfalls

Failing to cover all the provisions mentioned.

Dealing with the domestic provisions but failing to understand the way that the ECHR affects domestic law.

QUESTION 43

Why was detention without trial under Pt 4 of the Anti-Terrorism, Crime and Security Act 2001, introduced and abandoned? Comment on the compatibility of its replacements

8   Credit will be given for avoiding the assumption that the HRA is likely to have a dramatic effect on the scheme and for giving supporting examples.

with the guarantees of the European Convention on Human Rights, received into UK law under the Human Rights Act 1998?

How to Answer this Question

This is a fairly tricky essay question that asks you to deal with the controversial detention without trial scheme under Pt 4 of the Anti-Terrorism Crime and Security Act 2001, the findings of the House of Lords in relation to it in the case of *A and Ors* (2004), and its replacement – control orders – in the Prevention of Terrorism Act 2005. The 2005 scheme has been challenged successfully in relation to the ECHR rights, so that aspects of the 2005 scheme must be dealt with. The scheme under the 2005 Act has now been abandoned in favour of the Terrorism Prevention and Investigative Measures Act 2011 (TPIMs). So you need to consider whether the TPIMs scheme in reality merely introduces a new form of control order which may also show incompatibility with certain Convention rights. However, since s 3 HRA has been used to impose compatibility between the control orders' scheme and the Convention rights, especially Article 6, the same may be said of the TPIMs scheme. Thus the question of incompatibility is much more complex than it was in relation to Pt 4.

Answer Structure

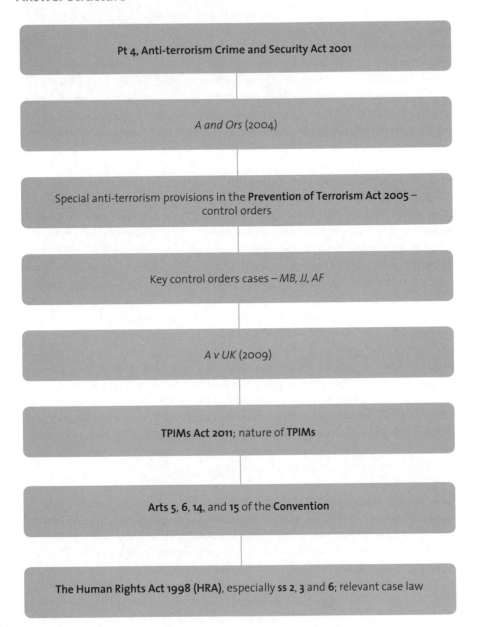

Pt 4, Anti-terrorism Crime and Security Act 2001

A and Ors (2004)

Special anti-terrorism provisions in the **Prevention of Terrorism Act 2005** – control orders

Key control orders cases – *MB, JJ, AF*

A v UK (2009)

TPIMs Act 2011; nature of **TPIMs**

Arts **5**, **6**, **14**, and **15** of the **Convention**

The Human Rights Act 1998 (HRA), especially **ss 2**, **3** and **6**; relevant case law

ANSWER

The problem faced by the Labour Government in 2001 was presented after 9/11 to Parliament and a number of parliamentary committees in the following terms: a dilemma arises in respect of the presence of persons in the UK who are suspected of being international terrorists and as therefore posing a grave security problem, but who cannot be placed on trial due to the sensitivity of the evidence and the high standard of proof. At the same time, they cannot be deported to their country of origin, because there are grounds to think that they would there be subject to torture or inhuman and degrading treatment, since to do so would violate Art 3 of the European Convention on Human Rights (ECHR) – due to *Chahal v UK* (1996).

Article 5(1) of the Convention protects the right to liberty and security of the person, afforded further effect in domestic law under the Human Rights Act 1998 (HRA). There is an exception under Art 5(1)(f) allowing for detention of 'a person against whom action is being taken with a view to deportation or extradition', but it was considered that it would not cover lengthy detentions during which deportation proceedings would not be ongoing. Thus, the Government presented itself as caught between the provisions of Arts 3 and 5, in relation to a number of suspected international terrorists, including persons with links to al-Qaeda, based in Britain, and therefore as having to find a compromise that would allow for their detention. The solution was to introduce a scheme allowing for indefinite detention without trial and at the same time to derogate from Art 5(1).

Under the detention without trial scheme under Pt 4 of the Anti-Terrorism, Crime and Security Act 2001 (ATCSA), detention depended – in effect – on certification by the Home Secretary as a substitute for a trial in respect of non-British citizens (who were therefore subject to immigration controls). The Government considered that the Pt 4 ATCSA provisions would be incompatible with Art 5(1) of the ECHR, afforded further effect in domestic law under the HRA, and therefore entered a derogation to Art 5(1), under s 14 HRA, within the terms of Art 15 of the Convention.

The House of Lords considered the detention scheme in *A and Ors v Secretary of State for the Home Dept* (2004). They did conclude that it was open to the Government to find that there was a state of emergency within the terms of Art 15 – that was viewed as a largely political judgment. On the question of proportionality – whether the measures went no further than required by the exigencies of the situation under Art 15 – the Lords made the point that ss 21 and 23 ATCSA did not rationally address the threat to the security of the United Kingdom presented by al-Qaeda terrorists and their supporters because the scheme did not address the threat presented by UK nationals, and it permitted foreign nationals suspected of being al-Qaeda terrorists or their supporters to pursue their activities abroad if there was any country to which they were able to go, and also the sections permitted on their face the certification and detention of persons who were not suspected of presenting any threat to the security of the United Kingdom as al-Qaeda terrorists or supporters.

Further, since the different treatment could not be justified, the scheme was found to violate Arts 14 and 5 read together on the basis of differentiating between groups of suspected international terrorists on the basis of nationality – this was found to be the key weakness of the scheme. The derogation order was quashed and a declaration of incompatibility between Arts 14 and 5 and s 23 was made. The Government accepted that it could no longer sustain the scheme; it eventually bowed to the pressure and introduced a new scheme under the Prevention of Terrorism Act 2005 (PTA); in that Act, Parliament also repealed the key provisions of Pt 4.

The PTA scheme provided for lesser measures to be used – not detention without trial but control orders (although, at their most stringent, control orders could have allowed for detention without trial). Under s 1(3), a control order made against an individual could impose any obligations that the Secretary of State or the court considered necessary for purposes connected with preventing or restricting involvement by that individual in terrorism-related activity.

Literally any obligation up to and including house arrest could be imposed. Control orders fell into the categories of derogating control orders and non-derogating ones; the distinction between derogating ones and non-derogating ones was not made in the Act – a non-derogating order was merely defined as one made by the Secretary of State and which did not breach Article 5 ECHR. The derogating orders would have required again a derogation from Art 5 since certain measures – in particular 24-hour house arrest – are viewed as incompatible with the right to liberty and possibly other Articles.

Under s 2, the Home Secretary could make a control order that imposed non-derogating obligations if he/she had reasonable grounds for suspecting that an individual was involved in terrorist-related activity – this was similar to the standard of proof under Pt 4 of the ATCSA and so represented a standard well below the criminal standard of proof – the definition of terrorism was that from the Terrorism Act 2000 s 1; the order could be for up to 12 months, and could be renewed. The courts had a greater role in the supervision of non-derogating control orders – it had to give permission. Also appeal could be made to a court against the order. Only non-derogating orders were introduced. Thus they were orders imposing obligations (such as 16-hours-a-day house detention combined with other restrictions) deemed by the Secretary of State not to breach Art 5.

In *SSHD v MB and AF* (2007), the House of Lords read into the rules under s 3 HRA a proviso that the procedures overall must be such as to ensure a fair trial under Art 6. The view of the majority was that procedural fairness was fact-specific and did not always depend on minimum disclosure. The Government should not be forced to disclose truly sensitive information, It was found, but more of what was being withheld at that time could and should be disclosed and the Special Advocates could do more to challenge whatever *was* disclosed. The overall conclusion was then that in most cases the system could and would operate with a sufficient degree of fairness even where no minimum disclosure of the case against the controlee was made to him so that he could give full instructions to the Special Advocate. So it was found that there was no need to declare the procedural rules incompatible with Art 6. Reliance on closed material could only be on the terms that appropriate safeguards were in place and the provisions of the 2005 Act for the use of a special advocate and rules of court constituted such appropriate safeguards. So the Lords imposed an Art 6 compliance on the scheme via s 3 HRA, which had not previously been present.

Strasbourg intervened in its seminal decision in *A v UK* (2009) on the 2001 system of detention without trial. Its findings as to the fairness of the procedure in such cases, which was substantially identical to that used in control order cases, were clearly of direct relevance to the latter. The Court found that where the open material consisted purely of general assertions and the decision to uphold detention was based solely or to a decisive degree on closed material, the proceedings *could not be fair*. In such instances, the role of the Special Advocates, unable to take instructions on the secret evidence, could not render the system Convention-compliant.

In *Secretary of State for the Home Department v AF* (2009) the House of Lords accepted Strasbourg's guidance in full and found that it was now clear that Art 6 required that the suspect have knowledge of the essence of the case against him, so as to be able to give effective instructions to the Special Advocates. They employed s 3 HRA to impose that change on the rules.

In *Secretary of State for the Home Department v JJ* (2007) the appellants were subjected to house detention for 18 hours and other restrictions. The majority found that the difference between deprivation of and restriction on liberty was one of degree, not of substance, and it was for the court to assess into which category a particular case fell; the court's task, Lord Bingham said, was to take account of a range of criteria from the Strasbourg case of *Guzzardi* (1980). On that basis the majority found that the orders created a deprivation of liberty. But 16 hours of house detention were found by one Law Lord not to create such a deprivation. So the control orders scheme remained broadly intact.

When the Supreme Court considered *SSHD v AP* (2010), the factor of forced relocation added to 16 hours' house detention was found to tip the balance so as to create a deprivation of liberty under Art 5; thus the court quashed the control order. Lord Brown, with whom the other judges agreed, reaffirmed his finding in *JJ* as to the acceptability of 16-hour house detention under Art 5.

After *AF* (2009), if the gist of the case against him was in the closed material and so was not revealed to the controlee, the Government view was that only light-touch control orders could be employed on the basis that they did not require compliance with the disclosure principle.

The non-derogating control orders regime could continue to be used but in a weakened form. The Coalition Government reviewed counter-terror measures, including control orders and decided to introduce new measures, termed terrorism prevention and investigative measures in the Terrorism Prevention and Investigative Measures Act 2011.[9] The Government decided that preventive measures were still needed against a small group of suspects who could be neither deported nor prosecuted.

The fact that the judges had not decisively rejected the control orders scheme and had found in *JJ* and in the Supreme Court in *AP* that 16 hours' house detention per day does not necessarily amount to a deprivation of liberty under Article 5(1) ECHR left the option of imposing overnight house arrest combined with other restrictions open to the Government. So the decision was made to introduce TPIMs, which are basically fairly light touch control orders in terms of the restrictions they can impose. They continue to impose house detention, but it is termed an 'overnight residence requirement'. That means that the house detention could be for 12 or more hours per day, but presumably must cover the hours when persons would normally be asleep. Since control orders normally also covered those hours (although they might also extend into the working day), the difference is not very great. TPIMs can also impose a range of other restrictions and surveillance measures. Like control orders, a TPIMs order may include restrictions on: association or communication with others; employment or studies; whether a person may enter a specified area or place; whether a person may travel overseas; a person's ability to transfer property; a person's use of or access to financial services. Like control orders, a TPIMs order may also involve the requirement on a person to: report regularly to a police station; wear an electronic tag; have his photograph taken by police. Further, as with control orders, a person under a TPIMs order may have: his residence, person and property searched by police in a variety of circumstances; and have his fingerprints and DNA taken by police without consent. However, at present it appears that the imposition of forced relocation will not be included, probably partly as a result of the Supreme Court decision in *AP*. The TPIMs legislation was presented to Parliament on the basis that it is ECHR-compliant. But it can be questioned whether a range of restrictions on liberty, including around 12 hours house detention a day, backed up by criminal sanctions, might in future be found to create a deprivation of liberty

The Coalition Government, in introducing TPIMs, made little effort to consider adopting a procedure that adhered more closely to Article 6 standards. The procedure under the 2011 Act for imposing terrorism, prevention and investigation measures differs very little in terms of disclosure – and in other due process respects – from the control orders procedure. But s 3 HRA could be used, as it was in relation to control orders, to impose Article 6 compliance on the scheme via interpretation.[10]

---

9   Candidates will gain credit for showing understanding of the more subtle problems of **ECHR**-compliance posed by both control orders and **TPIMs**.

10 Candidates will gain credit for showing appreciation of the role of **s3 HRA** in this scheme.

The control orders and TPIMs regimes came closer to complying with the ECHR than Part 4 did. But it appears that the TPIMs regime, like the control orders one, relies on presupposing a dilution of ECHR rights, or at least on interpretations of them in tension with the existing Strasbourg stance. It places the judges once again in the difficult position the control orders scheme created since they may again find themselves likely to be asked to use the HRA to ensure that the legislation is interpreted (under s 3) or applied (under s 6) in a manner that does adhere more closely to the rights.

Aim Higher

It could be pointed out in terms of enhanced ECHR compatibility, that the Government in framing the TPIMs scheme stated that account was being taken of the need to ensure that the use of TPIMs was not obstructive to prosecution. Thus the attempt has been made to *associate* the use of TPIMs with the criminal process. Nevertheless, TPIMs can allow the imposition of a range of measures, including house detention, which not only raise concerns in human rights terms, but also are not obviously likely to be efficacious in evidence-gathering terms.

Common Pitfalls

It is important for candidates to look closely at the issue of ECHR compatibility; some candidates may embark on a too-descriptive survey of the provisions.

Freedom of Assembly and Public Order

12

INTRODUCTION

This chapter is concerned with the conflict between the need, on the one hand, to maintain order and, on the other, to protect freedom of assembly. The topic lends itself readily to problem questions or essays, but in either case, its concern will be with those provisions of the criminal law most applicable in the context of demonstrations, marches or meetings. The common law power to prevent a breach of the peace is still extensively used. Students should be aware of recent decisions on this power (*Laporte* (2006), *Austin* (2009), *Austin v UK* (2012)). The Public Order Act 1986, as amended, is still the most significant statute, but it is also particularly important to bear in mind the public order provisions of the Criminal Justice and Public Order Act 1994 (CJPOA). The Serious and Organised Crime Act 2005 ss 132–138 could be mentioned in a general question about freedom of assembly or in a specific question relating to demonstrations in the vicinity of Parliament. The Criminal Justice and Police Act 2001 could be mentioned in relation to harassing behaviour directed at persons in dwellings. The Racial and Religious Hatred Act 2006 added Pt 3A to the Public Order Act, covering inciting hatred against persons on religious grounds; the Criminal Justice and Immigration Act 2008 s 74 and Schedule 16 amended Part 3A to make provision about hatred against a group of persons defined by reference to sexual orientation. These provisions would only be relevant if issues of hate speech were to arise in a question.

The relevance of any particular provision obviously depends on the wording of the question; there are a very large number of public order provisions and questions are unlikely to cover all of them. Police powers (covered in Chapter 11), may also be relevant. Obviously, different courses will emphasise different areas of public order law. Given that there are a very large number of provisions in this area, a course is likely to concentrate only on a selected range of provisions.

Problem questions sometimes call on the student to discuss *any* issues that may arise, as opposed to considering criminal liability only, in which case, any tortious liability incurred by members of an assembly or by police officers may arise as well as the possible use of powers based on the breach of the peace doctrine. The possibility of judicial review of police decisions may also arise.

At the present time, the **Human Rights Act 1998 (HRA)** is of course especially important and is relevant in all essay or problem questions on public protest and assembly. Examiners will expect at least some (even if fairly brief) discussion of its relevance and impact. **Arts 10** and **11** of the **European Convention on Human Rights (ECHR)**, which provide guarantees of freedom of expression and of peaceful assembly respectively, were received into UK law once the **HRA** came fully into force in 2000. (Note that **Art 10** protects 'expression', not merely 'speech', thus covering many forms of expressive activity, including forms of public protest.) Therefore, **Arts 10** and **11** and other **Convention** Articles relevant in this area have been directly applicable in UK courts for over ten years, and should be taken into account in interpreting and applying common law and statutory provisions affecting public protest. **Section 3(1)** of the **HRA** requires: 'So far as it is possible to do so, primary and subordinate legislation must be read and given effect in a way which is compatible with the **Convention** rights.' **Section 3(2)(b)** reads: 'this section does not affect the validity, continuing operation or enforcement of any incompatible primary legislation.' **Section 3(1)** goes well beyond the pre-**HRA** obligation to resolve ambiguity in statutes by reference to the **ECHR**. Thus, all statutes affecting freedom of assembly and public protest therefore need to be interpreted so as to be in harmony with the **Convention**, *if* that is needed due to Strasbourg jurisprudence, and is at all possible. Obviously, since **Arts 10** and **11** are qualified by a second paragraph allowing restraint on expression and assembly if 'necessary in a democratic society' for the prevention of disorder or crime, the statutory provisions may not need reinterpretation under s 3. So far under the **HRA**, that has been the case.

Under s 6 **HRA**, **Convention** guarantees are binding only against public authorities; these are defined as bodies that have a partly public function. In the context of public protest, this will normally mean that if the police, local authorities or other public bodies use powers deriving from any legal source, they must ensure that they exercise their powers within the limits imposed under **Arts 10** and **11**. If they prevent or limit peaceful public protest unjustifiably, those Articles could be relied on in any court action against the protesters, or the protesters could bring an action against them under s 7(1)(a) of the **HRA** relying on **Art 11**, probably combined with **Art 10**. In some circumstances **Art 5**, protecting the right to liberty, might be relevant. **Section 7(1)(b)** means that if the protesters are prosecuted or sued, they can rely on those Articles and can seek reinterpretation of the legal provision involved under s 3 **HRA**. Depending on the interpretation afforded to those Articles, including the exceptions to them, the protesters might be successful unless a statutory provision absolutely unambiguously supported the limitation or banning of the protest, or unless in the circumstances it was found that no **Convention** right was applicable. Where a statute limiting or affecting public protest is applied, the court is likely to rely on ss 3 and 6 of the **HRA**; where a common law provision creating such a limitation is relevant, the court will rely on s 6 alone. (For further discussion, see Chapter 9.)

Checklist ✔

Students should have general knowledge of the background to the **Public Order Act 1986**, as amended, and the public order provisions of the **Criminal Justice and Public Order Act 1994**; also – in relation to questions relating to demonstrations in the vicinity of Parliament or general questions about the current range of public order provisions – some knowledge of the **Serious and Organised Crime Act 2005** is needed. In particular, familiarity with the following areas is useful, depending on the areas the course in question has concentrated on:

- the freedom of assembly and public protest jurisprudence under **Arts 10** and **11** of the **European Convention on Human Rights**;
- the **Human Rights Act 1998**, especially **ss 3** and **6**;
- the notice requirements under **s 11** of the **Public Order Act 1986**;
- the conditions that can be imposed under **ss 12** and **14** of the **1986 Act**, as amended, on processions and assemblies;
- the banning power under **ss 13** and **14A** of the Act;
- liability under **ss 3, 4, 4A** and **5** of the Act;
- liability for assault on, or obstruction of, a police officer under **s 89** of the **Police Act 1996**;
- the common law power to prevent a breach of the peace;
- public nuisance;
- the obstruction of the highway under **s 137** of the **Highways Act 1980**;
- the public order provisions of **Pt V** and **s 154** of the **Criminal Justice and Public Order Act 1994**;
- **ss 132–138** of the **Serious and Organised Crime Act 2005** (only relevant if a question relates to demonstrations in the vicinity of Parliament);
- the **Criminal Justice and Police Act 2001** (only relevant in relation to harassing behaviour directed at persons in dwellings);
- the **Public Order Act Part 3A** (only relevant if a question mentions religious or sexual orientation hate speech).

QUESTION 44

Clare is a member of the City Youth Club. She and 40 other teenagers attend the youth club on Friday evening and are told that it has to close down that night due to sudden drastic cuts in funding imposed by the council. All of the teenagers immediately walk out of the club in protest and assemble on the pavement outside. While they are angrily discussing the closure of the club, Edwin and Fred, two police officers in uniform, approach the group.

Clare begins to address the group, telling them that they must remain peaceful in order to air their grievances more effectively. Edwin tells her that she must disperse part of the group if she wants to hold a meeting. She asks some of the teenagers to leave, but takes no action when they make no attempt to do so. The meeting continues and becomes more heated. Clare then suggests that they should march through the town.

The group sets off, Clare leading. Traffic is held up for 10 minutes as the group enters the town. Edwin asks Clare to disperse half the group of marchers. Clare asks two of the teenagers to leave, but takes no further action when they fail to comply with her request. Edwin then says that she will have to give him the names and addresses of the members of the group. She refuses, and Edwin then informs Clare that he is arresting her for failing to comply with his orders.

▶ Consider the criminal liability, if any, incurred by Clare. Take account of the **Human Rights Act** where relevant.

How to Answer the Question

This is a fairly typical problem question confined to quite a narrow compass, dealing with issues that arise mainly but not entirely under the Public Order Act 1986 (POA) in respect of marches and assemblies. It also requires an awareness of the provisions of Arts 10 and 11 as interpreted at Strasbourg, and of their possible impact on UK law under the Human Rights Act 1998 (HRA). If any of the statutory provisions considered leave open any room at all for a different interpretation (not only on the grounds of ambiguity), they could if necessary be reinterpreted in harmony with Arts 10 and 11 of the European Convention on Human Rights (ECHR).

It is very important to note that the answer is confined to the question of possible criminal liability incurred by Clare. Possible tortious liability incurred by Clare or the police officers is therefore irrelevant, as is the possibility that Clare could seek to challenge the police decisions by way of judicial review. Breach of the peace is not technically a criminal offence, so it is also irrelevant. The demands of Arts 10 and 11 as received into UK law under the HRA will be relevant at a number of points.

Applying the Law

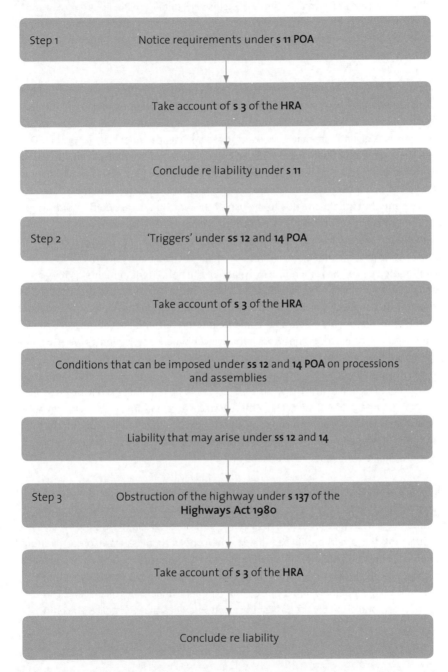

Step 1   Notice requirements under **s 11 POA**
Take account of **s 3** of the **HRA**
Conclude re liability under **s 11**
Step 2   'Triggers' under **ss 12** and **14 POA**
Take account of **s 3** of the **HRA**
Conditions that can be imposed under **ss 12** and **14 POA** on processions and assemblies
Liability that may arise under **ss 12** and **14**
Step 3   Obstruction of the highway under **s 137** of the **Highways Act 1980**
Take account of **s 3** of the **HRA**
Conclude re liability

This flow chart highlights the main issues surrounding the Human Rights Act 1998 and the Public Order Act 1986 that need to be considered in your answer.

ANSWER

Liability in this case arises mainly, but not exclusively, under the Public Order Act 1986 (POA). Since the question demands consideration of possible restrictions on protest and assembly, the requirements of Arts 10 and 11 as received into UK law under the Human Rights Act 1998 (HRA) must be taken into account.

Under s 11 of the POA, advance notice of a procession must be given if it falls within one of three categories. This march falls within s 11(1)(a), as it is intended to demonstrate opposition to the action of the local authority in closing the youth club. As no notice of the march was given, Clare may have committed an offence under s 11(7)(a) of the POA as she is the organiser of the march. However, the notice requirement does not apply under s 11(1) if it was not reasonably practicable to give any advance notice. This provision was intended to exempt spontaneous demonstrations such as this one from the notice requirements, but is defective due to the use of the word 'any'. This word would suggest that a phone call made five minutes before the march sets off would fulfil the requirements, thereby exempting very few marches. Although the march sets off suddenly, it is possible that Clare had time to make such a phone call; on a strict interpretation of s 11, she is therefore in breach of the notice requirements, as it was reasonably practicable for her to fulfil them.[1] However, it can be argued that notice was informally and impliedly given to the police officers already on the scene, or alternatively that the term 'reasonably practicable' could be interpreted, under s 3 of the HRA, so as to exempt spontaneous processions from liability even where a few minutes were available to give notice, because to fail to do so would be out of harmony with Art 11, which protects freedom of peaceful assembly (*Ezelin v France* (1991)) since peaceful spontaneous marches could incur liability. The word 'written' could be read into s 11 relying on s 3 (see *Ghaidan v Mendoza* (2004)) and clearly there was insufficient time to give written notice. (See also the *Kay* case (2008) on adopting a restrictive approach to s 11 POA, on the basis that the POA is a penal statute.)[2] Thus, assuming that either argument was accepted by the court, liability would not arise under s 11.

Clare may attract liability under s 14(4) of the POA, as she was the organiser of a public assembly, but failed to comply with the condition imposed by the most senior police officer present at the scene (Edwin) to disperse part of the group (where the officers are of equal rank, this condition will be fulfilled when one of them issues an order). It should be noted that as the group was in a public place and comprised more than two persons, it constituted a public assembly under s 16 of the POA, as amended. Edwin can impose conditions on the assembly only if one of four 'triggers' under s 14(1) is present. The third of these, and arguably the easiest to satisfy, provides that the police officer in

---

1   Candidates gain credit for applying the law closely to the facts throughout.
2   Candidates gain credit for considering a reinterpretation of the provisions under s 3 HRA, and then applying the newly reinterpreted provision – in this case s 11 POA – to the facts.

question must reasonably believe that 'serious disruption to the life of the community' may be caused by the assembly. In the case of *Reid* (1987), it was determined that the 'triggers' should be strictly interpreted: the words used should not be diluted. It would appear to be in accordance with **Art 11**, and indeed **Art 10** (see *Steel v UK* (1998)) to adopt such an interpretation under **s 3** of the **HRA**, since otherwise an interference with assemblies outside the legitimate aims of **para 2** of **Arts 10** and **11** might be enabled to occur.

However, in *R (Brehony) v Chief Constable of Greater Manchester* (2005), a regular demonstration had occurred outside a branch of Marks and Spencer, protesting about the firm's support for the government of Israel. The Chief Constable had issued a notice under **s 14** requiring the demonstration to move to a different location due to the disruption that it would be likely to cause to shoppers over the Christmas period. The judge refused the application for judicial review on the basis that, in **Arts 10** and **11** terms, the restraint was, proportionate to the aim of maintaining public order, pursued. This decision confirms that 'serious disruption to the life of the community' can mean mere anticipated inconvenience to shoppers. On this argument, Edwin may have had a power to impose conditions on the assembly and the condition imposed is one allowed for under **s 14** – to limit the number of persons in the assembly (see *DPP v Jones* (2002)). Liability may therefore arise under **s 14(4)** unless Clare could successfully argue that the failure to comply with the condition imposed arose due to circumstances beyond her control.

Will Clare incur liability under **s 12(4)** of the **POA**, as she was the organiser of a public procession, but failed to comply with the conditions imposed by Edwin to provide the names and addresses of the group or to disperse part of it? Edwin can impose conditions on the procession only if one of the four 'triggers' under **s 12(1)** is present. The triggers are identical to those under **s 14(1)**. The third of these may possibly arise, following *Brehony*. The group of teenagers was marching through the town; in such circumstances, it may be more readily argued that serious disruption to the life of the community may reasonably be apprehended. Such disruption could be argued for either on the basis that passers-by may be jostled by the group, especially if it has grown more excitable, or on the basis that traffic may be seriously disrupted. The fact that traffic has already been held up for 10 minutes may support a reasonable belief that such disruption may occur. Serious obstruction of the traffic might arguably amount to some disruption of the life of the community. Both possibilities taken together could found a reasonable apprehension that the life of the community will be seriously disrupted.

However, courts are required under both **ss 6** and **3** of the **HRA** to determine that the nature of the risk anticipated is one that would constitute one of the legitimate aims for limiting the primary rights under **Arts 11** and **10**. The vague and ambiguous phrase, 'serious disruption to the life of the community', could be reinterpreted under **s 3** of the **HRA** by reference to **Arts 11(2)** and **10(2)** of the **ECHR**. The grounds for imposing the conditions would have to be justified, either on the basis of protecting 'the rights of others' or because the 'serious disruption' feared amounted to 'disorder' for the purposes of those second paragraphs. Following *Brehony*, it seems probable that a court would be satisfied that serious disruption could reasonably be apprehended, and that in asserting a power to impose conditions the police did not breach Arts 10 or 11. However, the discretion as to the imposition of the conditions in s 12 could be viewed narrowly (either under Arts 10 or 11 or on ordinary principles of statutory construction). It could be argued that the restrictions are necessary in order to protect the rights of others. However, arguably, they are disproportionate to that aim, bearing in mind the importance of freedom of assembly (*Ezelin*). In particular, a requirement to provide names and addresses appears to be disproportionate to the aim in view, since it is unclear that it could serve that aim. In order to avoid breaching Arts 10 and 11, a court that took this view could adopt a strict interpretation of s 12, possibly finding either that the behaviour in question is not serious enough and/or that the condition could not be viewed as 'necessary'.

On the other hand, a court could rely on *Christians Against Racism and Fascism v UK* (1980), in which a ban on a peaceful assembly was not found to breach Art 11. A fortiori, a mere imposition of conditions might be found to be proportionate within the terms of Art 11(2). Following this argument, and bearing *Brehony* in mind, Edwin would be entitled to impose conditions on the march. The conditions imposed would have to relate to the disruption apprehended; this may be said of the requirement to disperse half the group, but not of the order that Clare should disclose the names and addresses of the group. Thus, liability may arise only in respect of the failure to comply with the former condition. Clare made some attempt to comply with it but did not succeed; she would, therefore, following this argument, incur liability under s 12(4) unless she can show that the failure arose due to circumstances outside her control. Although the powers of an organiser to disperse members of a march are limited, it may be argued that in approaching only two members of the group, Clare made in any event a token effort only; it is therefore arguable that she has committed an offence under s 12(4).

Clare may further have incurred liability under s 137 of the Highways Act 1980, which provides that a person will be guilty of an offence if he 'without lawful authority or excuse in any way wilfully obstructs the free passage of the highway'. In *Arrowsmith v Jenkins* (1963), it was held that minor obstruction of traffic can lead to liability under the Highways Act. However, the question of the purpose of the obstruction was given greater prominence in *Hirst and Agu v Chief Constable of West Yorkshire* (1986): it was said that courts should have regard to the freedom to demonstrate.

This approach was to an extent confirmed by *DPP v Jones* (1999), where the House of Lords recognised that a demonstration need not be treated as an improper use of the highway where it does not cause obstruction to other users. Such an approach is, of course, given added weight by the need for the courts to give appropriate weight, by virtue of s 3 of the HRA, to the rights of freedom of expression and assembly in Arts 10 and 11 of the ECHR. One possibility would be to interpret the uncertain term 'excuse' in order to seek to ensure harmony between s 137 of the Highways Act and Arts 10 and 11 under s 3 of the HRA, since otherwise s 137 would allow interferences with peaceful, albeit obstructive, assemblies, arguably contrary to the findings of the European Court of Human Rights in *Steel* and in *Ezelin*. On this basis, the brevity of the obstruction, and its purpose as part of a legitimate protest, suggest that the march amounted to a reasonable use of the highway. The stronger argument seems to be that liability under the Highways Act for inciting the group to obstruct the highway will not be established.

Thus, in conclusion, Clare is most likely to attract liability under ss 14(4) and 12(4) of the POA.

Common Pitfalls

Students sometimes recite the law fairly accurately but then apply it very briefly to the facts, jumping to the conclusion too rapidly that liability is established/not established.

Students sometimes discuss the law in relation to the facts but fail to come to a conclusion as to liability.

QUESTION 45

The Asian community in Northton become increasingly concerned about apparent racism in Northton City Council employment practices. A number of council workers have recently been made redundant; a disproportionate number of them are Asians. A group of 40 Asians decides to hold a demonstration outside the Civic Centre on the lawns and courtyard in front of it. On the appointed day, they assemble, nominate Ali and Rashid as their leaders, and shout at workers going into the Centre, telling them not to go in but to join the demonstration. When the workers do not respond, some of the Asians, including Ali, become angrier; they shout and wave their fists threateningly at some of the workers, but make no attempt to impede them physically. Some of the workers appear to be intimidated.

One of the Asians, Sharma, tries to persuade workers not to enter the Civic Centre and to support the anti-racism protest, but eventually becomes involved in a heated argument with a group of white workers. He continues more angrily to attempt to persuade them not to enter; they threaten to beat him up if the Asian group continues with its efforts.

Three police officers arrive on the scene. One of them, John, arrests Sharma, stating that this is for breach of the peace since the group of white workers is about to become violent. Sharma tries to leave, pushing John aside in the process; John seizes Sharma's arm. Belinda, one of the police officers, orders Ali to disperse half of the group; when he makes no effort to comply, she says that she is arresting him for failing to comply with the order. She also orders Rashid to leave the area. He fails to do so.

▶ Discuss.

How to Answer this Question

This question is partly concerned with liability that may arise in respect of assemblies under the Public Order Act 1986 (POA), as amended, and under ss 68 and 69 of the Criminal Justice and Public Order Act 1994 (CJPOA). The common law power to prevent a breach of the peace is significant in the question. The statutory provisions considered should be interpreted in harmony with Arts 10 and 11 of the European Convention on Human Rights (ECHR) (and any other relevant Articles) under s 3 of the Human Rights Act 1998 (HRA) if reinterpretation is needed; the common law doctrine of breach of the peace must be interpreted and applied in accordance with the duty of the court under s 6 of the HRA. It should be borne in mind that the problem concerns an assembly only, and not a march. Further, the assembly is not taking place on the highway. Therefore, liability particularly associated with marches and with assemblies on the highway will not arise. Note that a broad, wide-ranging discussion is called for due to the use of the word 'discuss' rather than 'advise x'.

Applying the Law

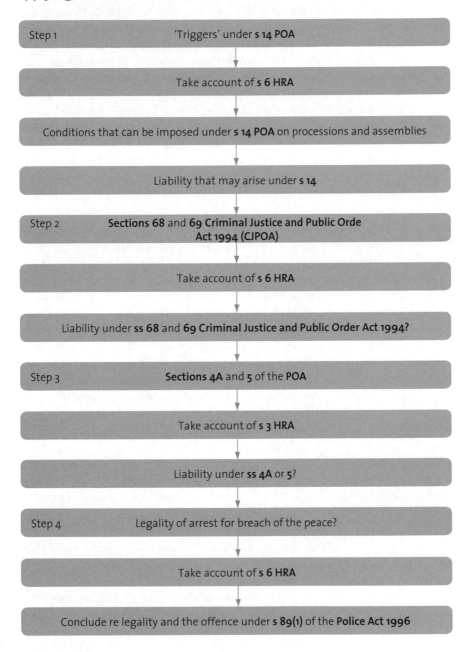

Step 1 — 'Triggers' under **s 14 POA**

Take account of **s 6 HRA**

Conditions that can be imposed under **s 14 POA** on processions and assemblies

Liability that may arise under **s 14**

Step 2 — **Sections 68** and **69 Criminal Justice and Public Orde Act 1994 (CJPOA)**

Take account of **s 6 HRA**

Liability under **ss 68** and **69 Criminal Justice and Public Order Act 1994?**

Step 3 — **Sections 4A** and **5 of the POA**

Take account of **s 3 HRA**

Liability under **ss 4A** or **5**?

Step 4 — Legality of arrest for breach of the peace?

Take account of **s 6 HRA**

Conclude re legality and the offence under **s 89(1)** of the **Police Act 1996**

ANSWER

Liability in this case may arise mainly, but not exclusively, under the Public Order Act 1986 (POA), as amended. Since the question demands consideration of possible restrictions on protest and assembly, the requirements of Arts 10, 11, as received into UK law under the Human Rights Act 1998 (HRA) must be taken into account. Article 14, which provides protection from discrimination in the context of another right, will also be considered briefly.

Ali may attract liability under s 14(4) of the POA, as he was the organiser of a public assembly, but failed to comply with the condition imposed by the most senior police officer present at the scene (where the officers are of equal rank, this condition will be fulfilled when one of them issues an order) to disperse half of the group. It should be noted that as the group was in a public place and comprised more than two persons, it constituted a public assembly under s 16 of the POA, as amended. Belinda can impose conditions on the assembly only if one of four 'triggers' under s 14(1) is present. The fourth 'trigger', arising under s 14(1)(b), requires that the senior police officer present must reasonably believe that the purpose of the assembly is 'the intimidation of others with a view to compelling them not to do an act they have a right to do or to do an act they have a right not to do'.

The fourth 'trigger' seems to be most clearly indicated. In the case of *Reid* (1987), it was determined that the triggers should be strictly interpreted: the words used should not be diluted. In *Reid*, the defendants shouted, raised their arms and waved their fingers; it was determined that such behaviour might cause discomfort but not intimidation and that the two concepts could not be equated. In *News Group Newspapers Ltd v SOGAT 82* (1986), it was held that mere abuse and shouting did not amount to a threat of violence. In the instant case, it could be argued that the Asians' behaviour in merely shouting at the Civic Centre workers could not amount to intimidation, but that in making threatening gestures with their fists, it crossed the boundary between discomfort and intimidation.

However, the imposition of conditions, the arrest of Ali and (potentially) the imposition of criminal liability under s 14 create interferences with the rights under Arts 11 and 10 of assembly and expression (*Steel v UK* (1998)). Therefore, it must be asked whether the demands of s 14 as applied in this instance are in accordance with those rights. In *Ezelin v France* (1991), the Court found that the freedom to take part in a peaceful assembly is of such importance that it cannot be restricted in any way, so long as the person concerned does not himself commit any reprehensible act. It may be argued that the intimidation of others is reprehensible and that therefore the tests under Art 11(2) (and Art 10(2)) are satisfied by the application of s 14 in this instance, taking account of s 6 HRA. The lenient stance taken towards the application of the third trigger in *R (Brehony) v Chief Constable of Greater Manchester* (2005) indicates that this stance would probably also be taken here.[3]

---

3   Examinees would gain credit for demonstrating an understanding of the courts' tendency to show deference to the decisions of police officers on the ground.

On that basis, it appears that Belinda had the power to impose a condition on the assembly. Thus, Ali's arrest appears to be justified under s 14(7) and he may be likely to incur liability under s 14(4). Other members of the Asian group who were aware of the condition may commit the offence under s 14(5).

Ali, Rashid, and possibly other members of the Asian group may also incur liability under s 68 of the Criminal Justice and Public Order Act 1994 (CJPOA). The section requires, first, that the defendant has trespassed. This seems to be satisfied, since Ali, Rashid and the other protestors appear to have exceeded the terms of an implied licence to be in the courtyard, and the courtyard is not excluded from s 68 since it is arguably 'land in the open air' – it is clearly not part of the highway (s 68(5)(a)). Second, it must be shown that the defendant intended to disrupt or obstruct a lawful activity or to intimidate persons so as to deter them from that activity. This last requirement may also be satisfied by the Asians' behaviour in shouting at the workers entering the Civic Centre. The broad view of s 68 taken in *Winder* (1996) indicates that a court would not scrutinise the application of s 68 to the facts too closely. Rashid (and possibly other Asians aware of John's order that members of the assembly should disperse) may also commit the offence under s 69 of failing to leave land after a direction to do so is given, founded on a reasonable belief that the offence under s 68 is being committed. Belinda tells Rashid to leave the land and he refuses to do so.

However, these possibilities of liability under ss 68 and 69 must be considered in relation to the HRA. The European Court of Human Rights made a clear finding in *Steel* (1998), confirmed in *Hashman* (2000), that protest that takes the form of physical obstruction nevertheless falls within the protection of Art 10 – and presumably Art 11 if a group is involved. It seems clear from the findings in *Steel* as to the first and second applicants, and from the Commission decision in *G v Federal Republic of Germany* (1980), that where a protestor is engaged in obstructive, albeit non-violent activity, arrest and imprisonment are in principle justifiable under the Convention. It is arguable, therefore, that the imposition of liability in this instance is compatible with the duty of the court under s 6 of the HRA.[4] On this basis, liability under s 69 would also be established since it is dependent on establishing a reasonable belief that the offence under s 68 has been committed.

It could also be argued that in shouting and waving their fists at the Civic Centre workers, Ali and the other demonstrators may incur liability under s 5 of the POA. Their behaviour must amount to 'threatening, abusive or insulting words or behaviour or disorderly behaviour', which takes place 'in the hearing or sight of a person likely to be caused harassment, alarm or distress thereby'. The word 'likely' imports an objective test into the section: it is necessary to show that a person was present at the scene, but not that he

---

4   Examinees would gain credit for demonstrating an understanding that reliance on the ECHR and HRA
     does not mean that liability Is necessarily hard to establish.

actually experienced the feelings in question. The demonstrators shout and gesture aggressively; this behaviour may clearly be termed disorderly or even threatening, and it is arguable, given the width of the concept of harassment, that it would be likely to cause feelings of harassment, although probably not of alarm, to the workers. It appears then that the demonstrators may incur liability under s 5, subject to the argument below as to the *mens rea* requirement under s 6(4). On the same argument, liability under s 4A of the POA may be established, assuming that they *intended* to cause harassment and did cause it. It should be noted, however, that in *Dehal v DPP* (2005) it was found that s 4 should be interpreted restrictively when applied to public protest due to the impact of the HRA, and Arts 10 and 11.

However, it is necessary to consider whether ss 4A and 5, interpreted as covering the behaviour in question, are compatible with Arts 10 and 11 under s 3 of the HRA (see *Percy v DPP* (2001)). Compatibility may be achieved by affording a broad interpretation to the defence of reasonableness in both sections (ss 5(3)(c) and 4A(3)(b)). However, in the context under discussion, the demonstrators appear to have intended to intimidate others, rather than to make points that others could find offensive. It is arguable that the instant behaviour would fall outside the meaning of 'reasonable', even bearing the requirements of Arts 10 and 11 in mind.

Under s 6(4), it must be established in respect of s 5 that the defendant intended his words, etc., to be threatening, abusive or insulting or was aware that they might be. Under s 4A, intent to cause harassment alone is needed. In *DPP v Clarke* (1992), it was found that to establish liability under s 5, it is insufficient to show only that the defendant intended to or was aware that he might cause harassment, alarm or distress; it must also be shown that he intended his conduct to be threatening, abusive or insulting or was aware that it might be. It therefore places a significant curb on the ability of s 5 (and to an extent, impliedly of s 4A) to interfere with Art 10 and Art 11 rights. Persons participating in forceful demonstrations may sometimes be able to show that behaviour that could be termed disorderly and which might be capable of causing harassment to others was intended only to make a point, and that they had not realised that others might find it threatening, abusive or insulting. This does not appear to be the case here, since the threats appear to be used not in order to make a point forcefully, but to intimidate.

Sharma may have committed a breach of the peace or his behaviour might have given rise to a reasonable belief that a breach of the peace was threatened; breach of the peace is not in itself a criminal offence, but it would justify the arrest of Sharma by John. If the arrest was lawful, Sharma's action in pushing John away would be an assault on an officer in the execution of his duty, an offence under s 89(1) of the Police Act 1996. In *Howell* (1981), the court said that a breach of the peace will arise if a positive act is done or is threatened to be done that harms a person or, in his presence, his property, or is likely to cause such harm, or which puts a person in fear of such harm. In *Nicol v DPP* (1996), it was found that a natural consequence of lawful conduct could be violence in another only where the defendant rather than the other person could be said to be acting unreasonably and, further, that unless rights had been infringed, it would not be reasonable for those others to react violently. However, in *Redmond-Bate v DPP* (1999), it was found that, taking **Art 10** into account, the court should ask where the threat was coming from; the person causing the threat should be arrested. The threat would appear to be coming from the white workers. Therefore, it may be argued that the police breached their duty under s 6 of the **HRA** in arresting Sharma, since they did not comply with **Art 10** (and arguably **Art 14** – the right to non-discrimination, which arises in the context of another right). The court's findings in *Steel v UK* (1998) may be taken to suggest that the power to prevent a breach of the peace may infringe **Arts 5, 10** and **11** when used against an entirely peaceful protestor. The decision in *Laporte* (2006) would support this argument.

However, in *Austin v UK* (2012) the Court considered that even the extreme measure of 'kettling' employed against a peaceful protester could be justified when the police were trying to deal with a crowd containing unruly elements. **Article 5** was not found to apply in *Austin*. But **Art 5** would clearly be applicable in this instance since Sharma was arrested. In the instant case, Sharma may have remained peaceful, albeit 'heated' and angry. On this interpretation, therefore, which would accord with the court's duty to shape the common law in accordance with the **ECHR** under s 6 of the **HRA**, Sharma should not have been arrested unless the police evidence is that a breach of the peace was imminent which could be averted by his arrest. Following *Redmond-Bate* that would probably not be found to be the case; on that basis Sharma has not committed the offence under s 89(1) of the **Police Act 1996**.[5] He could sue John in tort for assault if the arrest is found to be unlawful. Following this argument, it is therefore possible that if the protestors who used intimidatory tactics had been arrested for breach of the peace, their arrests would not have breached **Art 10**.

Aim Higher ★

The points re **ss 5** and **4A POA** could have been considered. In more depth and consideration could have been given to cases such as *Hammond* (2004), *Percy v DPP* (2001).

The case of *Ollinger v Austria* (2008) could be considered in relation to **ss 68** and **14 POA**.

---

5   Examinees would gain credit for demonstrating that the position as regards police intervention on grounds of breach of the peace is complex, and for showing understanding of the role of **s 6 HRA**.

QUESTION 46

The restraints on assemblies of ss 11–14A of the Public Order Act 1986 (POA), as amended, create a balance between the public interest in freedom of assembly and the need to maintain public order that is in harmony with Arts 10 and 11 of the ECHR. Therefore no reinterpretation of those provisions under section 3 of the Human Rights Act 1998 is necessary.

▶ Discuss.

How to Answer this Question

The Public Order Act 1986 (POA) remains the central statute in this area, but its amendment by the Criminal Justice and Public Order Act 1994 (CJPOA) created a significant new area of liability. The general public order scheme now created by the two statutes is very likely to appear on examination papers. This essay question requires a sound knowledge of certain key POA provisions that are particularly relevant to public assembly and protest. Section 16 POA was amended by the Anti-Social Behaviour Act 2003 so that an assembly is now a meeting of two or more persons in a public place. It also requires an awareness of the provisions of Arts 10 and 11 as interpreted at Strasbourg, and of their potential impact on this area of UK law under the Human Rights Act 1998 (HRA). It is suggested that a distinction should initially be drawn between prior and subsequent restraints contained in the POA as amended. The provisions in question operate to a significant extent as prior restraints.

Answer Structure

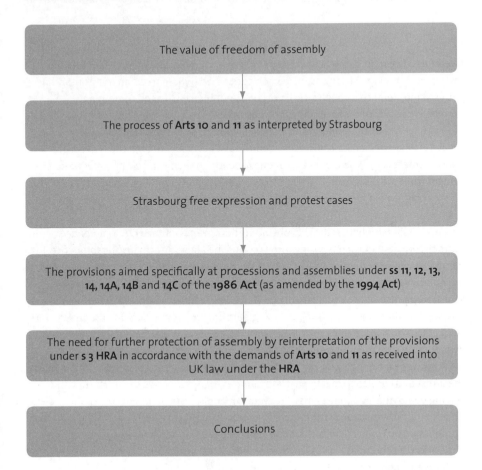

The value of freedom of assembly

The process of **Arts 10** and **11** as interpreted by Strasbourg

Strasbourg free expression and protest cases

The provisions aimed specifically at processions and assemblies under **ss 11, 12, 13, 14, 14A, 14B and 14C** of the **1986 Act** (as amended by the **1994 Act**)

The need for further protection of assembly by reinterpretation of the provisions under **s 3 HRA** in accordance with the demands of **Arts 10** and **11** as received into UK law under the **HRA**

Conclusions

ANSWER

The restraints available under ss 11–14A of the Public Order Act 1986 (POA), as amended by the Criminal Justice and Public Order Act 1994 (CJPOA), affect demonstrations, marches and meetings. Arts 10 and 11 of the ECHR, afforded further effect in domestic law under the Human Rights Act 1998 (HRA), seek to avoid suppression of protest in providing guarantees of freedom of expression and of peaceful assembly, subject to exceptions under Arts 10(2) and 11(2), which allow restraints on protests and demonstrations to be justified only if they are prescribed by law, have a legitimate aim, and are 'necessary in a democratic society'. The European Court of Human Rights (ECtHR) has found that the right to organise public meetings is 'fundamental' (*Rassemblement Jurassien Unite Jurassienne v Switzerland* (1979)). All forms of protest that can be viewed as the expression of an opinion fall within Art 10, according to the findings of the Court in *Steel v UK* (1998).

In *Ezelin v France* (1991), the Court found that Art 11 had been violated: it found that the freedom to take part in a peaceful assembly is of such importance that it cannot be restricted in any way, so long as the person concerned (whose freedom of assembly has suffered interference through arrest, etc.) does not himself/herself commit any reprehensible act. This stance was confirmed in *Cetinkaya v Turkey* (2005). *Ollinger v Austria* (2008) took the stance that a ban on a counter-demonstration was unlawful where the police could quite readily have been able to keep the two groups apart. Domestically, where protest is in question, there seems to be a preparedness, evident from the decision in *DPP v Percy* (2001) and *Laporte* (2007), to accept that Arts 10 and 11 apply, even if the protest in general includes offensive or disorderly elements.

This essay will ask whether the UK controls under ss 11–14C of the POA as amended are in harmony with Arts 10 and 11, taking into account the above Strasbourg jurisprudence. In general, it will be argued, contrary to the statement included in the title,[6] that ss 12–14A are not fully in accord with the demands of Arts 10 and 11 of the ECHR, although the Strasbourg jurisprudence could hardly be viewed as radical. Under all of those provisions, it is possible that those organising or taking part in protests and demonstrations can be subject to criminal penalties and hence to an interference with their Arts 10 and 11 rights, even though they themselves were behaving wholly peacefully. Thus, the effects of ss 12–14A appear to be contrary to the statement of principle set out in *Ezelin*, above, since the arrest and conviction of demonstrators under them cannot be seen to be directly serving one of the legitimate aims of preventing public disorder or ensuring public safety under para 2 of Arts 10 and 11. But there is a consistent line of case law from the European Commission on Human Rights that indicates that bans – and therefore a fortiori the imposition of conditions – on assemblies and marches are in principle compatible with Art 11, even where they criminalise wholly peaceful protests (*Pendragon v UK* (1998); *Chappell v UK* (1987)) or prevent what would have been peaceful demonstrations from taking place at all (*Christians Against Racism and Fascism v UK* (1980)). On the other hand, Mead considers that the Strasbourg Court may more recently be taking a 'more expansionist' stance – and this is considered below.[7]

Sections 12 and 13 POA are underpinned by s 11, which provides that the organisers of a march (not a meeting) must give advance notice of it to the police. The notice must specify the date, time and proposed route of the procession and give the name and address of the person proposing to organise it. Under s 11(7), the organisers may be guilty

---

6   Candidates will gain credit for taking a specific stance in relation to the title since the title invited an answer agreeing with the statement or disagreeing with it.

7   Candidates will gain credit by making reference to academic writing on this subject.

of an offence if the notice requirement has not been satisfied or if the march deviates from the date, time or route specified. Clearly, s 11 may have some deterrence value to organisers; such persons obviously bear a heavy responsibility in ensuring that any deviation does not occur. It can be argued that the word 'any' should not be interpreted so strictly as to exclude spontaneous processions where only a few minutes were available to give notice, because to do so would defeat the intention behind including the provision. If read in combination with the requirements as to giving notice by hand or in writing, it should be interpreted to mean 'any written notice' under s 3 of the HRA. If it were not so interpreted, it might be argued that s 11 breaches the guarantees of freedom of assembly under Art 11 and of expression under Art 10, since it could lead to the criminalisation of the organisers of a peaceful spontaneous march. Such an interpretation would seem to be in accordance with the findings in *Ezelin v France* and with the *Kay* case, in which a strict stance was taken towards s 11.

The power to impose conditions on public assemblies under s 14 and on processions under s 12 can be exercised in one of four situations: the senior police officer in question must reasonably believe that serious public disorder, serious damage to property or serious disruption to the life of the community may be caused by the procession. The fourth 'trigger' condition, arising under ss 12 and 14(1)(b) requires that the senior police officer must reasonably believe that the purpose of the assembly is 'the intimidation of others with a view to compelling them not to do an act they have a right to do or to do an act they have a right not to do'.

'Serious disruption to the life of the community' is a very wide phrase and clearly offers the police broad scope for interpretation. In *R (Brehony) v Chief Constable of Greater Manchester* (2005), a regular demonstration had occurred outside a branch of Marks and Spencer, protesting about the firm's support for the government of Israel; a counter-demonstration had also occurred, supporting the government. The Chief Constable had issued a notice under s 14 requiring the demonstration to move to a different location due to the disruption that it would be likely to cause to shoppers over the Christmas period. The judge refused the application for judicial review on the basis that, in Arts 10 and 11 terms, the restraint was proportionate to the aim pursued, of maintaining public order. This decision confirms that 'serious disruption to the life of the community' can mean mere anticipated inconvenience to shoppers. It would be possible to rely on s 3 HRA and Art 11 to curb the width of the term, taking account of *Ollinger v Austria* (2008). It would also be possible to rely on s 6 HRA and *Ollinger* in relation to the police use of the powers in the circumstances.

The conditions which may be imposed under s 14 are much more limited in scope than those that can be imposed under s 12, presumably because it was thought that marches presented more of a threat to public order than meetings. The use of s 14 is more likely, therefore, to be justified under Arts 10 or 11 para 2 since the assembly can still occur (*Ollinger*).

Under s13, a ban must be imposed on a march if it is thought that it may result in serious public disorder. This power is open to criticism, in that once a banning order has been imposed, it prevents all marches in the area that it covers for its duration. Thus, a projected march likely to be of an entirely peaceful character would be caught by a ban aimed at a violent march. Section 13 could be reinterpreted under s3 HRA in order to achieve compatibility with Arts 10 and 11 in various ways. For example, it could be argued that a power to seek an order to ban all marches could be interpreted as a power to ban all marches espousing a particular message, using s3 of the HRA creatively, as the House of Lords did in *R v A* (2001) and *Ghaidan v Mendoza* (2004).

It is arguable that s3 HRA could be relied on to limit the banning power to the particular marches giving rise to fear of serious public disorder, or to challenge a particular ban (*Guneri v Turkey* (2005)). However, the banning power is rarely used and given that its trigger relies on apprehending serious public disorder (albeit not In respect of all groups banned) a ban is likely to be found to be justified under Arts 10 or 11 para 2.

Originally, the 1986 Act contained no power to ban assemblies, possibly because it was thought that such a power would be too draconian, but provision to allow for such bans was inserted into it by s70 of the CJPOA. The banning power, arising under s14A, provides that a chief officer of police may apply for a banning order if he reasonably believes that an assembly is likely to be trespassory and may result in serious disruption to the life of the community or damage to certain types of building and structure. If an order is made, it will subsist for four days and operate within a radius of five miles around the area in question.

The meaning and ambit of s14A were considered in *Jones and Lloyd v DPP* (1997), which concerned an assembly on the road leading to Stonehenge, at a time when a s14A order was in force. The key finding of the House of Lords was that since *the particular assembly in question* had been found by the tribunal in fact to be a reasonable user of the highway, it was therefore not trespassory and so not caught by the s14A order. The Lords' conclusion was that the demands of this 'right' to assemble are satisfied, provided merely that an assembly on the highway is not invariably tortious. This interpretation did little, it is suggested, to ensure that s14A is compatible with Arts 10 and 11, since it allows interferences with peaceful assemblies.

Under s14A, attention could focus upon scrutiny of the risk of 'serious disruption to the life of the community' in granting the original ban. This method could also be used to bring ss12 and 14 into line with the Convention. A court could consider whether the nature of the risk anticipated is one that would constitute one of the legitimate aims for limiting the primary rights under Arts 11 and 10. This vague and ambiguous phrase could be reinterpreted under s3 of the HRA by reference to Arts 11(2) and 10(2) of the Convention. The ban or conditions would have to be found to be necessary and proportionate to the legitimate aim applicable. Thus, s3 has the potential to be used to limit and structure the tests allowing for the use of these curbs on protests. However, the decision in *Brehony* does not encourage the idea that the judiciary would be eager to take this course. *R (on the application of Gillan) v Commissioner of Metropolitan Police* (2006) also encourages a pessimistic view: the House of Lords found that, assuming that Art 10 was applicable in an instance in which a protester had been stopped and searched – arguably an interference that had occurred in order to impede him in joining the protest – the exception for the prevention of crime under para 2 was satisfied, without engaging in any proportionality analysis. However, the more expansionist approach evident in such cases as *Guneri v Turkey* (2005) and *Ollinger v Austria* (2008) would suggest that at the least the proportionality analysis must be conducted under s 6 HRA in relation to any particular set of facts.

It is concluded that the far-reaching nature of the public order scheme under discussion argues strongly for establishing further protection for freedom of assembly under the HRA, by reinterpretation of a number of the provisions under s 3. The scheme is to an extent pursuing legitimate aims – the prevention of disorder and crime – under Arts 10 and 11, but insofar as certain of its provisions allow for interference with peaceful assemblies, it appears, as indicated, that in certain respects it goes further than is necessary in a democratic society. However, ironically, the very fact that the scheme employs imprecise phrases such as 'serious', possibly in an attempt to afford maximum discretion to the police, works against it in favour of freedom of protest, since it could render the task of reinterpretation under s 3 of the HRA relatively straightforward. However, these possible reinterpretations of these provisions have not yet been undertaken under the HRA. But the application of the provisions In particular instances could be challenged via s 6 HRA.[8]

Aim Higher ★

In relation to **s 14A** there are strong grounds to justify a development of the ruling from *DPP v Jones*: the civil trespass finding could be modified: a court could find that if an assembly is peaceful and non-obstructive, it must always be termed reasonable and therefore non-trespassory, and so outside the terms of any **s 14A** order in force.

Candidates will gain credit by making further reference to academic writing on this subject – e.g. to Fenwick, Geddis.

Cetinkaya v Turkey (2005) could be considered.

---

8   Candidates will gain credit for showing an understanding of the difference between **s 3** and **s 6**, and addressing thereby the key issue raised by the title.

Common Pitfalls ✗

Students must focus on **s 3 HRA** and clear, possible changes that could be created to the statutory provisions, based on Strasbourg jurisprudence, not on general criticisms of the provisions.

Index